Aprilia RSV Mille

Service and Repair Manual

by Matthew Coombs

Models covered

Aprilia RSV Mille, 1998 to 2003
Aprilia RSV Mille R, 1999 to 2003

(4255 - 256)

© **Haynes Publishing 2005**

A book in the **Haynes Service and Repair Manual Series**

ISBN 1 84425 255 8

British Library Cataloguing in Publication Data
A catalogue record for this book is available from the British Library

Library of Congress Control Number 2005920360

Printed in the USA

Haynes Publishing
Sparkford, Yeovil, Somerset BA22 7JJ, England

Haynes North America, Inc
861 Lawrence Drive, Newbury Park, California 91320, USA

Editions Haynes
4, Rue de l'Abreuvoir
92415 COURBEVOIE CEDEX, France

Haynes Publishing Nordiska AB
Box 1504, 751 45 UPPSALA, Sweden

Contents

Contents

The Factory

Before the first Mille, all Aprilias had followed the same development pattern, a brought-in engine housed in a kit of parts sourced from various localities and wrapped in smart bodywork that was very much the factory's own contribution. Their very first bikes, motocrossers, used Sachs motors; their first GP 250s used tuned Rotax motors, and the 250 cc road bikes styled after the racers used Suzuki RGV motors.

The Mille arrived with a 60-degree Rotax V-twin motor and with a grand plan to take on the world of Superbike racing. All this just 25 years after the factory made its first complete motorcycle.

Along the way the little company, tiny by Japanese standards and small compared to BMW and even Ducati, showed flair and original thinking. They went 250 cc GP racing with Loris Reggiani and won a GP in 1987 – at home in Misano. It took them until '92 to win their first world title, with Alex Gramigni in the 125 cc class. A hat-trick of titles from Max Biaggi (1994 to 1996) really made Aprilia the dominant force in the smaller class of GP racing, and today the production of 125 and 250cc racers is a profit centre for the factory. A keen eye for the trends in the hyper fashion-conscious Italian home market saw a very successful succession of scooters and little two-strokes, many of them echoing the styling of the GP racers.

By the time Aprilia were true championship contenders the original Rotax motors were almost unrecognisable. The factory's Dutch tuning guru Jan Witteveen kept faith with his belief in disc valve induction in the face of Honda and Yamaha's reed valves and was an early believer in backwards rotating crankshafts. If you can't get a factory Honda in the small classes of GPs then you have to buy an Aprilia if you want to get on the rostrum.

Away from the race track Aprilia did a deal with BMW that saw them assembling the German firm's F650 in Italy, the first time BMW had entrusted their reputation for build quality to a foreign company. They also employed noted designer Philippe Starck to style the Moto 6.5, a bike aimed at style-conscious city riders. Ironically, it wasn't a sales success largely due to the BMW. The factory was also quick to take advantage of Italy's fascination with the Paris-Dakar rally, both with small two-strokes and with the 600 cc Tuareg using the ubiquitous Rotax four-valve single in a package that looked as if it could be ridden in the Rally yet was also a very useful road bike.

The arrival of the Mille gave Aprilia another string to their bow and opened up the possibility of some serious income from export markets including, vitally, the USA. The Mille was an immediate critical success. On the racing front, the company went racing in 1999 with vastly experienced Aussie Peter Goddard in the World Superbike Championship with occasional back-up from factory tester Alessandro Antonello for what everyone said was a development year. Goddard notched a few respectable points finishes and for 2000 Aprilia got serious with Troy Corser as the lead rider. Fresh from being released by Ducati to make room for Ben Bostrom, Corser was anxious to prove a point to the other Italian V-twin manufacturer. He proved several, taking Aprilia's first Superpole at the first round of the year, their first rostrum in the second race, and their first victory at the second round. He went on to win another four races in the season including a double at Misano, the track always regarded as Ducati's home event. Winning the first race of the following round gave him the rare distinction of three victories in consecutive races, and in a year when all four Japanese factories as well as the two Italians were fielding strong works teams. Troy finished the year in third place overall behind only Colin Edwards and Noriyuki Haga. The 2002 season looked to be shaping as a possible championship year when Troy set Superpole and then won both races at the first round of the year. However, it was a false dawn. He didn't win another race and there were signs of friction between rider and team. Aprilia's

The 2000 RSV1000 Mille

The 2002 RSV1000 Mille

The 2000 RSV-R Mille

The 2003 RSV-R Mille

other rider, Regis Laconi, won the last race of the year, but that was it.

With hindsight, this can be seen as a critical moment. Aprilia were about to spend money on launching themselves onto the American domestic market. Success in Superbike racing would help the marketing push enormously.

There was talk of Aprilia entering their works team in the American Superbike Championship in 2002, a rumour that resurfaced a year later with the added possibility the British Superbike Championship as the target. Non of this ever happened, indeed the factory did not go Superbike racing anywhere. Instead, the factory put all its eggs in the new four-stroke MotoGP basket with the most radical design on the grid. The RS Cube was an in-line triple with much Formula 1 technology, notably pneumatically-operated valves. Unfortunately the F1 model of producing bulk power and then controlling it with electronics did not work. The basic design was flawed and the bike was tens of kilograms overweight, thus missing out on the minimum weight break the regulations gave triples. Frankly, it was a disaster and certainly contributed to the financial woes that eventually saw the company taken over by Piaggio.

The Mille is Superbike racing's great maybe. In its first year of serious competition Aprilia gave Ducati a good hiding, beating them in the riders' championship. The road bikes were reckoned to be much more suited to the real world than the V-twin opposition, which consisted of the Suzuki TL1000 and the Ducati 916. Sales in the UK and the USA were very encouraging and magazine reviews unanimously positive. Compared to its fellow Italian, the Aprilia was easier to live with, more reliable, better finished and much cheaper. All the foundations were laid for a serious assault on a lucrative section of the Superbike market. All the ingredients were there: success in Word Superbike and the cachet of Italian design. Trackday heroes could upgrade to the RSV-R with its Ohlins suspension, forged wheels and carbon-fibre bodywork, while real racers could go for the SP version with 143 bhp short-stroke motor and a frame with adjustable engine position, headstock and swinging arm pivot.

With all that innovation and clever marketing, how come the factory found itself in financial trouble soon after the Millennium? Was it the ill-fated venture into MotoGP instead of consolidating success in World Superbike racing? Was it the collapse in the Italian domestic market for mopeds and scooters? In truth it was probably a mix of both.

Acknowledgements

Our thanks are due to Bridge Motorcycles of Exeter who supplied the motorcycle featured in the illustrations throughout this manual and to Kickstart Motorcycles of Port Talbot who provided technical advice. We would also like to thank NGK Spark Plugs (UK) Ltd for supplying the colour spark plug condition photographs, the Avon Rubber Company for supplying information on tyre fitting and Draper Tools Ltd for some of the workshop tools shown.

Thanks are also due to Julian Ryder who wrote the introduction 'The Factory'.

About this manual

The aim of this manual is to help you get the best value from your motorcycle. It can do so in several ways. It can help you decide what work must be done, even if you choose to have it done by a dealer; it provides information and procedures for routine maintenance and servicing; and it offers diagnostic and repair procedures to follow when trouble occurs.

We hope you use the manual to tackle the work yourself. For many simpler jobs, doing it yourself may be quicker than arranging an appointment to get the motorcycle into a dealer and making the trips to leave it and pick it up. More importantly, a lot of money can be saved by avoiding the expense the shop must pass on to you to cover its labour and overhead costs. An added benefit is the sense of satisfaction and accomplishment that you feel after doing the job yourself.

References to the left or right side of the motorcycle assume you are sitting on the seat, facing forward.

We take great pride in the accuracy of information given in this manual, but motorcycle manufacturers make alterations and design changes during the production run of a particular motorcycle of which they do not inform us. No liability can be accepted by the authors or publishers for loss, damage or injury caused by any errors in, or omissions from, the information given.

Dimensions and weights

Overall length
    1998 to 2000 models . . . . 2080 mm
    2001 to 2003 models . . . . 2070 mm
Overall width
    1998 to 2000 models . . . . 720 mm
    2001 to 2003 models . . . . 725 mm
Overall height . . . . 1170 mm
Wheelbase . . . . 1415 mm
Seat height . . . . 820 mm
Ground clearance . . . . 130 mm
Weight (wet)
    RSV Mille . . . . 221 kg
    RSV Mille R . . . . 211 kg
Seat height . . . . 710 mm
Ground clearance (minimum) . . . . 145 mm
Weight (with oil and full fuel tank) . . . . 274 kg

Engine

Type	Four-stroke 60° V-twin
Capacity	997.6 cc
Bore	97.0 mm
Stroke	67.5 mm
Compression ratio	11.4 to 1
Cooling system	Liquid cooled
Clutch	Wet multi-plate with vacuum-actuated back-torque limiter and hydraulic release
Transmission	Six-speed constant mesh
Final drive	Chain and sprockets
Camshafts	DOHC, chain and gear-driven
Fuel system	Electronic fuel injection
Exhaust system	Two-into-one
Ignition system	Digital electronic

Chassis

Frame type	Aluminium with engine as stressed member
Rake and Trail	
1998 to 2000 models	25°, 97 mm
2001 to 2003 models	25°, 99 mm
Fuel tank capacity	
Total (inc. reserve)	
1998 to 2000 models	20 litres
2001 to 2003 models	18 litres
Reserve	4.5 litres
Front suspension	
RSV Mille	
Type	Oil-damped, coil sprung upside-down 43 mm telescopic forks by Showa
Travel	120 mm
Adjustment	Spring pre-load, rebound and compression damping
RSV Mille R	
Type	Oil-damped, coil sprung upside-down 43 mm telescopic forks by Ohlins
Travel	115 mm
Adjustment	Spring pre-load, rebound and compression damping
Rear suspension	
RSV Mille	
Type	Single coil sprung shock absorber by Boge-Sachs with rising rate linkage, aluminium swingarm
Travel (at axle)	128 mm
Adjustment	Spring pre-load, rebound damping and compression damping
RSV Mille R	
Type	Single coil sprung shock absorber by Ohlins with rising rate linkage, aluminium swingarm
Travel (at axle)	125 mm
Adjustment	Spring pre-load, rebound damping and compression damping
Wheels	Front 3.5 x 17 in and rear 6.0 x 17 in (RSV Mille cast alloy, RSV Mille R forged alloy)
Tyres (standard – refer to owners handbook or Aprilia dealer for other fittings)	
Front	120/70-ZR17 (58W)
Rear	190/50-ZR17 (73W)
Front brake	Twin 320 mm discs with twin opposed-piston calipers by Brembo
Rear brake	Single 220 mm disc with single opposed-piston caliper by Brembo

Aprilia RSV Mille

The RSV Mille was launched in October 1998.

It has a 60° V-twin liquid-cooled dry sump engine built by Rotax. Drive to the double overhead camshafts which actuate the four valves per cylinder is by gear and chain. The hydraulically-actuated clutch is a wet multi-plate unit with conventional springs, and with Aprilia's PPC (Pneumatic Power Clutch) back-torque limiter that uses the vacuum in the intake manifold to reduce spring pressure on the plates. The transmission is a six-speed constant-mesh unit. Drive to the rear wheel is by chain and sprockets. The engine runs twin balancer shafts to counter the vibration inherent in a 60° V-twin design.

Fuel is supplied to the electronic injection system by a pump housed inside the fuel tank. The ignition system is fully electronic, with both fuel and ignition systems being controlled by a single engine control unit or ECU. Each throttle body has a single butterfly valve and single injector, and each cylinder head has twin spark plugs.

The engine sits in an aluminium frame that uses the engine as a stressed member. Front suspension is by Showa oil-damped upside-down telescopic forks with adjustable spring pre-load and both rebound and compression damping. Rear suspension is by aluminium swingarm acting via a three-way linkage on a single Boge-Sachs shock absorber. The shock absorber is adjustable for spring pre-load and both rebound and compression damping.

The brake system is made by Brembo. The front brake has twin opposed piston hydraulic callipers, and the rear brake system has a single opposed piston hydraulic caliper.

The frame supports a full race fairing and a one-piece seat cowling.

In 2001 a few changes were made – the fairing was restyled to incorporate wind deflectors to improve airflow; a plastic fuel tank was fitted; power was increased slightly; the rear shock absorber was revised.

In 2002 Brembo Monobloc four pad front brake calipers were fitted – these have a separate brake pad for each piston in the caliper.

In 2003 the transmission gear ratios were changed; a new exhaust system was fitted; a new tail piece and front mudguard were fitted to improve airflow.

Aprilia RSV Mille R

The RSV Mille R was launched in October 1999.

It has the same engine and electronics as the standard model (see above).

The difference between the R version and the standard is mainly in the suspension. Ohlins front forks and rear shock absorber are fitted. Weight saving is achieved using lighter Oz wheels and carbon-fibre fairing panels. An Ohlins steering damper is also fitted.

In 2001 a few changes were made – the fairing was restyled to incorporate wind deflectors to improve airflow; a plastic fuel tank was fitted; power was increased slightly; the rear shock absorber was revised.

In 2002 Brembo Monobloc four pad front brake calipers were fitted – these have a separate brake pad for each piston in the caliper. A dual-seat rear sub-frame the same as on the standard version was fitted. A Noriyuki Haga race replica with increased power was launched.

In 2003 the transmission gear ratios were changed; the front forks were revised, having shorter sliders and longer tubes to induce some flex, and an external damping fluid reservoir; new radially-mounted front brake calipers were fitted; the frame was finished in matt black; a new tail piece and front mudguard were fitted to improve airflow; new heel guards were fitted; the handlebar end-weights were revised to reduce vibration. A Colin Edwards race replica with increased power was launched – it features a more pressurised airbox and larger 57 mm (instead of 51 mm) throttle bodies, and a racing exhaust and EPROM chip for the ECU.

Professional mechanics are trained in safe working procedures. However enthusiastic you may be about getting on with the job at hand, take the time to ensure that your safety is not put at risk. A moment's lack of attention can result in an accident, as can failure to observe simple precautions.

There will always be new ways of having accidents, and the following is not a comprehensive list of all dangers; it is intended rather to make you aware of the risks and to encourage a safe approach to all work you carry out on your bike.

Asbestos

● Certain friction, insulating, sealing and other products - such as brake pads, clutch linings, gaskets, etc. - contain asbestos. Extreme care must be taken to avoid inhalation of dust from such products since it is hazardous to health. If in doubt, assume that they do contain asbestos.

Fire

● Remember at all times that petrol is highly flammable. Never smoke or have any kind of naked flame around, when working on the vehicle. But the risk does not end there - a spark caused by an electrical short-circuit, by two metal surfaces contacting each other, by careless use of tools, or even by static electricity built up in your body under certain conditions, can ignite petrol vapour, which in a confined space is highly explosive. Never use petrol as a cleaning solvent. Use an approved safety solvent.

● Always disconnect the battery earth terminal before working on any part of the fuel or electrical system, and never risk spilling fuel on to a hot engine or exhaust.

● It is recommended that a fire extinguisher of a type suitable for fuel and electrical fires is kept handy in the garage or workplace at all times. Never try to extinguish a fuel or electrical fire with water.

Fumes

● Certain fumes are highly toxic and can quickly cause unconsciousness and even death if inhaled to any extent. Petrol vapour comes into this category, as do the vapours from certain solvents such as trichloro-ethylene. Any draining or pouring of such volatile fluids should be done in a well ventilated area.

● When using cleaning fluids and solvents, read the instructions carefully. Never use materials from unmarked containers - they may give off poisonous vapours.

● Never run the engine of a motor vehicle in an enclosed space such as a garage. Exhaust fumes contain carbon monoxide which is extremely poisonous; if you need to run the engine, always do so in the open air or at least have the rear of the vehicle outside the workplace.

The battery

● Never cause a spark, or allow a naked light near the vehicle's battery. It will normally be giving off a certain amount of hydrogen gas, which is highly explosive.

● Always disconnect the battery ground (earth) terminal before working on the fuel or electrical systems (except where noted).

● If possible, loosen the filler plugs or cover when charging the battery from an external source. Do not charge at an excessive rate or the battery may burst.

● Take care when topping up, cleaning or carrying the battery. The acid electrolyte, evenwhen diluted, is very corrosive and should not be allowed to contact the eyes or skin. Always wear rubber gloves and goggles or a face shield. If you ever need to prepare electrolyte yourself, always add the acid slowly to the water; never add the water to the acid.

Electricity

● When using an electric power tool, inspection light etc., always ensure that the appliance is correctly connected to its plug and that, where necessary, it is properly grounded (earthed). Do not use such appliances in damp conditions and, again, beware of creating a spark or applying excessive heat in the vicinity of fuel or fuel vapour. Also ensure that the appliances meet national safety standards.

● A severe electric shock can result from touching certain parts of the electrical system, such as the spark plug wires (HT leads), when the engine is running or being cranked, particularly if components are damp or the insulation is defective. Where an electronic ignition system is used, the secondary (HT) voltage is much higher and could prove fatal.

Remember...

✗ **Don't** start the engine without first ascertaining that the transmission is in neutral.

✗ **Don't** suddenly remove the pressure cap from a hot cooling system - cover it with a cloth and release the pressure gradually first, or you may get scalded by escaping coolant.

✗ **Don't** attempt to drain oil until you are sure it has cooled sufficiently to avoid scalding you.

✗ **Don't** grasp any part of the engine or exhaust system without first ascertaining that it is cool enough not to burn you.

✗ **Don't** allow brake fluid or antifreeze to contact the machine's paintwork or plastic components.

✗ **Don't** siphon toxic liquids such as fuel, hydraulic fluid or antifreeze by mouth, or allow them to remain on your skin.

✗ **Don't** inhale dust - it may be injurious to health (see Asbestos heading).

✗ **Don't** allow any spilled oil or grease to remain on the floor - wipe it up right away, before someone slips on it.

✗ **Don't** use ill-fitting spanners or other tools which may slip and cause injury.

✗ **Don't** lift a heavy component which may be beyond your capability - get assistance.

✗ **Don't** rush to finish a job or take unverified short cuts.

✗ **Don't** allow children or animals in or around an unattended vehicle.

✗ **Don't** inflate a tyre above the recommended pressure. Apart from overstressing the carcass, in extreme cases the tyre may blow off forcibly.

✔ **Do** ensure that the machine is supported securely at all times. This is especially important when the machine is blocked up to aid wheel or fork removal.

✔ **Do** take care when attempting to loosen a stubborn nut or bolt. It is generally better to pull on a spanner, rather than push, so that if you slip, you fall away from the machine rather than onto it.

✔ **Do** wear eye protection when using power tools such as drill, sander, bench grinder etc.

✔ **Do** use a barrier cream on your hands prior to undertaking dirty jobs - it will protect your skin from infection as well as making the dirt easier to remove afterwards; but make sure your hands aren't left slippery. Note that long-term contact with used engine oil can be a health hazard.

✔ **Do** keep loose clothing (cuffs, ties etc. and long hair) well out of the way of moving mechanical parts.

✔ **Do** remove rings, wristwatch etc., before working on the vehicle - especially the electrical system.

✔ **Do** keep your work area tidy - it is only too easy to fall over articles left lying around.

✔ **Do** exercise caution when compressing springs for removal or installation. Ensure that the tension is applied and released in a controlled manner, using suitable tools which preclude the possibility of the spring escaping violently.

✔ **Do** ensure that any lifting tackle used has a safe working load rating adequate for the job.

✔ **Do** get someone to check periodically that all is well, when working alone on the vehicle.

✔ **Do** carry out work in a logical sequence and check that everything is correctly assembled and tightened afterwards.

✔ **Do** remember that your vehicle's safety affects that of yourself and others. If in doubt on any point, get professional advice.

● If in spite of following these precautions, you are unfortunate enough to injure yourself, seek medical attention as soon as possible.

The frame number is stamped into the right-hand side of the steering head

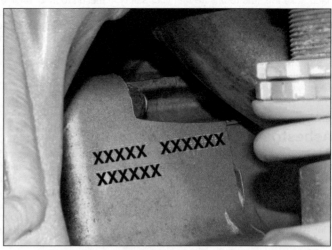

The engine number is stamped into the back of the crankcase on the left-hand side

Frame and engine numbers

The frame serial number is stamped into the right-hand side of the steering head. The engine number is stamped into the back of the crankcase. Both of these numbers should be recorded and kept in a safe place so they can be furnished to law enforcement officials in the event of a theft.

The frame and engine serial numbers should also be kept in a handy place (such as with your driver's licence) so they are always available when purchasing or ordering parts for your machine.

Buying spare parts

Once you have found the identification numbers, record them for reference when buying parts. Since the manufacturers change specifications, parts and vendors (companies that manufacture various components on the machine), providing the ID numbers is the only way to be reasonably sure that you are buying the correct parts.

Whenever possible, take the worn part to the dealer so direct comparison with the new component can be made. Along the trail from the manufacturer to the parts shelf, there are numerous places that the part can end up with the wrong number or be listed incorrectly.

The two places to purchase new parts for your motorcycle – the franchised or main dealer and the parts/accessories store – differ in the type of parts they carry. While dealers can obtain every single genuine part for your motorcycle, the accessory store is usually limited to normal high wear items such as chains and sprockets, brake pads, spark plugs and cables, and to tune-up parts and various engine gaskets, etc. Rarely will an accessory outlet have major suspension components, camshafts, transmission gears, or engine cases.

Used parts can be obtained from breakers yards for roughly half the price of new ones, but you can't always be sure of what you're getting. Once again, take your worn part to the breaker for direct comparison, or when ordering by mail order make sure that you can return it if you are not happy.

Whether buying new, used or rebuilt parts, the best course is to deal directly with someone who specialises in Aprilia.

Note: *The daily (pre-ride) checks outlined in the owner's manual covers those items which should be inspected on a daily basis.*

Coolant level

> **Warning: DO NOT remove the cooling system filler neck cap to add coolant. Topping up is done via the coolant reservoir tank filler. DO NOT leave open containers of coolant about, as it is poisonous.**

Before you start:
✔ Make sure you have a supply of coolant available (a mixture of 50% distilled water and 50% corrosion inhibited ethylene glycol anti-freeze is needed – do not use tap water, unless in an emergency, and then make sure it is soft water).
✔ Always check the coolant level when the engine is COLD. If the engine has been running allow it cool down fully before checking the level.
✔ Support the motorcycle upright on level ground. Use an auxiliary stand if necessary, but note that both wheels should be on the ground.

Bike care:
● Use only the specified coolant mixture. It is important that anti-freeze is used in the system all year round, and not just in the winter. Do not top the system up using only distilled water, as the system will become too diluted.
● Do not overfill the reservoir tank. If the coolant is significantly above the F (full) level line at any time, the surplus should be siphoned or drained off to prevent the possibility of it being expelled out of the overflow hose.
● If the coolant level falls steadily, check the system for leaks (see Chapter 1). If no leaks are found and the level continues to fall, it is recommended that the machine is taken to a dealer for a pressure test.

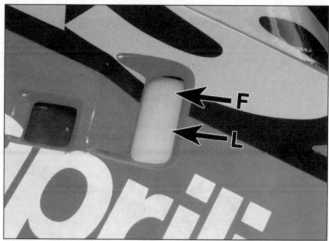

1 The coolant reservoir is located behind the fairing right-hand side panel, and is visible via the aperture in the panel (arrowed). With the motorcycle vertical, the coolant level should lie between the FULL and LOW level lines (arrowed) on the reservoir.

2 If the coolant level is on or below the Low level line, remove the reservoir filler cap.

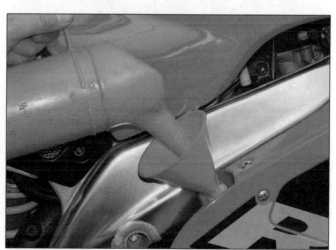

3 Top the reservoir up with the recommended coolant mixture to bring the level almost up to the FULL line, using a suitable funnel if necessary. Fit the cap.

Engine oil level

The correct oil

● Modern, high-revving engines place great demands on their oil. It is very important that you always top up with a good quality oil of the specified type and viscosity, and do not overfill the engine.

Oil type	API grade SG
Oil viscosity	SAE 15W50*

*If you are using the motorcycle constantly in extreme conditions of heat or cold, other more suitable viscosity ranges may be used – refer to the viscosity chart to select the oil best suited to your conditions.

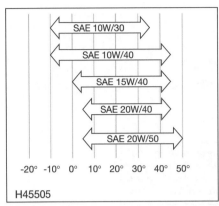

SAE 10W/30
SAE 10W/40
SAE 15W/40
SAE 20W/40
SAE 20W/50

-20° -10° 0° 10° 20° 30° 40° 50°

H45505

Oil viscosity chart; select the oil best suited to the conditions.

Before you start:

✔ The oil level must be checked with the engine warm. Take the motorcycle on a short run to allow it to reach normal operating temperature.

Caution: Do not run the engine in an enclosed space such as a garage or workshop.

✔ Stop the engine and support the motorcycle upright on level ground. Use an auxiliary stand if necessary, but note that both wheels should be on the ground. Allow it to stand undisturbed for a few minutes to allow the oil level to stabilise.

Bike care:

● If you have to add oil frequently, check whether you have any oil leaks from the engine joints, oil seals and gaskets. If not, the engine could be burning oil, in which case there will be white smoke coming out of the exhaust – (see *Fault Finding*).

1 The oil level inspection pipe (arrowed) is located on the oil tank and is visible via the apertures in the left-hand fairing side panel. Wipe the pipe and level marker clean if necessary.

2 With the motorcycle vertical, the oil level in the pipe should lie between the MAX and MIN level lines (arrowed) on the level marker (fairing side panel removed for clarity).

3 If the level is close to, on or below the MIN line, remove the left-hand fairing side panel (see Chapter 8). Unscrew the oil filler cap from the oil tank. Check the condition of the O-ring and replace it with a new one if it is damaged, deformed or deteriorated.

4 Using a suitable funnel if necessary, top up the engine with the recommended grade and type of oil to bring the level almost up to the MAX line on the inspection window. Do not overfill. Install the left-hand fairing side panel on completion (see Chapter 8).

Clutch fluid level

> ⚠️ **Brake and clutch hydraulic fluid can harm your eyes and damage painted surfaces, so use extreme caution when handling and pouring it and cover surrounding surfaces with rag. Do not use fluid that has been standing open for some time, as it is hygroscopic (absorbs moisture from the air) which can cause a loss of clutch effectiveness.**

Before you start:

✔ Make sure you have a supply of DOT 5.1 glycol-based hydraulic fluid. DOT 5.1 is compatible with, and a later generation of, DOT 4. **Do not** use DOT 5 silicone fluid.
✔ Wrap a rag around the reservoir to ensure that any spillage does not come into contact with painted surfaces.
✔ Support the motorcycle upright on level ground. Use an auxiliary stand if necessary, but note that both wheels should be on the ground. Turn the handlebars as required so the reservoir is level.

Bike care:

● If the fluid reservoir requires repeated topping-up there could be a leak somewhere in the system, which must be investigated immediately.
● Check for signs of fluid leakage from the hydraulic hose and clutch release mechanism components – if found, rectify immediately (see Chapter 2).
● Check the operation of the clutch before taking the machine on the road; if there is evidence of air in the system (spongy feel to the lever), it must be bled (see Chapter 2).

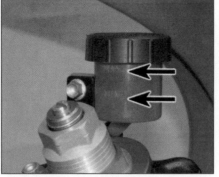

1 The clutch fluid level, visible through the reservoir body, must lie between the MAX and MIN level lines (arrowed).

2 If the level is below the MIN line, unscrew the reservoir cap and remove the diaphragm plate and diaphragm.

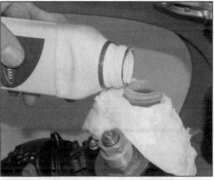

3 Top up with new clean hydraulic fluid, until the level is almost up to the MAX level line on the reservoir.

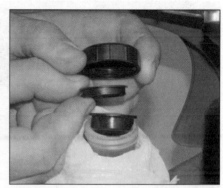

4 Ensure that the diaphragm is correctly seated before installing the plate and cap.

Suspension, steering and drive chain

Suspension and Steering:

● Check that the front and rear suspension operates smoothly without binding (see Chapter 1).
● Check that the suspension is adjusted as required, where applicable (see Chapter 6).
● Check that the steering moves smoothly from lock-to-lock, and that there is no freeplay.

Drive chain:

● Check that the chain isn't too loose or too tight, and adjust it if necessary (see Chapter 1).
● If the chain looks dry, lubricate it (see Chapter 1).

Legal and safety checks

Lighting and signalling:

● Take a minute to check that the headlight, tail light, brake light, licence plate light (where fitted), instrument lights and turn signals all work correctly.
● Check that the horn sounds when the button is pressed.
● A working speedometer, graduated in mph, is a statutory requirement in the UK.

Safety:

● Check that the throttle grip rotates smoothly when opened and snaps shut when released, in all steering positions. Also check for the correct amount of freeplay (see Chapter 1).
● Check that the brake lever and pedal, clutch lever and gearchange lever operate smoothly. Lubricate them at the specified intervals or when necessary (see Chapter 1).
● Check that the engine shuts off when the kill switch is operated. Check the starter interlock circuit (see Chapter 1).

● Check that the sidestand return springs hold the stand up securely when retracted.

Fuel:

● This may seem obvious, but check that you have enough fuel to complete your journey. If you notice signs of fuel leakage – rectify the cause immediately.
● Ensure you use the correct grade fuel – see Chapter 4 Specifications.

Brake fluid levels

⚠️ *Warning: Brake hydraulic fluid can harm your eyes and damage painted surfaces, so use extreme caution when handling and pouring it and cover surrounding surfaces with rag. Do not use fluid that has been standing open for some time, as it is hygroscopic (absorbs moisture from the air) which can cause a dangerous loss of braking effectiveness.*

Before you start:

✔ Make sure you have a supply of DOT 5.1 glycol-based hydraulic fluid. DOT 5.1 is compatible with, and a later generation of, DOT 4. **Do not** use DOT 5 silicone fluid.

✔ Wrap a rag around the reservoir being worked on to ensure that any spillage does not come into contact with painted surfaces.

✔ Support the motorcycle upright on level ground when checking the fluid levels. Use an auxiliary stand if necessary, but note that both wheels should be on the ground. When checking the fluid in the front reservoir turn the handlebars as required so the reservoir is level.

Bike care:

● The fluid in the front and rear brake master cylinder reservoirs will drop as the brake pads wear down. If the fluid level is low check the brake pads for wear (see Chapter 1).

● If either fluid reservoir requires repeated topping-up there could be a leak somewhere in the system, which must be investigated immediately.

● Check for signs of fluid leakage from the hydraulic hoses and/or brake system components – if found, rectify immediately (see Chapter 7).

● Check the operation of both brakes before taking the machine on the road; if there is evidence of air in the system (spongy feel to lever or pedal), it must be bled (see Chapter 7).

FRONT

1 The front brake fluid level, visible through the reservoir body, must lie between the MAX and MIN level lines (arrowed).

2 If the level is on or below the MIN line, undo the reservoir cap screws using a short or angled screwdriver. Take care not to dislodge the captive nuts (arrowed) near the base of the reservoir. Remove the cap and rubber diaphragm.

3 Top the reservoir up with new clean hydraulic fluid, until the level is almost up to the MAX level line on the reservoir. Do not overfill.

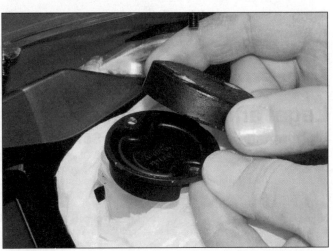

4 Wipe any moisture drops off the rubber diaphragm using an absorbent lint-free cloth. Ensure that the diaphragm is correctly seated before installing the cap. Secure the cap with the screws.

REAR

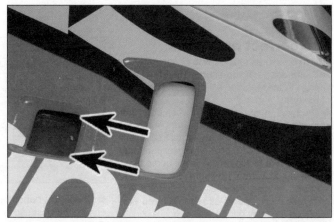

5 The rear brake fluid level is visible via the aperture in the right-hand fairing side panel – it must lie between the MAX and MIN level lines (arrowed). If the level is on or below the MIN line, remove the right-hand fairing side panel (see Chapter 8).

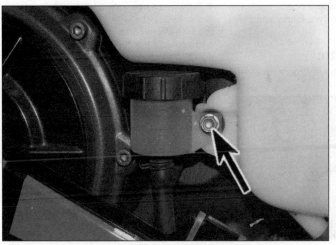

6 Unscrew the reservoir mounting bolt (arrowed) and draw the reservoir out from under the coolant reservoir.

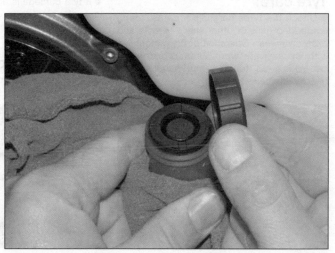

7 Wrap a rag round the reservoir then unscrew the cap and remove the diaphragm plate and rubber diaphragm.

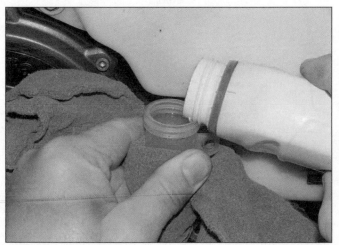

8 Top the reservoir up with new clean hydraulic fluid, until the level is almost up to the MAX level line. Do not overfill.

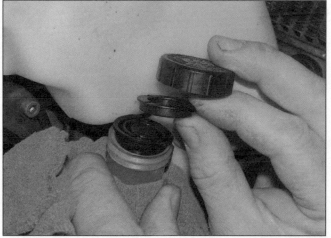

9 Wipe any moisture drops off the rubber diaphragm using an absorbent lint-free cloth. Ensure that the diaphragm is correctly seated before installing the plate and cap. Secure the reservoir with its bolt, then install the fairing side panel.

Tyres

The correct pressures:

● Tyre pressures change with air temperature and atmospheric pressure, therefore any change in the weather will affect the pressure of the tyre.

● The tyres must be checked when **cold**, not immediately after riding. Note that incorrect tyre pressures will cause abnormal tread wear and unsafe handling. Low tyre pressures may cause the tyre to slip on the rim or come off.

● Use an accurate pressure gauge. Many forecourt gauges are wildly inaccurate. If you buy your own, spend as much as you can justify on a quality gauge.

● Proper air pressure will increase tyre life and provide maximum stability and ride comfort.

Tyre care:

● Check the tyres carefully for cuts, tears, embedded nails or other sharp objects and excessive wear. Operation of the motorcycle with excessively worn tyres is extremely hazardous, as traction and handling are directly affected.

Loading	Front	Rear
1998 and 1999 models		
Rider only	33 psi (2.3 Bar)	36 psi (2.5 Bar)
Rider and passenger	36 psi (2.5 Bar)	40 psi (2.8 Bar)
2000 to 2002 models		
Rider only	32 psi (2.2 Bar)	36 psi (2.5 Bar)
Rider and passenger	35 psi (2.4 Bar)	39 psi (2.7 Bar)
2003 models		
Rider only	33 psi (2.3 Bar)	36 psi (2.5 Bar)
Rider and passenger	36 psi (2.5 Bar)	40 psi (2.8 Bar)

● Check the condition of the tyre valve and ensure the dust cap is in place.

● Pick out any stones or nails which may have become embedded in the tyre tread. If left, they will eventually penetrate through the casing and cause a puncture.

● If tyre damage is apparent, or unexplained loss of pressure is experienced, seek the advice of a motorcycle tyre fitting specialist without delay.

Tyre tread depth:

● At the time of writing UK law requires that tread depth must be at least 1 mm over 3/4 of the tread breadth all the way around the tyre, with no bald patches. Most riders, however, consider a miniumum tread depth of 2 mm to be a safer limit. Aprilia recommend a minimum of 2 mm on each tyre, with this figure being 3 mm for US market models.

● Many tyres now incorporate wear indicators in the tread. Identify the location marking on the tyre sidewall to locate the indicator bar and replace the tyre if the tread has worn down to the bar – some tyres have wear bars near the edge as well as in the centre.

1 Remove the dust cap from the valve. Check the tyre pressures when **cold**. Do not forget to fit the cap after checking the pressure.

2 Measure tread depth at the centre of the tyre using a depth gauge.

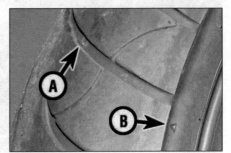

3 Tyre tread wear indicator bar (A) and its location marking (B – usually either an arrow, a triangle or the letters TWI) on the sidewall.

Chapter 1
Routine maintenance and servicing

Contents

Degrees of difficulty

Easy, suitable for novice with little experience		**Fairly easy,** suitable for beginner with some experience

Fairly difficult, suitable for competent DIY mechanic

Difficult, suitable for experienced DIY mechanic

Very difficult, suitable for expert DIY or professional

Engine

Engine idle speed .... 1250 ± 100 rpm
Spark plugs
    Type .... NGK DCPR9E (copper-core) or NGK DCPR9EVX (platinum tipped)
    Electrode gap .... 0.6 to 0.7 mm
Valve clearances (COLD engine)
    Intake valves .... 0.12 to 0.17 mm
    Exhaust valves .... 0.23 to 0.28 mm
Throttle body synchronisation
    Vacuum reading .... 270 to 330 mbar
    CO reading
        Non-catalytic models .... 0.8 to 1.3%
        Catalytic models .... 1.5 to 2.0%
Cylinder compression .... see Section 34
Oil pressure (at oil pressure switch) .... 7.25 psi (0.5 Bar) at idle speed with engine at normal operating temperature

Miscellaneous

Drive chain
    Slack .... 25 mm with bike on auxiliary stand (wheel off ground)
    Stretch limit (17 pin length – see text) .... 255.5 mm
Throttle twistgrip freeplay .... 2 to 3 mm
Fast idle lever freeplay .... 2 to 3 mm
Tyre pressures (cold) .... see *Daily (pre-ride) checks*

Recommended lubricants and fluids

Fuel grade
    European models .... Unleaded, minimum 95 RON (Research Octane Number)
    US and Canada models .... Unleaded, minimum 90 ((R+M) /2 method)
Engine/transmission oil type .... API grade SG motor oil
Engine/transmission oil viscosity .... SAE 15W50 (but see *Daily (pre-ride) checks*)
Engine/transmission oil capacity
    Oil change .... 3.7 litres
    Oil and filter change .... 3.9 litres
Coolant type .... 50% distilled water, 50% corrosion inhibited ethylene glycol anti-freeze
Coolant capacity (inc. reservoir) .... Approx. 2.5 litres
Brake and clutch fluid .... DOT 5.1 glycol-based hydraulic fluid. DOT 5.1 is compatible with, and a later generation of, DOT 4. **Do not** use DOT 5 silicone fluid.
Drive chain .... chain lubricant suitable for O-ring chains
Steering head bearings .... multi-purpose grease
Swingarm pivot bearings .... multi-purpose grease
Suspension linkage bearings .... multi-purpose grease
Bearing seal lips .... multi-purpose grease
Gearchange lever/rear brake pedal/footrest pivots .... multi-purpose grease
Brake and clutch lever pivots .... engine oil
Sidestand pivot .... multi-purpose grease
Throttle grip .... engine oil
Front brake lever piston tip .... silicone grease
Cables .... engine oil or cable lubricant

Torque settings

Coolant drain bolts
    Water pump drain bolt .... 12 Nm
    Radiator drain bolts .... 10 Nm
Engine oil drain bolts
    Engine drain bolt .... 12 Nm
    Oil tank drain bolt .... 15 Nm
Handlebar positioning bolts .... 11 Nm
Handlebar clamp bolts .... 25 Nm
Intake duct bolts .... 19 Nm
Oil filter cover bolts .... 11 Nm
Oil tank strainer .... 30 Nm
Rear axle nut .... 90 to 100 Nm
Spark plugs .... 20 Nm
Steering head bearing adjuster nut (see text) .... 40 Nm
Steering stem nut
    1998 to 2000 models with plain nut .... 80 Nm
    2001 to 2003 models with drilled nut .... 100 Nm
Top yoke fork clamp bolts .... 25 Nm

Note: *The daily (pre-ride) checks as outlined in your owner's manual cover those items which should be inspected on a daily basis. Always perform the pre-ride inspection at every maintenance interval (in addition to the procedures listed). The intervals listed below are the intervals recommended by the manufacturer for each particular operation during the model years covered in this manual. Your owner's manual may have different intervals for your model. As each service interval is reached a **service** message appears on the instrument cluster – this indicates that a service is due. To eliminate the **service** message after the service has been performed, press the LAP button on the left-hand switch housing and then the R button on the instrument cluster and hold both in for about five seconds.*

Daily (pre-ride)

See *'Daily (pre-ride) checks'* at the beginning of this manual.

After the initial 625 miles (1000 km)

Note: *This check is usually performed by an Aprilia dealer after the first 625 miles (1000 km) from new. Thereafter, maintenance is carried out according to the following intervals of the schedule.*

Every 625 miles (1000 km)

☐ Check, adjust, clean and lubricate the drive chain (Section 1)

Every 1250 miles (2000 km)

☐ Check the brake pads for wear (Section 2)

Every 4000 miles (6400 km)

☐ Change the front fork oil – RSV-R models (Section 27)

After the initial 4500 miles (7500 km)

☐ Change the front fork oil – RSV models (Section 27)

Every 4500 miles (7500 km) or 12 months

Carry out all the items under the Daily (pre-ride) checks and the 625 mile (1000 km) check, plus the following:

☐ Check and clean the air filter element (Section 3)
☐ Check the spark plugs (Section 4)
☐ Check the fuel hoses and fuel system components (Section 5)
☐ Change the engine oil and engine oil filter (Section 6)
☐ Check and adjust the engine idle speed (Section 7)
☐ Check throttle and fast idle cable operation and freeplay (Section 8)
☐ Check the operation of the clutch (Section 9)
☐ Check the cooling system (Section 10)
☐ Check for drive chain and sprocket wear (Section 11)

Every 4500 miles (7500 km) or 12 months (continued)

☐ Check the operation of the brakes, and for fluid leakage (Section 12)
☐ Check the tyre and wheel condition (Section 13)
☐ Check the tightness of all nuts and bolts (Section 14)
☐ Check and lubricate the sidestand, lever pivots and cables (Section 15)
☐ Check the battery (Section 16)
☐ Check throttle body synchronisation and exhaust CO level (Section 17)
☐ Check the steering head bearing freeplay (Section 18)
☐ Check the front and rear suspension (Section 19)
☐ Check the wheel bearings (Section 20)
☐ Check and adjust the headlight aim (Section 21)
☐ Check the sidestand and the starter interlock circuit operation (Section 22)

Every 9000 miles (15,000 km) or 24 months

Carry out all the items under the 4500 mile (7500 km) check, plus the following:

☐ Replace the spark plugs with new ones (Section 23)
☐ Check the valve clearances (Section 24)
☐ Replace the air filter element with a new one (Section 25)
☐ Clean the oil tank strainer (Section 26)

Every 14,000 miles (22,000 km) or 24 months

☐ Change the front fork oil – RSV models (Section 27)

Every two years

☐ Change the brake fluid (Section 28)
☐ Change the clutch fluid (Section 29)
☐ Change the coolant (Section 30)

Every four years

☐ Replace the brake hoses with new ones (Section 31)
☐ Replace the clutch hose with a new one (Section 32)
☐ Replace the fuel system hoses with new ones (Section 33)

Non-scheduled maintenance

☐ Check the cylinder compression (Section 34)
☐ Check the engine oil pressure (Section 35)

Component locations on right side

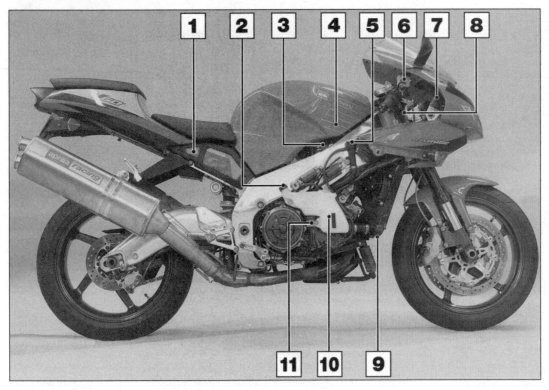

1 Battery
2 Coolant reservoir filler cap
3 Idle speed adjuster
4 Air filter
5 Cooling system filler neck cap
6 Front brake fluid reservoir
7 Secondary circuit fuses
8 Throttle cable upper adjusters
9 Coolant drain bolt on radiator (each side)
10 Coolant drain bolt on water pump (behind reservoir)
11 Rear brake fluid reservoir

Component locations on left side

1 Clutch fluid reservoir
2 Steering head bearing adjuster
3 Engine oil tank filler cap
4 Main fuses
5 Drive chain adjuster (each side)
6 Engine oil drain bolt on filter cover
7 Engine oil filter
8 Engine oil drain bolt on oil tank
9 Engine oil level inspection pipe

1 This Chapter is designed to help the home mechanic maintain his/her motorcycle for safety, economy, long life and peak performance.

2 Deciding where to start or plug into the routine maintenance schedule depends on several factors. If your motorcycle has been maintained according to the warranty standards and has just come out of warranty, start routine maintenance as it coincides with the next mileage or time interval. If you have owned the machine for some time but have never performed any maintenance on it, start at the nearest interval and include some additional procedures to ensure that nothing important is overlooked. If you have just had a major engine overhaul, then start the maintenance routine from the beginning. If you have a used machine and have no knowledge of its history or maintenance record, combine all the checks into one large service initially and then settle into the specified maintenance schedule.

3 Before beginning any maintenance or repair, the machine should be cleaned thoroughly, especially around the oil filter and drain plug, valve covers, and body panels. Cleaning will help ensure that dirt does not contaminate the engine and will allow you to detect wear and damage that could otherwise easily go unnoticed.

4 Certain maintenance information is sometimes printed on labels attached to the motorcycle. If the information on the labels differs from that included here, use the information on the label.

Every 625 miles (1000 km)

1 Drive chain check, adjustment, cleaning and lubrication

Check

1 A neglected drive chain won't last long and will quickly damage the sprockets. Routine chain adjustment and lubrication isn't difficult and will ensure maximum chain and sprocket life.

2 To check the chain, place the bike on an auxiliary stand so the rear wheel is off the ground and shift the transmission into neutral. Make sure the ignition switch is OFF. Do not check chain slack with bike resting on its sidestand.

3 Push up on the bottom run of the chain midway between the two sprockets and measure the amount of slack, then compare your measurement to that listed in this Chapter's Specifications **(see illustration)**. As the chain stretches with wear, adjustment will be necessary (see below). Since the chain will rarely wear evenly, rotate the wheel so that another section of chain can be checked; do this several times to check the entire length of chain, and mark the tightest spot.

Caution: Riding the bike with excess slack in the chain could lead to damage.

4 In some cases where lubrication has been neglected, corrosion and galling may cause the links to bind and kink, which effectively shortens the chain's length and makes it tight. Thoroughly clean and work free any such links, then highlight them with a marker pen or paint. After the bike has been ridden repeat the measurement for slack in the highlighted area. If the chain has kinked again and is still tight, replace it with a new one. A rusty, kinked or worn chain will damage the sprockets and can damage transmission bearings. If in any doubt as to the condition of a chain, it is far better to install a new one than risk damage to other components and possibly yourself.

5 Check the entire length of the chain for damaged rollers, loose links and pins, and missing O-rings, and replace it with a new one if necessary. **Note:** *Never install a new chain* on old sprockets, and never use the old chain if you install new sprockets – replace the chain and sprockets as a set. Refer to Section 10 for sprocket checks and chain stretch checks.

Adjustment

6 Rotate the wheel so that the chain is positioned with the tightest point at the centre of its bottom run.

7 Slacken the rear axle nut **(see illustration)**.

8 Slacken the locknut on each adjuster bolt, then turn the adjuster bolt on each side evenly until the amount of slack specified at the beginning of the Chapter is obtained at the centre of the bottom run of the chain **(see illustration)**. Following adjustment, check that the front edge of each chain adjustment marker is in the same position in relation to the index lines on the swingarm **(see illustration)**. It is important the **same** index line on each side aligns with the front edge of the marker; if not, the rear wheel will be out of alignment with the front. If there is a discrepancy in the marker positions, adjust one of them so that its position is exactly the same as the other. Check the chain slack as described above and readjust if necessary.

9 Tighten the axle nut to the torque setting specified at the beginning of the Chapter **(see illustration 1.7)**. Recheck the adjustment as above, then check that the wheel runs freely. Note that the torque setting specified is lower than that specified by Aprilia. The reason for this is that there have been a significant number of rear wheel bearing failures the cause of which has been identified as an overtight axle nut.

1.3 Measuring drive chain slack

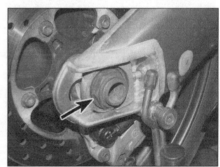

1.7 Slacken the axle nut (arrowed)

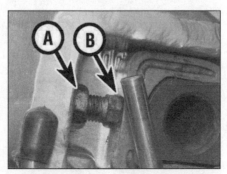

1.8a Slacken the locknut (A) and turn the adjuster bolt (B) as required

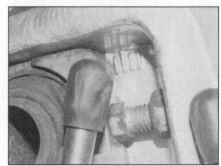

1.8b Make sure the adjustment markers are in the same position relative to the index lines on each side of the swingarm

1.11 Apply the specified lubricant to the overlap between the sideplates

Cleaning and lubrication

10 If required, wash the chain in paraffin (kerosene) or a suitable non-flammable or high flash-point solvent that will not damage the O-rings, using a soft brush to work any dirt out if necessary. Wipe the cleaner off the chain and allow it to dry, using compressed air if available. If the chain is excessively dirty it should be removed from the machine and allowed to soak in the paraffin or solvent (see Chapter 6).

Caution: **Don't use petrol (gasoline), an unsuitable solvent or other cleaning fluids which might damage the internal sealing properties of the chain. Don't use high-pressure water to clean the chain. The entire process shouldn't take longer than ten minutes, otherwise the O-rings could be damaged.**

11 The best time to lubricate the chain is after the motorcycle has been ridden. When the chain is warm, the lubricant will penetrate the joints between the sideplates better than when cold. **Note:** *Aprilia specifies an aerosol chain lube that it is suitable for O-ring or X-ring (sealed) chains; do not use any other chain lubricants – the solvents could damage the chain's sealing rings. Apply the oil to the area where the sideplates overlap – not the middle of the rollers* **(see illustration).**

 HAYNES HINT *Ideally apply the lubricant to the top of the lower chain run, so centrifugal force will work the oil into the chain when the bike is moving. After applying the lubricant, let it soak in a few minutes before wiping off any excess.*

 Warning: Take care not to get any lubricant on the tyres or brake system components. If any of the lubricant inadvertently contacts them, clean it off thoroughly using a suitable solvent or dedicated brake cleaner before riding the machine.

Every 1250 miles (2000 km)

2 Brake pad wear check

1 Visually check the amount of friction material remaining on each brake pad in each caliper. Do not assume that the condition of one pad in one side of one caliper reflects the condition of all the pads. On 1998 to 2000 models the best way to view the front brake pads is by looking up at the underside of each caliper. On 2001 to 2003 models look at the front calipers from the back of the fork **(see illustration).** On all models view the rear caliper from the back **(see illustration).**

2 The thickness of friction material remaining is the definitive way of judging wear, and there should never be less than 1.0 mm (though many consider that to be an absolute minimum and prefer to change pads at around 1.5 mm). If necessary remove the pads from the caliper (see Chapter 7) and measure the thickness of material. On 1998 to 2000 models also check that the material on the front pads is worn evenly across the pad – if not one of the pistons is sticking or has seized.

3 On some makes of pad there is a wear indicator groove or cut-out in the friction material that should be plainly visible from the most obvious vantage point, but note that an accumulation of road dirt and brake dust could make them difficult to see. Once the groove is no longer visible or the cut-out has been reached the pad is worn and must be replaced with a new one.

4 If the pads are worn they must be replaced with new ones. If the pads are excessively worn, check the brake discs (see Chapter 7).

5 Refer to Chapter 7 for details of pad removal and installation. Always replace the pads in both front calipers at the same time to ensure even braking.

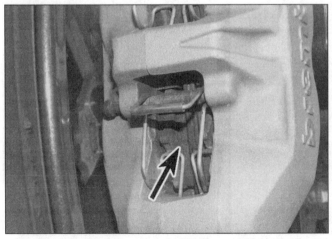

2.1a Visually check the amount of friction material in the front calipers (arrow) – 2001 model shown . . .

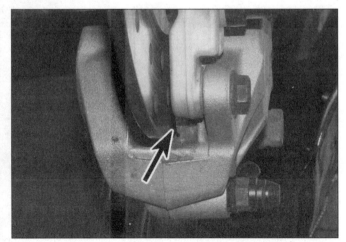

2.1b . . . and in the rear caliper (arrow)

Every 4500 miles (7500 km) or 12 months

3 Air filter check and cleaning

1 Raise the fuel tank (see Chapter 4).
2 Unscrew the bolts securing the air filter cover and remove it **(see illustrations)**.
3 Remove the filter from the housing, noting how it fits **(see illustration)**.
4 Tap the filter on a hard surface to dislodge any large particles of dirt. If compressed air is available, use it to blow through the element, directing it in the opposite direction of normal airflow, i.e. from the outside towards the inside.

 If using compressed air to clean the filter, place either your hand, a rag, or a piece of card on the inside to prevent any dust and debris being blown from one side of the element into the other.

Caution: If the machine is continually ridden in dusty conditions, the filter should be cleaned more frequently.
5 Check the filter for signs of damage. If the element is torn or cannot be cleaned, or is obviously beyond further use, replace it with a new one. Do not use solvents to try and clean the element. Do not run the engine without a filter.
6 Fit the filter in the housing, making sure it is correctly seated.
7 Check the condition of the rubber gasket in the groove in the cover or housing and replace it with a new one if it is damaged, deformed or deteriorated. Make sure the gasket is correctly seated in its groove. Fit the cover and secure it with its bolts.
8 Pull the bung out of the drain tube on the rear right-hand side of the air filter housing and allow any residue to drain **(see illustration)**. Refit the bung.
9 Lower the fuel tank (see Chapter 4).

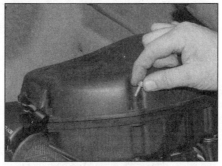

3.2a Unscrew the bolts . . .

3.3 Remove the filter from the housing

4 Spark plug check

⚠️ **Warning: Make sure the engine is cool before removing the spark plugs.**
Caution: Do not interchange the spark plug caps on each head – each cap must be fitted to its correct plug.
1 Each cylinder head has two spark plugs **(see illustration)**. Make sure your spark plug socket is the correct size before attempting to remove the plugs – a suitable one is supplied in the motorcycle's tool kit which is stored under the seat.
2 Raise the fuel tank (see Chapter 4).

3.2b . . . and remove the cover

3.8 Pull out the bung (arrowed) and drain the tube

3 To provide best access to the front cylinder plugs remove the air filter housing (see Chapter 4).
4 Work on one plug at a time. Pull the cap off the spark plug **(see illustration)**.
5 Clean the area around the base of the plug to prevent any dirt falling into the engine. Using either the plug removing tool and the 13 mm spanner supplied in the bike's toolkit, or a deep socket or aftermarket plug wrench, unscrew and remove the plug from the cylinder head **(see illustration)**.
6 Inspect the electrodes for wear. Look for excessive deposits and evidence of a cracked or chipped insulator around the centre electrode. Compare your spark plugs to the colour spark plug reading chart at the end of this manual. Check the threads, the washer

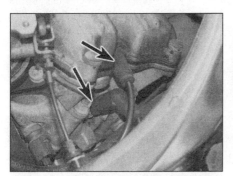

4.1 Each cylinder has two plugs (arrowed) – front cylinder shown

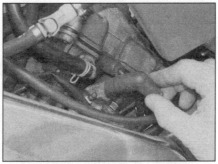

4.4 Pull the cap off the spark plug . . .

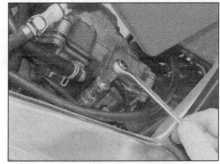

4.5 . . . then unscrew and remove the plug

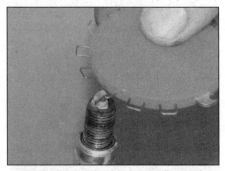

4.7a A wire type gauge is recommended to measure the spark plug electrode gap

4.7b A blade type feeler gauge can also be used

4.7c Adjusting the electrode gap on a standard type plug

and the ceramic insulator body for cracks and other damage.

7 Check the gap between the electrodes preferably using a wire type gauge, or alternatively a feeler gauge **(see illustrations)**. Compare the gap to that specified (see Specifications). If the standard copper-core plug is fitted (NGK DCPR9E) the gap can be adjusted by bending the side electrode, whilst being careful not to chip or crack the insulator nose **(see illustration)**. If a platinum-tipped plug is fitted (NGK DCPR9EVX) the side electrode should not be bent to adjust the gap as its surface will be damaged – if the gap is not as specified replace the spark plugs with new ones.

8 If the electrodes are not excessively worn, if no cracks or chips are visible in the insulator, and if the deposits can be easily removed with a soft brush, the plugs can be re-used. If in doubt concerning the condition of one or more of the plugs, replace them all with new ones as the expense is minimal.

Caution: Do not use a hard wire brush or sandblasting to clean the plugs – the electrodes are easily eroded. Use a toothbrush in conjunction with a suitable solvent, then use compressed air to dry the plug and blow out any particles.

9 Before installing the plugs, refer to the Specifications at the beginning of the Chapter and make sure they are the correct type and heat range. Make sure the washer is in place before installing the plug. Fit the plug into the end of the tool, then use the tool to insert the plug **(see illustration)**. Since the cylinder head is made of aluminium, which is a soft metal

and easily damaged, thread the plug as far as possible into the head turning the tool by hand. Once the plug is finger-tight, the job can be finished with a spanner on the tool supplied or a socket drive **(see illustration 4.5)**. If a torque wrench can be applied, tighten the spark plugs to the torque setting specified at the beginning of the Chapter. Otherwise, tighten them according the instructions on the box – generally if new plugs are being used, tighten them by 1/2 a turn after the washer has seated, and if the old plugs are being reused, tighten them by 1/8 to 1/4 turn after they have seated. Do not over-tighten them.

> **HAYNES HiNT**
> *You can slip a short length of hose over the end of the plug to use as a tool to thread it into place. The hose will grip the plug well enough to turn it, but will start to slip if the plug begins to cross-thread in the hole – this will prevent damaged threads.*

10 Fit the spark plug cap, making sure it locates correctly onto the plug **(see illustration 4.4)**. After all plugs have been checked lower the fuel tank (see Chapter 4).

> **HAYNES HiNT**
> *Stripped plug threads in the cylinder head can be repaired with a wire thread insert – see 'Tools and Workshop Tips' in the Reference section.*

5 Fuel system check

> ⚠️ *Warning: Petrol (gasoline) is extremely flammable, so take extra precautions when you work on any part of the fuel system. Don't smoke or allow open flames or bare light bulbs near the work area, and don't work in a garage where a natural gas-type appliance is present. If you spill any fuel on your skin, rinse it off immediately with soap and water. When you perform any kind of work on the fuel system, wear safety glasses and have a fire extinguisher suitable for a Class B type fire (flammable liquids) on hand.*

1 Raise the fuel tank (see Chapter 4). Check the tank, the fuel pump base and gasket and the fuel supply and return hoses for signs of leakage, deterioration or damage; in particular check that there is no leakage from the fuel hoses. Replace any hoses that are cracked or deteriorated with new ones. Similarly check all the vacuum hoses and the crankcase breather hose between the rear cylinder head and the air filter housing **(see illustration)**. On California models also check the EVAP system hoses (refer to Chapter 4 for details of this system).

2 If there is leakage from the fuel pump base, remove the pump and replace the O-ring with a new one (see Chapter 4).

3 Also check for signs of fuel leakage between the injectors and the throttle bodies. If there are, remove the injectors and install new O-rings and seals (see Chapter 4).

4 Installing a new fuel filter is advised after a particularly high mileage has been covered – Aprilia do not specify a replacement interval. It is also necessary if fuel starvation is suspected, in which case perform a fuel pressure check (see Chapter 4). On early models, with a metal fuel tank, check the condition of the inside of the fuel tank – if it is old and there is evidence of rust, remove, drain and clean the tank, then clean the strainer and fit a new filter (see Chapter 4).

4.9 Thread the plug in as far as possible by hand

5.1 Check all the fuel system hoses between the tank, the throttle bodies and the engine as described

6.3 Unscrew the oil filler cap

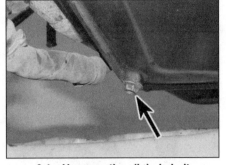

6.4a Unscrew the oil drain bolt (arrowed) . . .

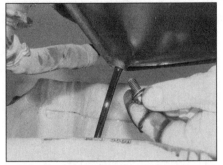

6.4b . . . and allow the oil to drain

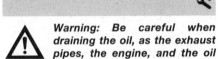

6 Engine oil and filter change

⚠️ *Warning: Be careful when draining the oil, as the exhaust pipes, the engine, and the oil itself can cause severe burns.*

1 Consistent routine oil and filter changes are the single most important maintenance procedure you can perform on a motorcycle. The oil not only lubricates the internal parts of the engine, transmission and clutch, but it also acts as a coolant, a cleaner, a sealant, and a protector. Because of these demands, the oil takes a terrific amount of abuse and should be replaced often with new oil of the recommended grade and type. Saving a little money on the difference in cost between good oil and cheap oil won't pay off if the

engine is damaged. The oil filter should be changed with every oil change.

2 Before changing the oil, warm up the engine so the oil will drain easily. Make sure the bike is on level ground. Remove the lower fairing (see Chapter 8).

3 Position a clean drain tray below the oil tank on the left-hand side of the engine. Unscrew the filler cap from the tank to vent it and to act as a reminder that there is no oil in the engine **(see illustration)**.

4 Unscrew the drain bolt from the bottom of the tank and allow the oil to flow into the drain tray **(see illustrations)**. Check the condition of the sealing washer on the drain bolt and replace it with a new one if it is damaged or worn – it is advisable to use a new one whatever the condition of the old one.

5 When the oil has completely drained, fit the bolt into the tank, preferably using a new sealing washer, and tighten it to the torque

setting specified at the beginning of the Chapter **(see illustration)**. Avoid overtightening, as it is quite easy to damage the threads in the tank.

6 Now place the drain tray below the oil filter cover, located on the engine to the rear of the oil tank. Unscrew the engine oil drain bolt and allow the residual oil in the engine to drain into the container **(see illustration)**. Clean any debris off the magnetic end of the bolt, then fit it back into the engine and tighten it to the specified torque.

7 Undo the filter cover bolts **(see illustration 6.6)** and remove the cover with its O-ring **(see illustration)**. Discard the O-ring – a new one should be used. Withdraw the filter, noting which way round it fits, and discard it **(see illustration)**.

8 Fit a new filter into the engine **(see illustration)**. Fit a new O-ring onto the cover, then install the cover and tighten its bolts to the specified torque **(see illustration)**.

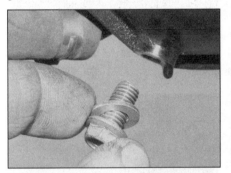

6.5 Install the drain plug using a new sealing washer and tighten it to the specified torque

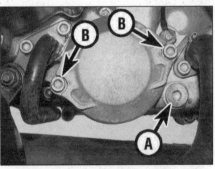

6.6 Engine oil drain bolt (A) and oil filter cover bolts (B)

6.7a Remove the cover and allow the oil to drain . . .

6.7b . . . then withdraw the filter

6.8a Install the new filter . . .

6.8b . . . then fit the cover using a new O-ring

6.9a Release the clamp (arrowed) and detach the hose . . .

6.9b . . . then unscrew, withdraw and clean the strainer – note the O-ring (arrowed)

9 With every second oil and filter change you should clean the strainer that is located inside the oil tank. Release the clamp securing the oil hose to the strainer union on the rear of the tank **(see illustration)**. Unscrew the strainer and withdraw it from the tank **(see illustration)**. Discard the O-ring. Clean the strainer using a suitable solvent then blow it through with compressed air. Install the strainer using a new O-ring and tighten it to the specified torque setting. Fit the hose, making sure it is in condition (use a new one if there are any signs of cracking or hardening), onto the strainer union and tighten the clamp to secure it.

10 Refill the oil tank to the proper level using the recommended type and amount of oil (see *Daily (pre-ride) checks*). Install the filler cap **(see illustration 6.3)**. Start the engine and let it run for two or three minutes (make sure that the oil pressure LED extinguishes after a few seconds). Shut it off, wait a few minutes, then check the oil level (see *Daily (pre-ride) checks*). If necessary, add more oil to bring the level in the pipe almost to the MAX line on the tank. Check around the drain bolts and the oil filter cover for leaks. A leak around the tank drain plug probably means a new washer is needed. A leak around the filter cover probably means a new O-ring is needed.

Saving a little money on the difference between good and cheap oils won't pay off if the engine is damaged as a result.

11 The old oil drained from the engine cannot be re-used and should be disposed of properly. Check with your local refuse disposal company, disposal facility or environmental agency to see whether they will accept the used oil for recycling. Don't pour used oil into drains or onto the ground.

Check the old oil carefully – if it is very metallic coloured, then the engine is experiencing wear from break-in (new engine) or from insufficient lubrication. If there are flakes or chips of metal in the oil, then something is drastically wrong internally and the engine will have to be disassembled for inspection and repair. If there are pieces of fibre-like material in the oil, the clutch is experiencing excessive wear and should be checked.

7 Idle speed check and adjustment

1 The idle speed should be checked and adjusted before and after the throttle bodies are synchronised (balanced), after checking the valve clearances, and when it is obviously too high or too low. Before adjusting the idle speed, make sure the spark plugs are clean and the gaps correct, and the air filter is clean. If a valve clearance check is part of the

service you are performing, do that first (see Section 24). Also, turn the handlebars from side-to-side and check the idle speed does not change as you do. If it does, the throttle cables may not be adjusted or routed correctly, or may be worn out. This is a dangerous condition that can cause loss of control of the bike. Be sure to correct this problem before proceeding.

2 The engine should be at normal operating temperature, which is usually reached after 10 to 15 minutes of stop-and-go riding. Place the motorcycle on its sidestand, and make sure the transmission is in neutral.

3 On early models up to frame no. ZD4MEE009YS000292 the idle speed adjuster is a screw on the throttle bodies that can be accessed using a long flat-bladed screwdriver via the rear of two small holes in the right-hand fuel tank trim panel, or alternatively by raising the fuel tank (see Chapter 4) and using a short screwdriver **(see illustration)**.

4 On all other models the idle speed adjuster is a knurled knob located on the right-hand side of the motorcycle between the fuel tank and the main frame beam **(see illustration)**. With the engine idling, adjust the speed by turning the screw or knob until the idle speed listed in this Chapter's Specifications is obtained. Turn the adjuster clockwise to increase idle speed, and anti-clockwise to decrease it.

5 Snap the throttle open and shut a few times, then recheck the idle speed. If necessary, repeat the adjustment procedure.

6 If a smooth, steady idle can't be achieved, the throttle bodies may need synchronising (see Section 17), or there could be a problem with the fuel injection system (see Chapter 4). Also check the intake duct rubbers for cracks or a loose clamp that will cause an air leak, resulting in a weak mixture.

8 Throttle and fast idle cable check

Throttle cables

1 Make sure the throttle grip rotates smoothly and freely from fully closed to fully open with the front wheel turned at various angles. The grip should return automatically from fully open to fully closed when released.

2 If the throttle sticks, this is probably due to a cable fault. Remove the cables (see Chapter 4) and lubricate them (see Section 15). Check that the inner cables slide freely and easily in the outer cables. If not, replace the cables with new ones. With the cables removed, make sure the throttle twistgrip rotates freely on the handlebar. Install the cables, making sure they are correctly routed. If this fails to improve the operation of the throttle, the cables must be replaced with new ones. Note that in very rare cases the fault could lie in the

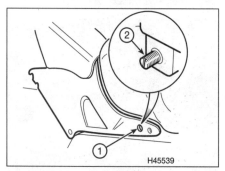

7.3 Insert a long screwdriver in the hole (1) to access the adjuster screw (2) - early models

7.4 Idle speed adjuster knob (arrowed) - late models

8.3 Twist the throttle and measure the amount of free rotation

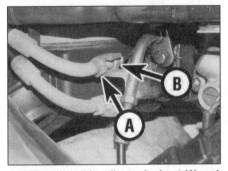

8.5 Throttle cable adjuster locknut (A) and adjuster (B)

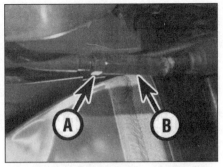

8.4 Slacken the adjuster locknut (A) and turn the adjuster (B) as described

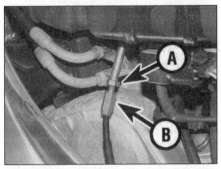

8.8 Fast idle cable adjuster locknut (A) and adjuster (B)

should not change. If it does, the cables may be routed incorrectly. Correct this condition before riding the bike.

6 Check that the throttle twistgrip operates smoothly and snaps shut quickly when released.

Fast idle cable

7 If the fast idle lever does not operate smoothly this is probably due to a cable fault, but also check the action at the throttle body end. If necessary remove the cable (see Chapter 4) and lubricate it (see Section 15). Check that the inner cable slides freely and easily in the outer cable. If not, replace the cable with a new one. With the cable removed, make sure the lever is able to move freely. Install the cable, making sure it is correctly routed.

8 With the lever operating smoothly, check for a small amount of freeplay in it before the cable actuates the mechanism, and compare the amount to that listed in this Chapter's Specifications. Adjust it if necessary using the adjuster at the throttle body end of the cable – raise the fuel tank (see Chapter 4) to access it. Slacken the locknut, then turn the adjuster as required until the specified amount of freeplay is evident, then retighten the locknut **(see illustration)**.

throttle bodies rather than the cables, necessitating their removal and inspection (see Chapter 4).

3 With the throttle operating smoothly, check for a small amount of freeplay in the cables, measured in terms of the amount of twistgrip rotation before the throttle opens, and compare the amount to that listed in this Chapter's Specifications **(see illustration)**. If it's incorrect, adjust the cables to correct it as follows.

4 Pull the rubber boot off the adjuster in the opening cable after it leaves the housing on the handlebar. Loosen the locknut then turn the adjuster until the specified amount of freeplay is obtained (see this Chapter's Specifications) **(see illustration)**. Retighten the locknut then slide the boot back on.

5 If the adjuster has reached its limit, or if major adjustment is required, reset the adjuster so that the freeplay is at a maximum

(i.e. the adjuster is fully turned in), then raise the fuel tank, and if required for best access remove the air filter housing (see Chapter 4), and adjust the cable at the throttle body end. Slacken the adjuster locknut on the top cable in the bracket and thread it fully up to the cable elbow **(see illustration)**. Push the adjuster into the bracket so the captive nut becomes free, then thread it up or down the adjuster as required until the freeplay is as specified – thread it towards the elbow to increase freeplay and away from it reduce it. Locate the adjuster in the bracket so the nut becomes captive then tighten the locknut against the bracket. Any fine alteration can be made at the handlebar end as in Step 4. If the cables cannot be adjusted as specified, install new ones (see Chapter 4).

 Warning: Turn the handlebars all the way through their travel with the engine idling. Idle speed

---

9 Clutch check

1 All models are fitted with an hydraulic clutch, for which there is no method of adjustment.

2 Check the fluid level in the reservoir (see *Daily (pre-ride) checks*).

3 Inspect the hydraulic and reservoir hoses and their connections for signs of fluid leakage, cracking, deterioration and wear **(see illustrations)**. Also check around the master cylinder pushrod end and the release cylinder body for leaks **(see illustration)**. Replace worn or damaged components with new ones (see Chapter 2).

4 Change the clutch fluid every two years (see Section 29), and replace the hose with a new one either if damaged or deteriorated, or

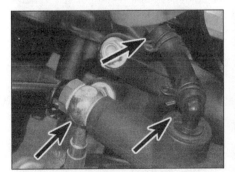

9.3a Check around the master cylinder and reservoir hose unions (arrowed) . . .

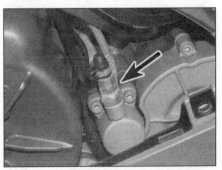

9.3b . . . and the release cylinder hose union (arrowed) for leaks

9.3c A leak around the pushrod end (arrowed) indicates a worn cup and seal

9.6 Clutch lever span adjuster – align the required setting number with the triangle on the lever

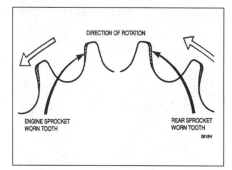

10.3 Check the hoses and unions. Also check the pump drain hole location (arrowed) for leakage – reservoir shown removed for clarity

10.8 Remove the filler cap

every four years irrespective of condition (see Section 32). If leakage is evident from the master cylinder it must be replaced with a new one as no individual components are available. A new seal is available for the release cylinder.

5 Check the operation of the clutch. If there is evidence of air in the system (spongy feel to the lever, difficulty in engaging gear, drag when in gear), bleed the clutch (see Chapter 2). If the lever feels stiff or sticky, overhaul the release mechanism (see Chapter 2).

6 The clutch lever has a span adjuster that alters the distance of the lever from the handlebar **(see illustration)**. Each setting is identified by a number on the adjuster, which must align with the triangle on the lever. Pull the lever away from the handlebar and turn the adjuster ring until the setting that best suits the rider is obtained.

10 Cooling system check

> ⚠ **Warning: The engine must be cool before beginning this procedure.**

1 Check the coolant level (see *Daily (pre-ride) checks*).

2 Remove the fairing side panels and the lower fairing (see Chapter 8).

3 Check the entire cooling system for evidence of leakage. Examine each rubber coolant hose along its entire length **(see illustration)**. Look for cracks, abrasions and other damage. Squeeze each hose at various points to see whether they are dried out or hard. They should feel firm, yet pliable, and return to their original shape when released. If necessary, replace them with new ones (see Chapter 3).

4 Check for evidence of leaks at each cooling system joint and around the pump on the right-hand side of the engine. Tighten the hose clips where possible or replace them with new ones where the clip-type are used to prevent future leaks. If the pump cover is leaking, check that the cover bolts are tight. If they are, replace the O-ring in the cover with a new one (see Chapter 3).

5 To prevent leakage of coolant from the cooling system to the lubrication system and vice versa, two seals are fitted on the pump shaft. There is a drain hole in the pump housing on the clutch cover **(see illustration 10.3)**. If either seal fails, the drain allows the coolant or oil to escape and prevents them mixing. In the event of both seals failing, the oil and coolant mix to form a white emulsion. The seal on the water pump side is of the mechanical type which bears on the rear face of the impeller. The second seal, which is mounted behind the mechanical seal is of the normal feathered lip type. Both seals are available separately. If on inspection there is evidence of leakage from the drain hole, remove the water pump and replace both seals with new ones. Refer to Chapter 3 for details.

6 Check the radiators for leaks and other damage. Leaks in the radiator leave tell-tale scale deposits or coolant stains on the outside of the core below the leak. If leaks are noted, remove the radiator(s) (see Chapter 3) and have it/them repaired or replace it/them with a new one.

Caution: Do not use a liquid leak stopping compound to try to repair leaks.

7 Check the radiator fins for mud, dirt and insects, which may impede the flow of air through the radiator. If the fins are dirty, remove the radiator (see Chapter 3) and clean it using water or low pressure compressed air directed through the fins from the inner side. If the fins are bent or distorted, straighten them

DIRECTION OF ROTATION

ENGINE SPROCKET
WORN TOOTH

REAR SPROCKET
WORN TOOTH

0618H

11.3 Check the sprockets in the areas indicated to see if they are worn

carefully with a screwdriver. If the air flow is restricted by bent or damaged fins over more than 20% of the surface area, replace the radiator with a new one.

8 Remove the cap from the filler neck **(see illustration)**. If you hear a hissing sound (indicating there is still pressure in the system), wait until it stops. Check the condition of the coolant in the system. If it is rust-coloured or if accumulations of scale are visible, drain and flush the system and refill it with new coolant (See Section 30). Check the cap for cracks and other damage. If in doubt replace it with a new one.

9 Check the antifreeze content of the coolant with an antifreeze hydrometer. Sometimes coolant looks like it's in good condition, but might be too weak to offer adequate protection. If the hydrometer indicates a weak mixture, drain, flush and refill the system (see Section 30).

10 Install the cap. Start the engine and let it reach normal operating temperature, then check for leaks again. As the coolant temperature increases, the electric fans (mounted on the back of each radiator) should come on automatically and the temperature should begin to drop. If it does not, refer to Chapter 3 and check the fans and fan circuits carefully.

11 If the coolant level is consistently low, and no evidence of leaks can be found, have the entire system pressure checked by an Aprilia dealer.

11 Drive chain and sprocket wear and chain stretch check

1 To check the chain, place the bike on an auxiliary stand so the rear wheel is off the ground and shift the transmission into neutral.

2 Check the entire length of the chain for damaged rollers, loose links and pins, and missing O-rings. Fit a new chain if damage is found. **Note:** *Never install a new chain on old sprockets, and never use the old chain if you install new sprockets – replace the chain and sprockets as a set.*

3 Remove the front sprocket cover (see Chapter 6). Check the teeth on the front sprocket and the rear sprocket for wear **(see illustration)**.

4 Inspect the drive chain slider on the front of the swingarm and the guide plate fitted with the sprocket cover for excessive wear and damage and replace them with new ones if necessary.

5 Measure the amount of chain stretch as follows:

6 Slacken the rear axle nut **(see illustration 1.7)**.

7 Slacken the locknut on each adjuster bolt, then turn the adjuster bolt on each side evenly until the chain is tight, but not taut **(see illustration 1.8a)**. Measure along the bottom run the length of 17 pins (from the centre of the 1st pin to the centre of the 17th pin) and compare the result to the stretch limit specified at the beginning of the Chapter **(see illustration)**. Rotate the rear wheel so that several sections of the chain can be measured, then calculate the average. If the chain stretch measurement exceeds the service limit it must be replaced with a new one (see Chapter 6).

8 If the chain is good, reset the adjusters so that there is the correct amount of freeplay, then tighten the axle nut to the specified torque setting (see Specifications).

12 Brake system check

1 A routine general check of the brake system will ensure that any problems are discovered and remedied before the rider's safety is jeopardised.

2 Check the brake lever and pedal for loose mountings, improper or rough action, excessive play, bends, and other damage. Lubricate the lever and pedal at the specified interval or as required (see Section 15). Replace any damaged parts with new ones (see Chapter 7).

3 Make sure all brake component fasteners are tight. Check the brake pads for wear (see Section 2) and make sure the fluid level in the reservoirs is correct (see *Daily (pre-ride) checks*). Look for leaks at the hose connections and check for cracks in the hoses **(see illustration)**. If the lever or pedal is spongy, bleed the brakes (see Chapter 7).

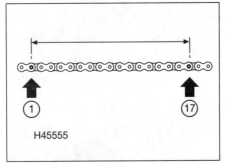

11.7 Measure the distance between the 1st and 17th pins to determine chain stretch

4 Make sure the brake light comes on when the brake lever or pedal is applied. Neither the front brake light switch, mounted on the underside of the master cylinder, nor the rear brake light switch, mounted on the inside of the pedal, are adjustable. If they fail to operate properly, check them (see Chapter 9).

5 The front brake lever has a span adjuster that alters the distance of the lever from the handlebar **(see illustration)**. Each setting is identified by a number on the adjuster, which must align with the triangle on the lever. Pull the lever away from the handlebar and turn the adjuster ring until the setting that best suits the rider is obtained.

6 The toe pin on the rear brake pedal is mounted eccentrically and can be adjusted to suit the rider's preference. Slacken the pinch bolt, then turn the pin until it is in the desired position **(see illustration)**. On completion tighten the pinch bolt securely. Replace the rubber on the pin with a new one if it is worn damaged or deteriorated. The gearchange lever has the same adjustability.

13 Tyre and wheel check

Tyres

1 Check the tyre condition and tread depth thoroughly – see *Daily (pre-ride) checks*.

Wheels

2 Cast wheels are virtually maintenance-free, but they should be kept clean and checked periodically for cracks and other damage. Also check the wheel runout and alignment (see Chapter 7). Never attempt to repair damaged cast wheels; they must be replaced with new ones. Check the valve rubber for signs of damage or deterioration and have it replaced if necessary. Also, make sure the valve stem cap is in place and tight.

14 Nut and bolt tightness check

1 Since vibration of the machine tends to loosen fasteners, all nuts, bolts, screws, etc. should be checked for proper tightness.

2 Pay particular attention to the following:
Spark plugs
Engine oil drain bolts and coolant drain bolts
Lever and pedal bolts
Footrest and sidestand bolts
Engine mounting bolts (refer to Chapter 2)
Shock absorber and suspension linkage bolts; swingarm pivot adjuster bolt, nut and locknut (refer to Chapter 6)
Handlebar clamp bolts and positioning bolts (refer to Chapter 6)
Front fork clamp bolts (top and bottom yoke) and fork top bolts
Steering stem nut
Steering damper bolts
Front wheel axle nut
Rear wheel axle nut
Front sprocket bolt and rear sprocket nuts
Brake caliper and master cylinder mounting bolts
Brake hose banjo bolts and caliper bleed valves
Brake disc bolts
Exhaust system bolts/nuts

3 If a torque wrench is available, use it along with the torque specifications at the beginning of this and other Chapters.

12.3 Flex the hoses and check for cracks, bulges and leaking fluid. Also check all connections for leaks

12.5 Brake lever span adjuster – align the required setting number with the triangle on the lever

12.6 Slacken the bolt (arrowed) and adjust the position as required

15 Stand, lever pivot and cable lubrication

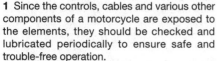

1 Since the controls, cables and various other components of a motorcycle are exposed to the elements, they should be checked and lubricated periodically to ensure safe and trouble-free operation.

2 The footrests, clutch and brake levers, brake pedal, and sidestand pivot should be lubricated frequently. In order for the lubricant to be applied where it will do the most good, the component should be disassembled. The lubricant recommended by Aprilia for each application is listed at the beginning of the Chapter. If chain or cable lubricant is being used, it can be applied to the pivot joint gaps and will usually work its way into the areas where friction occurs, so less disassembly of the component is needed (however it is always better to do so and clean off all corrosion, dirt and old lubricant first). If motor oil or light grease is being used, apply it sparingly as it may attract dirt (which could cause the controls to bind or wear at an accelerated rate). **Note:** *One of the best lubricants for the control lever pivots is a dry-film lubricant (available from many sources by different names).*

3 To lubricate the throttle and fast idle cables, disconnect the relevant cable at its upper end, then lubricate it with a pressure adapter (but note they don't fit well on flanged cable ends) and aerosol lubricant, or if one is not available, using the set-up shown **(see illustrations)**. See Chapter 4 for the fast idle and throttle cable removal procedures.

16 Battery check

1 All models are fitted with a sealed MF (maintenance free) battery. **Note:** *Do not attempt to remove the battery caps to check the electrolyte level or battery specific gravity. Removal will damage the caps, resulting in electrolyte leakage and battery damage.* All that should be done is to check that the terminals are clean and tight and that the casing is not damaged or leaking. See Chapter 9 for further details.

2 If the machine is not in regular use, remove the battery and give it a refresher charge every month to six weeks (see Chapter 9).

17 Throttle body synchronisation and exhaust CO check

 Warning: Petrol (gasoline) is extremely flammable, so take extra precautions when you work on any part of the fuel

15.3a Lubricating a cable with a pressure lubricator. Make sure the tool seals around the inner cable

system. Don't smoke or allow open flames or bare light bulbs near the work area, and don't work in a garage where a natural gas-type appliance is present. If you spill any fuel on your skin, rinse it off immediately with soap and water. When you perform any kind of work on the fuel system, wear safety glasses and have a fire extinguisher suitable for a Class B type fire (flammable liquids) on hand.

 Warning: Take great care not to burn your hands on the hot engine unit when accessing the throttle bodies and gauge take-off points on the intake ducts. Do not allow exhaust gases to build up in the work area; either perform the check outside or use an exhaust gas extraction system.

Note: *Throttle body vacuum synchronisation should always be carried out in conjunction with a CO level check to ensure that the throttle bodies are correctly set and that emissions regulations are complied with. An exhaust sample take-off probe that threads into a port in the exhaust downpipe of each cylinder is required (part No. 8140202), in conjunction with an exhaust gas analyser (part No. 8140578 (English version) or 8140196 (Italian version). You also need a set of vacuum gauges (available from Aprilia, part No.8140256) or calibrated tubes to indicate engine vacuum. The equipment used should be suitable for a twin cylinder engine and come complete with the necessary hoses to fit the take-off points. If this equipment is not available have the entire process carried out by an Aprilia dealer. While it is possible to carry out a vacuum synchronisation check and adjustment using readily available and inexpensive equipment, the fact that the vacuum reading for each throttle body is the same does not mean that the CO levels are correct. On models with an engine number up to 686064 a special intake duct adapter (part No. 8140267) that bolts in place of the standard duct is required for the front cylinder – the special duct provides a vacuum take-off union for the gauges.*

1 Throttle bodies that are out of synchronisation will result in increased fuel consumption, increased engine temperature,

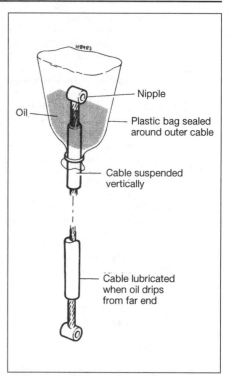

15.3b Lubricating a cable with a makeshift funnel and motor oil

erratic idling, less than ideal throttle response and higher vibration levels. If a valve clearance check is part of the service you are performing, do that first (see Section 24). Because of the nature of the synchronisation procedure and the need for special instruments (see **Note** above), most owners leave the task to an Aprilia dealer.

2 Start the engine and let it run until it reaches normal operating temperature, then check that the idle speed is correctly set, and adjust it if necessary (see Section 7).

3 Raise the fuel tank (see Chapter 4).

4 On models with an engine number up to 686064 remove the air filter housing, then displace the throttle bodies (see Chapter 4) – you should be able to do this without detaching the cables and disconnecting the hoses and wiring, but do so if required to avoid the possibility of damaging anything and to give more freedom of movement. Unscrew the bolts securing the front cylinder intake duct to the cylinder head and replace it with the special duct with the vacuum take-off union, making sure the union is on the right-hand side and tightening the bolts to the torque setting specified at the beginning of the Chapter **(see illustration)**. Install the throttle bodies and air filter housing (see Chapter 4).

5 On all models release the clamp and detach the hose from the vacuum take-off union on the right-hand side of the rear cylinder throttle body **(see illustration)**.

6 On models with engine number 686065-on

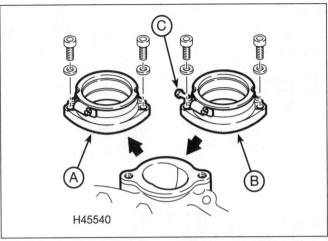

17.4 Remove the standard duct (A) and replace it with the special part (B) that has the vacuum take-off union (C)

17.5 Release the clamp and detach the hose

remove the blanking cap from the take-off union on the right-hand side of the front cylinder throttle body **(see illustration)**.

7 Connect the gauge hoses to the vacuum take-off unions. Make sure they are a good fit because any air leaks will result in false readings.

8 Unscrew the blanking plug from the exhaust take-off port in each cylinder exhaust header pipe **(see illustrations)**. Connect one of the exhaust sample probes to each of the ports, then connect the probes to the gas analyser – there should be instructions with the tools.

9 Start the engine, allow it to reach normal operating temperature and recheck the idle speed. If using vacuum gauges fitted with damping adjustment, set this so that the needle flutter is just eliminated but so that they can still respond to small changes in pressure.

10 The CO and vacuum readings for the cylinders should be the same, or at least within the range specified at the beginning of the Chapter.

11 On models with a frame number that starts ZD4ME, adjustment is made using the screw on each throttle body **(see illustration)**.

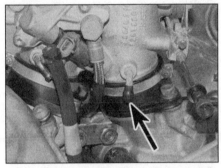

17.6 Remove the blanking cap (arrowed)

The same screw adjusts the CO level and the vacuum for its cylinder. Adjust each screw as required until the CO readings are as specified and so that the vacuum readings are as close as possible, but giving priority to the CO readings.

12 On models with a frame number that starts ZD4RP, adjustment is made using the screws on the ECU (engine control unit) **(see illustration)**. Remove the rider's seat and lift the rubber cover off the ECU to access the screws, which are in the front on the left-hand side. The same screw adjusts the CO level

17.8a Front cylinder header pipe blanking plug (arrowed)

and the vacuum for its cylinder. Adjust each screw as required until the CO and vacuum readings are within the range specified and as close to each other as possible, but giving priority to the CO readings.

13 Recheck the idle speed and adjust if necessary, then recheck the CO and vacuum readings and readjust if necessary. Repeat until all three (idle speed, CO and vacuum) are as specified. When adjustment is complete, stop the engine.

14 Remove the vacuum gauges and the exhaust probes.

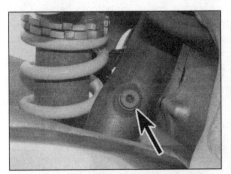

17.8b Rear cylinder header pipe blanking plug (arrowed)

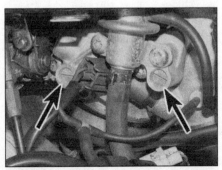

17.11 Synchronisation adjustment screws (arrowed) – models with a frame number that starts ZD4ME

17.12 On models with a frame number that starts ZD4RP the synchronisation adjustment screws (arrowed) are on the front of the ECU

18.5 Checking for play in the steering head bearings

18.7a Unscrew the handlebar positioning bolt on each side

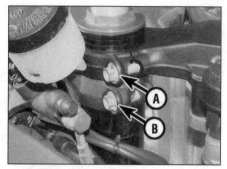

18.7b Fork clamp bolt (A), handlebar clamp bolt (B)

18.8a Unscrew the steering stem nut and remove the washer . . .

18.8b . . . and ease the yoke up off the forks

HAYNES HINT *Make sure you are not mistaking any movement between the bike and stand or jack, or between the stand or jack and the ground, for freeplay in the bearings. Do not pull and push the forks too hard – a gentle movement is all that is needed. Freeplay in the forks themselves due to worn bushes can also be misinterpreted as steering head bearing play – do not confuse the two.*

15 On models with an engine number up to 686064 remove the special intake duct and replace it with the original – do not leave the special one in place (see Step 4). Tighten the flange bolts to the specified torque.
16 On models with engine number 686065-on fit the blanking cap to the take-off union on the right-hand side of the front cylinder throttle body **(see illustration 17.6)**.
17 On all models fit the vacuum hose onto the rear cylinder throttle body union and secure it with its clamp, using a new one if necessary **(see illustration 17.5)**. Fit the blanking plug into each exhaust downpipe using a smear of ANTI-SEIZE MOTAGEPASTE AS 1800 on the threads **(see illustrations 17.8a and b)**.
18 Lower the fuel tank (see Chapter 4).

18 Steering head bearing freeplay check and adjustment

1 Steering head bearings can become dented, rough or loose during normal use of the machine, particularly if the bike is ridden hard or often only on the back wheel! Worn, loose or tight steering head bearings can cause severe handling problems, a condition that is potentially dangerous.

Check

2 Remove the steering damper (see Chapter 6). Remove the lower fairing (see Chapter 8).
3 Support the motorcycle on an auxiliary stand and raise the front wheel off the ground

using a jack with a block of wood between the jack head and the engine.
4 Point the front wheel straight-ahead and slowly move the handlebars from side-to-side. Any dents or roughness in the bearing races will be felt and the bars will not move smoothly and freely. Again point the wheel straight ahead, and tap the front of the wheel to one side. The wheel should 'fall' under its own weight to the limit of its lock, indicating that the bearings are not too tight. Check for similar movement to the other side. If the steering doesn't perform as described, and it's not due to the resistance of cables or hoses, then the bearings should be adjusted as described below.
5 Next, grasp the bottom of the forks and gently pull and push them forward and backward **(see illustration)**. Any looseness or freeplay in the steering head bearings will be felt as front-to-rear movement of the forks. If play is felt, adjust the bearings as described below.

Adjustment

6 Remove the fairing if required to give more room to work and prevent the possibility of damage should a tool slip (see Chapter 8). Cover the fuel tank in plenty of rag to prevent damage, or to be absolutely certain, raise it (see Chapter 4).
7 Unscrew the positioning bolt securing each handlebar to the underside of the top yoke **(see illustration)**. Slacken the fork clamp bolts in the top yoke **(see illustration)**.
8 Unscrew and remove the steering stem nut and its washer **(see illustration)**. Ease the top yoke up off the forks and place it aside using some rag to protect other components, and making sure no strain is placed on the ignition switch wiring **(see illustration)**.
9 Carefully bend down each of the lock washer tabs located in the notches in the adjuster locknut (the top nut) **(see illustration)**. Unscrew and remove the locknut – it may not be more than finger-tight, but use a drift located in one of the notches or a suitable C-spanner if necessary **(see illustration)**.

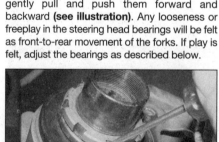

18.9a Bend down the tabs . . . .

18.9b . . . then unscrew the locknut . . .

18.9c . . . and remove the lock washer

18.10 Adjust the bearings as described using either a drift or a C-spanner

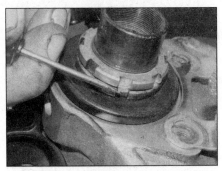

18.13 Bend the tabs up into the lock washer notches

Remove the lock washer, noting how it's other tabs locate in the notches in the adjuster nut **(see illustration)**. Check the condition of the lock washer and replace it with a new one if any of the tabs look fatigued by the bending process – Aprilia recommend using a new one as a matter of course.

10 Using either the C-spanner or drift, slacken the adjuster nut slightly until pressure is just released, then tighten it until all freeplay is removed, yet the steering is able to move freely **(see illustration)**. The object is to set the adjuster nut so that the bearings are under a very light loading, just enough to remove any freeplay, but not so much that the steering does not move freely from side to side as described in the check procedure above. If the Aprilia service tool (part No. 8140203) or a suitable peg spanner (which can be made by cutting castellations into an old socket) is available, tighten the adjuster nut to the torque setting specified at the beginning of the Chapter. However do not rely on the torque setting method alone and assume the loading to be correct – check the physical feel as described as well.

11 If the bearings cannot be correctly adjusted, disassemble the steering head and check the bearings and races (see Chapter 6). *Caution: Take great care not to apply excessive pressure because this will cause premature failure of the bearings.*

12 With the bearings correctly adjusted, install the lock washer, using a new one if the tabs are weakened or cracked, onto the adjuster nut and fit two opposite tabs into the slots in the adjuster nut **(see illustration 18.9c)**.

13 Hold the adjuster nut to prevent it moving, then install the locknut and tighten it finger-tight **(see illustration 18.9b)**. Tighten the locknut further (but no more than 90°) until its notches align with the remaining lock washer tabs, making sure the adjuster nut does not turn as well (though that is unlikely). Secure the locknut in position by bending up the remaining lock washer tabs into its notches **(see illustration)**.

14 Slacken each handlebar clamp bolt **(see illustration 18.7b)**. Fit the top yoke onto the steering stem and forks **(see illustration 18.8b)**. Install the steering stem nut with its

washer and tighten it to the torque setting specified at the beginning of the Chapter **(see illustration 18.8a)**. Now tighten both the top yoke fork clamp bolts to the specified torque **(see illustration 18.7b)**.

15 Install the handlebar positioning bolts and tighten them to the specified torque **(see illustration 18.7a)**. Now tighten the handlebar clamp bolts to the specified torque **(see illustration 18.7b)**.

16 Check the bearing adjustment as described above and re-adjust if necessary.

17 Install the fuel tank if raised or removed (see Chapter 4), and the fairing if removed (see Chapter 8).

Steering head bearing lubrication

18 Over a period of time the grease will harden or may be washed out of the bearings by incorrect use of jet washes.

19 Aprilia do not specify a particular service interval for this procedure, but every so often, and particularly if jet washes have been used or the bike has been ridden in wet weather often, you should disassemble the steering head for re-greasing of the bearings. Refer to Chapter 6 for details.

19 Suspension check

1 The suspension components must be maintained in top operating condition to ensure rider safety. Loose, worn or damaged suspension parts decrease the motorcycle's stability and control.

Front suspension

2 While standing alongside the motorcycle, and with it off the stand and upright, apply the front brake and push on the handlebars to compress the forks several times. See if they move up-and-down smoothly without binding. If binding is felt, the forks should be disassembled and inspected (see Chapter 6).

3 Inspect the area below and around each dust seal for signs of oil leakage, pitting and corrosion, then carefully lever the seals out using a flat-bladed screwdriver and inspect

the area around the fork seal **(see illustration)**. If leakage is evident, the seals in each fork must be replaced with new ones (see Chapter 6). If there is pitting of the chrome tubes (RSV Mille) within the extent of fork travel, you should consider replacing them with new ones as it will eventually cause the seals to fail. If there is evidence of corrosion between the seal retaining ring and its groove spray the area with a penetrative lubricant, otherwise the ring will be difficult to remove if needed. Press the dust seal back into place on completion.

4 Check the tightness of all suspension nuts and bolts to be sure none have worked loose, applying the torque settings at the beginning of Chapter 6 if you have a torque wrench.

Rear suspension

5 Inspect the rear shock absorber for damage and fluid leakage and tightness of its mountings. If leakage is found, the shock must be replaced with a new one (see Chapter 6).

6 With the aid of an assistant to support the bike, compress the rear suspension several times. It should move up and down freely without binding. If any binding is felt, the worn or faulty component must be identified and checked (see Chapter 6). The problem could be due to either the shock absorber, the suspension linkage components or the swingarm components.

7 Support the motorcycle on an auxiliary stand so that the rear wheel is off the ground. Grab the swingarm and rock it from side to

19.3 Check for oil leakage and pitting of the fork tubes (arrowed)

19.7 Checking for play in the swingarm bearings

19.8 Checking for play in the rear suspension mountings and linkage bearings

19.11 Example of ruined bearings and seals due to water ingress

side – there should be no discernible movement at the rear **(see illustration)**. If there's a little movement or a slight clicking can be heard, inspect the tightness of all the swingarm and rear suspension mounting bolts and nuts, referring to the procedures and torque settings specified at the beginning of Chapter 6, and re-check for movement.

8 Next, grasp the top of the rear wheel and pull it upwards – there should be no discernible freeplay before the shock absorber begins to compress **(see illustration)**. Any freeplay felt in either check indicates worn bearings in the suspension linkage or swingarm, or worn suspension mountings. The worn components must be identified and replaced with new ones (see Chapter 6).

9 To make an accurate assessment of the swingarm bearings, remove the rear wheel (see Chapter 7) and the bolt securing the suspension linkage assembly to the swingarm (see Chapter 6). Grasp the rear of the swingarm with one hand and place your other hand at the junction of the swingarm and the frame. Try to move the rear of the swingarm from side-to-side. Any wear (play) in the bearings should be felt as movement between the swingarm and the frame at the front. If there is any play the swingarm will be felt to move forward and backward at the front (not from side-to-side). Next, move the swingarm up and down through its full travel. It should move freely, without any binding or rough spots. If there is any play in the swingarm or if it does not move freely, remove the bearings for inspection (see Chapter 6).

Swingarm and suspension linkage bearing lubrication

10 Over a period of time the grease will harden or may be washed out of the bearings by incorrect use of jet washes or dirt will penetrate the bearings due to failed seals.

11 Aprilia do not specify a particular service interval for this procedure, but every so often, and particularly if jet washes have been used or the bike has been ridden in wet weather often, you should remove the swingarm and suspension linkage as described in Chapter 6 for inspection and greasing or replacement of the bearings. The suspension is not equipped with grease nipples. On the model photographed, the suspension linkage plate bearings in the swingarm had been completely destroyed by water penetration **(see illustration)**.

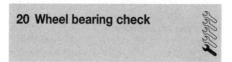

20 Wheel bearing check

1 Wheel bearings will wear over a long period of time and worn bearings can result in handling problems.

2 Support the motorcycle upright using an auxiliary stand, and support it so that the wheel being checked is off the ground. Check for any play in the bearings by pushing and pulling the wheel against the axle – turn the steering to full lock to keep it steady when checking the front wheel **(see illustration)**. Also spin the wheel and check that it rotates smoothly.

3 If any play is detected in the hub, or if the wheel does not rotate smoothly and freely (and this is not due to brake or transmission drag), remove the wheels and check the bearings for wear or damage (see Chapter 7). If in doubt replace them with new ones.

4 Beware of not overtightening the rear wheel axle nut. Overtightening has been found to lead to early bearing failure due to an excessive load being placed on the bearings and central spacer. Refer to Section 1 for more details.

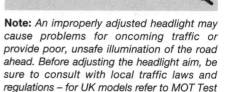

21 Headlight aim adjustment

Note: *An improperly adjusted headlight may cause problems for oncoming traffic or provide poor, unsafe illumination of the road ahead. Before adjusting the headlight aim, be sure to consult with local traffic laws and regulations – for UK models refer to MOT Test Checks in the Reference section.*

1 The headlight beam(s) can adjusted both horizontally and vertically. Before making any adjustment, check that the tyre pressures are correct and the suspension is adjusted as required. Make any adjustments to the headlight aim with the machine on level ground, with the fuel tank half full and with an assistant sitting on the seat. If the bike is usually ridden with a passenger on the back, have a second assistant to do this.

2 Vertical adjustment is made by turning the adjuster screw on the bottom of the headlight unit – reach under the fairing to access it **(see illustration)**. Turn the screw clockwise to raise the beam and anti-clockwise to lower it.

3 Horizontal adjustment of the right-hand main beam is made by turning the adjuster screw on the top right of the headlight unit – use a Phillips screwdriver inserted between the end of the instrument cluster and the fusebox. Turn the screw clockwise to move the beam to the left, and anti-clockwise to move it to the right **(see illustration 21.2)**.

4 Horizontal adjustment of the left-hand main beam is made by turning the adjuster screw on the top left of the headlight unit – use a Phillips screwdriver inserted between the end

20.2 Checking for play in the wheel bearings

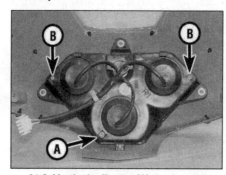

21.2 Vertical adjuster (A), horizontal adjusters (B)

of the instrument cluster and the relay box. Turn the screw clockwise to move the beam to the right, and anti-clockwise to move it to the left **(see illustration 21.2)**.

22 Sidestand and starter interlock circuit

1 Check the stand springs for damage and distortion. The springs must be capable of

retracting the stand fully and holding it retracted when the motorcycle is in use. If a spring is sagged or broken it must be replaced with a new one.

2 Lubricate the stand pivots regularly (see Section 15).

3 Check the stand and its mount for bends and cracks, and that the bracket bolts and pivot bolt nut are tight. If necessary stands can often be repaired by welding.

4 Check the operation of the starter interlock circuit by shifting the transmission into neutral, retracting the stand and starting the

engine. Pull in the clutch lever and select a gear. Extend the sidestand. The engine should stop as the sidestand is extended, and the sidestand warning light in the instrument cluster should come on. Also check that the engine cannot be started when the sidestand is down and the engine is in gear, and that the engine stops if a gear is selected with the engine running and the sidestand down. If the circuit does not operate as described, check the various switches (sidestand, neutral and clutch) and the diodes in the circuit (see Chapter 9).

Every 9000 miles (15,000 km) or 24 months

Carry out all the items under the 4500 mile (7500 km) check, plus the following:

23 Spark plug renewal

1 Remove the old spark plugs as described in Section 4 and install new ones.

24 Valve clearance check and adjustment

1 The engine must be completely cool for this maintenance procedure, so let the machine sit overnight before beginning.

2 Remove the spark plugs to allow the engine to be turned over easier (see Section 4).

3 Remove the valve covers (see Chapter 2).

4 Unscrew the crankshaft end cap from the alternator cover **(see illustration)**. Discard the O-ring as a new one should be used.

5 Make a chart or sketch of all valve positions so that a note of each clearance can be made against the relevant valve.

6 Start with the front cylinder. Turn the engine using a 14 mm hex bit on the alternator rotor bolt, turning it in an anti-clockwise direction only until the camshaft lobes are pointing away from each other at a slight upwards angle from the cylinder head **(see illustrations)**.

7 With the engine in this position, check the clearances on both the intake and exhaust valves. Insert a feeler gauge of the same thickness as the correct valve clearance (see Specifications, noting that there is a difference between intake and exhaust) between the base of each camshaft lobe and the top of the cam follower on each valve and check that it is a firm sliding fit – you should feel a slight drag when the you pull the gauge out **(see illustration)**. If not, use the feeler gauges to obtain the exact clearance. Record the measured clearance on the chart.

8 Now do the rear cylinder. Rotate the engine anti-clockwise using the 14 mm hex bit on the

alternator rotor bolt **(see illustration 24.6a)** until the camshaft lobes are pointing away from each other at a slight upwards angle from the cylinder head **(see illustration 24.6b)**. Check and adjust the valve clearance as described in Step 7.

9 When all clearances have been measured and charted, identify whether the clearance on any valve falls outside the specified range. If any do, the shim must be replaced with one of a thickness that will restore the correct clearance.

10 Shim replacement requires removal of the camshaft(s) (see Chapter 2). There is no need to remove both camshafts if shims from only

one side of the cylinder need replacing. Place rags over the spark plug hole and the cam chain tunnel to prevent a shim from dropping into the engine on removal. Work on one valve at a time to prevent the possibility of mixing up the followers, which must be returned to their original location. If you want to remove more than one shim and follower at a time, store them in a marked container or bag, denoting which cylinder and which valve the follower and shim are from, so that they do not get mixed up.

11 With the camshaft removed, remove the cam follower of the valve in question, then retrieve the shim from the inside of the follower

24.4 Remove the crankshaft end cap

24.6a Turn the engine anti-clockwise using a hex bit on the timing rotor bolt . . .

24.6b . . . until the camshaft lobes (arrowed) are positioned as shown

24.7 Insert the feeler gauge between the base of the lobe and the top of the follower as shown

24.11a Carefully lift out the follower using fingers, a lapping tool or a magnet . . .

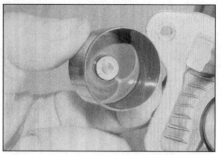

24.11b . . . and retrieve the shim from inside it . . .

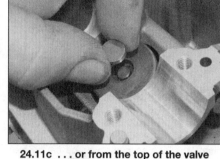

24.11c . . . or from the top of the valve

(see illustrations). The follower is best removed with a magnet or using the suction created by a valve lapping tool, but fingers may suffice, and long nosed pliers can be used with care – do not grip the follower tightly as you could score it. If the shim is not in the follower, pick it out of the top of the valve spring retainer using either a magnet, a screwdriver with a dab of grease on it (the shim will stick to the grease), or a very small screwdriver and a pair of pliers. Do not allow the shim to fall into the engine.

12 A size mark should be stamped on one face of the shim – a shim marked 275 is 2.75 mm thick. If the mark is not visible measure the shim thickness using a micrometer **(see illustration)**. Shims are available in 0.025 mm increments from 2.30 to 3.00 mm. If the shim thickness is less than its denomination, this must be taken into account when selecting a new shim.

13 Calculate the required replacement shim size using the formula $a = (b - c) + d$, where a is the required shim size, b is the measured valve clearance, c is the specified valve clearance, and d is the existing shim thickness. For example:

The measured clearance of an intake valve is 0.20 mm, so b = 0.20.

The specified clearance range for an inlet valve is 0.12 to 0.17 mm, the mid-point being 0.145 mm, so c = 0.145.

The thickness of the existing shim is 2.450 mm, so d = 2.45.

Therefore, the required replacement shim 'a' = 0.20 – 0.145 + 2.45 (a = 2.505 mm). The nearest available shim size is therefore 2.5, denoted 250.

Note: *If the required replacement shim is greater than 3.00 mm (the largest available),*

24.12 The size should be marked on the shim but can also be verified with a micrometer

the valve is probably not seating correctly due to a build-up of carbon deposits and should be checked and cleaned or resurfaced as required (see Chapter 2).

14 Obtain the replacement shim, then lubricate it with molybdenum disulphide oil (a 50/50 mixture of molybdenum disulphide grease and engine oil) and fit it into the recess in the top of the valve spring retainer with the size mark facing down **(see illustration 24.11c)**.

15 Check that the shim is correctly seated, then lubricate the follower with molybdenum disulphide oil and install it onto the valve, making sure it fits squarely in its bore **(see illustration 24.11a)**. Repeat the process for any other valves until the clearances are correct, then install the camshafts (see Chapter 2).

16 Rotate the crankshaft anti-clockwise several turns to seat the new shim(s) **(see illustration 24.6a)**, then check the clearances again.

17 Install all disturbed components in a reverse of the removal sequence, referring to the relevant Chapters. Install the crankshaft end cap using a new O-ring **(see illustration)**.

24.17 Fit a new O-ring then install the cap

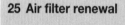

25 Air filter renewal

Caution: If the machine is continually ridden in wet or dusty conditions, the filter should be replaced more frequently.

1 Refer to the procedure in Section 3 and replace the air filter with a new one.

26 Oil tank strainer clean

 Warning: Be careful when draining the oil, as the exhaust pipes, the engine, and the oil itself can cause severe burns.

1 Refer to Section 6, Step 9 and clean the strainer in the oil tank in conjunction with changing the oil and engine main oil filter.

Every 14,000 miles (22,000 km) or 24 months

27 Front fork oil change

RSV models

Change the fork oil after the first 4500 miles (7500 km) from new, then every 14,000 miles (22,000 km) or 24 months thereafter.

1 Fork oil degrades over a period of time and loses its damping qualities. Refer to the fork oil change procedure in Chapter 6. The forks do not need to be completely disassembled.

RSV-R models

Change the fork oil every 4000 miles (7500 km)

2 The tolerances built into the forks used on

R models are so close that it is essential that the oil is changed religiously every 4000 miles (7500 km). Failure to do so could result in damaged forks and a costly replacement. Note that work on the forks must only be undertaken by an Ohlins service centre. Refer to your Aprilia dealer for further details. No procedures are given in this manual for these forks.

Every two years

28 Brake fluid change

1 The brake fluid should be replaced at the prescribed interval or whenever a master cylinder or caliper overhaul is carried out. Refer to the brake bleeding section in Chapter 7, noting that all old fluid must be pumped from the fluid reservoir and hydraulic hoses before filling with new fluid.

> **HAYNES HINT** *Old hydraulic fluid is invariably much darker in colour than new fluid, making it easy to see when all old fluid has been expelled from the system.*

29 Clutch fluid change

1 The clutch fluid should be replaced at the prescribed interval or whenever a master cylinder or release cylinder overhaul is carried out. Refer to the clutch bleeding section in Chapter 2, noting that all old fluid must be pumped from the fluid reservoir and hydraulic hose before filling with new fluid.

30 Cooling system draining, flushing and refilling

⚠ *Warning: Allow the engine to cool completely before performing this maintenance operation. Also, don't allow antifreeze to come into contact with your skin or the painted surfaces of the motorcycle. Rinse off spills immediately with plenty of water. Antifreeze is highly toxic if ingested. Never leave antifreeze lying around in an open container or in puddles on the floor; children and pets are attracted by its sweet smell and may drink it. Check with local authorities (councils) about disposing of antifreeze. Many communities have collection centres which will see that antifreeze is disposed of safely. Antifreeze is also combustible, so don't store it near open flames.*

Draining

1 Remove the lower fairing (see Chapter 8).
2 Make sure the engine is cold. Remove the coolant reservoir (see Chapter 3).
3 Slowly unscrew the cap from the top of the cooling system filler neck **(see illustration 10.8)**. If you hear a hissing sound (indicating there is still pressure in the system), wait until it stops.
4 Position a suitable container capable of holding at least 2.5 litres beneath the water pump on the right-hand side of the engine. Unscrew the drain bolt and allow the coolant to completely drain from the system **(see illustration)**. Retain the drain bolt sealing washer for use during flushing, but note that a new one must be used on final installation.
5 Now position the container under the right-hand radiator. Unscrew the drain bolt from the bottom and allow the coolant to drain **(see illustration)**. Repeat the procedure for the left-hand radiator. Again retain the drain bolt sealing washers for use during flushing, but note that new ones must be used on final installation.

Flushing

6 Flush the system with clean tap water by inserting a garden hose in the filler neck. Allow the water to run through the system until it is clear and flows out cleanly. If the radiators are extremely corroded, remove them (see Chapter 3) and have them cleaned by a specialist.
7 Clean the drain holes then install the drain bolts using the old sealing washers. Install the reservoir and connect the hose (see Chapter 3).
8 Fill the cooling system with clean water mixed with a flushing compound. Make sure the flushing compound is compatible with aluminium components, and follow the manufacturer's instructions carefully. Fit the filler cap and the reservoir cap.
9 Start the engine and allow it to reach normal operating temperature. Let it run for about ten minutes.
10 Stop the engine. Let it cool for a while, then cover the filler cap with a heavy rag and slowly unscrew it, releasing any pressure that may be present in the system. Once the hissing stops, remove the cap completely.
11 Drain the system once again (see Steps 2 to 5).
12 Fill the system with clean water and repeat the procedure in Steps 6 to 11.

Refilling

13 Install the three drain bolts using a suitable non-permanent thread locking compound (Aprilia recommend Loctite 574 for the water pump drain bolt and Loctite 572 for the radiator drain bolts) and new sealing washers and tighten them to the torque settings specified at the beginning of the Chapter. Install the reservoir (see Chapter 3).
14 Fill the system via the filler neck with the proper coolant mixture (see this Chapter's Specifications), until it reaches the base of the neck **(see illustration)**. **Note:** *Pour the coolant in slowly to minimise the amount of air entering the system. Also fill the reservoir almost up to the MAX line, then fit the cap.*
15 When the system is full (all the way up to the base of the radiator filler neck), flex and squeeze the large bore coolant hoses to encourage coolant around the system and air out of it. If necessary top the system up to the base of the filler neck. Fit the cap.
16 Start the engine and allow it to idle for a few minutes. Flick the throttle twistgrip part open 3 or 4 times, so that the engine speed rises to approximately 4000 – 5000 rpm, then stop the engine. This process will bleed any trapped air bubbles from the system. Give the thermostat housing a few taps and lift the bike of its stand and wiggle it about to free any trapped bubbles.
17 Let the engine cool then remove the filler cap as described in Step 3. Check that the coolant level is still up to the base of the upper radiator filler neck. If it's low, add the

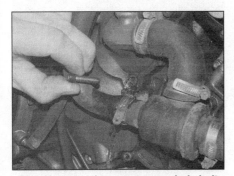

30.4 Unscrew the water pump drain bolt and allow the coolant to drain

30.5 Unscrew the radiator drain bolts and allow the coolant to drain

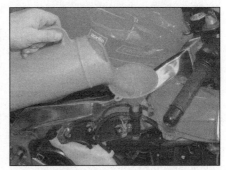

30.14 Fill the cooling system as described

specified mixture until it reaches the base of the filler neck. Refit the cap.

18 Check the coolant level in the reservoir and top it up if necessary.

19 Check the system for leaks. Install the lower fairing (see Chapter 8).

20 Do not dispose of the old coolant by pouring it down the drain. Instead pour it into a heavy plastic container, cap it tightly and take it into an authorised disposal site or service station – see **Warning** at the beginning of this Section.

Every four years

31 Brake hose renewal

1 The hoses deteriorate with age and should be replaced with new ones regardless of their apparent condition. Refer to Chapter 7 and disconnect the brake hoses from the master cylinders and calipers. Always replace the banjo union sealing washers with new ones.

32 Clutch hose renewal

1 The hose deteriorates with age and should be replaced with a new one regardless of its apparent condition. Refer to Chapter 2 and disconnect the hose from the master cylinder and release cylinder. Always replace the banjo union sealing washers with new ones.

33 Fuel hose renewal

⚠️ *Warning: Petrol (gasoline) is extremely flammable, so take extra precautions when you work on any part of the fuel system. Don't smoke or allow open flames or bare light bulbs near the work area, and don't work in a garage where a natural gas-type appliance is present. If you spill any fuel on your skin, rinse it off immediately with soap and water. When you perform any kind of work on the fuel system, wear safety glasses and have a fire extinguisher suitable for a Class B type fire (flammable liquids) on hand.*

1 The fuel system hoses should be replaced with new ones at the first signs of cracking or hardening, or at the specified interval regardless of their apparent condition. This includes all the vent and drain hoses, and the vacuum hoses. On California models you should also replace the EVAP system hoses with new ones (see Chapter 4).

2 Remove the air filter housing (see Chapter 4). Disconnect the hoses, noting the routing of each hose and where and how it connects (see Chapter 4, referring to the relevant Section). It is advisable to make a sketch of the various hoses before removing them to ensure they are correctly installed.

3 Secure each new hose to its unions using new clamps or sealing washers where fitted. Refer to Chapter 4 for torque settings for the fuel supply hose. Run the engine and check for leaks before taking the machine out on the road.

Non-scheduled maintenance

34 Cylinder compression check

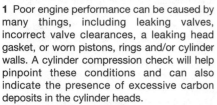

1 Poor engine performance can be caused by many things, including leaking valves, incorrect valve clearances, a leaking head gasket, or worn pistons, rings and/or cylinder walls. A cylinder compression check will help pinpoint these conditions and can also indicate the presence of excessive carbon deposits in the cylinder heads.

2 The only tools required are a compression gauge and a spark plug wrench. A compression gauge with a threaded end for the spark plug hole is preferable to the type that requires hand pressure to maintain a tight seal. Depending on the outcome of the initial test, a squirt-type oil can may also be needed.

3 Make sure the valve clearances are correctly set (see Section 24) and that the cylinder head fasteners are tightened to the correct torque setting (see Chapter 2).

4 Refer to *Fault Finding Equipment* in the Reference section for details of the compression test. Aprilia do not provide any figures for standard and minimum running compression, however an engine in good condition should show 150 to 180 psi, and anything less than 120 psi is in need of attention. Also look for large differences between the cylinders, even if neither is too low in itself.

35 Engine oil pressure check

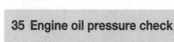

1 The oil pressure warning light should come on when the ignition (main) switch is turned ON and extinguish a few seconds after the engine is started – this serves as a check that the warning light bulb is sound. If the oil pressure light comes on whilst the engine is running, low oil pressure is indicated – stop the engine immediately and carry out an oil level check *(see Daily (pre-ride) checks)*.

2 An oil pressure check must be carried out if the warning light comes on when the engine is running yet the oil level is good (Step 1). It can also provide useful information about the condition of the engine's lubrication system.

3 To check the oil pressure, a suitable gauge and adapter (which screws into the crankcase) will be needed. Aprilia can provide the components (part No. 8140181) for this purpose, or one can be obtained commercially. You will also need a container and some rags to catch and mop up any residual oil that is lost between removing the oil pressure switch and installing the gauge. Check the engine oil level after installing the gauge and replenish if necessary (see *Daily (pre-ride) checks*).

4 Remove the lower fairing (see Chapter 8).

5 Remove the oil pressure switch (see Chapter 9), and swiftly screw the gauge assembly in its place.

6 Warm the engine up to normal operating temperature.

7 With the engine idling check the gauge reading. The oil pressure should be similar to that given in the Specifications at the start of this Chapter. Stop the engine.

8 Unscrew the gauge assembly and immediately install the oil pressure switch (see Chapter 9).

9 If the pressure is significantly lower than the standard, either the oil pump or its drive mechanism may be faulty, the pressure relief valve may be stuck open, the oil filter in the engine or the oil tank strainer may be blocked, or there could be severe engine wear. Also make sure the correct grade oil is being used. Begin diagnosis by checking the oil filter and strainer, then the oil pump and relief valve (see Chapter 2). If those items check out okay, chances are the bearing oil clearances are excessive and the engine needs to be overhauled.

10 If the pressure is too high, either an oil passage is clogged, the relief valve is stuck closed or the wrong grade of oil is being used.

11 Check the oil level (see *Daily (pre-ride) checks*). Install the lower fairing (see Chapter 8).

Chapter 2
Engine, clutch and transmission

Contents

Degrees of difficulty

Easy, suitable for novice with little experience	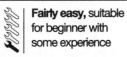	Fairly easy, suitable for beginner with some experience		Fairly difficult, suitable for competent DIY mechanic		Difficult, suitable for experienced DIY mechanic	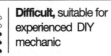	Very difficult, suitable for expert DIY or professional	

Specifications

General

Type	Four-stroke 60° V-twin
Capacity	997.6 cc
Bore	97.0 mm
Stroke	67.5 mm
Compression ratio	11.4 to 1
Camshafts	DOHC, chain and gear-driven
Clutch	Wet multi-plate with vacuum-actuated back-torque limiter and hydraulic release
Cooling system	Liquid cooled
Transmission	Six-speed constant mesh
Final drive	Chain and sprockets
Engine weight	approx. 65 kg

Camshafts and followers

Camshaft bearing oil clearance (max)	0.060 mm
Camshaft journal diameter (min)	23.950 mm
Camshaft journal holder internal diameter (max)	24.040 mm
Camshaft end-float (max)	0.40 mm
Camshaft journal width (max)	27.77 mm
Camshaft journal holder width (min)	27.10 mm
Follower play in bore (max)	0.08 mm
Follower diameter (min)	33.44 mm
Follower bore diameter (max)	33.58 mm

Cam chains and gears/sprockets

Cam chain driven gear/sprocket ID (max) .... 22.015 mm
Cam chain driven gear plate shaft OD (min) .... 15.98 mm
Cam chain stretch limit (20 pin length – see text) .... 166.2 mm

Cam chain tensioners

Tensioner bore in cylinder block (max) .... 14.07 mm
Tensioner-to-bore in cylinder block clearance (max) .... 0.08 mm

Valves, guides and springs

Valve size
    Intake valve .... 36 mm
    Exhaust valve .... 31 mm
Valve clearances .... see Chapter 1
Stem diameter (min)
    Intake valve .... 5.950 mm
    Exhaust valve .... 5.935 mm
New guide bore diameter (use 6 mm F7 reamer) .... 6.006 to 6.018 mm
Guide bore diameter (max) .... 6.05 mm
Guide protrusion from head .... 13.1 to 13.5 mm
Seat width (max)
    Intake valve
        Standard .... 1.05 to 1.35 mm
        Wear limit (max)
            1998 to 2000 models .... 1.6 mm
            2001 to 2003 models .... 1.5 mm
    Exhaust valve
        Standard .... 1.25 to 1.55 mm
        Wear limit (max) .... 1.8 mm
Radial runout at head (max) .... 0.05 mm
Stem runout (max) .... 0.05 mm
Spring free lengths (min)
    Outer spring .... 43.4 mm
    Inner spring .... 40.9 mm

Cylinders

Bore diameter
    Size A
        Standard .... 97.000 to 97.012 mm
        Wear limit .... 97.027 mm
    Size B
        Standard .... 97.012 to 97.025 mm
        Wear limit .... 97.040 mm
Bore taper (max) .... 0.04 mm
Bore ovality (max) .... 0.04 mm
Gasket face warpage (max) .... 0.04 mm

Pistons

Piston diameter (max – measured 10 mm up from skirt, at 90° to piston pin axis)
    1998 to 2000 models
        Red piston .... 96.918 mm
        Green piston .... 96.930 mm
    2001 to 2003 models
        Red piston .... 96.890 mm
        Green piston .... 96.900 mm
Piston-to-bore clearance (max)
    1998 to 2000 models .... 0.090 mm
    2001 to 2003 models .... 0.120 mm
Piston pin diameter (min) .... 21.998 mm
Piston pin bore diameter (max) .... 22.018 mm
Connecting rod small-end internal diameter (min) .... 22.030 mm

Piston rings

Ring thickness (min – see illustration with text)
    Top ring .... 0.85 mm
    2nd ring .... 1.20 mm
    Oil ring .... 2.45 mm
Ring-to-groove clearance (max) – all rings .... 0.12 mm
End gap (installed – max) .... 1.00 mm

Clutch – 1998 to 2000 models

Note: *The 2001-on specification clutch assembly can be fitted retrospectively on 1998 to 2000 models provided the components are not intermixed. Refer to an Aprilia dealer for details.*

Friction plate quantity
    Type A 8
    Type B (blue coded) 1
Friction plate tab width (min) . . . . 13.7 mm
Friction plate warpage (max) . . . . 0.15 mm
Plain plate quantity
    up to engine no. 689953 10
    from engine no. 689954
        Type A 9
        Type B (hardened – one tooth missing or notch in outer rim) 1
Plain plate warpage (max) . . . . 0.15 mm
Plate assembly thickness (min) . . . . 44.9 mm
Pressure plate warpage (max) . . . . 0.1 mm
Pressure plate thickness (min) . . . . 33.5 mm
Spring free length (min) . . . . 43.0 mm
Primary driven gear bush internal diameter (max) . . . . 30.060 mm

Clutch – 2001 to 2003 models

Friction plate
    Quantity 9
    Tab width (min) . . . . 13.7 mm
    Warpage (max) . . . . 0.15 mm
Plain plate
    Quantity
        Type A 9
        Type B (hardened – one tooth missing or notch in outer rim) 1
    Warpage (max) . . . . 0.15 mm
Plate assembly thickness (min) . . . . 44.9 mm
Pressure plate warpage (max) . . . . 0.1 mm
Pressure plate thickness (min) . . . . 33.5 mm
Spring free length (min) . . . . 43.0 mm
Primary driven gear bush internal diameter (max) . . . . 30.060 mm

Lubrication system

Oil type, viscosity and capacity . . . . see Chapter 1
Oil pressure . . . . see Chapter 1
Oil pump
    Inner rotor tip-to-outer rotor clearance (max) . . . . 0.20 mm
    Outer rotor-to-housing clearance (max) . . . . 0.25 mm
    Rotor end-float (max) . . . . 0.15 mm
Pressure relief valve
    Plunger diameter (min) . . . . 9.975 mm
    Bore diameter (max) . . . . 10.035 mm
    Spring free length (min) . . . . 56.0 mm

Starter clutch

Driven gear bearing journal diameter on crankshaft (min) . . . . 34.960 mm
Driven gear internal diameter (max) . . . . 35.07 mm
Reduction gear internal diameter (max) . . . . 10.10 mm
Idle gear internal diameter (max) . . . . 10.08 mm
Gear shaft external diameter (min) . . . . 9.990 mm

Crankshaft and bearings

In crankcase
    Main bearing housing internal diameter (max) . . . . 46.035 mm
    Main journal diameter (min) . . . . 45.955 mm
    Main bearing oil clearance (max) . . . . 0.06 mm
In clutch cover
    End bearing housing internal diameter (max) . . . . 30.040 mm
    End journal diameter (min) . . . . 29.970 mm
    End bearing oil clearance (max) . . . . 0.065 mm
End-float (crankcases assembled) . . . . 0.50 mm
Runout (max) . . . . 0.020 mm

Balancer shafts and bearings

Front balancer shaft
  In crankcase
    Bearing housing internal diameter (max) . . . .   32.060 mm
    Journal diameter (min) . . . .   31.980 mm
    Bearing oil clearance (max) . . . .   0.06 mm
  In clutch cover
    End bearing housing internal diameter (max) . . . .   20.060 mm
    End journal diameter (min) . . . .   19.990 mm
    End bearing oil clearance (max) . . . .   0.06 mm
Rear balancer shaft
  Ball bearing journal diameter (min) . . . .   14.97 mm
  Bearing housing diameter (max) . . . .   34.98 mm
  Shaft radial play in plain bearing . . . .   0.7 mm

Connecting rods and big-end bearings

Big-end side clearance (max) . . . .   0.60 mm
Big-end internal diameter (max) . . . .   42.050 mm
Crankpin diameter (min) . . . .   41.98 mm
Big-end bearing oil clearance . . . .   0.07 mm
Radial play . . . .   0.020 to 0.045 mm
For connecting rod small-end specifications see under 'Pistons'.

Gearchange mechanism, selector drum and forks

Selector fork end thickness (min) . . . .   3.95 mm
Pinion groove width (max) . . . .   4.35 mm
Fork-to-groove clearance (max) . . . .   0.15 mm
Fork guide pin diameter (min) . . . .   5.850 mm
Selector fork shaft runout (max) . . . .   0.02 mm
Gearchange shaft runout (max) . . . .   0.25 mm

Transmission

All RSV models and RSV-R models to 2002
  Primary reduction . . . .   1.935 to 1 (57/31T)
  Final reduction . . . .   2.470 to 1 (42/17T)
  1st gear . . . .   2.500 to 1 (35/14T)
  2nd gear . . . .   1.750 to 1 (28/16T)
  3rd gear . . . .   1.368 to 1 (26/19T)
  4th gear . . . .   1.090 to 1 (24/22T)
  5th gear . . . .   0.956 to 1 (22/23T)
  6th gear . . . .   0.851 to 1 (23/27T)
2003 RSV-R models
  Primary reduction . . . .   1.935 to 1 (57/31T)
  Final reduction . . . .   2.470 to 1 (42/17T)
  1st gear . . . .   2.267 to 1 (34/15T)
  2nd gear . . . .   1.632 to 1 (31/19T)
  3rd gear . . . .   1.300 to 1 (26/20T)
  4th gear . . . .   1.090 to 1 (24/22T)
  5th gear . . . .   0.960 to 1 (24/25T)
  6th gear . . . .   0.885 to 1 (23/26T)
Input shaft
  Diameter at right-hand bearing (min) . . . .   29.965 mm
  Diameter at left-hand bearing (min) . . . .   24.972 mm
  Diameter at 5th gear pinion (min) . . . .   29.030 mm
  Internal diameter of 5th gear pinion (max) . . . .   29.125 mm
  Diameter at 6th gear pinion (min) . . . .   24.978 mm
  Internal diameter of 6th gear pinion (max) . . . .   29.022 mm
Output shaft
  Diameter at right-hand bearing (min) . . . .   19.972 mm
  Diameter at left-hand bearing (min) . . . .   29.915 mm
  Diameter at 2nd gear pinion (min) . . . .   29.030 mm
  Internal diameter of 2nd gear pinion (max) . . . .   29.125 mm
  Diameter at 1st, 3rd and 4th gear pinions (min) . . . .   24.978 mm
  Internal diameter of 1st, 3rd and 4th gear pinions (max) . . . .   29.022 mm

Torque settings

Balancer shafts
    Front balancer shaft nut .... 150 Nm
    Rear balancer shaft holder bolts .... 11 Nm
    Rear balancer shaft nut .... 50 Nm
Cam chain drive gear bolt to front balancer shaft .... 50 Nm
Cam chain driven gear plate bolts
    Front cylinder plate
        Top bolts (8 mm) .... 25 Nm
        Bottom bolt (6 mm) .... 11 Nm
    Rear cylinder plate (all bolts 8 mm) .... 25 Nm
Cam chain tensioner cap bolt .... 20 Nm
Cam chain top guide bolts .... 11 Nm
Camshaft holder bolts .... 11 Nm
Camshaft sprocket/balancer gear bolts .... 11 Nm
Clutch hose banjo bolts .... 20 Nm
Clutch diaphragm plate nut .... 30 Nm
Clutch damper spring plate bolts/nuts .... 30 Nm
Clutch inner cover bolts
    6 mm bolts .... 11 Nm
    8 mm bolts .... 19 Nm
Clutch nut .... 170 Nm
Clutch outer cover bolts .... 5 Nm
Clutch pressure plate bolts .... 11 Nm
Clutch release cylinder bleed valve .... 15 Nm
Clutch release cylinder bolts .... 12 Nm
Connecting rod bolts
    Initial setting .... 2 Nm
    Mid setting .... 30 Nm
    Final setting .... + 70°
Crankcase bolts .... 11 Nm
Cylinder head joining plate bolts/nuts .... 40 Nm
Cylinder head-to-block bolts
    Painted block .... 27 Nm
    Unpainted block .... 29 Nm
Cylinder head 10 mm nuts
    Painted head
        Nuts on outside of head .... 53 Nm
        Nuts in cam chain tunnel .... 58 Nm
    Unpainted head .... 58 Nm
Cylinder head 6 mm bolts .... 12 Nm
Cylinder block studs .... 10 Nm
Engine mounting bolts
    Adjuster bolts .... 11 Nm
    Adjuster bolt locknuts .... 50 Nm
    Front mounting bolts – 1998 to 2000 models .... 40 Nm
    Front mounting bolts – 2001 to 2003 models .... 50 Nm
    All other mounting bolts/nuts .... 50 Nm
Engine sprocket bolt .... 50 Nm
Gearchange selector drum cam plate bolt .... 11 Nm
Gearchange stopper arm bolt .... 11 Nm
Oil pipe and hose union bolts to engine .... 10 Nm
Oil level inspection pipe banjo bolts .... 20 Nm
Oil pump bolts .... 11 Nm
Primary drive gear nut .... 230 Nm
Primary driven gear bolts/nuts .... 30 Nm
Selector drum bearing retainer screws .... 11 Nm
Starter clutch bolts .... 30 Nm
Transmission shaft bearing retainer screws .... 11 Nm
Valve cover bolts .... 9 Nm

1 General information

The engine/transmission unit is a liquid-cooled 60° V-twin, fitted parallel with the frame. The engine has four valves per cylinder, operated by double overhead camshafts. The camshafts are driven by both gear and chain off the crankshaft.

The engine/transmission unit is constructed in aluminium alloy and the crankcase is divided vertically. The crankcase incorporates a dry sump, pressure fed lubrication system, and houses an oil pump gear driven off the clutch housing. The water pump is gear driven off the front balancer shaft. The one-piece forged crankshaft runs in two main bearings and one end bearing in the clutch cover. The left-hand end of the crankshaft carries the alternator rotor. The ignition timing triggers are incorporated in the alternator rotor.

The engine runs two balancer shafts, the front one being gear driven off the crankshaft, and the rear one being driven a gear on the rear cylinder exhaust camshaft.

The clutch is a wet multi-plate and is gear driven off the crankshaft. The transmission is a six-speed constant mesh unit. Final drive to the rear wheel is by chain and sprockets.

2 Component access

Operations possible with the engine in the frame

The components and assemblies listed below can be removed without having to remove the engine/transmission assembly from the frame. If however, a number of areas require attention at the same time, removal of the engine is recommended.

*Although the rear cylinder head/block assembly can be removed with the engine in the frame this is not advised – not only is access very limited but there is likelihood of piston ring breakage as the head/block assembly is installed over the piston.

Oil cooler
Valve covers
Cam chain tensioners
Camshafts and followers
Cam chains and drive gears
Rear balancer shaft
Rear cylinder head and cylinder*
Rear piston*
Water pump
Clutch
Oil pump
Primary drive gear
Alternator
Starter clutch and gears
Crankshaft position sensor
Gearchange mechanism
Starter motor
Oil pressure switch
Neutral switch

Operations requiring engine removal

It is necessary to remove the engine/transmission assembly from the frame and separate the crankcase halves to gain access to the following components:

Front cylinder head and cylinder block
Front piston
Connecting rods
Crankshaft
Front balancer shaft
Transmission shafts
Selector drum and forks

3 Major engine repair – general information

1 It is not always easy to determine when or if an engine should be completely overhauled, as a number of factors must be considered.

2 High mileage is not necessarily an indication that an overhaul is needed, while low mileage, on the other hand, does not preclude the need for an overhaul. Frequency of servicing is probably the single most important consideration. An engine that has regular and frequent oil and filter changes, as well as other required maintenance, will most likely give many miles of reliable service. Conversely, a neglected engine, or one which has not been run in properly, may require an overhaul very early in its life.

3 Exhaust smoke and excessive oil consumption are both indications that piston rings and/or valve guides are in need of attention, although make sure that the fault is not due to oil leakage.

4 If the engine is making obvious knocking or rumbling noises, the connecting rods and/or main bearings are probably at fault.

5 Loss of power, rough running, excessive valve train noise and high fuel consumption may also point to the need for an overhaul, especially if they are all present at the same time. If a complete tune-up does not remedy the situation, major mechanical work is the only solution.

6 An engine overhaul generally involves restoring the internal parts to the specifications of a new engine. The piston rings and main and connecting rod bearings are usually renewed during a major overhaul. Generally the valve seats are re-ground, since they are usually in less than perfect condition at this point. The end result should be a like new engine that will give as many trouble-free miles as the original.

7 Before beginning the engine overhaul, read through the related procedures to familiarise yourself with the scope and requirements of the job. Overhauling an engine is not all that difficult, but it is time consuming. Plan on the motorcycle being tied up for a minimum of two weeks. Check on the availability of parts and make sure that any necessary special tools, equipment and supplies are obtained in advance.

8 Most work can be done with typical workshop hand tools, although a number of precision measuring tools are required for inspecting parts to determine if they must be renewed. Often a dealer will handle the inspection of parts and offer advice concerning reconditioning and renewal. As a general rule, time is the primary cost of an overhaul so it does not pay to install worn or substandard parts.

9 As a final note, to ensure maximum life and minimum trouble from a rebuilt engine, everything must be assembled with care in a spotlessly clean environment.

4 Engine removal and installation

Caution: The engine is very heavy. Engine removal and installation should be carried out with the aid of at least one assistant; personal injury or damage could occur if the engine falls or is dropped. An hydraulic or mechanical floor jack should be used to support and lower or raise the engine – an hydraulic trolley jack is the best as its wheels enable free movement of the engine while it is still supported.

Removal

Note 1: *Where the clip-type (as opposed to the screw-type) hose clamps are used on the oil cooler and tank hoses, fuel system hoses*

A peg spanner is required to slacken and tighten the adjuster bolt locknuts on the upper and lower rear engine mounting bolts on the right-hand side. If the Aprilia service tool (Pt. No. 8140203 or a pattern equivalent, shown on the left) is not available, a suitable one can be made by cutting an old socket (shown on the right) of the correct size. Note that the tool shown on the left combines two sizes in one tool (the other size fits the locknut on the swingarm).

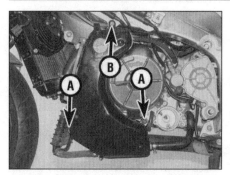

4.9a Oil tank mounting nuts (A) and mounting bolt (B)

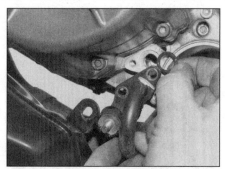

4.9b Unscrew the bolts, detach the pipe and remove the O-ring

4.9c Unscrew the hose/pipe support bolt (arrowed)

and coolant hoses, a flat-bladed screwdriver is the best way of releasing them, but note that to rejoin this type of clamp a special pair of pliers makes the job much easier. Also note that these clamps should only be used once, and so new ones should be obtained for the installation procedure.

Note 2: *Where nuts and bolts are exposed, for example oil cooler and tank mountings, it is worth spraying them with some penetrating fluid/lubricant (such as WD40) before trying to undo them.*

1 Support the bike securely in an upright position using an auxiliary stand. Work can be made easier by raising the machine to a suitable working height on an hydraulic ramp or other suitable platform. Make sure the motorcycle is secure and will not topple over (also see *Tools and Workshop Tips* in the Reference section).

2 If the engine is dirty, particularly around its mountings, wash it thoroughly before starting any major dismantling work. This makes working on the engine much easier and rules out the possibility of caked on lumps of dirt falling into some vital component.

3 Remove the lower fairing and fairing side panels (see Chapter 8).

4 Remove the seats (see Chapter 8).

5 Disconnect the battery leads (see Chapter 9).

6 Drain the engine oil and remove the oil filter (see Chapter 1).

7 Drain the coolant (see Chapter 1).

4.9d Release the clamp (arrowed) and detach the hose

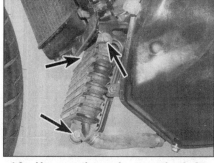

4.9e Unscrew the cooler mounting bolts (arrowed) . . .

8 Remove the fuel tank, the air filter housing and the throttle bodies (see Chapter 4). Plug the engine intake ducts with clean rag.

9 Unscrew the nuts securing the bottom of the oil tank to its mounting brackets **(see illustration)**. Unscrew the bolts securing the oil pipe from the oil cooler to the left-hand side of the engine **(see illustration)**. Detach the pipe and discard the O-ring. Also unscrew the bolt securing the oil cooler hose/pipe support piece to the right-hand side of the engine **(see illustration)**. Release the clamp securing the oil hose from the oil tank to the left-hand side of the engine and pull the hose off its union **(see illustration)**. Unscrew the bolts securing the oil cooler to its brackets,

noting the collars **(see illustration)**. Unscrew the bolt securing the top of the oil tank **(see illustration 4.9a)** and remove the tank, cooler and hoses/pipe as an assembly **(see illustration)**. Remove the rubber support bush fitted over the alternator cover bolt **(see illustration)**.

10 Release the clamps securing all the hoses to both radiators and detach them, noting which fits where. Unscrew the nuts and bolts securing the radiator bottom mounting bracket to the engine **(see illustration)**. Unscrew the radiator upper mounting bolts and remove the radiators together, leaving them joined together by the top interconnecting hose and the bottom

4.9f . . . and remove the tank and cooler together

4.9g Remove the rubber support bush (arrowed)

4.10a Unscrew the nuts and the bolts securing the bottom bracket to the engine . . .

4.10b . . . then unscrew the upper mounting bolts (right-hand bolt arrowed) . . .

4.10c . . . and remove the radiators together

4.10d Remove the thermostat (arrowed) with all its hoses . . .

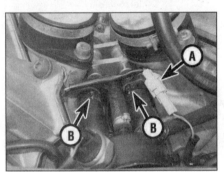

4.10e . . . then remove the filler neck (arrowed) with its hoses

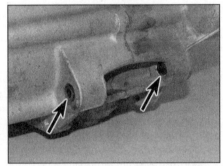

4.10f Disconnect the fan switch wiring connectors (arrowed)

4.10g Disconnect the CMP wiring connector (A) then release the clamps (B) and detach the hoses and remove the manifold

4.10h Remove the bushes (arrowed)

mounting bracket (see illustrations). Also remove the coolant reservoir (see Chapter 3). Remove the thermostat along with all the hoses that attach to it, detaching the hoses at their other end (see illustration). Also remove the filler neck hose assembly, noting the cable ties that hold the wiring loom to it (see illustration). Disconnect the wiring connectors from the fan switch in the three-way manifold (see illustration). Disconnect the camshaft position (CMP) sensor wiring connector, then release the clamps securing the short hoses to their unions on the engine then remove the manifold along with its hoses, noting their routing (see illustration). Remove the two bushes for the radiator and oil tank mounting bracket from the front of the engine for safekeeping (see illustration).

11 Remove the exhaust system (Chapter 4).

12 Make an alignment mark between the gearchange shaft end and the slit in the lever clamp, then unscrew the pinch bolt and slide the lever off the shaft (see illustration).

13 Displace the clutch release cylinder and secure it clear of the engine – there is no need to detach the hose (see Chapter 2). Remove the front sprocket (see Chapter 6).

14 Pull the spark plug caps off the plugs. Detach the wiring connectors from the coils on the right-hand frame beam, noting which fits where (see illustration). Unscrew the bolts securing the coil bracket to the frame and

4.12 Unscrew the pinch bolt (arrowed) and remove the gearchange lever

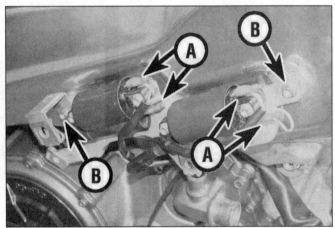

4.14 Disconnect the wiring connectors (A) then unscrew the bolts (B) and remove the coil assembly

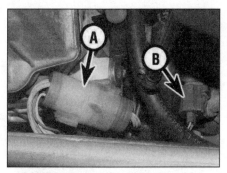

4.15 Disconnect the alternator wiring connector (A) and the connector (B) from the ECT sensor in each head

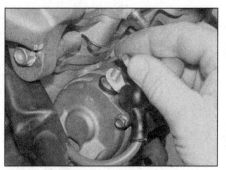

4.16 Pull the boot back, unscrew the nut and detach the starter lead

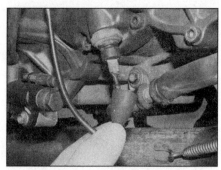

4.17 Pull the boot down and detach the oil pressure switch wire

remove the coil assembly, noting the routing of the HT leads to the front cylinder.

15 Disconnect the alternator wiring connector **(see illustration)**. Disconnect the wiring connector from the engine coolant temperature (ECT) sensor in each cylinder head. If you are performing a full engine strip or a procedure that involves removing the alternator rotor, it is worth doing so now as the bolt is tight and the rotor can be difficult to get off the shaft – doing so with the engine still in the frame means you don't have to hold and support it. Refer to Chapter 9 to remove it.

16 Pull back the rubber boot covering the starter motor terminal, then unscrew the nut and detach the lead **(see illustration)**. Remove the starter motor now if required (see Chapter 9), or do so after the engine has been removed if necessary.

17 Pull the rubber boot off the oil pressure switch, then pull the wiring connector off the terminal **(see illustration)**.

18 Undo the neutral switch terminal screw and detach the wire **(see illustration)**.

19 Unscrew the bolt securing the earth lead to the right-hand side of the rear cylinder block and detach the lead **(see illustration)**.

20 Remove the rear brake pedal – there is no need to detach the master cylinder pushrod, but take care when drawing it out of the cylinder (see Chapter 6). Displace the rear brake master cylinder and reservoir from the right-hand side of the engine and secure it clear, making sure no strain is placed on the hoses and the reservoir is kept upright (see Chapter 7). Trace the wiring from the rear brake

switch and disconnect it at the connector – feed the wiring down to the switch, noting its routing **(see illustration)**. Unscrew the bolts securing the pedal bracket and remove it along with the switch **(see illustration)**.

21 At this point, position an hydraulic or mechanical jack under the engine with a block of wood between the jack head and engine **(see illustration)**. Make sure the jack is centrally positioned so the engine will not topple in any direction when the last mounting bolt is removed. Raise the jack to take the weight of the engine, but make sure it is not lifting the bike and taking the weight of that as well. The idea is to support the engine so that there is no pressure on any of the mounting bolts once they have been slackened, so they can be easily withdrawn. Note that it may be necessary to adjust the jack as some of the

bolts are removed to relieve the stress transferred to the other bolts. Note that if you have an engine hoist you can fit it to the engine in place of the brackets joining the two intake ducts on the cylinder heads using the Aprilia tool (part No. 8140183) – tighten the bolts to 40 Nm and make sure the equipment used is capable of lifting 70 kg.

> **HAYNES HiNT** *After removing each engine mounting bolt, make a note of its location and fit any adjuster, locknut, nut, washer or spacer that goes with the bolt back onto it, in the correct order and way round – this will ensure that everything can be reassembled with ease later on.*

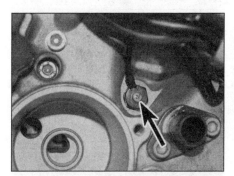

4.18 Undo the screw (arrowed) and detach the neutral switch wire

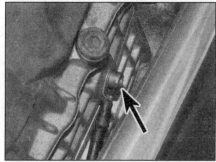

4.19 Unscrew the bolt (arrowed) and detach the earth lead

4.20a Disconnect the rear brake switch wiring connector (arrowed) . . .

4.20b . . . then unscrew the bolts (arrowed) and remove the bracket

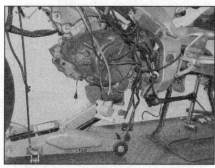

4.21 Place a jack under the engine to support it

4.22 Unscrew the nut and withdraw the lower rear bolt

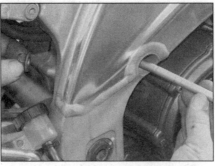

4.23 Unscrew the nut and withdraw the upper rear bolt

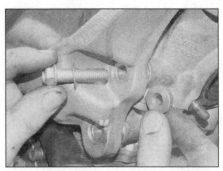

4.24 Unscrew and remove the right front mounting bolts, washers and spacers

22 Unscrew the nut on the inside of the right-hand lower rear mounting bolt then remove the bolt **(see illustration)**.
23 Unscrew the nut on the inside of the right-hand upper rear mounting bolt then remove the bolt **(see illustration)**.
24 Unscrew the two front mounting bolts on the right-hand side, noting the washers, and remove the spacers from between the engine and frame **(see illustration)**.
25 Unscrew the two front mounting bolts on the left-hand side, noting the washers **(see illustration)**.
26 Slacken the locknuts on the upper and lower rear mounting adjuster bolts using the Aprilia tool or a suitable peg spanner (see **Tool Tip** on page 2•6). The locknuts can remain loose on the adjuster bolts, or can be removed if required. Now unscrew the adjuster bolts using a hex bit until they

contact the inside of the frame **(see illustration)**.
27 Make sure the engine is supported by the jack, and have an assistant hold it. Unscrew the nut on the inside of the left-hand lower rear mounting bolt then remove the bolt **(see illustration)**.
28 Unscrew the nut on the inside of the left-hand upper rear mounting bolt then remove the bolt and the spacer that fits between the engine and frame **(see illustrations)**.
29 Check that all wiring, cables and hoses are disconnected and well clear. Carefully manoeuvre the engine forwards until the bottom right-hand side is clear of the frame, freeing the drive chain from around the output shaft if not already done, then rotate it backwards (anti-clockwise as looked from the right-hand side) so the back drops and the right-hand side of the front cylinder clears the

frame. If using a trolley jack make sure it does not slide away as you rotate the engine – have an assistant ready for this. If using a mechanical jack make sure it does not topple over. Lower the engine on the jack and when the jack is fully lowered, lift the engine off it, remove the jack, and manoeuvre the engine out of the left-hand side of the frame.
30 If required thread the adjuster bolts back into and through the frame and remove them from the inside, noting which fits where as they are different.

Installation

31 If removed, fit the rear mounting adjuster bolts into the right-hand side of the frame, threading them in from the inside until the flanged ends contact the frame.
32 Manoeuvre the engine into position under the frame and lift it onto the jack **(see illustration 4.21)**. Raise the engine, taking care not to catch any part of the engine on the frame, and loop the drive chain around the output shaft as early as possible. Raise and move the engine in a reverse of the way it was removed. When the mounting bolt holes are aligned slide the left-hand upper and lower rear mounting bolts through, not forgetting the spacer that fits between the frame and the engine with the upper bolt **(see illustrations 4.28b and 4.27)**. Fit the nut onto the end of each bolt and tighten them finger-tight.
33 Install the front mounting bolts on the left-hand side with their washers and tighten them finger-tight **(see illustration 4.25)**. Now tighten the lower and upper rear mounting

4.25 Unscrew and remove the left front mounting bolts and washers

4.26 Unscrew the adjuster bolts using a hex bit

4.27 Unscrew the nut and withdraw the lower rear bolt

4.28a Unscrew the nut . . .

4.28b . . . then withdraw the upper rear bolt and remove the spacer

bolts on the left-hand side to the torque setting specified at the beginning of the Chapter, counter-holding the nuts to prevent them turning. Now tighten the front mounting bolts on the left-hand side to the specified torque setting.

34 Install the front mounting bolts on the right-hand side with their washers and the spacers that fit between the frame and the engine and tighten them to the specified torque setting **(see illustration 4.24)**.

35 Tighten the upper and lower rear mounting adjuster bolts on the right-hand side to the specified torque setting using a hex bit **(see illustration 4.26)**.

36 If removed, thread the locknuts onto the adjuster bolts. Tighten the locknuts to the specified torque using the Aprilia tool or a suitable peg spanner as on removal (see **Tool Tip** above). It is advisable to make a reference mark between the adjuster bolts and the frame to make sure they do not turn as the locknuts are being tightened.

37 Install the upper and lower rear mounting bolts and nuts and tighten the bolts to the specified torque, counter-holding the nuts to prevent them turning **(see illustrations 4.23 and 4.22)**.

38 The remainder of the installation procedure is the reverse of removal, noting the following points:

● Use new gaskets on the exhaust pipe connections.
● When fitting the gearchange lever onto the shaft, align the slit in the arm with mark made on the shaft, and tighten the pinch bolt securely **(see illustration 4.12)**.
● Make sure all wires, cables and hoses are correctly routed and connected, and secured by any clips or ties.
● Do not forget to fit the rubber support bush for the oil tank over the alternator cover bolt **(see illustration 4.9g)**.
● Make sure the bushes for the radiator and oil tank bracket are in their bores in the front of the engine.
● Do not forget to connect the earth lead to the right-hand side of the rear cylinder block **(see illustration 4.19)**.
● Refill the engine with oil and coolant (see Chapter 1).
● Adjust the throttle cable freeplay.
● Adjust the drive chain (see Chapter 1).
● If the engine has been disassembled refer to the final Section of this Chapter for initial starting and running procedures. Adjust the idle speed (see Chapter 1).

5 Engine disassembly and reassembly – general information

Disassembly

1 Before disassembling the engine, thoroughly clean and degrease its external surfaces. This will prevent contamination of the engine internals, and will also make working a lot easier and cleaner. A high flash-point solvent, such as paraffin (kerosene) can be used, or better still, a proprietary engine degreaser such as Gunk. Use old paintbrushes and toothbrushes to work the solvent into the various recesses of the casings. Take care to exclude solvent or water from the electrical components and intake and exhaust ports.

 Warning: The use of petrol (gasoline) as a cleaning agent should be avoided because of the risk of fire.

2 When clean and dry, position the engine on the workbench, leaving suitable clear area for working. Make sure the engine is stable – some strategically placed blocks of wood under the crankcase or engine covers will help support it and keep it stable while you work. Gather a selection of small containers, plastic bags and some labels so that parts can be grouped together in an easily identifiable manner. Also get some paper and a pen so that notes can be taken. You will also need a supply of clean rag, which should be as absorbent as possible.

3 Before commencing work, read through the appropriate section so that some idea of the necessary procedure can be gained. When removing components note that great force is seldom required, unless specified (checking the specified torque setting of the particular bolt being removed will indicate how tight it is, and therefore how much force should be needed). In many cases, a component's reluctance to be removed is indicative of an incorrect approach or removal method – if in any doubt, re-check with the text.

4 When disassembling the engine, keep 'mated' parts together (including gears, cylinder bores, pistons, connecting rods, valves, etc. that have been in contact with each other during engine operation). These 'mated' parts must be reused or replaced as an assembly. It is worth obtaining a large sheet of card and marking it according to the layout of the engine so that parts can be placed on it and stored in relation to their position in the engine as they are removed.

5 A complete engine/transmission disassembly should be done in the following general order with reference to the appropriate Sections.

Remove the starter motor (see Chapter 9)
Remove the valve covers
Remove the front cylinder head and block
Remove the front piston
Remove the alternator rotor and starter clutch (see Chapter 9)
Remove the front cylinder cam chain and drive gear assembly
Remove the starter reduction and idle gears
Remove the rear cylinder head and block
Remove the rear piston
Remove the clutch
Remove the primary drive gear and front balancer shaft gears
Remove the rear cylinder cam chain and drive gear
Remove the oil pump
Remove the gearchange mechanism
Separate the crankcase halves
Remove the front balancer shaft
Remove the crankshaft and the connecting rods
Remove the selector drum and forks and the transmission shafts/gears

Reassembly

6 Reassembly is accomplished by reversing the general disassembly sequence. After assembling the crankcases, build up the rear cylinder components as far as the valve cover (cam chain and its drive gear/sprocket, piston, cylinder block and cylinder head, camshafts), before installing any of the front cylinder components. This ensures that the timing for the rear cylinder is not disturbed until necessary, and that the engine is then turned by the correct amount for installation of the front cylinder components.

6 Oil cooler and oil tank

Note 1: *The oil cooler can be removed with the engine in the frame. If the engine has been removed, ignore the steps which do not apply.*
Note 2: *The clip-type hose clamps used on the oil cooler and tank hoses are best released using a flat-bladed screwdriver, but note that to rejoin this type of clamp a special pair of pliers makes the job much easier. Also note that these clamps should only be used once, and so new ones should be obtained for the installation procedure.*
Note 3: *Spray the exposed tank and cooler nuts and bolts with some penetrating fluid/lubricant (such as WD40) before trying to undo them.*

Removal

1 The cooler is located on the front of the engine. Remove the lower fairing (see Chapter 8). Drain the engine oil (see Chapter 1).

2 To remove the cooler without its feed and return hoses, release the clamps securing the hoses and pull them off their unions on the cooler. Unscrew the bolts securing the oil cooler to its brackets, noting the collars in the mounting grommets **(see illustration 4.9e)**.

3 To remove the cooler with its feed and return hoses, unscrew the nut securing the bottom of the oil tank to its rear mounting bracket **(see illustration 4.9a)**. Unscrew the bolts securing the oil pipe from the oil cooler to the left-hand side of the engine **(see illustration 4.9b)**. Detach the pipe and discard the O-ring. Also unscrew the bolt securing the oil cooler hose/pipe joining piece to the right-hand side of the engine **(see illustration 4.9c)**. Release the clamp securing the hose to the oil tank and pull it off its union.

6.5 Oil tank hose union bolts (arrowed)

7.2a Valve cover bolts (arrowed)

Unscrew the bolts securing the oil cooler to its brackets, noting the collars in the mounting grommets **(see illustration 4.9e)**.

4 To remove the hoses but leave the cooler in place, release the clamps securing the hoses and pull them off their unions.

5 To remove the oil tank, release the clamps securing the hoses and pull them off their unions, detaching them from the tank or the cooler and engine as required **(see illustration 4.9a)**. Unscrew the nuts and the bolt securing the oil tank and remove it, noting the collar with the top mounting bolt. Remove the rubber support bush fitted over the alternator cover bolt **(see illustration 4.9g)**. If required unscrew the bolts securing the tank hose union on the engine and remove it **(see illustration)**. Discard the O-ring as a new one must be used.

Inspection

6 Check the cooler fins for mud, dirt and insects which may impede the flow of air through it. If the fins are dirty, clean them using water or low pressure compressed air directed from the inner side. If the fins are bent or distorted, straighten them carefully with a screwdriver. If the air flow is restricted by bent or damaged fins over more than 20% of the surface area, replace the cooler with a new one.

7 Check the condition of the hoses and replace them with new ones if they are damaged, deformed or show signs of

cracking. Check the condition of the oil level inspection pipe on the oil tank and replace it with a new one if necessary, using new sealing washers on each side of the banjo unions and tightening the banjo bolts to the torque setting specified at the beginning of the chapter.

Installation

8 Installation is the reverse of removal, noting the following:

● Check the condition of the cooler and tank mounting grommets and rubber bushes and replace them with new ones if they are damaged or deteriorated. Make sure the collars are in the mounting grommets.

● The clip type clamps should be replaced with new ones.

● Install the oil pipe and hose unions on the engine using new O-rings and tighten their bolts to the torque setting specified at the beginning of the Chapter.

● Do not forget to fit the rubber support bush for the oil tank over the alternator cover bolt **(see illustration 4.9g)**.

● Fill the engine with oil (see Chapter 1).

7 Valve covers

Note: *The valve covers can be removed with*

the engine in the frame. If the engine has been removed, ignore the steps which do not apply.

Removal

1 Remove the fuel tank, the air filter housing and the throttle bodies (see Chapter 4).

2 Unscrew the valve cover bolts **(see illustration)**. Check the condition of the sealing washers on the bolts and replace the bolt/washer assemblies with new ones if necessary – the washers are not listed as being available separately **(see illustration)**.

3 Lift the valve cover off the cylinder head **(see illustration)**. If it is stuck, do not try to lever it off with a screwdriver. Tap it gently around the sides with a rubber hammer or block of wood to dislodge it.

4 The cover gasket is normally glued into the groove in the cover, and is best left there if reusable (but note that it is always advisable to use a new one). If the gasket is in any way damaged, deformed or deteriorated, replace it with a new one.

Installation

5 Clean the mating surface of the cylinder head with solvent, removing any traces of old sealant.

6 If a new gasket is being used, clean any traces of old glue or sealant from the groove in the cover and clean it with solvent. Fit the new cover gasket into the groove, using a smear of grease to help stick it in place **(see illustration)**.

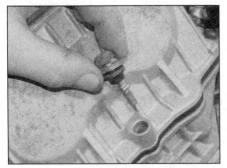

7.2b Check the condition of the sealing washers

7.3 Lift the valve cover off the head

7.6 Fit the new gasket into the groove

8.3 Unscrew the crankshaft end cap

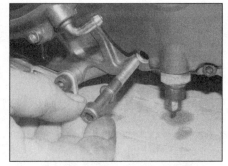

8.4 Unscrew the clutch cover bolt

8.5a Turn the engine anti-clockwise using a hex bit on the rotor bolt . . .

If the old gasket is being reused, make sure its mating surface is clean and sound.

7 Position the valve cover on the cylinder head, making sure the gasket stays in place **(see illustration 7.3)**. Install the cover bolts, using new ones if necessary (see Step 2) and tighten them to the torque setting specified at the beginning of the Chapter.

8 Install the throttle bodies, the air filter housing and the fuel tank (see Chapter 4).

8 Camshafts, rear balancer shaft and followers

Note 1: *The camshafts and followers can be removed with the engine in the frame.*

Note 2: *To ensure that the engine is precisely positioned at top dead centre (TDC) on the compression stroke for the cylinder being worked on, two holes are cut into the crankshaft right-hand web into which the rounded end of the Aprilia special tool (part No. 0240880) or an equivalent made from an 8 mm bolt locates* **(see illustrations 8.6a, b and c)**. *Either obtain the special holding tool or fabricate your own with the end rounded off as shown before commencing this procedure. If you make your own ensure the bolt is strong – we used a car cylinder head bolt which is strengthened (ask your local car repair workshop for one).*

Removal

1 Remove the spark plugs to allow the engine to be turned over easier (see Chapter 1).

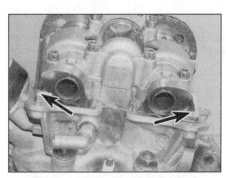

8.5b . . . until the camshaft lobes . . .

2 Remove the valve covers (see Section 7). If the camshafts from only head are to be removed, only remove the relevant cover.

3 Unscrew the crankshaft end cap from the alternator cover **(see illustration)**. Discard the O-ring as a new one should be used.

4 Unscrew the clutch cover bolt that is just below the oil pressure switch **(see illustration)**. Discard the sealing washer as a new one must be used.

Front cylinder head camshafts

Note: *If the camshafts from both cylinder heads are being removed, start with the front.*

5 Turn the engine using a 14 mm hex bit on the alternator rotor bolt; turn it in an anti-clockwise direction only until the piston is at TDC (top dead centre) on the compression stroke, at which point the camshaft lobes are pointing away from each other at a slight upwards angle from the cylinder head, the line

8.5c . . . and the IN and EX timing marks are positioned as shown

above the IN mark on the intake camshaft sprocket should be facing in and in line with the line above the EX mark on the exhaust camshaft sprocket **(see illustrations)**.

6 Thread either the Aprilia special tool or a home-made equivalent (see **Note 2** above) into the clutch cover bolt hole until it locates in the hole in the crankshaft – you should be able to feel the point at which it locates by jiggling the crankshaft back and forth a very small amount either side of its current position (see Step 5) as you thread the holding bolt in **(see illustrations)**. When you can't turn the crankshaft any more the tool end has located in the hole. Do not over-tighten the bolt – hand-tight is sufficient. If the only work you are doing on the engine is to remove the front cylinder camshafts or other front cylinder components, do not remove the holding tool after removing the camshafts – this will keep the engine in its correct position for the

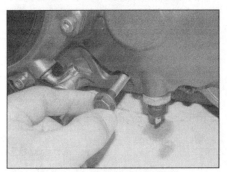

8.6a Thread the tool in . . .

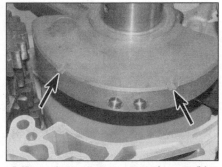

8.6b . . . there are two cutouts (arrowed) in the crank web, one for each cylinder TDC . . .

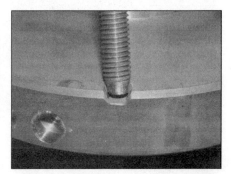

8.6c . . . into which the shaped end of the tool locates and locks the crankshaft

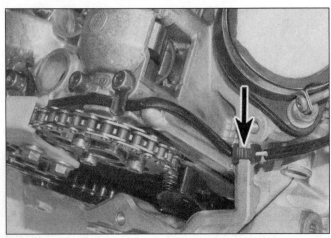

8.11 Free the grommet (arrowed) from its cutout

8.12a Unscrew the camshaft holder bolts, noting how the washer holds the wiring (A) . . .

installation of all removed components. If the rear cylinder is being worked on as well, remove any other front cylinder components (cylinder head, piston, cam chain) before starting on the rear cylinder, then follow the procedure from Step 16. If no work is being done on the rear cylinder, from here on the only reason to remove the holding tool is if the clutch cover is being removed, in which case the tool should be reinstalled immediately afterwards, or unless so directed in the text (e.g. for checking of freedom of movement of a component or assembly that has just been installed), in which case the tool must be reinstalled immediately afterwards.

7 Remove the cam chain tensioner (see Section 9).

8 Remove the cam chain top guide (see Section 9).

9 Mark each camshaft according to its location (i.e. intake or exhaust) so they cannot be inadvertently interchanged. If you are going to detach the sprockets from the camshafts, also mark them according to location, and make an alignment mark between the sprocket and the camshaft as an aid to installation.

10 If required, unscrew the bolts securing each camshaft sprocket, then slip each sprocket off the end of its camshaft and disengage it from the chain. Tie the chain over

the front of its tunnel to prevent it dropping down. Note the differences in the sprockets – the exhaust camshaft one has a square trigger for the camshaft position sensor, while the intake sprocket has a square hole.

11 If required, remove the camshaft position sensor (see Chapter 4). If you prefer to leave it on the camshaft holder, and the engine is in the frame, trace the wiring from the sensor and disconnect it at the connector **(see illustration 4.10g)**, then free the wiring grommet from its cut-out in the head **(see illustration)**.

12 Unscrew the bolts securing the holder, slackening them evenly and a little at a time in a criss-cross pattern **(see illustration)**. Remove the bolts with their washers, noting which fits where (there are different lengths), and note how one bolt secures the cam position sensor wiring with a tabbed washer. Lift the holder off the camshafts **(see illustration)**. Fit the bolts with their washers back into their holes in the holder as an aid to installation. Retrieve the two dowels from either the holder or the head if they are loose, otherwise leave them in place. Do not try and remove them if they are tight.

13 Lift the camshafts off the head, noting how they fit, and disengaging the sprockets from the chain if they weren't removed earlier **(see illustration)**. If not already done tie the

chain over the front of its tunnel to prevent it dropping down.

14 If required remove the cam chain guide blade (see Section 9).

15 If required, remove the followers and shims (see Step 27). On completion cover the top of the cylinder head with a rag to prevent anything falling into the engine.

Rear cylinder head camshafts

Note: *If the camshafts from both cylinder heads are being removed, start with the front.*

16 Turn the engine using a 14 mm hex bit on the alternator rotor bolt; turn it in an anticlockwise direction only until the piston is at TDC (top dead centre) on the compression stroke, at which point the camshaft lobes are pointing away from each other at a slight upwards angle from the cylinder head, the line above the IN mark on the intake camshaft sprocket should be facing and in line with the line above the EX mark on the exhaust camshaft sprocket **(see illustration 8.5a and b)** – due to the position of the rear balancer shaft driven gear the EX mark cannot be seen, but as long as the IN mark is correctly positioned you can assume so is the EX mark **(see illustration 8.5c for clarity)**.

Caution: If the front camshafts have been removed, lift the front cam chain up in your hand and allow it to turn freely as you turn the engine, otherwise it could get jammed around its bottom sprocket.

17 Thread either the Aprilia special tool or a home-made equivalent (see **Note 2** above) into the clutch cover bolt hole until it locates in the hole in the crankshaft – you should be able to feel the point at which it locates by jiggling the crankshaft back and forth a very small amount either side of its current position (see Step 5) as you thread the holding bolt in **(see illustrations 8.6a, b and c)**. When you can't turn the crankshaft any more the tool end has located in the hole. Do not overtighten the bolt – hand-tight is sufficient. If the only work you are doing on the engine is to

8.12b . . . and remove the holder

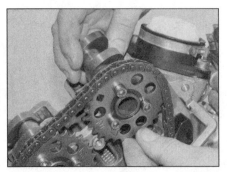

8.13 Remove the camshafts from the head

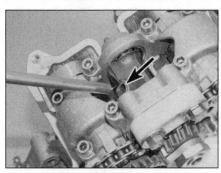

8.19a Counter-hold the shaft by inserting a rod in the hole (arrowed) . . .

8.19b . . . and hold the rod while unscrewing the nut

8.19c Remove the key (arrowed) if it is loose

remove the front and/or rear cylinder camshafts, do not remove the holding tool after removing the camshafts – this will keep the engine in its correct position for the installation of all removed components. From here on the only reason to remove the holding tool is if the clutch cover is being removed, in which case the tool should be reinstalled immediately afterwards, or if the crankcases are being separated, or unless so directed in the text (for checking of freedom of movement of a component or assembly that has just been installed), in which case the tool must be reinstalled immediately afterwards.

18 Remove the cam chain tensioner (see Section 9).

19 Insert a suitable rod in the hole in the rear balancer shaft and use it counter-hold the shaft, then unscrew the nut on its end **(see illustrations)**. Remove the counter-weight, noting how it fits **(see illustration 8.50b)**.

Slide the driven gear off the shaft, noting how it locates on the Woodruff key **(see illustration 8.50a)**. Remove the key from its slot if loose, taking care not to drop it down the cam chain tunnel **(see illustration)**.

20 Mark each camshaft according to its location (i.e. intake or exhaust) so they cannot be inadvertently interchanged. Also mark the sprockets according to location, and make an alignment mark between the intake camshaft and its sprocket, and between the exhaust camshaft and its sprocket and the balancer shaft drive gear, as an aid to installation.

21 Unscrew the bolts securing the camshaft sprocket to the intake camshaft and the bolts securing the gear and sprocket to the exhaust camshaft, then slip each off the end of its camshaft and disengage it from the chain **(see illustration)**. Do not intermix the bolts – they are different and must be fitted with their original components. Tie the chain over the

front of its tunnel to prevent it dropping down.

22 Unscrew the bolts securing the balancer shaft bearing housing and remove the cam chain top guide located on the top bolt lugs **(see illustration)**. Draw the housing out of the camshaft holder **(see illustration)**. Discard the O-rings. Note. Draw the balancer shaft out **(see illustration)**.

23 Unscrew the bolts securing the camshaft holder, slackening them evenly and a little at a time in a criss-cross pattern **(see illustration)**. Remove the bolts with their washers, noting which fits where (there are different lengths). Lift the holder off the camshafts. Fit the bolts with their washers back into their holes in the holder as an aid to installation. Retrieve the two dowels from either the holder or the head if they are loose, otherwise leave them in place. Do not try and remove them if they are tight.

24 Lift the camshafts off the head, noting how they fit **(see illustration)**.

8.21 Unscrew the bolts (arrowed) and remove the sprockets and gear

8.22a Unscrew the bolts (arrowed) . . .

8.22b . . . then remove the bearing housing . . .

8.22c . . . and withdraw the balancer shaft

8.23 Unscrew the bolts and remove the holder . . .

8.24 . . . then remove the camshafts

8.27a Carefully lift out the follower using fingers, a lapping tool or a magnet . . .

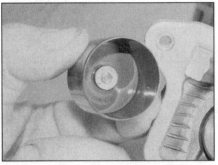

8.27b . . . and retrieve the shim from inside it . . .

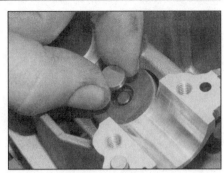

8.27c . . . or from the top of the valve

25 If required remove the cam chain guide blade (see Section 9).

26 On completion cover the top of the cylinder head with a rag to prevent anything falling into the engine.

Followers and shims

27 If you are removing the followers and shims, obtain a container which is divided into eight compartments (or two containers divided into four), and label each compartment with the identity of a valve location in the cylinder head, for example the front cylinder, intake camshaft, left-hand valve could be marked F-I-L. If a container is not available, use labelled plastic bags. Lift each cam follower out of the cylinder head using either a magnet or the suction created by a valve lapping tool, though fingers may suffice, and long nosed pliers can be used with care – do not grip the follower tightly as you could score it **(see illustration)**. Retrieve the shim from either the inside of the follower or pick it out of the top of the valve, using either a magnet, a small screwdriver with a dab of grease on it (the shim will stick to the grease), or a screwdriver and a pair of pliers **(see illustrations)**. Do not allow the shim to fall into the engine. Store the follower and its shim in its correct compartment in the container, or in its labelled bag.

Inspection

Note: *Before discarding the camshafts or the cylinder head and camshaft holders because of wear or damage, check with local machine shops specialising in motorcycle engineering*

work. In the case of the camshafts, it may be possible for cam lobes to be welded, reground and hardened, at a cost far lower than that of a new camshaft. Due to the cost of a new cylinder head, it is recommended that all options be explored.

28 Inspect the bearing surfaces in the camshaft holders and cylinder head and the corresponding journals on the camshafts. Look for score marks, deep scratches and evidence of spalling (a pitted appearance). Check the oil passages for clogging.

29 Check the camshaft lobes for heat discoloration (blue appearance), score marks, chipped areas, flat spots and spalling. Also check the lobe contact surfaces on the cam followers. If damage is noted or wear is excessive, the camshaft must be replaced with a new one.

30 Next, check the camshaft journal oil clearances preferably using Plastigauge (but note that if none is available the oil clearance can be obtained by measuring the journal diameter and holder/head bore as described in Step 34, then calculating the difference, though this method is not as accurate). Note that Plastigauge comes in two different sizes, graded according to a range of clearances it can measure – make sure you order the correct one according to the oil clearance figure specified.

Refer to Tools and Workshop Tips in the Reference section for details of how to read a micrometer and dial gauge.

31 Check one camshaft at a time. Clean the camshaft and the bearing surfaces in the cylinder head and camshaft holder with a clean lint-free cloth, then lay the camshaft in its correct location in the head, making sure that the lobes are not contacting the followers (if not removed) or valve stem ends – if they are the shaft will turn as the holder bolts are tightened which will disturb the Plastigauge and lead to a false reading.

32 Cut two strips of Plastigauge and lay one piece on each journal, parallel with the camshaft centreline. Make sure the camshaft holder dowels are installed. Install the holder and tighten the bolts evenly and a little at a time in a criss-cross sequence, making sure the holder is pulled down squarely onto the dowels, to the torque setting specified at the beginning of the Chapter. While doing this, don't let the camshaft rotate, or the Plastigauge will be disturbed and you will have to start again.

33 Now unscrew the camshaft holder bolts evenly and a little at a time in a criss-cross sequence, and lift off the holder.

34 To determine the oil clearance, compare the crushed Plastigauge (at its widest point) on each journal to the scale printed on the Plastigauge container. Compare the results to this Chapter's Specifications. If the oil clearance is greater than specified, measure the diameter of the camshaft journal with a micrometer **(see illustration)**. If the journal diameter is less than the specified limit, replace the camshaft with a new one and recheck the clearance. If the clearance is still too great, or if the camshaft journal is within its limit, replace the cylinder head and holder as a set with new ones. If required the holder/cylinder head bore sizes can be measured with the camshafts removed and the holder tightened down, using a small bore gauge and micrometer, comparing the results to the specifications **(see illustration)**.

35 Measure the width of each camshaft journal and its corresponding surface on the head and holder and compare the results to the Specifications. Replace any components that are worn with new ones.

36 Inspect the outer surfaces of the cam followers for evidence of scoring or other damage **(see illustration)**. If a follower is in

8.34a Measure the diameter of the journal with a micrometer

8.34b Measure the internal diameter using a bore gauge as shown

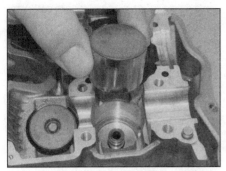

8.36 Check the followers and their bores as described

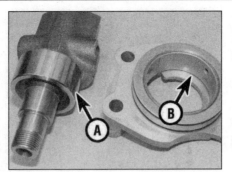

8.38a Check the balancer shaft journal (A) and the shells in the housing (B)

8.38b Check the bearing (arrowed) and the seal behind it

poor condition, it is probable that the bore in which it works is also damaged. Check for clearance between the followers and their bores. Measure the external diameter of each follower and the internal diameter of the bore. Replace any followers or the head itself if worn beyond their specified limits. If the bores are seriously out-of-round or tapered, a new cylinder head is needed.

37 Check each camshaft sprocket for cracks and wear or other damage, replacing it with a new one if necessary. If the sprocket teeth are worn, check the cam chain and its drive gears and sprockets as well. If wear this severe is apparent, the entire engine should be disassembled for inspection.

38 Check the main journal on the rear balancer shaft and the bearing shells in the housing for wear and damage **(see illustration)**. Fit the shaft into the housing and check the amount of radial play. Measure the diameter of the housing – take the measurement in the middle of the housing as it is tapered. Replace the bearing housing with a new one if wear exceeds the limits – the shells are not available separately from the holder. Measure the diameter of the shaft end where it fits into the ball bearing, and check the bearing itself **(see illustration)**. Refer to *Tools and Workshop Tips* in the reference section for details on bearing checks and

removal and installation methods. Check the oil seal that is behind the bearing and replace it with a new one if necessary.

Installation

Followers and shims

39 Lubricate each shim with molybdenum disulphide oil (a 50/50 mixture of molybdenum disulphide grease and engine oil) and fit it into its recess in the top of the valve spring retainer with the size mark facing down **(see illustration 8.27c)**. It is essential that the correct shim is installed otherwise the valve clearances will be incorrect.

40 Check that the shim is correctly seated, then lubricate the follower with molybdenum disulphide oil and install it onto the valve, making sure it fits squarely in its bore **(see illustration 8.27a)**. Repeat the process for all other valves.

Rear cylinder head camshafts

Note: *If the camshafts from both cylinder heads have removed, install the rear cylinder ones first.*

41 If both cylinders or only the rear cylinder has been worked on, the engine should already be correctly aligned and locked with the holding tool for installation of the rear cylinder camshafts. If the tool has been removed, refit it (see Step 17). If the engine

has been turned after the tool was removed, realign it so that the rear cylinder piston is at TDC on its compression stroke by looking into the cylinder via the spark plug hole while you turn the engine anti-clockwise using the hex key on the rotor bolt – when you can see the top of the piston at its highest point fit the holding tool as described in Step 17. If the engine has been completely stripped then the holding tool should already be in place for the complete rear cylinder rebuild according to the procedures described for installation of the cam chain and its drive gear/sprocket, piston, cylinder block and cylinder head.

42 If removed install the cam chain guide blade (see Section 9).

43 Apply molybdenum disulphide oil (a mixture of 50% molybdenum disulphide grease and 50% engine oil) to the camshaft journals. Lay each camshaft onto the cylinder head, making sure each is returned to its original position according to the markings made on removal, and positioning them so that the lobes are pointing away from each other at a slight upwards angle from the cylinder head **(see illustration and 8.24)**.

44 If removed, fit the two locating dowels into the cylinder head. Fit the holder onto the camshafts, locating it onto the dowels **(see illustration)**. Install the bolts with their washers and tighten them finger-tight – make

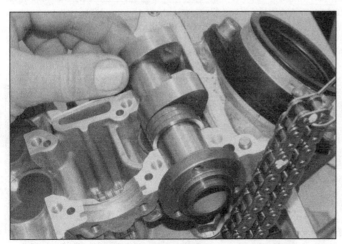

8.43 Locate the camshafts, positioning the lobes as shown

8.44 Fit the holder, locating it on the dowels (arrowed)

8.45 Fit the bearing housing into the holder and over the shaft journal

8.46a Fit the exhaust camshaft sprocket . . .

8.46b . . . followed by the intake sprocket, aligning the marks as shown and described

sure the bolts and their washers are returned to their original location **(see illustration 8.23)**. Now tighten them evenly and a little at a time in a criss-cross pattern, making sure the holder is drawn down evenly and does not bind, to the torque setting specified at the beginning of the Chapter.

Caution: Whilst tightening the bolts, make sure each holder is being pulled squarely down and is not binding on the dowels or tilting to one side – if it does, adjust the relevant bolts until the holder is again square to the head. The holder is likely to break if it's not tightened down evenly and squarely.

45 Slide the rear balancer shaft into the camshaft holder, locating its end in the ball bearing **(see illustration 8.22c)**. Fit two new O-rings onto the outside of the balancer shaft

holder and smear them with clean oil **(see illustration 8.22b)**. Apply molybdenum disulphide oil (a mixture of 50% molybdenum disulphide grease and 50% engine oil) to the bearing shells on the inside of the holder. Slide the holder onto the shaft and locate it in the camshaft holder, making sure the O-rings stay in place **(see illustration)**. If removed fit the cam chain top guide onto the lugs for the top bolts. Install the bolts with their washers and tighten them to the specified torque setting **(see illustration 8.22a)**.

46 Check that the camshaft lobes are still pointing away from each other at a slight upwards angle from the cylinder head. Locate the exhaust camshaft sprocket onto the camshaft, aligning the bolts holes (they are offset so the sprocket can only fit one way) **(see illustration)**. Adjust the position of the camshaft either way to set the line above the EX mark on the sprocket facing in and parallel with the head. Keeping the rear run of the chain taut lay it round the sprocket and under the top guide. Now fit the intake camshaft sprocket, so that the line above the IN mark is facing in and parallel with the EX mark, engaging it with the chain as you fit it onto the camshaft **(see illustration)**. Make sure the chain is taut between the sprockets so that any slack is in the front run where it will be taken up by the tensioner when installed.

47 Re-check that the marks are aligned correctly and that all chain slack is in the front run, then apply a suitable non-permanent

thread locking compound to the intake camshaft sprocket bolts and tighten them to the specified torque – the bolts for this sprocket are shorter than those for the exhaust sprocket and balancer drive gear on the other camshaft **(see illustration)**.

48 Fit the balancer drive gear onto the exhaust camshaft sprocket, aligning it so the punch mark on its outer face rim is roughly at the 2 o'clock position (the gear can only fit one way as the bolt holes are offset) **(see illustration)**. Apply a suitable non-permanent thread locking compound to the gear/sprocket bolts and tighten them to the specified torque.

49 Install the cam chain tensioner (see Section 9).

50 If removed fit the Woodruff key into its slot in the balancer shaft – stuff some rag into the chain tunnel in case you drop the key **(see illustration 8.19c)**. Set the shaft so the key is roughly in the 7 o'clock position. Slide the balancer driven gear onto the shaft, aligning the punch mark on its outer face rim with that on the drive gear, adjusting the position of the shaft as required so the slot in the gear locates over the woodruff key **(see illustration)**. Slide the counter-weight onto the shaft with its sharp sided face on the inside, aligning its slot with the key **(see illustration)**. Apply a suitable non-permanent thread locking compound to the nut and tighten it to the specified torque setting counter-holding the shaft using a rod through

8.47 Fit the bolts and tighten them to the specified torque

8.48 Fit the drive gear and tighten the bolts to the specified torque

8.50a Fit the driven gear, aligning the punch marks . . .

8.50b . . . then fit the counter-weight . . .

8.50c . . . and secure them with the nut

8.55a Fit the exhaust camshaft . . .

8.55b . . . followed by the intake camshaft, aligning them as shown and described

the shaft as before **(see illustration and 8.19a and b)**.

Front cylinder head camshafts

Note: *If the camshafts from both cylinder heads have removed, install the rear cylinder ones first.*

51 If only the front cylinder has been worked on, the engine should already be correctly aligned and locked with the holding tool for installation of the front cylinder camshafts. If the tool has been removed, refit it (see Step 6). If the engine has been turned after the tool was removed, realign it so that the rear cylinder piston is at TDC on its compression stroke as described in Step 16 (remove the rear valve cover to see the camshafts – see Section 7), then turn the engine 60° anti-clockwise using a 14 mm hex bit on the alternator rotor bolt until the front piston is at TDC – you can tell by looking into the cylinder via the spark plug hole while you turn the engine, and when you can see the top of the piston at its highest point fit the holding tool as described in Step 6. If both cylinders have been worked on and you have completed the rear cylinder camshaft installation, turn the engine 60° anti-clockwise using a 14 mm hex bit on the alternator rotor bolt until the front piston is at TDC – you can tell by looking into the cylinder via the spark plug hole while you turn the engine, and when you can see the top of the piston at its highest point fit the holding tool as described in Step 6. *Caution: If you are turning the engine, lift the front cam chain up in your hand and allow it to turn freely as you turn the engine, otherwise it could get jammed around its bottom sprocket.*

52 If removed install the cam chain guide blade (see Section 9).

53 Apply molybdenum disulphide oil (a mixture of 50% molybdenum disulphide grease and 50% engine oil) to the camshaft journals.

54 If the sprockets have been removed from the camshafts, lay each camshaft onto the cylinder head, making sure each is returned to its original position according to the markings made on removal, and positioning them so that the lobes are pointing away from each other at a slight upwards angle from the cylinder head.

55 If the sprockets are on the shafts, lay the

exhaust camshaft in the head so the lobes are pointing forwards at a slight upwards angle from the cylinder head and so the line above the EX mark on the sprocket is facing back and parallel with the head **(see illustration)**. Keeping the front run of the chain taut lay it round the sprocket. Now lay the intake camshaft on the head so the lobes are pointing backwards at a slight upwards angle from the cylinder head, engaging the sprocket with the chain as you do, making sure the chain is tight between the sprockets so that any slack is in the rear run where it will be taken up by the tensioner when installed, and aligning the shaft so that the line above the IN mark on the sprocket is facing in and parallel with the EX mark **(see illustration and 8.5c)**.

56 If removed, fit the two locating dowels into the cylinder head. Fit the holder onto the camshafts, locating it onto the dowels **(see illustration 8.12b)**. Install the bolts with their washers and tighten them finger-tight – make sure the bolts and their washers are returned to their original location, and make sure that if it wasn't removed the camshaft position sensor wiring is correctly routed and secured by the tabbed washer on the rear outer bolt **(see illustration 8.12a)**. Now tighten the bolts evenly and a little at a time in a criss-cross pattern, making sure the holder is drawn down evenly and does not bind, to the torque setting specified at the beginning of the Chapter. *Caution: Whilst tightening the bolts, make sure each holder is being pulled squarely down and is not binding on the dowels or tilting to one side – if it does, adjust the relevant bolts until the holder is again square to the head. The holder is likely to break if it's not tightened down evenly and squarely.*

57 If the sprockets have been removed from the camshafts, check that the camshaft lobes are still pointing away from each other at a slight upwards angle from the cylinder head **(see illustration 8.5b)**. Locate the exhaust camshaft sprocket onto the camshaft, aligning the bolts holes (they are offset so the sprocket can only fit one way). Adjust the position of the camshaft either way to set the line above the EX mark on the sprocket facing in and parallel with the head. Keeping the front run of the chain taut lay it round the sprocket. Now fit the intake camshaft sprocket, so that the line

above the IN mark is facing in and parallel with the EX mark, engaging it with the chain as you fit it onto the camshaft. Make sure the chain is taut between the sprockets so that any slack is in the rear run where it will be taken up by the tensioner when installed. Re-check that the marks are aligned correctly and that all chain slack is in the rear run, then apply a suitable non-permanent thread locking compound to the camshaft sprocket bolts and tighten them to the specified torque.

58 Install the cam chain tensioner (see Section 9).

59 If removed, install the camshaft position sensor (see Chapter 4). If you did not remove it, and the engine is in the frame, fit the wiring grommet into its cut-out in the head using a dab of sealant, then connect the wiring connector **(see illustrations 8.11 and 4.10g)**.

60 Install the cam chain top guide (see Section 9).

On completion

61 Remove the crankshaft holding tool **(see illustration 8.6a)**.

62 Rotate the engine anti-clockwise through two full turns (720°) and re-check that the valve timing marks for both cylinders are correctly aligned (see Steps 5 and 16). Re-install the holding tool when each cylinder is at TDC to confirm correct alignment. When you are satisfied that everything is as it should be, remove the holding tool, fit the clutch cover bolt using a new sealing washer and tighten it to the specified torque **(see illustration 8.4)**.

63 Check the valve clearances (Chapter 1) and adjust if necessary.

64 Install the crankshaft end cap using a new O-ring **(see illustration)**.

8.64 Install the end cap using a new O-ring

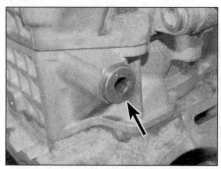

9.2 Unscrew the cap bolt (arrowed) . . .

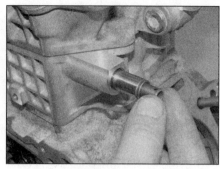

9.3 . . . and withdraw the tensioner

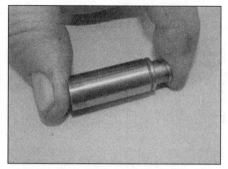

9.6 Check the action of the tensioner by compressing it

65 Coat the camshaft lobes with clean oil. Install the valve covers (see Section 7).
66 Install the spark plugs (see Chapter 1).
67 Check the engine oil level and top up if necessary (see *Daily (pre-ride) checks*).

9 Cam chain tensioners and blades

Note: *The cam chain tensioners can be removed with the engine in the frame. If the engine has been removed, ignore the steps that do not apply.*

Tensioners

Removal

1 Set the cylinder being worked on at TDC on its compression stroke before removing a tensioner, and remove only one tensioner a time – turning the engine with one removed to align it for removal of the other could cause the slack chain to jump on its sprocket. Remove the valve cover(s) (see Section 7), and the crankshaft end cap from the alternator cover **(see illustration 8.3)**. Turn the engine in an anti-clockwise direction to align the timing marks (see Section 8, Step 5 for the front cylinder marks, and Step 16 for the rear cylinder marks).
2 Unscrew the tensioner cap bolt and remove the sealing washer **(see illustration)**.
3 Withdraw the tensioner, noting which way round it fits **(see illustration)**. Do not rotate the engine with the tensioner removed.
4 Discard the sealing washer as a new one must be used on installation.

Inspection

5 Examine the tensioner components for signs of wear and damage. Measure the internal diameter of the tensioner bore in the cylinder block using a small bore gauge and micrometer, and measure the diameter of the tensioner piston. Subtract one from the other to obtain the clearance. If the result is greater than the limit specified replace the tensioner with a new one assuming the bore diameter is within limits.
6 Press the ends of the tensioner together and check that it moves smoothly and that the spring pressure is good **(see illustration)**. Replace the tensioner with a new one if necessary.

Installation

7 Ensure the cylinder block surface is clean and dry.
8 Lubricate the tensioner with oil then fit it into the engine with its wider end going in first **(see illustration 9.3)**.
9 Install the cap bolt with a new sealing washer and tighten it to the torque setting specified at the beginning of the Chapter **(see illustration)**.
10 Rotate the engine anti-clockwise through two full turns (720º) and check the timing marks for both cylinders are correctly aligned (see Section 8, Step 5 for the front cylinder marks, and Step 16 for the rear cylinder marks). Install the valve cover(s). Install the timing inspection cap using a new O-ring **(see illustration 8.64)**.

Blades

Removal

11 Remove the valve cover(s) (see Section 7).
12 To remove the top guide, unscrew its bolts **(see illustrations)**. On the front cylinder note how the camshaft position sensor wiring routes under the tab on the inner face of the guide. On the rear cylinder note the washers with the bolts.
13 To remove the guide blade from the front of the front cylinder and the rear of the rear cylinder, simply lift it off its seat and draw it out **(see illustration)**.
14 To remove the tensioner blade, follow the procedure in Section 10 to remove the cam

9.9 Fit a new sealing washer with the cap bolt

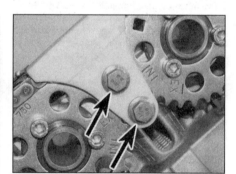

9.12a Top guide bolts (arrowed) – front cylinder

9.12b Top guide bolts (arrowed) – rear cylinder

9.13 Lift the blade out of the tunnel

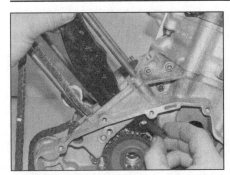

9.14 Withdraw the pivot piece and remove the blade

9.16 Make sure the sensor wiring is correctly routed (arrowed)

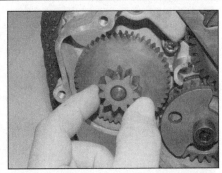

10.4a Remove the reduction gear and its shaft

chain driven gear plate. Withdraw the blade pivot piece then lift the blade out of the tunnel (see illustration).

Inspection

15 Examine the top guide and blades for signs of wear and damage, and replace them with new ones if necessary.

Installation

16 To install the top guide, on the front cylinder make sure the camshaft position sensor wiring routes under the tab on the inner face of the guide (see illustration). On the rear cylinder do not forget the washers with the bolts. Tighten the bolts to the torque setting specified at the beginning of the Chapter.

17 To install the guide blade in the front of the front cylinder and the rear of the rear cylinder slide it into place between the chain and the cylinder head and block, making sure it seats correctly (see illustration 9.13).

18 To install the tensioner blade, lubricate the pivot piece with oil, then locate the blade in the tunnel and slide the pivot in (see illustration 9.14). Install the cam chain drive gear plate (see Section 10, following the relevant Steps for the cylinder being worked on). Fit the sprocket onto the intake camshaft, following the relevant installation Steps in Section 9 for the cylinder being worked on to ensure the valve timing is correct.

10 Cam chains and drive gears

Note 1: *The cam chains can be removed with the engine in the frame. If the engine has been removed and/or partially stripped ignore the Steps which do not apply.*

Note 2: *To ensure that the engine is precisely positioned at top dead centre (TDC) on the compression stroke for the cylinder being worked on, two holes are cut into the crankshaft right-hand web into which the rounded end of the Aprilia special tool (part No. 0240880) or an equivalent made from an 8 mm bolt locates (see illustrations 8.6a, b and c). Either obtain the special holding tool or fabricate your own with the end rounded off as shown before commencing this procedure.*

10.4b Unscrew the bolt and remove the outer counter-weight, the gear, and the inner counter-weight

If you make your own ensure the bolt is strong – we used a car cylinder head bolt which is strengthened (ask you local car repair workshop for one).

Removal

1 Drain the engine oil and, unless you are only removing the front cylinder cam chain, the coolant (see Chapter 1).

2 Remove the sprockets from the camshafts for the cylinder being worked on, following procedure in Section 8 (Steps 1 to 4 for both cylinders, then Steps 5 to 10 for the front cylinder and Steps 16 to 21 for the rear cylinder) – the camshafts can stay in place but the relevant steps up to the point of removing the sprockets must be followed to ensure the valve timing is correct.

3 Mark the outside of the chain so that it can be installed so that it runs in the same direction as before.

10.5a Slide the drive gear off the shaft

10.4c Remove the key (arrowed) if it is loose

4 To remove the front cylinder cam chain and drive gear, remove the alternator rotor, bringing the starter driven gear with it (see Chapter 9). Remove the starter reduction gear and its shaft (see illustration). Unscrew the bolt securing the cam chain drive gear on the end of the front balancer shaft, then remove the outer counter-weight, the drive gear, and if required the inner counter-weight, noting how they all locate on the Woodruff key in the shaft (see illustration). Remove the key if it is loose (see illustration).

5 To remove the rear cylinder cam chain and drive gear, remove the clutch (see Section 16), and the primary drive gear and front balancer gears (see Section 20). If required slide the cam chain drive gear off the end of the crankshaft, noting how it locates on the Woodruff key (see illustration). Remove the key if it is loose (see illustration).

6 Unscrew the bolts securing the driven gear

10.5b Remove the key if it is loose

10.6a Front cylinder gear plate bolts (arrowed)

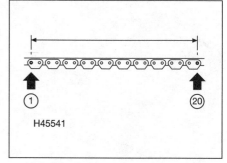

10.6b Note the wave washers and bolt locations

10.8 Check the amount of stretch by measuring as shown

plate, noting which fits where, and the wave washers fitted with all bolts except the bottom one for the front cylinder plate **(see illustrations)**. Remove the plate, noting the needle bearings on the shaft that the gear runs on **(see illustration 10.24 or 10.17b)**. Remove the cam chain tensioner blade **(see illustration 9.14)**. Remove the gear and lift the chain out of the tunnel **(see illustration 10.22 or 10.15c)**. Note the washer fitted on the back of the gear/sprocket **(see illustration 10.15a)**.

7 Remove the dowels from the crankcase if they are loose – two are fitted with the rear cylinder plate on all models, but only with the front cylinder plate up to engine number 527353.

Inspection

8 Check the chains for binding, kinks and any obvious damage and replace them with new ones if necessary. Check the chain for stretch by measuring the length of 20 pins (from the centre of the 1st pin to the centre of the 20th pin) and compare the result to the stretch limit specified at the beginning of the Chapter **(see illustration)**.

9 Check the sprocket and gear teeth for wear and damage, including those on the driven sprockets. If new ones are being fitted, fit new chains as a matter of course.

10 Check that the needle bearings rotate freely and smoothly and without excessive freeplay between the shaft and the gear/sprocket. Measure the outside diameter of the gear plate shaft and the internal diameter of the gear/sprocket and replace them with new ones if worn beyond the limit specified. Replace the bearings with new ones if necessary.

Installation

Note: *If the cam chains and drive gears for both cylinders have been removed, install the rear cylinder ones first, and install all the rear cylinder components up to and including the camshafts and its sprockets, leaving only the valve cover uninstalled, then proceed with the front cylinder cam chain and drive gear and all*

remaining components. This ensures the timing will be correct.

11 If the whole engine has been stripped, position the crankshaft so that the rear cylinder connecting rod is at its highest point. Now thread either the Aprilia special tool or a home-made equivalent (see **Note 2** above) into the clutch cover bolt hole in the crankcase until it locates in the hole in the crankshaft – you should be able to feel the point at which it locates by jiggling the crankshaft back and forth a very small amount either side of its current position as you thread the holding bolt in **(see illustration)**. When you can't turn the crankshaft any more the tool end has located in the hole. Do not over-tighten the bolt – hand-tight is sufficient. Commence the rear cylinder rebuild with installation of the cam chain and its drive gear/sprocket as from Step 15.

12 If both cylinders or just the rear cylinder have been worked on, the engine should already be correctly aligned and locked with the holding bolt for installation of the rear cylinder cam chain and drive gear and all other removed components. If both cam chains have been removed but the front piston, block, head and camshafts are in place do not remove the tool and turn the engine.

13 If only the front cylinder has been worked on, the engine should already be correctly aligned and locked with the holding bolt for installation of the front cylinder cam chain and drive gear and all other removed components.

14 If the engine has been completely stripped and the rear cylinder rebuild has been completed up to valve cover installation, remove the holding tool, then turn the engine 300° anti-clockwise using a socket on the primary drive gear nut (you cannot use the alternator bolt as the rotor has not yet been installed) from its rear cylinder rebuild position, so that the front cylinder connecting rod is at TDC. Now thread either the Aprilia special tool or a home-made equivalent (see **Note 2** above) into the clutch cover bolt hole in the crankcase until it locates in the hole in the crankshaft – you should be able to feel the point at which it locates by jiggling the crankshaft back and forth a very small amount either side of its current position as you thread the holding bolt in **(see illustration 10.11)**. When you can't turn the crankshaft any more the tool end has located in the hole. Do not over-tighten the bolt – hand-tight is sufficient. Commence the front cylinder rebuild with installation of the cam chain and its drive gear/sprocket as from Step 22.

Rear cylinder cam chain and gears

15 If removed, fit the driven gear plate dowels into the crankcase. Fit the washer onto the back of the gear/sprocket, using a smear of grease to stick it in place **(see illustration)**. Slip the chain into the tunnel then engage the sprocket with it and locate the gear/sprocket against the crankcase, making sure the washer stays in place, and if not removed the driven gear meshes correctly

10.11 Thread the tool into the engine

10.15a Use some grease to stick the washer to the gear/sprocket

10.15b Engage the sprocket with the chain . . .

10.15c . . . and position it on the crankcase . . .

10.15d . . . aligning the punch mark with the line

with the drive gear, and aligning the punch mark on the driven gear with the mark on the crankcase **(see illustrations)**.

16 Install the cam chain tensioner blade (see Section 9).

17 Fit the needle bearings onto the gear plate shaft and lubricate them with clean engine oil **(see illustration)**. Align the gear/sprocket with its bore in the crankcase and slide the shaft through, making sure the washer stays in place, and making sure the driven gear punch mark remains aligned with the mark on the crankcase **(see illustration and 10.15d)**. Install the bolts with their wave washers, noting that the longer gold coloured bolt fits through the tensioner blade pivot piece **(see illustration 10.6b)**. Tighten the bolts to the torque setting specified at the beginning of the Chapter.

18 If removed fit the Woodruff key into the crankshaft, then slide the drive gear onto it, engaging it with the driven gear, and making sure the driven gear punch mark still aligns with the mark on the crankcase **(see illustrations 10.5b and a, 10.15d)**. Install the balancer gears and the primary drive gear (see Section 20).

19 Fit the sprockets onto the camshafts, following the procedure in Section 8 (Steps 46 to 50 and 60 to 66).

20 Install the clutch (see Section 16).

21 Add the engine oil and the coolant (see Chapter 1).

Front cylinder cam chain and gears

22 Up to engine number 527353, and if removed, fit the driven gear plate dowels into the crankcase. Fit the washer onto the back of the gear/sprocket, using a smear of grease to stick it in place **(see illustration 10.15a)**. Slip the chain into the tunnel then engage the sprocket with it and locate the gear/sprocket against the crankcase, making sure the washer stays in place, and if not removed the driven gear meshes correctly with the drive gear **(see illustration)**.

23 If removed, install the cam chain tensioner blade (see Section 9).

24 Fit the needle bearings onto the gear plate shaft and lubricate them with clean engine oil. Align the gear/sprocket with its bore in the crankcase and slide the shaft through, making

sure the washer stays in place **(see illustration)**. Install the upper bolts with their wave washers noting that the longer gold coloured bolt fits through the tensioner blade pivot piece. Apply a suitable non-permanent thread locking compound to the lower 6 mm bolt and install it. Tighten the bolts to the torque settings specified at the beginning of the Chapter.

25 Rotate the driven gear and chain so the punch mark on the driven gear aligns with the mark or projection on the gear plate **(see illustration)**. Fit the Woodruff key into the balancer shaft **(see illustration 10.4c)**, then install the inner counterweight (with a notch cut into its inner rim for the key), the drive gear, making sure it engages correctly with the driven gear and the punch mark remains

10.17a Fit the bearings onto the shaft . . .

10.17b . . . then fit the plate through the gear and into the crankcase

10.22 Engage the sprocket with the chain and position it on the crankcase

10.24 Fit the bearings onto the shaft then fit the plate through the gear and into the crankcase

10.25a Turn the gear to align the punch mark with the line or projection

10.25b Fit the inner counter-weight . . .

10.25c . . . the drive gear . . .

10.25d . . . and the outer counter-weight, locating the end of the key (A) in the hole (B)

correctly aligned with the mark or projection on the plate **(see illustrations)**. Fit the outer counterweight, making sure the square hole on its inner face locates over the end of the key **(see illustration)**. Apply a non-permanent thread locking compound to the bolt and tighten it to the specified torque **(see illustration 10.4b)**.

26 Fit the sprockets onto the camshafts, following the procedure in Section 8 (Steps 57 to 66).

27 Install the starter reduction gear and its shaft **(see illustration 10.4a)**. Install the starter driven gear and alternator rotor (see Chapter 9).

28 Add the engine oil and the coolant if drained (see Chapter 1).

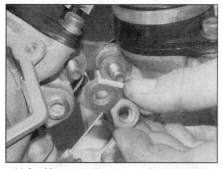

11.9a Unscrew the nuts and remove the plate . . .

11 Cylinder head and block removal and installation

Caution: The engine must be completely cool before beginning this procedure or the cylinder head may become warped.

Note 1: *The rear cylinder head can be removed with the engine in the frame, although this is not advised (see Section 2). If the engine has been removed, ignore the steps that don't apply. To remove the front or both cylinder heads the engine must be removed from the frame (see Section 4).*

Note 2: *The cylinder head and block are removed as an assembly and separated after removal if required. This is because the bolts holding them together go up into the underside of the head and are not accessible with the block on the crankcase.*

Removal

1 To remove the front or both cylinder heads remove the engine from the frame (see Section 4).

2 To remove the rear cylinder head only, and if you have elected not to remove the engine from the frame, remove the throttle bodies and the exhaust system (see Chapter 4).

3 Remove the valve cover (see Section 7).

4 Remove the spark plugs (see Chapter 1).

5 If both heads and blocks are being removed, start with the front cylinder and complete all work on that, including removing the piston and the cam chain and its driven gear if required, before starting the rear cylinder. If you are removing both heads but leaving the pistons on the connecting rods, take care to support the front piston when realigning the engine for removal of the rear head as it is easy for the rings to catch on the crankcase, in which case they could break and fall inside.

6 If required remove the camshafts for the cylinder being worked on, though if you prefer to leave them in place just detach the sprockets from them, following the procedure in Section 8 (Steps 1 to 4 for both cylinders, then Steps 5 to 10 for the front cylinder and Steps 16 to 21 for the rear cylinder). If you are planning to overhaul the head, remove the camshafts and also the followers and shims.

7 If not already done remove the cam chain guide blade (see Section 9).

8 If the engine is in the frame, unscrew the bolt securing the earth lead to the right-hand side of the rear cylinder block and detach the lead **(see illustration 4.19)**.

9 Unscrew the nuts and remove the adjacent plate joining the two cylinder heads between the intake ducts, then unscrew the bolts and remove the other plate **(see illustrations)**.

10 Unscrew the two 6 mm bolts in the cam chain tunnel **(see illustration)**.

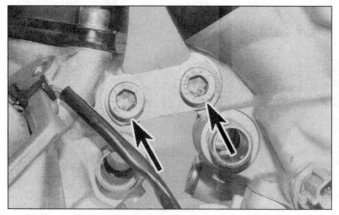

11.9b . . . then unscrew the bolts (arrowed) and remove the other plate

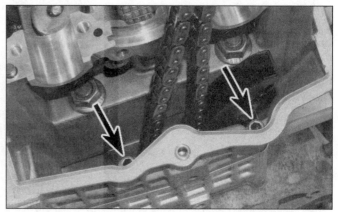

11.10 Unscrew the two 6 mm bolts (arrowed)

11.11a Outer cylinder head nuts (arrowed)

11.11b Inner cylinder head nuts (arrowed)

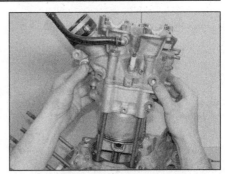

11.12 Carefully lift the head and block up off the crankcase and piston

11 Each cylinder head is secured by four 10 mm nuts **(see illustrations)**. Unscrew the four nuts, slackening them evenly and a little at a time in a criss-cross pattern until they are all loose. Remove the nuts, taking care not to drop any of them down the cam chain tunnel.

12 Pull the cylinder head and block up together off the crankcase **(see illustration)**. If they are stuck, tap around the base of the block with a soft-faced mallet. Do not try to free them by inserting a screwdriver between the block and the crankcase – you'll damage the sealing surfaces. Protrusions from the block can be used as leverage points with care if necessary. Pass the cam chain down through the tunnel as you lift the assembly, and take care not to allow the connecting rod to knock against the crankcase once the piston is free. Try not to let the chain fall into the crankcase – hang it over the edge of the tunnel (secure it with a piece of wire or metal bar to prevent it from slipping back if necessary). Mark both the head and block with an 'F' or 'R' according to location so as not to muddle them up.

13 Remove the old gasket and discard it **(see illustration 11.24b)**. Stuff some rag around each connecting rod under the piston to support them and prevent anything falling into the crankcase. Remove the two dowels if they are loose **(see illustration 11.24b)**. If either appears to be missing it is probably stuck in the underside of the block.

14 If required, unscrew the four bolts securing the block to the head and separate them **(see illustration)**. If they are stuck, tap around the joint with a soft-faced mallet. Do not try to separate them by inserting a screwdriver between them – you'll damage the sealing

surfaces. Protrusions from the head and block can be used as leverage points with care if necessary. Discard the gasket as a new one must be used **(see illustration 11.20)**. Remove the two dowels if they are loose.

15 Check the cylinder head gasket and the mating surfaces on the cylinder head and block for signs of leakage, which could indicate warpage. Similarly check the base gasket and the mating surfaces on the block and crankcase for signs of leakage.

16 Refer to Section 12 to check the cylinder head, and to Section 13 to check the block.

17 Clean all traces of old gasket material from the cylinder head and block and crankcase. If a scraper is used, take care not to scratch or gouge the soft aluminium. Be careful not to let any of the gasket material drop into the crankcase.

Installation

Note: *If the heads and blocks for both cylinders have been removed, install the rear cylinder ones first, and install all the rear cylinder components up to and including the camshafts and its sprockets, leaving only the valve cover uninstalled, then proceed with the front cylinder cam chain and drive gear and all remaining components. This ensures the timing will be correct.*

18 Check that the cylinder head studs are tight in the crankcase. If any are loose, remove them, then clean their threads and apply a suitable non-permanent thread locking compound and tighten them to the torque setting specified at the beginning of the Chapter. Refer to Section 2 'Fasteners' of

Tools and Workshop Tips in the Reference section at the end of this manual for details of how to slacken and tighten studs using two nuts locked together.

19 If both heads and blocks were removed, build up the rear cylinder first. Check that the crankshaft is positioned so the piston for the cylinder being worked on is at TDC and the crankshaft is locked in position with the holding tool as described and fitted when removing the camshafts or their sprockets (see Section 8), or when installing the cam chain and gear and piston if a full engine strip has been done (see Sections 10 and 14).

20 If the head and block were separated, make sure you have the correct ones for the cylinder being worked on according to the 'F' and 'R' marks made on removal. Fit the two dowels into the block if removed and push them firmly home. Ensure both cylinder head and block mating surfaces are clean then lay a new gasket onto the dowels **(see illustration)**. The gasket can only fit one way, so if the holes do not line up properly the gasket is upside down. Never re-use the old gasket.

21 Fit the head onto the block, making sure it locates onto the dowels, then turn the assembly over **(see illustration)**. Install the four bolts and tighten them evenly and a little at a time in a criss-cross sequence to the specified torque setting, noting that there is a different setting depending on whether you have an unpainted or a painted block **(see illustration 11.14)**.

22 Check that the mating surfaces of the cylinder block and crankcase are free from oil or pieces of old gasket.

11.14 Unscrew the bolts (arrowed) and separate the head and block

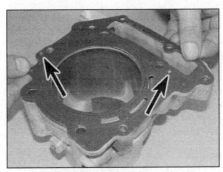

11.20 Lay the gasket over the dowels (arrowed) . . .

11.21 . . . then fit the head onto the block

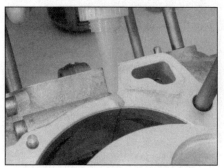

11.24a Apply the sealant around the joints . . .

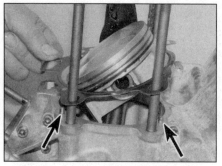

11.24b . . . then lay the gasket over the dowels (arrowed)

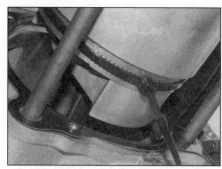

11.25 A strip cable-tied around the rings worked well to guide the rings into the bore

23 If removed, fit the dowels into the crankcase and push them firmly home **(see illustration 11.24b)**.

24 Remove the rags from around the piston, taking care not to let the connecting rod fall against the rim of the crankcase. Apply a smear of suitable sealant (such as Loctite 574) to the area around the joint between each crankcase half **(see illustration)**. Lay the new base gasket in place, locating it over the dowels **(see illustration)**. The gasket can only fit one way, so if all the holes do not line up properly it is the wrong way round. Never re-use the old gasket.

25 Ensure the piston ring end gaps are positioned correctly before fitting the cylinder block (see Section 15). Lubricate the cylinder bore, piston and piston rings with clean engine oil. If available, fit a piston ring compressor onto the piston to ease its entry into the bore as the cylinder is lowered. If a dedicated tool is not available wrap a strip of thin metal (we used the ring from a large jubilee clip) around and cable-tie it in place as shown to compress the rings – as the block lowers it will automatically push the clamp down **(see illustration)**. There is a good lead-in for the rings, enabling them to be hand-fed into the bore, but the extra weight of the head on the block means that it is possible for the assembly to drop quicker than you expect as a ring slips in, whereupon it can easily catch the next ring and break it, with the broken piece most likely falling into the crankcase. If possible, (and it is highly advisable due to the

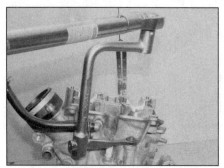

11.30 An offset tool is needed to torque the head down

combined weight of the block and head), have an assistant support the cylinder while the rings are fed in.

26 Carefully lower the block and head onto the piston so the crown fits into the bore and the cam chain tensioner blade enters the tunnel **(see illustration 11.12)**. Gently push the cylinder down, making sure it enters the bore squarely and does not get cocked sideways. If you are doing this without a piston ring compressor, carefully compress and feed each ring into the bore as the cylinder is lowered. Do not use force if it appears to be stuck as the piston and/or rings will be damaged. If a compressor was used, remove it once the rings are in the bore.

27 Feed the cam chain up the tunnel. It is helpful to have an assistant to pass the chain up and slip a piece of wire through it to prevent it falling back into the engine. Keep the chain taut to prevent it becoming disengaged from the drive sprocket.

28 When the piston crown and rings are correctly installed in the bore and the chain is up the tunnel, press the cylinder down onto the base gasket, making sure the dowels locate.

29 Lubricate the threads and undersides of the 10 mm nuts with clean oil. Install the nuts and the 6 mm bolts and tighten them finger-tight **(see illustrations 11.10, 11.11a and b)**.

30 Now tighten the nuts and bolts evenly and a little at a time in a criss-cross sequence to the specified torque setting(s), noting that there are different settings depending on whether you have an unpainted or a painted head. Access to the nuts using a torque wrench and standard socket is restricted – we used an offset tool (available from any good stockist) as shown to get round this problem **(see illustration)**.

31 Install the followers and shims and the camshafts if removed, otherwise fit the sprockets onto the camshafts (see Section 8).

32 If not already done install the cam chain guide blade (see Section 9).

33 If both blocks and heads were removed, now build up the front cylinder in the same way as the rear. When repositioning the engine make sure it turns freely, indicating that the rear cylinder build was good.

34 Fit the plates joining the two cylinder heads between the intake ducts and tighten the bolts and nuts to the specified torque **(see illustrations 11.9b and a)**.

35 If the engine is in the frame, connect the earth lead to the right-hand side of the rear cylinder block and tighten its bolt **(see illustration 4.19)**.

36 Install all other components that have been removed in a reverse of the removal procedure, referring to the relevant sections and Chapters where necessary. Tighten the engine mounting bolts to the specified torque settings.

12 Cylinder head and valve overhaul

1 Because of the complex nature of this job and the special tools and equipment required, most owners leave servicing of the valves, valve seats and valve guides to a professional.

2 With the correct tools (a valve spring compressor is essential – make sure it is suitable for motorcycle work), you can also remove the valves and associated components from the cylinder head, clean them and check them for wear to assess the extent of the work needed, and, unless seat cutting or guide replacement is required, grind in the valves and reassemble them in the head.

3 A dealer service department or specialist can replace the guides and re-cut the valve seats.

4 After the valve service has been performed, be sure to clean it very thoroughly before installation on the engine to remove any metal particles or abrasive grit that may still be present from the valve service operations. Use compressed air, if available, to blow out all the holes and passages.

Disassembly

5 Before proceeding, arrange to label and store the valves along with their related components in such a way that they can be returned to their original locations without

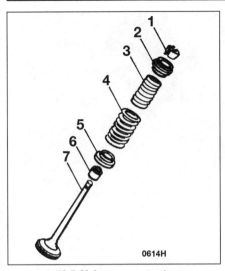

12.5 Valve components

1 Collets	5 Spring seat
2 Spring retainer	6 Valve stem oil
3 Inner valve spring	seal
4 Outer valve spring	7 Valve

getting mixed up **(see illustration)**. A good way to do this is to use the same containers as the followers and shims are stored in (see Section 8), or to obtain two separate containers (one for the rear head and one for the front), each divided into four compartments, and label each compartment with the location of a valve, i.e. intake or exhaust camshaft, left or right valve. If a

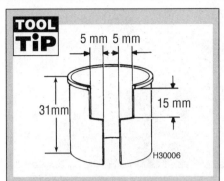

Protect the bore in the cylinder head from scratches by the valve spring compressor using a shield made from a 35mm film canister cut to the dimensions shown

container is not available, use labelled plastic bags (egg cartons also do very well!).

6 Remove the cylinder head and block, then separate them (see Section 11). Clean all traces of old gasket material from the cylinder head. If a scraper is used, take care not to scratch or gouge the soft aluminium; refer to *Tools and Workshop Tips* for details of gasket removal methods.

7 First locate the valve spring compressor on each end of the valve assembly, making sure it is the correct size **(see illustration)**. On the underside of the head make sure the plate on the compressor only contacts the valve and not the soft aluminium of the head – if the

plate is too big for the valve, use a spacer between them **(see illustration)**. On the top of the valve the adaptor needs to be about the same size as the spring retainer – if it is too big it will contact the follower bore and mark it, and if it is too small it will be difficult to remove and install the collets **(see illustration)**. If your adaptor is too big or small, change it for one that is a good fit.

8 Compress the springs on the first valve – do not compress them any more than is necessary to free the collets. Remove the collets, using either needle-nose pliers, tweezers, a mechanic's telescopic magnet, or a screwdriver with a dab of grease on it **(see illustration)**. Carefully release the valve spring compressor and remove it. Remove the spring retainer, noting which way up it fits **(see illustration 12.32b)**. Remove the springs, noting that the closer wound coils are at the bottom and that the top ends have painted marks **(see illustration 12.32a)**. Press down on the top of the valve stem and draw the valve out from the underside of the head **(see illustration 12.30)**. If the valve binds in the guide (won't pull through), push it back into the head and deburr the area around the collet groove with a very fine file or whetstone **(see illustration)**.

9 Once the valve has been removed pull the valve stem seal off the top of the valve guide with pliers or a dedicated tool and discard it – never reuse the old seals **(see illustration)**. Remove the spring seat using the same tool or a mechanic's telescopic magnet, or turn

12.7a Fit the valve spring compressor . . .

12.7b . . . making sure it locates correctly on the valve . . .

12.7c . . . and on the spring retainer

12.8a Remove the collets as described

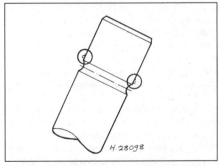

12.8b Remove any burrs (circled) if the valve stem won't pull through the guide

12.9a Pull the oil seal off the top of the guide . . .

12.9b ... then remove the spring seat

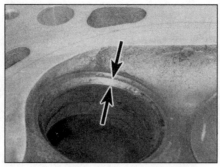

12.16 Measure the valve seat width (between the arrows)

12.17 Measure the valve stem diameter with a micrometer

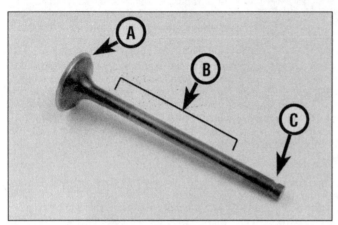

12.18 Check the valve face (A), stem (B) and collet groove (C) for signs of wear and damage

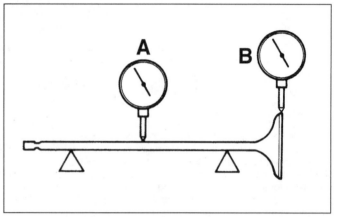

12.19 Measure the valve stem runout (A) and the valve head runout (B)

the head upside down and tip it out, taking care not to lose it **(see illustration)**.

10 Repeat the procedure for the remaining valves. Remember to keep the parts for each valve together and in order so they can be reinstalled in the same location.

11 Next, clean the cylinder head with solvent and dry it thoroughly. Compressed air will speed the drying process and ensure that all holes and recessed areas are reached.

12 Clean all of the valve springs, collets, retainers and spring seats with solvent and dry them thoroughly. Do the parts from one valve at a time so they don't get mixed up.

13 Scrape off any deposits that may have formed on the valve, then use a motorised wire brush to remove deposits from the valve heads and stems. Again, make sure the valves do not get mixed up.

Inspection

14 Inspect the head very carefully for cracks and other damage. If cracks are found, a new head will be required. Check the camshaft bearing surfaces for wear and evidence of seizure. Check the camshafts and holder for wear as well (see Section 8).

15 Using a precision straight-edge and a feeler gauge set to the warpage limit listed in the specifications at the beginning of the Chapter, check the head gasket mating surface for warpage. Refer to *Tools and Workshop Tips* in the Reference section for details of how to use the straight-edge.

16 Examine the valve seats in the combustion chamber. If they are pitted, cracked or burned, the head will require work beyond the scope of the home mechanic. Measure the valve seat width and compare it to this Chapter's Specifications **(see illustration)**. If it exceeds the service limit, or if it varies around its circumference, overhaul is required.

17 Clean the valve guide to remove any carbon build-up, then measure the inside diameter of the guide with a small hole gauge and micrometer. Measure the guide at the ends and at the centre to determine if it is worn in a bell-mouth pattern (more wear at the ends). Also measure the valve stem diameter **(see illustration)**. Replace whichever component is worn beyond its specifications with a new one. If the valve guide is within specifications, but is worn unevenly, replace it with a new one.

18 Carefully inspect each valve face, stem and collet groove area for cracks, pits and burned spots **(see illustration)**.

19 Rotate the valve and check for any obvious indication that it is bent, in which case it must be replaced with a new one. Using V-blocks and a dial gauge, measure the valve stem runout and the valve head runout and compare the results to the specifications **(see illustration)**. If either measurement exceeds the service limit specified, the valve must be replaced with a new one.

20 Check the end of the stem for pitting and excessive wear and replace the valve with a new one is necessary. The stem end can be ground down slightly, provided that the amount of stem above the collet groove after grinding is sufficient.

21 Check the end of each valve spring for wear and pitting. Measure the spring free lengths and compare them to the specifications **(see illustration)**. If any spring is shorter than specified it has sagged and

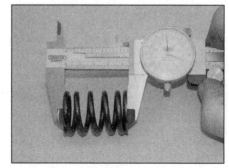

12.21 Measure the free length of the valve springs and check them for squareness

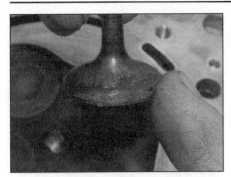

12.25 Apply the lapping compound sparingly, in small dabs, to the valve face only

12.26 Rotate the valve grinding tool back and forth between the palms of your hands

12.29 Fit the spring seat, making sure it is the correct way up

must be replaced with a new one. Also place the spring upright on a flat surface and check it for bend by placing a ruler against it, or alternatively lay it against a set square. If the bend in any spring is excessive, it must be replaced with a new one. Always replace the inner and outer springs as a set, never singly.

22 Check the spring seats, retainers and collets for obvious wear and cracks. Any questionable parts should not be reused, as extensive damage will occur in the event of failure during engine operation.

23 If the inspection indicates that no overhaul work is required, the valve components can be reinstalled in the head.

Reassembly

24 Unless a valve service has been performed, before installing the valves in the head they should be ground in (lapped) to ensure a positive seal between the valves and seats. This procedure requires coarse and fine valve grinding compound and a valve grinding tool (either hand-held or drill driven – note that some drill-driven tools specify using only a fine grinding compound). If a grinding tool is not available, a piece of rubber or plastic hose can be slipped over the valve stem (after the valve has been installed in the guide) and used to turn the valve.

25 Apply a small amount of coarse grinding compound to the valve face **(see illustration)**. Smear some molybdenum disulphide oil (a

50/50 mixture of molybdenum disulphide grease and engine oil) to the valve stem, then slip the valve into the guide **(see illustration 12.30)**. Note: *Make sure each valve is installed in its correct guide and be careful not to get any grinding compound on the valve stem.* Attach the grinding tool to the valve.

26 If a hand tool is being used rotate the tool between the palms of your hands. Use a back-and-forth motion (as though rubbing your hands together) rather than a circular motion (i.e. so that the valve rotates alternately clockwise and anti-clockwise rather than in one direction only) **(see illustration)**. If a motorised tool is being used, follow its instructions for use and take note of the correct drive speed for it – if your drill runs too fast and is not variable, use a hand tool instead. Lift the valve off the seat and turn it at regular intervals to distribute the grinding compound properly. Continue the grinding procedure until the valve face and seat contact area is of uniform width, and unbroken around the entire circumference.

27 Carefully remove the valve and wipe off all traces of grinding compound, making sure none gets in the guide. Use solvent to clean the valve and wipe the seat area thoroughly with a solvent soaked cloth.

28 Repeat the procedure with fine valve grinding compound, then use solvent to clean the valve and flush the guide, and wipe the seat area thoroughly with a solvent soaked cloth. Repeat the entire procedure for the

remaining valves. On completion thoroughly clean the entire head again, then blow through all passages with compressed air. Make sure all traces of the grinding compound have been removed before assembling the head.

29 Working on one valve at a time, lay the spring seat in place in the cylinder head, making sure the shouldered side faces up **(see illustration)**.

30 Coat the valve stem with molybdenum disulphide oil (a 50/50 mixture of molybdenum disulphide grease and engine oil), then install it into its guide **(see illustration)**. Check that the valve moves up and down freely in the guide.

31 Hold the valve against the underside of the head to prevent it dropping out, then fit a new valve stem oil seal onto the valve stem, rotating it slightly as you do **(see illustration)**. Slide the seal down the stem and press it onto the top of the guide using an appropriately sized deep socket – finger pressure is sufficient to get it to clip into place **(see illustration)**. Don't remove the seal again or it will be damaged. Having the valve in place when you fit the seal allows the stem to be used as a guide and negates the possibility of twisting or cocking and damaging it as you press it onto the guide.

32 Next fit the inner spring, then the outer spring, with the painted end of the springs facing away from the head (if the paint has been wiped off fit the springs with the closer-wound coils facing down into the cylinder

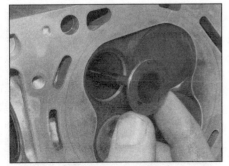

12.30 Lubricate the stem and insert the valve in the guide

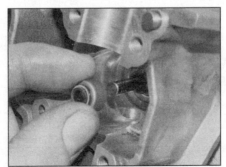

12.31a Fit a new valve stem seal . . .

12.31b . . . using a deep socket to press it into place

12.32a Fit the valve springs . . .

12.32b . . . then fit the spring retainer

12.34 Tap the stem end to make sure that both collets are locked into the groove

head **(see illustration)**. Fit the spring retainer, with its shouldered side facing down so that it fits into the top of the springs **(see illustration)**.

33 Compress the valve springs with the spring compressor, making sure it is correctly located onto each end of the valve assembly (see Step 7) **(see illustrations 12.7a, b and c)**. Do not compress the springs any more than is necessary to slip the collets into place. The collets must be installed with the wider end at the top. Apply a small amount of grease to the collets to help hold them in place. Locate each collet in turn onto the valve stem, locating the ridge on its inside into the groove in the stem **(see illustration 12.8)**, then carefully release the compressor, making sure the collets seat and lock as you do. Check that the collets are securely locked in the retaining groove.

34 Support the cylinder head on blocks so the valves can't contact the workbench top, then tap the top of the valve stem using a brass drift and hammer **(see illustration)**. This will help seat the collets in the groove. If you don't have a brass drift, use a soft-faced

HAYNES HiNT *Check for proper sealing of the valves by pouring a small amount of solvent into each of the valve ports. If the solvent leaks past any valve into the combustion chamber area the valve grinding operation on that valve should be repeated.*

hammer and a piece of hard wood as an interface.

35 Repeat the procedure for the remaining valves. Remember to keep the parts for each valve together, and separate from the other valves, so they can be reinstalled in the same location. After the cylinder head and camshafts have been installed, check and adjust the valve clearances as required (see Chapter 1).

13 Cylinder block inspection and selection

Inspection

1 Do not attempt to separate the liner from the cylinder block.

2 Check the bore walls carefully for scratches and score marks (but do not confuse them with the fine cross-hatch lines produced by the cylinder honing process, which are normal, unless they have been worn away).

3 Clean any limescale build-up out of the coolant jacket around the cylinder.

4 Using a precision straight-edge and a feeler gauge set to the warpage limit listed in the specifications at the beginning of the Chapter, check the top mating surface of the cylinder for warpage. Refer to *Tools and Workshop Tips* in the Reference section for details of how to use the straight-edge. If warpage is excessive the cylinder block must be replaced with a new one (see Step 11).

5 Using a telescoping bore gauge and a

micrometer (see *Tools and Workshop Tips*), check the dimensions of each bore to assess the amount of wear, taper and ovality. Measure near the top (but below the level of the top piston ring at TDC), centre and bottom (but above the level of the oil ring at BDC) of the bore, both parallel to and across the crankshaft axis **(see illustrations)**. Compare the results to the specifications at the beginning of the Chapter. If the bores are worn, oval or tapered beyond the service limit they must be replaced with new ones (see Step 11) – reboring is not possible as the cylinders are Nikasil coated. Note that the Nikasil coating is highly wear resistant and should last the life of the engine.

6 If the precision measuring tools are not available, take the cylinders to an Aprilia dealer or specialist motorcycle repair shop for assessment and advice.

Selection

7 If a new cylinder block is being fitted, it must be selected according to the size grade of its piston. If a new piston is being fitted, it must be selected according to the size grade of its cylinder block. If both new cylinder blocks and pistons are being fitted, they will come as a matched pair along with a set of rings. Each cylinder block has the letter A or B stamped into its exhaust side near the cam chain tunnel **(see illustration)**. Each piston is colour-coded either RED or GREEN. A RED piston must be matched with an A cylinder block; a GREEN piston must be matched with a B cylinder block. New pistons come with a set of rings.

13.5a Use a bore gauge . . .

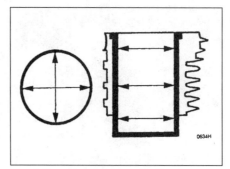

13.5b . . . and measure at the points shown

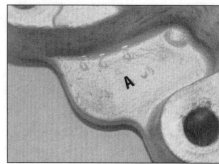

13.7 Each block is size graded using the letter A or B

14 Pistons

Note: *The rear piston can be removed with the engine in the frame although this is not recommended (see Section 2). If the engine has been removed, ignore the steps that don't apply. To remove the front or both pistons the engine must be removed from the frame (see Section 4).*

Removal

1 Remove the cylinder head and block (see Section 11).

2 Before removing the piston from the connecting rod, use a permanent felt marker pen to write the cylinder identity on the crown of the piston (or on the skirt if the piston is dirty and going to be cleaned). Also mark each piston crown or skirt with an arrow that points to the front of the engine – it is very important that each piston is returned to its original cylinder, and extremely important that it is the correct way round as the bore for the piston pin is offset slightly. There should be a piston size colour-code mark on the rear side of the piston crown, though it is unlikely to be visible. Stuff clean rag around the connecting rod to prevent a dropped circlip falling into the crankcase.

3 Carefully prise out the circlip on one side of the piston using needle-nose pliers or a small flat-bladed screwdriver inserted into the notch and located against the bent end of the circlip **(see illustration)**. Push the piston pin out from the other side to free the piston from the connecting rod **(see illustration)**. Remove the other circlip and discard them both as new ones must be used. When the piston has been removed, slide its pin back into its bore so that related parts do not get mixed up.

 HAYNES HiNT *If a piston pin is a tight fit in the piston bosses, soak a rag in boiling water then wring it out and wrap it around the piston – this will expand the alloy piston sufficiently to release its grip on the pin. If the piston pin is particularly stubborn, extract it using a drawbolt tool, but be careful to protect the piston's working surfaces.*

Inspection

4 Using your thumbs or a piston ring removal and installation tool, carefully remove the rings from the pistons **(see illustrations 15.11, 15.10b, and 15.9b and a)**. Do not nick or gouge the pistons in the process. Carefully note which way up each ring fits and in which groove as they must be installed in their original positions if being re-used – the top and middle rings can be identified by their different profiles and thickness **(see illustration 15.8a)**.

5 Scrape all traces of carbon from the tops of the pistons. A hand-held wire brush or a piece

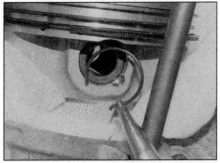

14.3a Prise the circlip out from one side of the piston

of fine emery cloth can be used once most of the deposits have been scraped away. Do not, under any circumstances, use a wire brush mounted in a drill motor to remove deposits from the pistons; the piston material is soft and will be eroded away by the wire brush.

6 Use a piston ring groove cleaning tool to remove any carbon deposits from the ring grooves. If a tool is not available, a piece broken off an old ring will do the job. Be very careful to remove only the carbon deposits. Do not remove any metal and do not nick or gouge the sides of the ring grooves.

7 Once the deposits have been removed, clean the pistons with solvent and dry them thoroughly. If the identification previously marked on the piston is cleaned off, be sure to re-mark it with the correct identity and orientation. Make sure the oil return holes below the oil ring groove are clear **(see illustration 15.8a)**.

8 Carefully inspect each piston for cracks around the skirt, at the pin bosses and at the ring lands. Normal piston wear appears as even, vertical wear on the thrust surfaces of the piston and slight looseness of the top ring in its groove. If the skirt is scored or scuffed, the engine may have been suffering from overheating and/or abnormal combustion, which caused excessively high operating temperatures. Check that the circlip grooves are not damaged.

9 A hole in the piston crown, an extreme to be sure, is an indication that abnormal combustion (pre-ignition) was occurring. Burned areas at the edge of the piston crown

14.10 Fit the ring into the groove and measure clearance with a feeler gauge

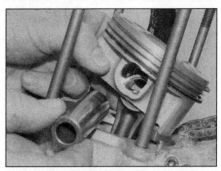

14.3b Push the piston pin out from the other side then withdraw it and remove the piston

are usually evidence of spark knock (detonation). If any of the above problems exist, the causes must be corrected or the damage will occur again. Obviously the piston must be replaced with a new one.

10 Measure the piston ring-to-groove clearance by laying each piston ring in its groove and slipping a feeler gauge in underneath it **(see illustration)**. Make sure you have the correct ring for the groove (see Step 4). Note that the top ring has an L shaped cross-section – measure the clearance at the flat section **(see illustration 15.8a)**. Check the clearance at three or four locations around the groove. If new rings are being used, measure the clearance using the new rings. If the clearance is greater than specified with the old rings, measure the thickness of the rings and replace them with new ones if worn below the specified limit, then check the clearance again. Note that the top ring has an L shaped cross-section – measure the thickness of the flat section. If the clearance is greater than that specified with new rings, or if the old rings are not worn, the piston is worn and must be replaced with a new one. If you are fitting new pistons, fit new rings with them rather than using the old ones.

11 Check the piston-to-bore clearance by measuring the bore (see Section 13) and the piston diameter. Make sure each piston is matched to its correct cylinder. Measure the piston 10 mm up from the bottom of the skirt and at 90° to the piston pin axis **(see illustration)**. Subtract the piston diameter from the bore diameter to obtain the

14.11 Measure the piston diameter with a micrometer

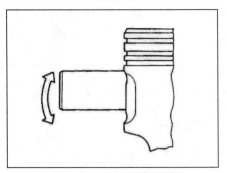

14.12a Slip the pin into the piston and check for freeplay between them

14.12c ... and the internal diameter of the bore in the piston

14.12b Measure the external diameter of the pin ...

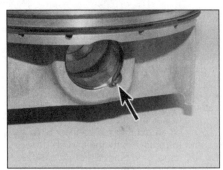

14.17 Locate the bent end in the removal notch (arrowed)

clearance. If it is greater than the specified maximum, replace whichever of the cylinder and/or piston is worn beyond its limits.

12 Apply clean engine oil to the piston pin, insert it into the piston and check for any freeplay between the two **(see illustration)**. Measure the pin external diameter at each end and the pin bore in the piston **(see illustrations)**. Calculate the difference to obtain the piston pin-to-piston pin bore clearance. Compare the result to the specifications at the beginning of the Chapter. If the clearance is greater than specified, replace the components that are worn beyond their specified limits with new ones (see Step 13). If not already done, repeat the measurements between the pin and the connecting rod small-end (see Section 29).

Selection

13 If a new piston is being fitted, it must be

selected according to the size grade of its cylinder block. If a new cylinder block is being fitted, it must be selected according to the size grade of its piston. If both new pistons and cylinder blocks are being fitted, they will come as a matched pair along with a set of rings. Each piston is colour-coded either RED or GREEN. Each cylinder block has the letter A or B stamped into its exhaust side near the cam chain tunnel **(see illustration 13.7)**. A RED piston must be matched with an A cylinder block; a GREEN piston must be matched with a B cylinder block. New pistons come with a set of rings.

Installation

14 Inspect and install the piston rings (see Section 15).
15 Lubricate the piston pin, the piston pin bore and the connecting rod small-end bore with molybdenum disulphide oil (a 50/50

mixture of molybdenum disulphide grease and clean engine oil).
16 When installing the pistons onto the connecting rods, make sure you have the correct piston for the cylinder being worked on, and that it is the correct way round according to your marks made on removal. Note that the colour-code mark on the crown of a new piston (and possibly visible on a re-installed piston) must face the rear of the engine.
17 Stuff clean rag around the connecting rod to prevent a dropped circlip falling into the crankcase. Install a *new* circlip in one side of the piston (do not re-use old circlips) – use only the Aprilia type circlips with the bent end, and locate the bent end in the removal notch **(see illustration)**. Compress the circlip only just enough to fit it and make sure it is properly seated in its groove. Line up the piston on its correct connecting rod, and insert the piston pin from the other side **(see illustration 14.3b)**. Secure the pin with the other *new* circlip **(see illustration 14.3a)**. Remove the rag the crankcase.
18 Install the cylinder head and block (see Section 13).

15 Piston rings

1 It is good practice to fit new piston rings when an engine is overhauled. Before installing the rings (new or old), check the installed end gaps of the top and second (middle) rings as follows.
2 If new rings are being used, lay out each piston with a new ring set and keep them together so the rings will be matched with the same piston and bore during the end gap measurement procedure and engine assembly. If the old rings are being reused, make sure they are matched with their correct piston and cylinder.
3 Insert the ring into the top of its bore and square it up with the bore walls by pushing it in with the top of the piston **(see illustrations)**. The ring should be about 20 mm below the top edge of the bore. Slip a feeler gauge between the ends of the ring and measure the gap **(see illustration)**. Compare

15.3a Fit the ring into the bore ...

15.3b ... then square it up using the piston ...

15.3c ... and measure the installed end gap

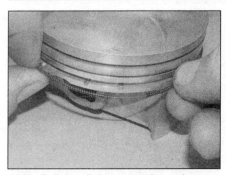

15.7a Pull the oil ring expander ends apart and fit it in its groove . . .

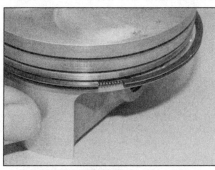

15.7b . . . then fit the scraper over it

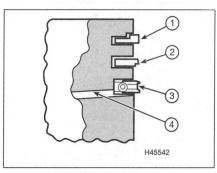

15.8a Top ring (1), middle ring (2), oil control ring (3), oil return hole (4)

the measurements to the specifications at the beginning of the Chapter.

4 If the gap is larger or smaller than specified, double check to make sure that you have the correct rings before proceeding. If the gap is too small, the ring ends may come in contact with each other during engine operation, which can cause serious damage. Excess end gap is not critical unless it exceeds the service limit. Again, double-check to make sure you have the correct rings for your engine and check that the bore is not worn (see Section 13).

5 Repeat the procedure for the other ring. Remember to keep the rings, pistons and bores matched up.

6 Once the ring end gaps have been checked, the rings can be installed on the pistons.

7 Install the oil control ring (lowest on the piston) first. It is composed of two separate components, namely the expander and the scraper. Slip the expander into its groove – pull the ends apart enough to slip it in and make sure the ends sit against each other correctly once in **(see illustration)**. Now ft the scraper ring over the expander making sure the expander locates against it correctly as shown **(see illustration and 15.8a)**. Set the ends of the expander and scraper on opposite sides of the piston. Check that the scraper can be turned smoothly in the ring groove.

8 The top and middle rings can be identified by their different profiles and thicknesses **(see**

illustration) – refer to the Specifications. Install the second (middle) ring next. Make sure it is the correct way up. Fit the 2nd ring into the middle groove in the piston **(see illustration)**. Do not expand the ring any more than is necessary to slide it into place. To avoid breaking the ring, use a piston ring installation tool, or alternatively pieces of old feeler gauge blades can be used as shown **(see illustration)**.

9 Finally, install the top ring in the same manner into the top groove in the piston **(see illustration)**.

10 Once the rings are correctly installed, check they move freely without snagging and stagger their end gaps at 120° intervals.

16 Clutch

Note 1: *The clutch can be removed with the engine in the frame. If the engine has already been removed, ignore the preliminary steps which don't apply.*
Note 2: *If you are just fitting a new set of clutch plates, you should be able to get away with just removing the circular clutch outer cover, though you will need to hook the plates out using a piece of bent wire or similar. To remove the whole clutch assembly you need to remove the clutch inner cover as well.*

Note 3: *Where the clip-type (as opposed to the screw-type) hose clamps are used on the coolant hoses, a flat-bladed screwdriver is the best way of releasing them, but note that to rejoin this type of clamp a special pair of pliers makes the job much easier. Also note that these clamps should only be used once, and so new ones should be obtained for the installation procedure.*

Removal

1 Drain the engine oil, and if you are removing the clutch inner cover also drain the coolant (see Chapter 1). Remove the coolant reservoir (see Chapter 3).

2 Remove the rear brake pedal – there is no need to detach the master cylinder pushrod, but take care when drawing it out of the cylinder (see Chapter 6). Displace the rear brake master cylinder and reservoir from the right-hand side of the engine and secure it clear, making sure no strain is placed on the hoses and the reservoir is kept upright (see Chapter 7). Trace the wiring from the rear brake switch and disconnect it at the connector – feed the wiring down to the switch, noting its routing **(see illustration 4.20a)**. Unscrew the bolts securing the pedal bracket and remove it along with the switch **(see illustration 4.20b)**.

3 If you are removing the clutch inner cover remove the starter motor (see Chapter 9). Remove the thermostat along with the large bore hoses that attach to it, detaching the

15.8b Fit the middle ring into its groove

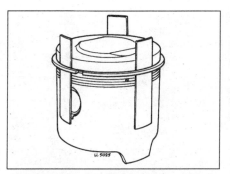

15.8c Use the pieces of feeler gauge blade as shown to guide the rings onto the piston

15.9 Fit the top ring into its groove

16.6 Clutch outer cover bolts (arrowed)

16.7 Offset the diaphragm tabs, then hold the hex and unscrew the nut

16.9a Unscrew the bolts, noting the shouldered washers, and remove the springs . . .

hoses from the water pump cover and the right-hand radiator **(see illustration 4.10d)**. Also detach the filler neck hose from the pump cover. Secure the small bore thermostat hose and the filler neck hose clear of the cover.

4 Release the clamp securing the vacuum hose to the clutch outer cover and detach the hose.

5 Pull the rubber boot off the oil pressure switch, then pull the wiring connector off the terminal **(see illustration 4.17)**.

6 Unscrew the clutch outer cover bolts and remove the cover **(see illustration)**.

7 Release the diaphragm tabs from the raised sections around the bolt holes and rotate the clutch so the tabs are clear – this will prevent the diaphragm catching and tearing if the clutch turns while unscrewing the diaphragm

plate nut **(see illustration)**. Counter-hold the clutch using a hex key in the centre of the shaft and unscrew the nut. Remove the outer washer, outer diaphragm plate, diaphragm, inner plate and inner washer, noting which way round they all fit **(see illustrations 16.37e, d, c, b and a)**.

8 If you want to remove the entire clutch assembly, refer to Chapter 3 and remove the water pump, which is housed in the clutch inner cover. There is no need to separate the pump from the cover after removal.

9 Working in a criss-cross pattern, and holding the clutch housing to prevent it turning, gradually slacken the clutch pressure plate bolts until spring pressure is released, then remove the bolts, shouldered washers, springs and the pressure plate **(see illustrations)**.

10 Withdraw the pushrod from the clutch **(see illustration)**.

11 Remove the clutch friction and plain plates one by one, keeping them in order, and using a bent piece of wire to hook them out where necessary **(see illustration 16.33d)**. Keep the plates assembled in their original order, even if you are replacing them with new ones, as there are different types – the old ones can be used as a guide to installing the new ones.

12 To remove the clutch nut the transmission input shaft must be locked. This can be done in several ways. If the engine is in the frame, engage 6th gear and have an assistant hold the rear brake on hard with the rear tyre in firm contact with the ground. Alternatively, the Aprilia service tool (Pt. No. 0277881) or a commercially available clutch holding tool can be used to stop the clutch centre from turning whilst the nut is slackened **(see illustration)**. With the shaft locked, unscrew the clutch nut, then remove the spring washer.

13 Slide the clutch centre off the shaft **(see illustration 16.31)**.

14 Slide the shaped thrust washer off the shaft **(see illustration 16.30)**.

15 Slide the clutch housing off the shaft **(see illustration)**.

16 Slide the thrust washer off the shaft **(see illustration 16.28)**.

Inspection

17 After an extended period of service the clutch friction plates will wear and promote

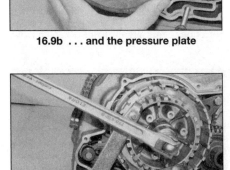

16.9b . . . and the pressure plate

16.10 Withdraw the pushrod

16.12 Unscrew the clutch nut as described – here a commercially available holding tool is being used

16.15 Slide the clutch housing off the shaft

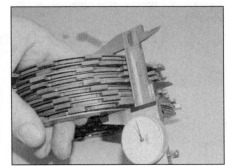

16.17 Measure the thickness of the complete pack of plates . . .

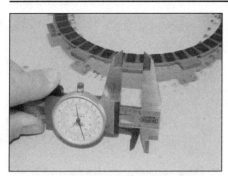

16.18 . . . and the width of the tabs

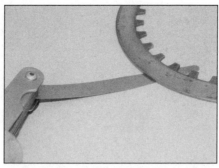

16.19 Check the plain plates for warpage

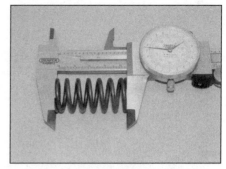

16.20a Measure the free length of the clutch springs . . .

clutch slip. Assemble the complete set of friction and plain plates and measure the thickness of the complete pack using a Vernier caliper **(see illustration)**. If the thickness is less than the service limit given in the Specifications at the beginning of the Chapter, the friction plates must be replaced with new ones as a set. Also, if any of the plates smell burnt or are glazed, they must be replaced as a set.

18 Measure the width of the friction plate tabs and replace any plates that are worn beyond the service limit specified with new ones **(see illustration)**.

19 The plain plates should not show any signs of excess heating (bluing). Check for warpage using a flat surface and feeler gauges **(see illustration)**. If any plate exceeds the maximum amount of warpage, or shows signs of bluing, all plain plates must be renewed as a set.

20 Measure the free length of each clutch spring using a Vernier caliper **(see illustration)**. If any spring is below the service limit specified, replace all the springs with new ones as a set. Also place the spring upright on a flat surface and check it for bend by placing a ruler against it, or alternatively lay it against a set square **(see illustration)**. If the bend in any spring is excessive, all springs must be replaced with new ones.

21 Inspect the edges of the tabs on the friction plates and the corresponding slots in the clutch housing for burrs and indentations

(see illustration). Similarly check for wear between the inner teeth of the plain plates and the slots in the clutch centre **(see illustration)**. Wear of this nature will cause clutch drag and slow disengagement during gear changes as the plates will snag when the pressure plate is lifted. With care a small amount of wear can be corrected by dressing with a fine file, but if wear is excessive (greater than 0.3 mm) new components should be installed.

22 Check the bush in the primary driven gear on the back of the clutch housing and the section of shaft it runs on for signs of wear (i.e. the oil retaining holes in its surface are not visible), damage or scoring, and replace them with new ones if necessary **(see illustration)**. Measure the internal diameter of the bush and replace the housing with a new one if the bush

has worn beyond its maximum diameter.

23 Check the clutch pressure plate, the lifter section on the pushrod, and the bearing for signs of roughness, wear or damage, and replace any parts with new ones as necessary **(see illustration)**. Check the pressure plate for warpage using a flat surface and feeler gauges. If any warpage exceeds the maximum amount replace it with a new one. Also measure the pressure plate thickness and compare it with that specified. Check the pushrod for bend and damaged ends.

24 Check the pushrod oil seal on the left-hand side of the engine for signs of leakage and replace it with a new one it if necessary. First displace the release cylinder (see Section 18), then remove the front sprocket cover and chain guide (see Chapter 6). Lever out the old seal using a seal hook or screwdriver, then

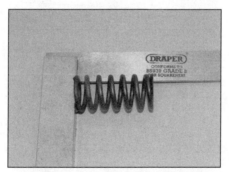

16.20b . . . and check them for bend

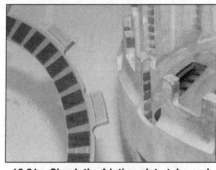

16.21a Check the friction plate tabs and clutch housing slots as described

16.21b Check the plain plate tongues and the clutch centre slots as described

16.22 Check the bush (arrowed) as described

16.23 Check the bearing (arrowed) and the pressure plate as described

16.24a Lever out the old seal . . .

16.24b . . . and fit a new one in

16.25a Check the damper springs as described

press or drive a new seal squarely into place **(see illustrations)**. Install the retainer plate and front sprocket cover (see Chapter 6), and the release cylinder (see Section 18).

25 Check the primary drive damper springs on the back of the clutch housing **(see illustration)**. If any are loose or damaged, slide the oil pump drive gear off, noting how its inner side locates against the drive tabs **(see illustration)**. On 1998 to 2000 models unscrew the bolts securing the spring plate and remove the plate. Remove the springs and their end bushes, noting how they are arranged and locate. Remove the primary drive gear, then remove the spring washer, noting which way up it fits, and the plain washer. On 2001 to 2003 models unscrew

the nuts securing the outer spring plate and remove the plate, noting the small hole that aligns with small holes in the primary driven gear and the inner spring plate – these holes must be aligned on reassembly **(see illustration)**. Remove the outer spring plate spacers, the springs and their end bushes, noting how they are arranged and locate. Remove the primary drive gear, then remove the spring washer, noting which way up it fits, and the inner spring plate. Replace any worn or damaged components with new ones as required – the springs should be replaced as a set rather than individually. On reassembly apply a suitable thread locking compound (such as Loctite 648) to the bolt or nut threads and tighten them to the torque

setting specified at the beginning of the Chapter.

26 Check the teeth of the primary driven gear on the back of the clutch housing and the corresponding teeth of the primary drive gear on the crankshaft **(see illustration 16.25a)**. Replace the gears as a set with new ones if worn or chipped teeth are discovered (see Step 22 for the driven gear and refer to Section 20 for the primary drive gear). Similarly check the oil pump drive gear on the back of the housing and its driven gear on the pump shaft **(see illustration 16.25b)**.

Installation

Note: *If the primary drive gear has been removed and not yet installed, do so before installing the clutch (see Section 20).*

27 If necessary, remove all traces of old gasket from the crankcase and inner clutch cover mating surfaces.

28 Slide the thrust washer onto the input shaft **(see illustration)**. Smear the shaft with molybdenum disulphide oil (50% molybdenum grease and 50% engine oil).

29 Slide the clutch housing onto the shaft, making sure the teeth on the oil pump drive gear engage with those on the driven gear, and the teeth on the primary driven gear engage with those on the primary drive gear **(see illustration)**. Try to turn the oil pump driven gear by hand to check that it has engaged correctly **(see illustration)**.

16.25b Lift the oil pump drive gear off, noting how it locates

16.25c Unscrew the nuts (arrowed) to remove the damper components

16.28 Slide the thrust washer onto the shaft . . .

16.29a . . . then install the clutch housing . . .

16.29b . . . and check that its gear teeth have engaged correctly

16.30 Slide the shaped thrust washer onto the shaft . . .

16.31 . . . followed by the clutch centre

16.32a Fit the spring washer . . .

30 Slide the shaped thrust washer onto the shaft **(see illustration)**.

31 Slide the clutch centre onto the shaft **(see illustration)**.

32 Slide the spring washer onto the shaft so that its inner rim is raised away from the engine **(see illustration)**. Apply a suitable thread locking compound (such as Loctite 648) to the clutch nut threads. Fit the nut, then using the method employed on removal to lock the input shaft (see Step 12), tighten the nut to the torque setting specified at the beginning of the Chapter **(see illustrations)**. **Note:** *Check that the clutch centre rotates freely after tightening the clutch nut.*

33 Build up the clutch friction and plain plates in the housing as follows: coat each clutch plate with engine oil before installing it;

on 1998 to 2000 models up to engine number 689953 first fit a plain plate, then fit a friction plate, then alternate between plain and friction plates, making sure that the outermost friction plate is the one with a blue coloured tab end, and locate the tabs of this plate in the shallow slots in the housing so they are offset from the others **(see illustrations)**; on 1998 to 2000 models from engine number 689954 and all models from 2001-on first fit the plain plate with the missing tooth or the cut-out in its outer rim **(see illustration)**, then fit a friction plate **(see illustration)**, then alternate between plain and friction plates, making sure that the outermost friction plate is the one with a blue coloured tab end, and locate the tabs of this plate in the shallow slots in the housing so

they are offset from the others **(see illustrations 16.33a and b)**.

34 Smear molybdenum grease onto each end of the pushrod and slide it into the input shaft **(see illustration 16.10)**. Lubricate the bearing in the pressure plate with clean oil **(see illustration 16.23)**.

35 Fit the pressure plate into the clutch centre, making sure it seats correctly **(see illustration 16.9b)**. Fit the clutch springs **(see illustration 16.9a)**. Fit the bolts, making sure the shouldered washers have the raised should facing in, and tighten the bolts evenly in a criss-cross sequence to the specified torque setting.

36 Refer to Chapter 3 and install the water pump, which is housed in the clutch inner cover.

16.32b . . . then fit the clutch nut . . .

16.32c . . . and tighten it to the specified torque

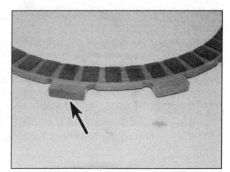

16.33a Identify the coloured tab (arrowed) . . .

16.33b . . . and fit the tabs into the shallow slots in the housing (arrowed)

16.33c The plain plate with the missing tooth or a notch (arrowed) goes first . . .

16.33d . . . then fit a friction plate

16.37a Fit the inner washer . . .

16.37b . . . and the inner diaphragm plate . . .

16.37c . . . then fit the diaphragm, offsetting the tabs as described

16.37d Fit the outer diaphragm plate . . .

16.37e . . . and the outer washer . . .

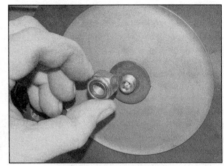

16.37f . . . then fit the nut . . .

16.37g . . . and tighten it as described

16.37h Locate the tabs over the raised sections . . .

16.38 . . . then fit the cover

37 Slide the inner washer and diaphragm plate onto the end of the shaft, with the curved rim of the plate located on the pressure plate **(see illustrations)**. Fit the diaphragm onto the shaft, aligning it so the holed tabs in its rim are away from the raised ends of the cover bolt holes **(see illustration)**. Fit the outer diaphragm plate with its curved rim facing away from the diaphragm **(see illustration)**. Fit the outer washer **(see illustration)**. Apply a suitable thread locking compound (such as Loctite 648) to the diaphragm nut threads and tighten it to the specified torque setting, counter-holding the shaft using a hex key located in the end as on removal **(see illustrations)**. Turn the clutch to align the holed tabs in its rim with the cover bolt holes, then locate the holes over the raised sections **(see illustration)**.

38 Fit the outer cover and tighten its bolts in a criss-cross sequence to the specified torque setting **(see illustration)**.
39 Install all remaining components (see Steps 5 to 1).
40 Refill the engine with oil and coolant if required (see Chapter 1).
41 Check the action of the release mechanism.

17 Clutch master cylinder

⚠ **Warning: Use care when working with brake/clutch fluid as it can injure your eyes and it will damage painted surfaces**

and plastic parts – cover surrounding components with rag, wipe up any spills immediately and wash the area with soap and water.
Note: *If you intend to change the clutch fluid as part of the master cylinder removal, drain the fluid completely from the system (see Section 19), as opposed to retaining the old fluid within it by blocking the hose as described (Step 8).*
1 If the master cylinder is leaking fluid past its piston seal, or if the clutch does not work properly when the lever is applied, and bleeding the system does not help (see Section 19), and the hydraulic hose is in good condition, then a new master cylinder is needed – rebuild kits and replacement cup and seal are not available. The only parts that can be replaced with new ones are the

17.3 Slacken the cap (arrowed)

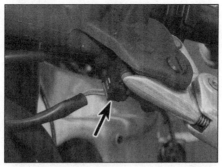

17.5 Carefully lever the switch (arrowed) off

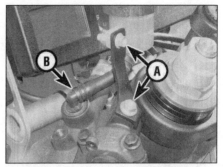

17.6 Unscrew either of the bolts (A) to free the reservoir. Reservoir hose clamp and union (B)

reservoir components, including its hose union and seal in the master cylinder.

2 Make sure you have some new DOT 5.1 glycol-based hydraulic brake and clutch fluid and some clean rags.

Removal

Note: *If the master cylinder is being displaced from the handlebar and not being removed completely or overhauled, follow Steps 4 and 9 only.*

3 Turn the handlebars as required so that the top of the reservoir is level. Slacken the reservoir cap and lightly tighten it again **(see illustration)**. Detach the fast idle lever housing from the master cylinder (see Chapter 4).

4 If a new master cylinder is being fitted, remove the clutch lever (see Chapter 6). If it is just being displaced the lever can remain in situ.

5 Remove the clutch switch by carefully levering it off the master cylinder using a small flat-bladed screwdriver – it is a push fit with expanding pegs locating in holes **(see illustration)**.

6 Unscrew the bolt securing the reservoir bracket to the handlebar, or the bolt securing the reservoir to its bracket, as required or preferred **(see illustration)**. Remove the reservoir cap, diaphragm plate and rubber diaphragm. If the system hasn't been drained, tip the brake fluid from the reservoir into a

suitable container. Wipe any remaining fluid out of the reservoir with a clean rag.

7 If required, separate the reservoir from the master cylinder by releasing the hose clamp and detaching the hose **(see illustration 17.6)**. If required pull the reservoir hose union out of the master cylinder.

8 If the master cylinder is being completely removed, unscrew the clutch hose banjo bolt and separate the hose from the cylinder, noting its alignment **(see illustration)**. Discard the sealing washers as they must be replaced with new ones. Either clamp the hose using a hose clamp, block it using another suitable short piece of hose fitted through the eye of the banjo union (it must be a fairly tight fit to seal it properly), or using a suitable bolt with sealing washers and a capped (domed) nut, or wrap some plastic food wrap tightly around (a finger cut off a latex glove also works well), the object being to minimise fluid loss and prevent dirt entering the system. Whatever you do, also cover the end of the hose in rag, just in case. If the master cylinder is just being displaced and not completely removed or overhauled, do not disconnect the hose.

9 Check for an alignment mark between the handlebar and the master cylinder clamp mating surfaces and make one if not already there **(see illustration 17.10)**. Unscrew the master cylinder clamp bolts, then lift the master cylinder and reservoir away from the handlebar **(see illustration)**.

Caution: Do not tip the master cylinder or brake fluid will run out.

Installation

10 Locate the master cylinder on the handlebar and fit the clamp with its triangular mark pointing forwards **(see illustration 17.9)**, aligning the clamp mating surfaces with the mark on the handlebar **(see illustration)**. Tighten the clamp bolts.

11 If detached, connect the clutch hose to the master cylinder, using new sealing washers on each side of the union, and aligning the hose as noted on removal **(see illustration 17.8)**. Tighten the banjo bolt to the specified torque setting.

12 If removed fit the reservoir hose union seal and union into the master cylinder **(see illustration 17.6)**. Fit the reservoir onto its bracket, or the bracket onto the handlebar as required. Connect the hose to its union and secure it with the clamp.

13 Install the fast idle lever housing and switch housing (see Chapter 4).

14 Press the clutch switch onto the master cylinder **(see illustration 17.5)**. If removed, install the clutch lever (see Chapter 6).

15 Fill the fluid reservoir with new brake/clutch fluid as described in *Daily (pre-ride) checks*. Bleed the air from the system (see Section 19).

16 Wipe any moisture off the rubber diaphragm with a clean lint-free cloth. Fit the

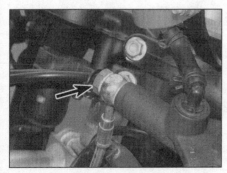

17.8 Clutch hose banjo bolt (arrowed)

17.9 Master cylinder clamp bolts (arrowed)

17.10 Align the mating surfaces with the mark (arrowed)

17.16 Fit the diaphragm, the plate and the cap

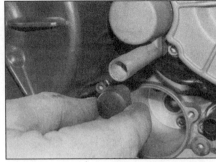

18.3 Remove the bung to access the lower bolt

18.4 Clutch hose banjo bolt hex (arrowed)

diaphragm onto the master cylinder reservoir, making sure it is correctly seated, and the diaphragm plate **(see illustration)**. Fit the cap.
17 Check the operation of the clutch before riding the motorcycle.

18 Clutch release cylinder

> **Warning: Use care when working with brake/clutch fluid as it can injure your eyes and it will damage painted surfaces and plastic parts – cover surrounding components with rag, wipe up any spills immediately and wash the area with soap and water. Disassembly, overhaul and reassembly of the clutch release cylinder must be done in a spotlessly clean work area to avoid contamination and possible failure of the hydraulic system components.**

Note: If you intend to change the clutch fluid as part of the release cylinder removal, drain the fluid completely from the system (see Section 19), as opposed to retaining the old fluid within it by blocking the hose as described (Step 4).

1 If the release cylinder is leaking fluid, or if the clutch does not work properly when the lever is applied, and bleeding the system does not help (see Section 19), and the hydraulic hose and master cylinder are in good condition, then a new release cylinder may be needed – the only part available is a new seal.
2 Make sure that you have some new DOT 5.1 glycol-based hydraulic brake and clutch fluid, and some clean rags.

Removal

3 Remove the lower fairing (see Chapter 8). Pull the rubber bung out of the fairing support post **(see illustration)**.
4 If the release cylinder is being completely removed, unscrew the clutch hose banjo bolt using the bottom hex (leaving the bleed valve threaded into the top of bolt) and separate the hose from the cylinder, noting its alignment **(see illustration)**. Discard the sealing washers as they must be replaced with new ones. Either block the hose using another suitable short piece of hose fitted through the eye of the banjo union (it must be a fairly tight fit to seal it properly), or using a suitable bolt with sealing washers and a capped (domed) nut, or wrap some plastic food wrap tightly around (a finger cut off a latex glove also works well), the object being to minimise fluid loss and

prevent dirt entering the system. Whatever you do, also cover the end of the hose in rag, just in case. If the release cylinder is just being displaced and not completely removed or overhauled, do not disconnect the hose.
Note: If you're planning to overhaul the release cylinder and don't have a source of compressed air to blow out the piston, the hydraulic system can be used to force the piston out of the body – reconnect the hose once the release cylinder has been removed, then disconnect it again once the piston has been pumped out.
5 Unscrew the release cylinder bolts and displace or remove the cylinder – it may come away by itself, or it may bring its mounting flange with it **(see illustrations)**. Remove the mounting flange if necessary, noting which way round it fits. Do not operate the clutch lever with the release cylinder removed.

> **HAYNES HINT** *If the release cylinder and flange are separated, wrap some cable ties around the piston and through the mounting bolt holes to prevent the piston creeping out, or from being displaced should the lever be accidentally pulled in.*

18.5a Unscrew the bolts (arrowed) . . .

18.5b . . . and remove the release cylinder – here the flange (arrowed) came with it

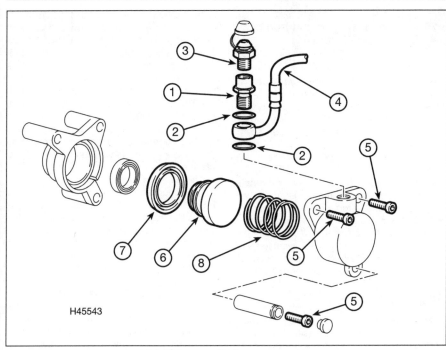

H45543

18.6 Release cylinder components

1 Banjo bolt
2 Sealing washers
3 Bleed valve
4 Hose
5 Mounting bolts
6 Piston
7 Seal
8 Spring

Overhaul

6 Have a supply of clean rags on hand, then expel the piston, either by reconnecting the clutch hose (see Step 4) and pumping the clutch lever, or by using a jet of compressed air directed into the fluid inlet **(see illustration)**. Withdraw the piston from the cylinder.

 Warning: Use only low air pressure, otherwise the piston may be forcibly expelled and cause damage or injury. Wrap the cylinder in a rag before applying the air. Never place your fingers in front of the piston in an attempt to catch or protect it when applying compressed air, as serious injury could result.

Caution: Do not try to remove the piston by levering it out, or by using pliers or any other grips.

7 Remove the piston seal from the groove in the piston, noting which way round it fits, and taking care not to mark the piston if using a metal tool. Discard it as new ones must be used.

8 Clean the piston and release cylinder bore with clean hydraulic fluid.

Caution: Do not, under any circumstances, use a petroleum-based solvent to clean hydraulic parts.

9 Inspect the piston and release cylinder bore for signs of corrosion, nicks and burrs and loss of plating. If surface defects are found, or if wear is evident, the release cylinder should be replaced with a new one.

10 Check the pushrod oil seal in the crankcase for signs of leakage and replace it with a new one if necessary (see Section 16, Step 24).

11 Lubricate the new piston seal with clean hydraulic fluid and fit it into the groove in the piston with the wider side facing its inner end. Fit the spring into the cylinder. Lubricate the piston and seal with clean hydraulic fluid and insert the assembly into the cylinder, making sure the spring stays in place and the rim of the seal does not turn inside out. Use your thumbs to press it fully in.

Installation

12 Wipe the outer end of the pushrod clean and smear some silicon grease onto it. Remove the cable ties from the release cylinder if used. Fit the mounting flange onto the crankcase if separated from the release cylinder **(see illustration 18.5b)**.

13 Install the cylinder and tighten the bolts to the torque setting specified at the beginning of the Chapter **(see illustration 18.5a)**.

14 If detached, connect the clutch hose to the master cylinder, using new sealing washers on each side of the union, and aligning the hose as noted on removal **(see illustration 18.4)**. Tighten the banjo bolt to the specified torque setting.

15 Bleed the system (see Section 19). Check for fluid leaks.

16 Fit the rubber bung into the fairing post **(see illustration 18.3)**. Install the lower fairing (see Chapter 8).

17 Check the operation of the clutch before riding the motorcycle.

19 Clutch release mechanism bleeding

 Warning: Use care when working with brake/clutch hydraulic fluid as it can injure your eyes and it will damage painted surfaces and plastic parts.

Bleeding

1 Bleeding the clutch is simply the process of removing all the air bubbles from the fluid reservoir, the hoses and the release cylinder. Bleeding is necessary whenever an hydraulic connection is loosened, when a component or hose is replaced, or when the master cylinder or release cylinder is overhauled. Leaks in the system may also allow air to enter, but leaking clutch fluid will reveal their presence and warn you of the need for repair.

2 Remove the left-hand fairing side panel (see Chapter 8). To bleed the clutch, you will need some new DOT 5.1 glycol-based brake and clutch fluid, a length of clear vinyl or plastic tubing, a small container partially filled with clean brake fluid, some rags and a ring spanner to fit the release cylinder bleed valve.

3 Cover the areas surrounding the master and release cylinders with rag to prevent damage in the event that brake fluid is spilled.

4 Unscrew the cap and remove the diaphragm plate and diaphragm **(see illustration 17.16)**. Slowly pump the clutch lever a few times until no air bubbles can be seen floating up from the holes in the bottom of the reservoir. Doing this bleeds the air from the master cylinder end of the line. Loosely refit the reservoir cap.

5 Remove the rubber cap from the top of the bleed valve **(see illustration)**. If using a ring spanner, fit it over the bleed valve now. Attach one end of the clear vinyl or plastic tubing to the bleed valve and submerge the other end in the brake fluid in the container.

6 Check the fluid level in the reservoir – do not allow it to drop below the lower mark during the bleeding process.

7 Carefully pump the clutch lever three or four times and hold it in while opening the release cylinder bleed valve. When the valve is

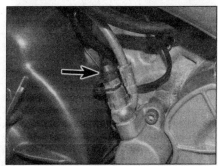

19.5 Clutch release cylinder bleed valve (arrowed)

opened, clutch fluid will flow into the clear tubing and the lever will move toward the handlebar.

8 Retighten the bleed valve, then release the clutch lever gradually. Repeat the process until no air bubbles are visible in the fluid leaving the release cylinder and the lever is firm when applied. On completion, disconnect the bleeding equipment, then tighten the bleed valve to the torque setting specified at the beginning of the chapter. Fit the rubber cap onto the top of the bleed valve.

9 Fit the rubber diaphragm onto the master cylinder reservoir, making sure it is correctly seated, and the diaphragm plate. Fit the cap. Wipe up any spilled brake fluid and check the entire system for leaks.

Changing the fluid

10 Changing the clutch fluid is a similar process to bleeding the clutch and requires the same materials, plus a suitable tool for siphoning the fluid out of the hydraulic reservoir (such as a syringe, though if one isn't available it is no problem to displace the reservoir and tip the fluid out as described in Section 17). Ensure that your container is large enough to take all the old fluid when it is flushed out of the system.

11 Follow Steps 3, 4 and 5, but after removing the reservoir cap, diaphragm plate and diaphragm, siphon or tip the old fluid out of the reservoir. Fill the reservoir with new brake fluid, then follow Step 7.

12 Retighten the bleed valve, then release the lever gradually. Keep the reservoir topped-up with new fluid to above the LOWER level at all times or air may enter the system and greatly increase the length of the task. Repeat the process until new fluid can be seen emerging from the bleed valve.

 HAYNES HINT *Old fluid is invariably darker in colour than new fluid, making it easy to see when all old fluid has been expelled from the system.*

13 Disconnect the hose, then tighten the bleed valve to the specified torque setting and fit the rubber cap.

14 Top-up the reservoir then install the diaphragm, plate and cap. Wipe up any spilled clutch fluid and check the entire system for leaks.

15 Check the operation of the clutch before riding the motorcycle.

Draining the system for overhaul

16 Draining the clutch fluid is again a similar process to bleeding the clutch. The quickest and easiest way is to use a commercially available vacuum-type bleeding tool – follow the manufacturer's instructions. Otherwise follow the procedure described above for changing the fluid, but quite simply do not put any new fluid into the reservoir – the system fills itself with air instead.

20 Primary drive gear and front balancer shaft gears

Note 1: *The primary drive gear can be removed with the engine in the frame.*
Note 2: *To lock the engine in the correct position (rear piston at TDC) for alignment of the crankshaft and the front balancer shaft a hole is cut into the crankshaft right-hand web into which the rounded end of the Aprilia special tool (part No. 0240880) or an equivalent made from an 8 mm bolt locates (see illustrations 8.6a, b and c). Either obtain the special holding tool or fabricate your own with the end rounded off as shown before commencing this procedure. If you make your own ensure the bolt is strong – we used a car cylinder head bolt which is strengthened (ask you local car repair workshop for one).*

Removal

1 Remove the spark plugs to allow the engine to be turned over easier (see Chapter 1). Remove the rear cylinder valve cover (see Section 7).

2 Unscrew the crankshaft end cap from the alternator cover **(see illustration 8.3)**. Discard the O-ring as a new one should be used.

3 Remove the clutch (see Section 16).

4 Turn the engine using a 14 mm hex bit on the alternator rotor bolt; turn it in an anti-clockwise direction only until the rear cylinder piston is at TDC (top dead centre) on the compression stroke, at which point the camshaft lobes are pointing away from each other at a slight upwards angle from the cylinder head, the line above the IN mark on the intake camshaft sprocket should be facing and in line with the line above the EX mark on the exhaust camshaft sprocket **(see illustrations 8.5a and b)** – due to the position of the rear balancer shaft driven gear the EX mark cannot be seen, but as long as the IN mark is correctly positioned you can assume so is the EX mark **(see illustration 8.5c for clarity)**.

5 Thread either the Aprilia special tool or a home-made equivalent (see **Note 2** above) into the clutch cover bolt hole that is just below the oil pressure switch until it locates in the hole in the crankshaft – you should be able to feel the point at which it locates by jiggling the crankshaft back and forth a very small amount either side of its current position (see Step 4) as you thread the holding bolt in **(see illustration 10.11)**. When you can't turn the crankshaft any more the tool end has located in the hole. Do not over-tighten the bolt – hand-tight is sufficient. Do not remove the holding tool – this will keep the engine in its correct position for installation (unless the engine is being completely stripped).

6 Unscrew the primary drive gear nut and remove the spring washer **(see illustrations)**. Slide the gear off the crankshaft, noting how it locates on the Woodruff key.

7 Unscrew the balancer shaft nut and remove the spring washer **(see illustrations)**. Slide the counterweight off the balancer shaft,

20.6a Unscrew the nut . . .

20.6b . . . remove the spring washer and slide the gear (arrowed) off the shaft

20.7a Unscrew the nut . . .

20.7b . . . and remove the spring washer

20.7c Remove the counter-weight, then slide the drive and driven gear pair off their shafts

20.9a Remove the outer washer ...

20.9b ... the water pump idle gear ...

20.9c ... the water pump drive gear ...

20.9d ... the inner washer ...

20.9e ... and the Woodruff key

noting how it locates on the Woodruff key **(see illustration)**.

8 Note how the punch marks on the balancer shaft drive and driven gears align, then grasp both gears and slide them off their shafts **(see illustration 20.7c)**.

9 If required, remove the outer washer from the balancer shaft, then remove the water pump idle gear, the water pump drive gear and the inner washer **(see illustrations)**. Remove the Woodruff key if it is loose **(see illustration)**.

Inspection

10 Check the teeth of the primary drive gear and the corresponding teeth of the primary driven gear on the back of the clutch housing. Similarly check the balancer shaft drive and driven gears and the water pump gears. If there is any sign of damage or wear between any gear pair, replace them both with new ones.

Installation

11 If removed from the balancer shaft, fit the Woodruff key into its slot, then slide the inner washer, with its flared side facing in, and water pump drive gear onto the shaft, locating the cut-outs over the key **(see illustrations 20.9e, d and c)**. Fit the water pump idle gear onto its post **(see illustration 20.9b)**. Fit the outer washer over the drive gear **(see illustration 20.9a)**.

12 Align the punch marks on the balancer shaft drive and driven gears and mesh their teeth, then slide both gears onto their shafts simultaneously, locating them over the keys **(see illustration)**.

13 Slide the counterweight onto the balancer shaft, locating it over the key **(see illustration 20.7c)**. Fit the spring washer and the nut and tighten the nut to the torque setting specified at the beginning of the Chapter **(see illustrations 20.7b and a)**.

14 Slide the primary drive gear onto the crankshaft with its shouldered side down, locating it over the key. Fit the spring washer **(see illustration 20.6b)**. Apply a suitable thread locking compound (such as Loctite 243) to the nut and tighten it to the torque setting specified at the beginning of the Chapter **(see illustration 20.6a)**.

15 Remove the holding tool.

16 Install the clutch (see Section 16).

17 Install the valve cover (see Section 7).

18 Install the crankshaft end cap using a new O-ring **(see illustration 8.64)**.

19 Install the spark plugs (see Chapter 1).

20.12 Slide the gears onto their shafts and the keys, aligning the punch marks (arrowed)

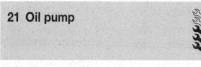

21 Oil pump

Note: *The oil pump can be removed with the engine in the frame.*

Pressure check

1 Perform an oil pressure check (see Chapter 1). If the pressure is as specified then the pump is good. If the pressure is lower than it should be, and all other possible causes (as listed in Chapter 1) have been eliminated, then the pump may be worn or faulty and the relevant components must be replaced with new ones.

Removal

2 Remove the clutch (see Section 16).

3 Remove the circlip securing the oil pump driven gear **(see illustration)**. Pull the gear to

21.3a Remove the circlip and pull the gear off ...

21.3b . . . then align the drive pin as shown and withdraw it

21.4a Unscrew the bolts . . .

21.4b . . . and remove the pump assembly

release it from its drive pin and slide it off the shaft. Turn the shaft so the drive pin aligns with the slot in the cover and draw the pin out **(see illustration)**.

4 Undo the oil pump bolts then grasp the shaft and pump cover and body and draw it off the crankcase as an assembly **(see illustrations)**. Remove the inner and outer rotors for the suction side of the pump from the crankcase (the inner one may have come with the pump and be on the inner end of the shaft) **(see illustrations 21.17b and a)**. Keep the rotors together and do not mix them up with the pressure rotors if the pump is disassembled.

Disassembly

5 Remove the drive pin from the inner end of the shaft.

6 Remove the pump cover.

7 Remove the inner and outer rotors for the pressure side of the pump from the pump body and keep them together so they can be installed the same way round.

8 Draw the shaft out of the pump and remove the pressure rotor drive pin.

Inspection

9 Clean all components in solvent and dry them using compressed air or lint-free cloth.

10 Check the pump body and cover for cracks and other damage.

11 Inspect the rotors, body, cover and crankcase for scoring and wear. If any damage, scoring or uneven or excessive wear is evident, replace the relevant components with new ones.

12 Fit the outer rotor of the suction pump back into the crankcase with the punch mark facing in **(see illustration 21.17a)**. Fit the

inner rotor into the outer rotor with the drive pin slot facing out **(see illustration 21.17b)**. Fit the drive pin into its hole in the shaft then slide the shaft into the rotor and crankcase, locating the pin in its slot **(see illustration 21.17c)**. With the rotors positioned as shown measure the clearance between the inner rotor tip and the outer rotor with a feeler gauge and compare it to the service limit listed in the specifications at the beginning of the Chapter **(see illustration)**. Also measure the clearance between the outer rotor and the rotor housing with a feeler gauge **(see illustration)**. If possible lay a straight-edge across the rotors and the crankcase and measure the clearance (rotor end-float) using feeler gauges. If any clearance measured is greater than the maximum listed, replace the rotors with new ones – they come as a set.

13 Fit the outer rotor of the pressure pump back into the pump body. Fit the inner rotor into the outer rotor with the drive pin slot facing in. Slide the shaft into the rotor and body. With the rotors positioned as shown measure the clearance between the inner rotor tip and the outer rotor with a feeler gauge and compare it to the service limit listed in the specifications at the beginning of the Chapter **(see illustration)**. Also measure the clearance between the outer rotor and the rotor housing with a feeler gauge **(see illustration)**. If possible lay a straight-edge across the rotors and the crankcase and measure the clearance (rotor end-float) using feeler gauges **(see illustration)**. If any clearance measured is

21.12a Measuring the inner rotor tip–to–outer rotor clearance for the suction pump

21.12b Measuring the outer rotor-to-housing clearance for the suction pump

21.13a Measuring the inner rotor tip–to–outer rotor clearance for the pressure pump

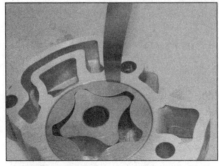

21.13b Measuring the outer rotor-to-housing clearance for the pressure pump

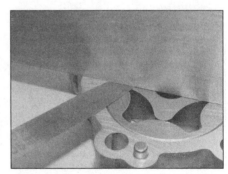

21.13c Measuring rotor end-float for the pressure pump

21.14 Checking the action of the relief valve plunger

21.17a Fit the outer rotor with the punch mark on the inside . . .

21.17b . . . then fit the inner rotor

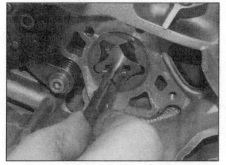

21.17c Locate the drive pin in the slots in the inner rotor

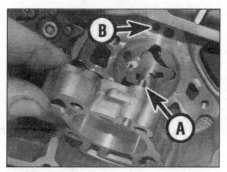

21.18 Fit the pump body over the shaft and against the crankcase, locating the pin (A) in its hole (B)

21.19a Fit the drive pin into its hole . . .

greater than the maximum listed, replace the rotors with new ones – they come as a set.

14 Check the action of the relief valve plunger by pressing against it with a screwdriver **(see illustration)**. Its movement, while limited by spring pressure, should be smooth. If required, unscrew the pressure relief valve cap, noting its set depth, how it is staked in place, and that there is a spring behind it, then remove the spring and plunger, noting which way round it fits. Check the plunger and its bore in the body for wear. Measure their diameters and replace them with new ones if worn beyond their specified limits. Measure the free length of the spring and replace it with a new one if it is shorter than the specified minimum.

Assembly and installation

15 If removed, coat the relief valve plunger with clean oil and insert it in the pump cover. Fit the spring. Apply a suitable thread locking compound (such as Loctite 648) to the cap threads. Thread it into the cover and set its outer surface 2 mm deep in the bore. Stake the cap in place as it was originally.

16 Clean the mating surfaces of the crankcase, pump body and cover with solvent and dry them. Lubricate the rotors with clean oil. Apply a thin film of Loctite 574 to the crankcase mating surface.

17 Fit the outer rotor of the suction pump into the crankcase with the punch mark facing in **(see illustration)**. Fit the inner rotor into the

outer rotor with the drive pin slot facing out **(see illustration)**. Fit the drive pin into its hole in the shaft then slide the shaft into the rotor and crankcase, locating the pin in its slot **(see illustration)**.

18 Make sure the locating pin is in the pump body. Fit the body over the shaft and locate it against the crankcase **(see illustration)**.

19 Fit the pressure pump drive pin into its slot in the shaft **(see illustration)**. Fit the inner rotor with its slot facing in onto the drive pin, then fit the outer rotor **(see illustrations)**.

20 Apply a thin film of Loctite 574 to the body mating surface, then fit the cover over the shaft and onto the body, locating it on the pin **(see illustration)**. Install the pump bolts and

21.19b . . . then fit the inner rotor onto the pin . . .

21.19c . . . and the outer rotor around the inner rotor

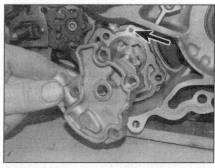

21.20 Fit the cover, locating it onto the pin (arrowed)

21.21 Press the gear on until it clicks onto the pin

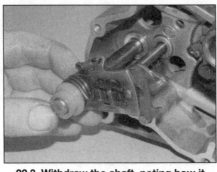

22.3 Withdraw the shaft, noting how it locates

22.4 Note the fitting of the spring ends and the roller, then unscrew the bolt (arrowed) and remove the arm

tighten them to the torque setting specified at the beginning of the Chapter.

21 Fit the drive pin into its slot, aligning it as before **(see illustration 21.3b)**. Press the driven gear onto the pin until it is felt to click into place. Secure it with its circlip **(see illustration 21.3a)**.

22 Install the clutch (see Section 16).

22 Gearchange mechanism

Note: *The gearchange mechanism can be removed with the engine in the frame. If the engine has already been removed, ignore the preliminary steps.*

Removal

1 Remove the clutch (see Section 16).

2 Make an alignment mark between the gearchange shaft end and the slit in the lever clamp, then unscrew the pinch bolt and slide the arm off the shaft **(see illustration 4.12)**.

3 Note how the gearchange selector arm locates onto the pins in the selector drum cam plate, and how the gearchange shaft centralising spring ends locate. Withdraw the gearchange shaft from the engine **(see illustration)**.

4 Note how the stopper arm spring ends locate and how the roller on the arm locates in the neutral detent on the selector drum cam, then unscrew the stopper arm bolt and remove the plain washer, the arm, the shouldered washer, and the spring, noting how they fit **(see illustration)**.

5 If required (e.g. for later removal of the selector drum), unscrew the bolt securing the cam plate to the selector drum and remove

the plate – use a screwdriver located across the pins to prevent the drum turning **(see illustration)**.

Inspection

6 Inspect the stopper arm and selector arm return springs and the shaft centralising spring **(see illustration)**. If they are fatigued, worn or damaged they must be replaced with new ones – the centralising spring on the shaft is retained by the nylon bush. Make sure the centralising spring post is tight in the crankcase.

7 Inspect the selector arm pawls and the pins on the cam plate for wear.

8 Check the stopper arm roller and the cam plate detents for wear. Check that the roller spins freely.

9 Check the gearchange shaft for distortion and damage to the splines. If the shaft is bent you can attempt to straighten it, but if the splines are damaged the shaft must be replaced with a new one. Also check the condition of the shaft oil seal in the cover. If it is damaged, deteriorated or shows signs of leakage a new one must be fitted. Lever out the old seal with a seal hook or screwdriver **(see illustration)**. Press or drive the new seal squarely into place, with its marked side facing out, using a seal driver or suitable socket **(see illustration)**.

Installation

10 Install the cam plate, locating its shaped inner face into the end of the selector drum **(see illustration)**. Apply a suitable thread

22.5 Selector drum cam plate bolt (arrowed)

22.6 Check all the springs for fatigue

22.9a Lever out the old seal . . .

22.9b . . . then fit the new one and press or drive it into place

22.10a Locate the plate on the end of the drum . . .

22.10b ... and secure it with the threadlocked bolt

22.11a Locate the return spring on its post ...

22.11b ... then install the stopper arm assembly

locking compound (such as Loctite 243) to the threads of the cam bolt and tighten it to the specified torque setting, locking the plate to prevent it turning as on removal **(see illustration)**.

11 Fit the return spring onto its post with its straight end seating on the crankcase **(see illustration)**. Fit the stopper arm bolt with its plain washer through the stopper arm, then fit the shouldered washer, with its shouldered side facing the arm. Apply the threadlock to the threads of the bolt. Hold the hooked end of the spring down with a screwdriver and fit the arm onto its mount, resting the arm in the hook and locating the roller in the neutral detent on the cam plate **(see illustration)**. Tighten the bolt to the torque setting specified at the beginning of the Chapter. Make sure the stopper arm is free to move and is returned by the pressure of the spring.

12 Smear some grease onto the lips of the shaft oil seal in the crankcase. Make sure the centralising spring ends are correctly located on each side of the tab on the lower pawl plate **(see illustration 22.6)**. Slide the shaft into its hole in the engine, making sure the centralising spring ends locate correctly each side of the locating pin in the crankcase **(see illustrations)**.

13 Install the gearchange lever, making sure it is correctly aligned **(see illustration 4.12)**. Install the clutch (see Section 16).

22.12a Slide the shaft in and locate the return spring ends on each side of the pin

22.12b The installed assembly should be as shown

Removal

2 Remove the alternator rotor (see Chapter 9) – the starter driven gear may come with it. If not slide it off the end of the crankshaft.

Inspection

3 If separated fit the starter driven gear into the back of the alternator rotor, turning the gear anti-clockwise as you do to spread the clutch sprags and allow it to enter. With the alternator rotor face down on a workbench, check that the starter driven gear rotates freely in an anti-clockwise direction and locks against the rotor in a clockwise direction **(see illustration)**. If it doesn't, the starter clutch should be dismantled for further investigation.

4 Withdraw the starter driven gear from the

starter clutch. If the gear appears stuck, rotate it anti-clockwise as you withdraw it to free it from the sprags.

5 Check the condition of the sprags inside the clutch housing and the corresponding surface on the driven gear hub **(see illustration)**. If they are damaged, marked or flattened at any point, or if the sprags are not securely held in their housing by their retaining springs, new components should be obtained – the starter clutch components (sprag assembly, housing and starter driven gear) are available individually. To separate the clutch housing and sprag assembly from the rotor, hold the rotor using a suitable spanner on its boss or using a holding strap and unscrew the bolts inside the rotor **(see**

23 Starter clutch

Note: *The starter clutch can be removed with the engine in the frame. If the engine has been removed, ignore the steps which do not apply.*

Check

1 The operation of the starter clutch can be checked while it is in situ. Remove the starter motor (see Chapter 9). Check that the reduction gear is able to rotate freely anti-clockwise as you look at it via the starter motor aperture, but locks when rotated clockwise. If not, the starter clutch is faulty and should be removed for inspection.

23.3 Make sure the driven gear turns freely in an anticlockwise direction as shown

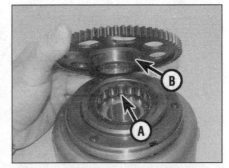

23.5a Check the sprags (A) and the surface of the hub (B)

23.5b Unscrew the bolts (arrowed) and separate the sprag assembly from the rotor as described

24.3a Release the circlip . . .

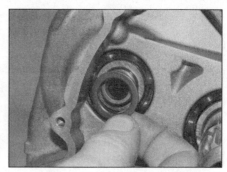

24.3b . . . and remove the washer

illustration). Separate the clutch housing from the back of the rotor. Remove the sprag assembly from the housing, noting which way round it fits and how it locates. Install the new assembly in a reverse sequence. Apply clean engine oil to the sprags. Apply a suitable non-permanent thread locking compound (such as Loctite 648) to the bolts and tighten them to the torque setting specified at the beginning of the Chapter.

6 Check the bush in the starter driven gear hub and its corresponding surface on the crankshaft. If the bush surfaces show signs of excessive wear (i.e. the oil retaining holes in its surface are not visible) replace the driven gear with a new one. Measure the internal diameter of the bush and the diameter of the crankshaft surface that it runs on to check the extent of wear and compare the results to the limits specified.

7 Check the teeth of the starter motor drive shaft, reduction gear, idle gear and starter driven gear. If worn or chipped teeth are discovered on related gears replace the relevant components with new ones. Check the idle and reduction gear shafts for damage, and check that the gears are not a loose fit. Measure the internal diameter of the gears and the external diameter of their shafts to check the extent of wear and compare the results to the limits specified.

Installation

8 Install the alternator rotor (see Chapter 9).

24 Crankcase separation and reassembly

Note: *Where an option to remove a component is given (i.e. if required, remove the oil pressure switch), it should be removed if a full engine strip, overhaul and rebuild is being carried out. However if the crankcases are being split solely to correct an isolated problem with a component or assembly not related to the optional component, then it can remain in place.*

Separation

1 To access the crankshaft and connecting rods, transmission shafts and selector drum and forks, front balancer shaft, and all related bearings, the engine must be removed from the frame (see Section 4) and the crankcase must be split into two parts.

2 Before the crankcases can be separated, remove the cylinder heads, cylinder blocks, pistons, starter motor, alternator and starter clutch, clutch, oil pump, gearchange mechanism (including the cam plate), primary drive and balancer shaft gears, and the cam chains and gears. See the relevant Sections of this and the other Chapters for details. Remove the crankshaft holding tool if not already done.

3 Remove the circlip from the right-hand end of the transmission output shaft then remove the thrust washer **(see illustrations)**.

4 If required remove the neutral switch and oil pressure switch (see Chapter 9).

5 Lay the engine on its right-hand side and support it on wooden blocks so the ends of the transmission input shaft and crankshaft are off the work surface. Unscrew the twenty bolts in the left-hand side of the crankcase, starting with the bolts on the perimeter and working to those in the middle, slackening them evenly and a little at a time in a criss-cross pattern until they are all loose, then remove the bolts **(see illustration)**.

> **HAYNES HINT** *As each bolt is removed, store it in its relative position in a cardboard template of the crankcase halves along with any washer or wiring clamp that goes with the bolt. This will ensure all bolts are installed in the correct location on reassembly.*

6 Carefully turn the engine over onto its left-hand side and support it on wooden blocks so the ends of the transmission output shaft and crankshaft are off the work surface.

7 Using a soft-faced hammer give the ends of the transmission shafts a couple of taps each. Carefully lift the right-hand crankcase half off the left-hand half, if necessary using a soft hammer to tap around the joint, the bore holes, and gently on the shaft ends, to separate the halves **(see illustration)**. You

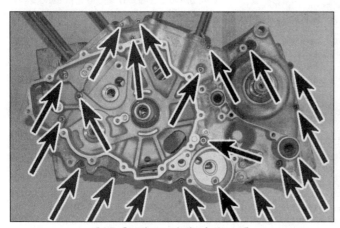

24.5 Crankcase bolts (arrowed)

24.7 Carefully separate the crankcase halves

24.10 Check that the thrust washer is on the end of the shaft

24.11 Make sure the connecting rods are positioned as shown

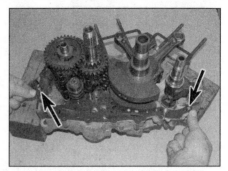

24.14 Make sure the dowels (arrowed) are installed, then fit the gasket

can also use a screwdriver against the leverage tabs. **Note:** *If the halves do not separate easily, make sure all fasteners have been removed. Do not try and separate the halves by levering between the crankcase mating surfaces as they are easily scored and will leak oil afterwards. If the transmission input shaft sticks in its bearing and is lifting with the crankcase, tap the end of it with a soft-faced hammer. If necessary, obtain an expanding clamp (brake piston expanders work very well) and some wood to protect the crankcase, then place the clamp in the cylinder opening and carefully expand the clamp to force the halves apart.* The right-hand side crankcase half will come away by itself, leaving the crankshaft, balancer shaft, transmission shafts, and selector drum and forks in the left-hand half.

8 Remove the gasket. Remove the two locating dowels from the crankcase if they are loose (they could be in either crankcase half), noting their locations **(see illustration 24.14)**. Check that the thrust washer is on the right-hand end of the transmission output shaft **(see illustration 24.10)**. If not, it is probably stuck to the bearing in the right-hand crankcase half. Refer to Section 25 for servicing of the crankcase halves and details on oil seal removal and installation – all seals should be replaced with new ones.

Reassembly

9 Remove any traces of old gasket from the crankcase mating surfaces.
10 Support the left-hand half on wooden blocks so the ends of the transmission output shaft and crankshaft are off the work surface. Ensure that all components and their bearings and new oil seals are in place in the right and left-hand crankcase halves. Check that the thrust washer is on the right-hand end of the transmission output shaft **(see illustration)**.
11 Make sure that each connecting rod is positioned correctly for its cylinder – the upper (right-hand) rod is for the front cylinder **(see illustration)**.
12 Generously lubricate the transmission shafts, selector drum and forks, and the crankshaft, particularly around the bearings, with molybdenum disulphide oil (a mixture of 50% molybdenum disulphide grease and

50% engine oil), then use a rag soaked in high flash-point solvent to wipe over the mating surfaces of both halves to remove all traces of oil.
13 Fit the two locating dowels in the left-hand crankcase half if removed **(see illustration 24.14)**.
14 Fit a new gasket onto the left-hand crankcase, fitting the joined section across the bores between the connecting rod ends, and locating it on the dowels **(see illustration)**. Make sure all the bolt holes align. Use a smear of grease on the gasket to help locate it if required.
Caution: Do not apply an excessive amount of sealant, as it will ooze out when the case halves are assembled and may obstruct oil passages.
15 Check again that all components are in position, then carefully fit the right-hand crankcase half onto the left-hand half **(see illustration 24.7)**. Make sure the dowels and shaft ends all locate correctly into the right-hand crankcase half, and that the gasket stays in place.
16 Check that the right-hand crankcase half is correctly seated. **Note:** *The crankcase halves should fit together without being forced, though a soft-faced hammer can be used gently to ease the halves together if required. If the casings are not correctly seated, remove the right-hand half and investigate the problem. Do not attempt to pull them together using the bolts as the casing could crack and be ruined.*
17 Carefully turn the engine over, making sure the halves remain joined. Clean the

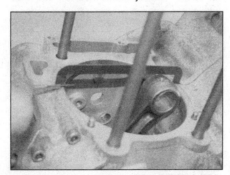

24.21 Cut the gasket bridges flush with the crankcase

threads of the crankcase bolts and install them in their original locations **(see illustration 24.5)**. Secure all bolts finger-tight at first, then tighten them evenly and a little at a time, starting with the inner bolts and working to the perimeter, to the torque setting specified at the beginning of the Chapter.
18 With all crankcase bolts tightened, check that the crankshaft, balancer shaft and transmission shafts rotate smoothly and easily. Select each gear in turn (you will have to fit the cam plate onto the selector drum and turn it by hand to do this) and check the operation of the transmission in each gear, then select neutral and check that the shafts can turn freely and independently of each other. If there are any signs of undue stiffness, tight or rough spots, or of any other problem, the fault must be rectified before proceeding further.
19 If removed install the neutral switch and oil pressure switch (see Chapter 9).
20 Fit the thrust washer onto the right-hand end of the transmission output shaft and secure it with the circlip **(see illustrations 24.3b and a)**.
21 Using a very sharp knife cut the gasket bridges flush with the crankcase mating surfaces at the bores **(see illustration)**.
22 Install all other removed assemblies in the reverse of the sequence given in Step 2. Refer to Section 25, Step 11 and fit a new transmission shaft oil seal.

25 Crankcase inspection and servicing

1 After the crankcases have been separated, remove the crankshaft and connecting rods, front balancer shaft, transmission shafts, and selector drum and forks, referring to the relevant Sections of this Chapter. Refer to Sections 30 and 31 and to *Tools and Workshop Tips* in the Reference Section for checks and information on the selector drum and transmission shaft bearings. Refer to Sections 26, 27, 28 and 29 and to *Tools and Workshop Tips* in the Reference Section for checks and information on the main and big-end bearings, and the balancer shaft bearings.

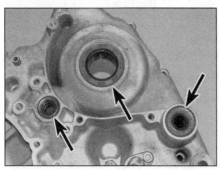

25.2 Remove the oil seals (arrowed)

25.3a Remove the oil spray pipe (arrowed) . . .

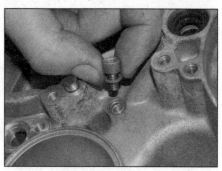

25.3b . . . the gallery bolt and its sealing washer . . .

2 Lever out the transmission output shaft oil seal, gearchange shaft oil seal and clutch pushrod oil seal using a seal hook or screwdriver **(see illustration)**.

3 Pull the piston oil spray pipe out of the crankcase – if it is tight use heat around its bore in the casing **(see illustration)**. Also remove the bolt from the bottom of the oil gallery on the outside of the left-hand crankcase half and withdraw the oil jet **(see illustrations)**. Discard the sealing washer. Clean the pipe and jet with solvent and blow them through with compressed air if available.

4 Remove the internal oil strainer, noting how it fits **(see illustration)**. Clean the gauze and check it for damage.

5 Remove all traces of old gasket from the mating surfaces. Clean up minor damage to the surfaces with a fine sharpening stone or grindstone.

6 Clean the crankcases thoroughly with new solvent and dry them with compressed air. Blow out all oil passages with compressed air **(see illustration)**.

Caution: Be very careful not to nick or gouge the crankcase mating surfaces or oil leaks will result. Check both crankcase halves very carefully for cracks and other damage.

7 Check that the cylinder block studs are tight in each crankcase half. If any are loose, remove them, then clean their threads and apply a suitable non-permanent thread locking compound and tighten them to the torque setting specified at the beginning of the Chapter. Refer to Section 2 'Fasteners' of *Tools and Workshop Tips* in the Reference

section at the end of this manual for details of how to slacken and tighten studs using two nuts locked together.

8 Small cracks or holes in aluminium castings can be repaired with an epoxy resin adhesive or a product known as Lumiweld as a temporary measure. Permanent repairs can only be done by TIG welding, and only a specialist in this process is in a position to advise on the economy or practical aspect of such a repair. If any damage is found that can't be repaired, renew the crankcase halves as a set.

9 Damaged threads can be economically reclaimed using a diamond section wire insert, for example of the Heli-Coil type (though there are other makes), which is easily fitted after drilling and re-tapping the affected thread.

10 Studs or screws that have sheared off below the surface of their bore can usually be removed with extractors, which consist of a tapered, left-hand thread screw of very hard steel. These are inserted into a pre-drilled hole in the stud, and usually succeed in dislodging the most stubborn stud or screw. If a stud has sheared above its bore line, it can be removed using a conventional stud extractor which avoids the need for drilling.

> **HAYNES HINT** *Refer to Tools and Workshop Tips for details of installing a thread insert and using screw extractors.*

11 Support the left-hand crankcase half on blocks of wood and fit a new clutch pushrod oil

seal and gearchange shaft oil seal, using a socket to drive them in until they seat in the bore – lubricate their outer rim with oil to ease their entry, and make sure they are fitted with the marked side facing out **(see illustration 25.2)**. Smear the seal lips with grease. Only fit the transmission output shaft oil seal after fitting the shafts and joining the crankcases as the shaft is likely to turn the seal lips inside out as you install it – the seal sits flush with is bore.

12 Install the oil strainer making sure it locates correctly **(see illustration 25.4)**.

13 Fit the oil jet into its passage, then fit a new sealing washer onto the bolt and tighten it **(see illustrations 25.3c and b)**. Fit the piston oil spray pipe into its bore if removed, applying Loctite 648 or equivalent to its end and locating the pin in its cut-out **(see illustration 25.3a)**.

14 Install all other components and assemblies, referring to Step 1 and the relevant Sections of this and the other Chapters, before reassembling the crankcase halves.

26 Main, balancer shaft and connecting rod bearing information

1 Even though main and connecting rod bearings and balancer shaft bearings are generally replaced with new ones during the engine overhaul, the old bearings should be retained for close examination as they may reveal valuable information about the condition of the engine.

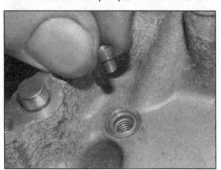

25.3c . . . and the oil jet

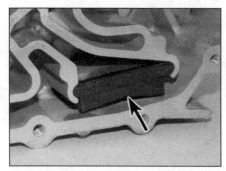

25.4 Pull the oil strainer (arrowed) out

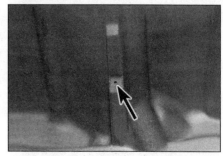

25.6 Make sure you blow through all oil passages – there are some small ones (arrowed) which are easy to miss

2 Bearing failure occurs mainly because of lack of lubrication, the presence of dirt or other foreign particles, overloading the engine and/or corrosion. Regardless of the cause of bearing failure, it must be corrected before the engine is reassembled to prevent it from happening again.

3 When examining the connecting rod bearings, remove them from the connecting rods and caps and lay them out on a clean surface in the same general position as their location on the crankshaft journals. This will enable you to match any noted bearing problems with the corresponding crankshaft journal.

4 Dirt and other foreign particles get into the engine in a variety of ways. It may be left in the engine during assembly or it may pass through filters or breathers. It may get into the oil and from there into the bearings. Metal chips from machining operations and normal engine wear are often present. Abrasives are sometimes left in engine components after reconditioning operations, especially when parts are not thoroughly cleaned using the proper cleaning methods. Whatever the source, these foreign objects often end up imbedded in the soft bearing material and are easily recognised. Large particles will not imbed in the bearing and will score or gouge the bearing and journal. The best prevention for this cause of bearing failure is to clean all parts thoroughly and keep everything spotlessly clean during engine reassembly. Frequent and regular oil and filter changes are also recommended.

5 Lack of lubrication or lubrication breakdown has a number of interrelated causes. Excessive heat (which thins the oil), overloading (which squeezes the oil from the bearing face) and oil leakage or throw off (from excessive bearing clearances, worn oil pump or high engine speeds) all contribute to lubrication breakdown. Blocked oil passages will also starve a bearing and destroy it. When lack of lubrication is the cause of bearing failure, the bearing material is wiped or extruded from the steel backing of the bearing. Temperatures may increase to the point where the steel backing and the journal turn blue from overheating.

> **HAYNES HINT** *Refer to Tools and Workshop Tips for bearing fault finding.*

6 Riding habits can have a definite effect on bearing life. Full throttle low speed operation, or labouring the engine, puts very high loads on bearings, which tend to squeeze out the oil film. These loads cause the bearings to flex, which produces fine cracks in the bearing face (fatigue failure). Eventually the bearing material will loosen in pieces and tear away from the steel backing. Short trip riding leads to corrosion of bearings, as insufficient engine heat is produced to drive off the condensed water and corrosive gases produced. These products collect in the engine oil, forming acid and sludge. As the oil is carried to the engine

bearings, the acid attacks and corrodes the bearing material.

7 Incorrect bearing installation during engine assembly will lead to bearing failure as well. Tight fitting bearings that leave insufficient bearing oil clearances result in oil starvation. Dirt or foreign particles trapped behind a bearing insert result in high spots on the bearing that lead to failure.

8 To avoid bearing problems, clean all parts thoroughly before reassembly, double check all bearing clearance measurements and lubricate the new bearings with clean engine oil during installation.

27 Crankshaft and main bearings

Removal

1 Separate the crankcase halves (see Section 24).

2 Lift the crankshaft out of the left-hand crankcase half **(see illustration)**. If it appears stuck, tap it gently using a soft-faced mallet.

3 If required, remove the connecting rods from the crankshaft (see Section 29).

Inspection

4 Clean the crankshaft with solvent, squirting through all the oil passages. If available, blow the crank dry with compressed air, and also blow through the oil passages.

5 Refer to Section 26 and examine the main bearings **(see illustration)**. If they are scored,

badly scuffed or appear to have been seized, new bearing shells must be installed (see below). Always renew the shells as a set. If they are badly damaged, check the corresponding crankshaft journal. Note that are also end bearings in the clutch inner cover that the right-hand end of the shaft runs in – be sure to check these as well **(see illustration)**. Evidence of extreme heat, such as discoloration, indicates that lubrication failure has occurred. Be sure to thoroughly check the oil pump and pressure relief valve as well as all oil holes and passages before reassembling the engine.

6 Inspect the crankshaft journals, paying particular attention where damaged bearings have been discovered. If the journals are scored or pitted in any way a new crankshaft will be required.

7 Place the crankshaft on V-blocks and check the runout at the main bearing journals using a dial gauge. Compare the reading to the maximum specified at the beginning of the Chapter. If the runout exceeds the limit, a new crankshaft must be installed.

Oil clearance check

8 Whether new bearing shells are being fitted or the original ones are being re-used, check the main bearing and end bearing oil clearance prior to reassembly.

9 Using a micrometer, measure the diameter of the crankshaft main and end bearing journals **(see illustration)**. Using a bore gauge and micrometer, measure the internal diameter of the main and end bearing bores with the bearings in place **(see illustrations 27.5a and b)**. Calculate the

27.2 Carefully lift the crankshaft out

27.5b . . . and the end bearing shells (arrowed) in the clutch cover

27.5a Check the crankshaft main bearing shells in each crankcase half . . .

27.9 Measure the journal diameter

difference between the two to determine the bearing oil clearance and compare the results to the specifications at the beginning of the Chapter. If the oil clearance exceeds the service limit, new main and/or end bearings must be selected and installed. Note that if the diameter of the crankshaft journal is below the range specified, it is worn and a new crankshaft must be installed. Always fit new main and end bearings if you fit a new crankshaft.

Main and end bearing selection

10 New main and end bearings are supplied on a selective fit basis according to the colour code marked on each crankcase half and on the clutch cover adjacent to the bearing housing. The colour code is either RED, BLUE or YELLOW, and the bearing shell colour code must match it. The colour code is marked on the side of each bearing shell. The dimensions relating to the particular codes are given below in case the marks on the crankcase are not visible.

Crankcase code (main bearing housing internal diameter)
RED – 49.899 to 49.908 mm
BLUE – 49.908 to 49.918 mm
YELLOW – 49.918 to 49.292 mm

Clutch cover code (end bearing housing internal diameter)
RED – 32.921 to 32.930 mm
BLUE – 32.930 to 32.940 mm
YELLOW – 32.940 to 32.951 mm

Main and end bearing removal and installation

11 Removal of the old main and end bearings and installation of new ones requires the use of an hydraulic press, an oven and an Aprilia special tool set in order to avoid damaging either the crankcases or the new bearings. It is therefore advised that removal of the old bearings and installation of new ones is undertaken by an Aprilia main dealer.

Installation

12 If removed, fit the connecting rods onto the crankshaft (see Section 29).
13 Apply molybdenum disulphide oil (a

mixture of 50% molybdenum disulphide grease and 50% engine oil) to the main bearings. Carefully lower the tapered (alternator) end of the crankshaft into position in the left-hand crankcase, making sure the lower (left-hand) connecting rod faces back in line with the rear cylinder, and the upper (right-hand) connecting rod faces forwards in line with the front cylinder **(see illustration 27.2)**.
14 Reassemble the crankcase halves (see Section 24).

---

28 Front balancer shaft and bearings

Removal

1 Separate the crankcase halves (see Section 24).
2 Lift the balancer shaft out of the left-hand crankcase half **(see illustration)**. If it appears stuck, tap it gently using a soft-faced mallet.

Inspection

3 Clean the shaft with solvent.
4 Refer to Section 26 and examine the bearings **(see illustration)**. If they are scored, badly scuffed or appear to have been seized, new bearing shells must be installed (see below). Always renew the shells as a set. If they are badly damaged, check the corresponding journal. Note that there are also end bearings in the clutch inner cover which the right-hand end of the shaft runs in – be sure to check these as well **(see illustration)**. Evidence of extreme heat, such as discoloration, indicates that lubrication failure has occurred. Be sure to thoroughly check the oil pump and pressure relief valve as well as all oil holes and passages before reassembling the engine.
5 Inspect the balancer shaft journals, paying particular attention where damaged bearings have been discovered **(see illustration 28.7)**. If the journals are scored or pitted in any way a new shaft will be required.

Oil clearance check

6 Whether new bearing shells are being fitted or the original ones are being re-used, check the crankcase bearing and end bearing oil clearance prior to reassembly.

28.2 Carefully lift the balancer shaft out

7 Using a micrometer, measure the diameter of the bearing journals **(see illustration)**. Using a bore gauge and micrometer, measure the internal diameter of the bearing bores with the bearings in place **(see illustration 28.4a and b)**. Calculate the difference between the two to determine the bearing oil clearance and compare the results to the specifications at the beginning of the Chapter. If the oil clearance exceeds the service limit, new bearings must be selected and installed. Note that if the diameter of the journal is below the range specified, it is worn and a new balancer shaft must be installed. Always fit new bearings if you fit a new shaft.

Bearing selection

8 New bearings are supplied on a selective fit basis according to the colour code marked on each crankcase half and on the clutch cover adjacent to the bearing housing. The colour code is either RED, BLUE or YELLOW, and the bearing shell colour-code must match it. The colour code is marked on the side of each bearing shell. The dimensions relating to the particular codes are given below in case the marks on the crankcase are not visible.

Crankcase code (bearing housing internal diameter)
RED – 35.909 to 35.918 mm
BLUE – 35.918 to 35.928 mm
YELLOW – 35.928 to 35.939 mm

Note: *No dimensions are given for the end bearings in the clutch cover – refer to an Aprilia dealer for advice.*

28.4a Check the balancer shaft bearing shells in each crankcase half . . .

28.4b . . . and the end bearing shells (arrowed) in the clutch cover

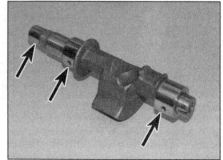

28.7 Measure the diameter of each journal (arrowed)

29.2 Measure the connecting rod side clearance

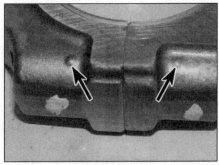

29.3a The raised dots (arrowed) must be on the same side . . .

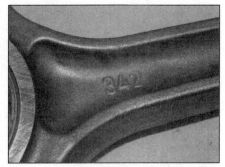

29.3b . . . and the number faces the middle of the crankshaft

Main and end bearing removal and installation

9 Removal of the old bearings and installation of new ones requires the use of an hydraulic press, an oven and an Aprilia special tool set in order to avoid damaging either the crankcases or the new bearings. It is therefore advised that removal of the old bearings and installation of new ones is undertaken by an Aprilia main dealer.

Installation

10 Apply molybdenum disulphide oil (a mixture of 50% molybdenum disulphide grease and 50% engine oil) to the bearings. Carefully lower the short end of the shaft with the internal threads into position in the left-hand crankcase **(see illustration 28.2)**.
11 Reassemble the crankcase halves (see Section 24).

29 Connecting rods

Removal

1 Remove the crankshaft (see Section 27).
2 Before removing the rods from the crankshaft, measure the big-end side clearance between the rods and the crank web with a feeler gauge **(see illustration)**. If

the clearance is greater than the service limit listed in this Chapter's Specifications, replace the rods with new ones.
3 Using paint or a felt marker pen, mark the relevant cylinder identity on each connecting rod (i.e. FRONT or REAR). The left-hand side (alternator end) of the crankpin holds the rear cylinder rod, and the right-hand side (primary drive gear end) of the crankpin holds the front cylinder rod. Mark across the cap-to-connecting rod join to ensure that the cap is fitted the correct way around on reassembly, though there should already be a raised dot on each that are matched **(see illustration)**. The number 342 marked on the side of the rod faces the middle of the crankshaft, so the numbers face each other **(see illustration and 29.16)**.
4 Unscrew the big-end cap bolts and separate the connecting rod, cap and both bearing shells from the crankpin **(see illustration)**. When the bolts are partially unscrewed tap their heads with a soft-faced hammer to separate the rod and cap if required. Keep the rod, cap, bolts and (if they are to be re-used) the bearing shells together in their correct positions to ensure correct installation. Note that on installation new bolts must be used, but the old ones can be used for checking the oil clearance.

Inspection

5 Check the connecting rods for cracks and other obvious damage.
6 Apply clean engine oil to the piston pin,

insert it into the connecting rod small-end and check for any freeplay between the two. Measure the pin OD in the middle and the small-end bore ID and compare the measurements to the specifications at the beginning of the Chapter **(see illustrations)**. Replace components that are worn beyond the specified limits with new ones.
7 Refer to Section 26 and examine the connecting rod bearing shells. If they are scored, badly scuffed or appear to have seized, new shells must be installed. Always renew the shells in the connecting rods as a set. If they are badly damaged, check the corresponding crankpin. Evidence of extreme heat, such as discoloration, indicates that lubrication failure has occurred. Be sure to thoroughly check the oil pump and pressure relief valve as well as all oil holes and passages before reassembling the engine.
8 Have the rods checked for twist and bend by an Aprilia dealer if you are in doubt about their straightness.

Oil clearance check

9 Whether new bearing shells are being fitted or the original ones are being re-used, check the connecting rod bearing oil clearance prior to reassembly. You can check both rods at the same time as long as doing so doesn't make you rotate one rod as the other is being fitted as this will distort the Plastigauge. If possible position or clamp the crankshaft and rods so they are stable and cannot move – a

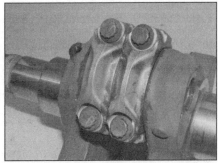

29.4 Unscrew the connecting rod big-end cap bolts and separate the rods from the shaft

29.6a Measure the external diameter of the pin . . .

29.6b . . . and the internal diameter of the connecting rod small-end

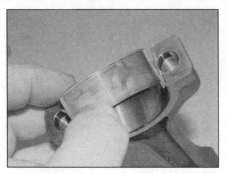

29.10 Remove the shells from the rod and cap

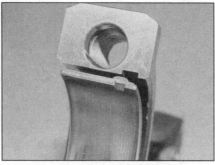

29.11 Fit the shell into its housing making sure the tab locates in the notch

29.14 Measure the diameter of the crankpin to see if it is worn

piston pin passed through both rod small-ends will help keep the rods together.

10 Remove the bearing shells from the connecting rod and cap **(see illustration)**. Clean the backs of the shells and their housing in the rod and cap.

11 Press the bearing shells into place, making sure they are in their original position if checking the original shells, and ensuring that the tab on each shell engages the notch in the rod or cap **(see illustration)**. Take care not to touch any shell's bearing surface with your fingers.

12 Cut a length of the Plastigauge (it should be slightly shorter than the width of the crankpin) and place it on the (cleaned) crankpin journal away from the oil holes. Lubricate under the connecting rod bolt heads with clean engine oil. Fit the connecting rod assemblies, shells and caps **(see illustrations 29.18 and 29.19a)**. Make sure the rods and caps are fitted the correct way around so the previously made markings align (see Step 3), and tighten the bearing cap bolts in three stages, first to the initial torque setting

specified at the beginning of the Chapter, then to the mid torque setting, and then to the final angle setting using a degree disc, whilst ensuring that the connecting rods do not rotate **(see illustration 29.19b)**. Now slacken the cap bolts and remove the connecting rod assemblies, again taking great care not to rotate the connecting rod.

13 Compare the width of the crushed Plastigauge at its widest point to the scale printed on the Plastigauge envelope to obtain the connecting rod bearing oil clearance.

14 If the clearance is not within the specified limits, the bearing shells may be the wrong grade (or excessively worn if the original shells are being re-used). Before deciding that different grade shells are needed, make sure that no dirt or oil was trapped between the bearing shells and the connecting rod or cap when the clearance was measured, and be certain that neither rod turned on the crankpin and distorted the strand of Plastigauge. If the clearance is excessive, even with new shells (of the correct size), measure the diameter of the crankpin and compare it to the specifications **(see illustration)**. If it is worn beyond the specified range, replace the crankshaft with a new one.

15 On completion carefully clean off all traces of the Plastigauge material from the crankpin and bearing shells.

Bearing shell selection

Note: *If fitting new connecting rods note that they are supplied with all three sizes of shell; the correct shells must be selected as described below.*

29.18 Fit the rod and cap onto the crankpin . . .

16 Fit the shells according to the amount of radial play in the rods. Radial play must be measured using an accurate dial gauge with the rods fitted on the crankshaft **(see illustration)**. Bearings are available in three thicknesses, RED, BLUE and YELLOW (see table). First install the RED coloured shells and fit the rods onto the crankshaft (see below – use the old bolts, and only use new bolts for the final installation when you know you have the correct shells), then measure the amount of radial play. If it exceeds the specified amount, remove the shells and replace them with BLUE or YELLOW ones according to the difference between the specified and measured amount of radial play so that the specified amount is restored. If the clearance is excessive even with YELLOW shells, replace the crankshaft with a new one.

Shell colour	Thickness
RED	1.471 to 1.476 mm
BLUE	1.476 to 1.481 mm
YELLOW	1.481 to 1.486 mm

Installation

17 Work on one rod at a time, and make sure it is installed on the correct side of the crankshaft, and the correct way round (see Step 3). Clean the backs of the shells and their housing in the rod and cap. If new shells are being fitted, ensure that all traces of any protective grease are cleaned off using paraffin (kerosene). Wipe the shells, cap and rod dry with a clean lint free cloth. Fit the bearing shells in the connecting rod and cap, making sure the tab on each shell engages the notch **(see illustration 29.11)**.

18 Lubricate each shell's bearing surface with molybdenum disulphide oil (a 50/50 mixture of molybdenum disulphide grease and clean engine oil). Fit the connecting rod onto the crankpin with its number facing the middle and fit the cap onto the rod so the raised dots align **(see illustration)**. Check to make sure that all components have been returned to their original locations using the marks made on disassembly.

19 Apply engine oil under the heads of the **new** connecting rod bolts. Fit the bolts and tighten them in three stages, first to the initial

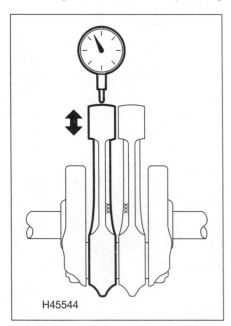

29.16 Measure the amount of radial play using a dial gauge

torque setting specified at the beginning of the Chapter, then to the mid torque setting and then to the final angle setting using a degree disc **(see illustrations)**.

20 Check that the rod rotates smoothly and freely on the crankpin. If there are any signs of roughness or tightness, remove the rod and re-check the oil clearance.

21 Install the crankshaft (see Section 27).

30 Selector drum and forks

Note 1: *To access the selector drum and forks the engine must be removed from the frame and the crankcases separated.*

Note 2: *On the model photographed the fork shafts were too tight in the crankcase to be removed without the aid of grips or pliers, which would probably score them and render them useless. Instead the selector drum and forks along with the transmission shafts were removed by grasping the whole lot in one and raising it until the forks were clear of their shafts* **(see illustration A below)**. *On installation the shafts, drum and forks were assembled on the bench and held together while locating the assembly in the crankcase* **(see illustration B below)**.

A: Grasp the whole assembly and lift it up off the selector fork shafts

B: Assemble the transmission shafts, drum and forks on the bench and slide the forks onto their shafts as you lower the assembly onto the crankcase

29.19a ... then fit the new and lubricated bolts ...

Removal

1 Separate the crankcase halves (Section 24).
2 The selector forks and their shafts are not marked for identification, so before removal mark them yourself using a felt pen according to where they fit and which way round.
3 Withdraw the output shaft selector fork shaft, then pivot the forks out of their tracks in the selector drum and remove them, noting how they locate in the grooves in their pinion **(see illustration)**. Once removed, slide the forks back onto the shafts in their correct order and way round.
4 Withdraw the input shaft selector fork shaft, then pivot the fork out of its track in the selector drum **(see illustration)**. Withdraw the selector drum from the crankcase. Now remove the fork noting how it locates in the groove in its pinion.

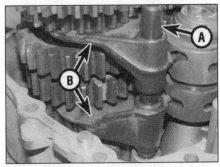

30.3 Withdraw the shaft (A) then remove the forks (B)

30.6a Measure the fork-to-groove side clearance using a feeler gauge

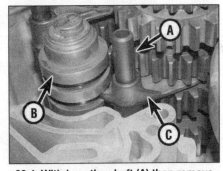

29.19b ... and tighten them as described

Inspection

5 Inspect the selector forks for any signs of wear or damage, especially around the fork ends where they engage with the groove in the gear pinion. Check closely to see if the forks are bent. If the forks are in any way damaged they must be replaced with new ones.
6 Slip each fork in turn into the groove in its gear pinion on the transmission shaft and measure the fork-to-groove clearance using a feeler gauge **(see illustration)**. Compare the results to the specifications at the beginning of the Chapter. If the clearance exceeds the service limit specified, measure the thickness of the fork ends and the width of the groove and compare the readings to the specifications **(see illustration)**. Replace whichever components that are worn beyond their specifications with new ones.

30.4 Withdraw the shaft (A) then remove the drum (B) and then the fork (C)

30.6b Measure the thickness of the fork ends and the width of its pinion groove

30.9 Check the drum grooves and fork guide pins

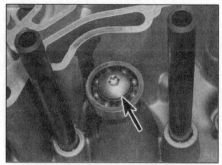

30.10a Selector drum bearing and its retaining screw (arrowed) – left-hand half

30.10b Selector drum bearing and its retaining screw (arrowed) – right-hand half

7 Check that the forks fit correctly on their shaft. They should move freely with a light fit but no appreciable freeplay. Measure the diameter of the shafts and compare the result to the specified minimum. Replace the forks and/or shafts with new ones if they are worn. Check that the fork shaft holes in the casing are neither worn nor damaged.

8 Check the selector fork shafts are straight by rolling them along a flat surface, or measure any runout using V-blocks and a dial gauge. A bent shaft will cause difficulty in selecting gears and make the gearchange action heavy. Replace the shafts with new ones if they are bent.

9 Inspect the selector drum grooves and selector fork guide pins for signs of wear or damage and replace them with new ones if necessary **(see illustration)**. Measure the diameter of the guide pins and compare the result to the minimum specified.

10 Check that the selector drum bearing in each crankcase half rotates freely and smoothly **(see illustrations)**. Remove the old bearing and fit a new one if necessary (see *Tools and Workshop Tips* in the Reference Section). Each bearing is held by a screw. On installation apply a suitable non-permanent thread locking compound to the screws and tighten them to the specified torque setting.

Installation

11 Apply molybdenum disulphide oil (a 50/50 mixture of molybdenum disulphide grease and clean engine oil) to the selector fork ends. Slide the middle fork into the groove of the

combined 3rd/4th gear pinion on the input shaft **(see illustration 30.4)**. Slide the drum into position in the crankcase, aligning it so that the raised section for the neutral switch is contacting the switch plunger **(see illustration)**. Locate the guide pin on the end of the fork into the middle groove in the selector drum.

12 Slide the left-hand (bottom) fork into the groove of the sixth gear pinion on the output shaft **(see illustration 30.3)**. Slide the right-hand (top) fork into the groove of the fifth gear pinion on the output shaft. Locating the guide pins on the ends of the forks into the bottom and top grooves in the selector drum – you may have to move the forks and their pinions up to achieve this. Lubricate the fork shaft and slide it through the forks.

13 Reassemble the crankcase halves (see Section 24).

31 Transmission shaft removal and installation

Note: *To access the transmission shafts the engine must be removed from the frame and the crankcases separated.*

Removal

1 Separate the crankcase halves (Section 24).
2 Remove the selector drum and forks (see Section 30).
3 Grasp the input shaft and output shaft and

withdraw them from the crankcase as an assembly, noting their relative positions and how they fit together. If the output shaft is tight in the crankcase, gently tap the bottom of the shaft using a soft-faced hammer or drift. Separate the shafts. Note the thrust washer on the right-hand end of the output shaft and take care not to lose it.

4 Lever the output shaft oil seal out of the right-hand crankcase **(see illustration)** – a new one must be used on installation, but do not install it until the shafts are installed and the crankcases have been rejoined (see Section 25).

5 If necessary, disassemble the transmission shafts and inspect them for wear or damage, and check the bearings (see Section 32).

Installation

6 Support the left-hand half of the crankcase on wooden blocks so that the end of the transmission output shaft does not contact the work surface as it is installed.

7 Lay the input shaft and output shaft side by side on the bench so that the pinions for each gear mesh together. Make sure that the shafts are the correct way round, in which case the smallest pinion on the input shaft meshes with the largest pinion on the output shaft. Lubricate the left-hand end of each shaft with clean engine oil.

8 Grasp the input shaft and output shaft and install them into the left-hand crankcase, making sure that both ends engage in their bearings. If the output shaft is tight in the bearing, gently tap on the end of the shaft to ease it in. Make sure that the thrust washer is on the right-hand end of the output shaft **(see illustration 24.10)**.

8 Install the selector drum and forks (see Section 30).
9 Join the crankcase halves (Section 24).

32 Transmission shaft overhaul

Note: *References to the right- and left-hand ends of the transmission shafts are made as though they are installed in the engine and the engine is the correct way up.*

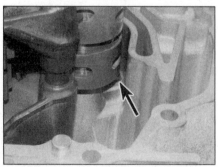

30.11 Locate the raised section against the neutral switch contact (arrowed)

31.4 Lever the oil seal out and discard it

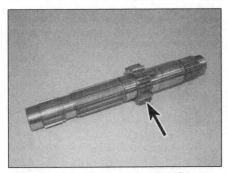

32.6 The 1st gear pinion (arrowed) is part of the shaft

32.11a Measure the internal diameter of the pinion . . .

32.11b . . . and the diameter of its section of the shaft

> **HAYNES HiNT**
> *When disassembling the transmission shafts, place the parts on a long rod or thread a wire through them to keep them in order and facing the proper direction.*

1 Remove the transmission shafts from the crankcase (see Section 31). Always disassemble the transmission shafts separately to avoid mixing up the components. Note that once removed the needle bearings that some of the pinions run on should be discarded and new ones fitted when rebuilding the shaft.

Input shaft disassembly

2 Slide the 2nd gear pinion off the shaft **(see illustration 32.19)**.

3 Remove the circlip securing the 6th gear pinion, then slide the splined washer and the pinion off the shaft **(see illustrations 32.18e, d and c)**. Spread the 6th gear pinion needle bearing then slide it off the shaft, followed by the splined washer **(see illustrations 32.18b and a)**.

4 Remove the circlip securing the combined 3rd/4th gear pinion, then slide the pinion off the shaft **(see illustrations 32.17b and a)**.

5 Remove the circlip securing the 5th gear pinion, then slide the thrust washer and the 5th gear pinion off the shaft **(see illustrations 32.16c, b and a)**.

6 The 1st gear pinion is integral with the shaft **(see illustration)**.

Input shaft inspection

7 Wash all of the components in clean solvent and dry them off.

8 Check the gear teeth for cracking chipping, pitting and other obvious wear or damage. Any pinion that is damaged as such must be replaced with a new one.

9 Inspect the dogs and the dog holes in the gears for cracks, chips, and excessive wear especially in the form of rounded edges. Make sure mating gears engage properly. Replace paired gears as a set if necessary.

10 Check for signs of scoring or bluing on the pinions and shaft. This could be caused by overheating due to inadequate lubrication. Check that all the oil holes and passages are clear. Replace any damaged pinions with new ones.

11 Check that each pinion moves freely on the shaft or its bearing but without undue freeplay. Where dimensions are given, measure the internal diameter of the pinion and the diameter of the section of shaft it runs on (see Specifications) **(see illustrations)**. If any component is worn replace it with a new one.

12 The shaft is unlikely to sustain damage unless the engine has seized, placing an unusually high loading on the transmission, or the machine has covered a very high mileage. Check the surface of the shaft, especially where a pinion turns on it, and replace it with a new one if it has scored or picked up, or if there are any cracks.

13 Check that the transmission shaft

bearings in each crankcase half rotate freely and smoothly and are tight in the casing **(see illustrations)**. Remove the old bearings and fit new ones if necessary (see *Tools and Workshop Tips* in the Reference Section). Each bearing in the left-hand half is held by a screw. On installation apply a suitable non-permanent thread locking compound to the screws and tighten them to the specified torque setting. If a bearing is sealed on one side that side must face out from the crankcase.

14 Discard all the circlips as new ones must be used.

Input shaft reassembly

15 During reassembly, apply molybdenum disulphide oil (a 50/50 mixture of molybdenum disulphide grease and clean engine oil) to the mating surfaces of the shaft, pinions and bearings. When installing the circlips, do not expand the ends any further than is necessary and locate them as shown, i.e. against a spline wall, not in the spline trenches. Install the stamped circlips so that their chamfered side faces the pinion it secures, i.e. so that its sharp edge faces the direction of thrust load (see *correct fitting of a stamped circlip* illustration in Tools and Workshop Tips of the Reference section). Use new needle bearings and do not expand their ends any more than necessary when installing them.

16 Slide the 5th gear pinion onto the left-hand end of the shaft with its dogs facing away from the integral 1st gear **(see illustration)**. Slide the thrust washer onto the shaft then fit the

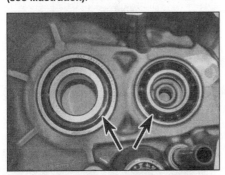

32.13a Check the shaft bearings (arrowed) . . .

32.13b . . . in each crankcase half

32.16a Slide the 5th gear pinion onto the shaft . . .

32.16b ... followed by the thrust washer ...

32.16c ... then fit the circlip

32.16d ... locating it in its groove

circlip, making sure that it locates correctly in its groove **(see illustrations)**.

17 Slide the combined 3rd/4th gear pinion onto the shaft, so that the smaller (3rd gear) pinion faces the 5th gear pinion dogs **(see illustration)**.

Fit the circlip, making sure that it locates correctly in its groove **(see illustrations)**.

18 Slide the splined washer onto the shaft **(see illustration)**. Slide the 6th gear pinion needle bearing onto the shaft, then slide the

pinion onto the bearing, with its dogs facing the 4th gear pinion **(see illustrations)**. Slide the splined washer onto the shaft then fit the circlip, making sure that it locates correctly in its groove **(see illustrations)**.

32.17a Slide the 3rd/4th gear pinion onto the shaft ...

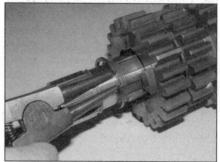

32.17b ... then fit the circlip ...

32.17c ... locating it in its groove

32.18a Slide the splined washer onto the shaft ...

32.18b ... then fit the needle bearing

32.18c Slide the 6th gear pinion onto the shaft ...

32.18d ... followed by the thrust washer ...

32.18e ... then fit the circlip ...

32.18f ... locating it in its groove

32.19 Slide the 2nd gear pinion onto the shaft

32.20 The assembled input shaft

32.28a Slide the 2nd gear pinion onto the shaft . . .

19 Slide the 2nd gear pinion onto the shaft **(see illustration)**.
20 Check that all components have been correctly installed **(see illustration)**.

Output shaft disassembly

21 Remove the thrust washer from the right-hand end of the shaft **(see illustration 32.33c)**.
22 Slide the 1st gear pinion off the shaft **(see illustration 32.33b)**. Spread the 1st gear pinion needle bearing then slide it off the shaft **(see illustration 32.33a)**, followed by the thrust washer and the 5th gear pinion **(see illustrations 32.32b and a)**.
23 Remove the circlip securing the 3rd gear pinion, then slide the splined washer, the 3rd gear pinion, the 4th gear pinion, their needle bearings, and the splined washer off the shaft **(see illustrations 32.31b and a and 32.30d, c, b and a)**.

24 Remove the circlip securing the 6th gear pinion, then slide the pinion off the shaft **(see illustrations 32.29b and a)**.
25 Remove the circlip securing the 2nd pinion, then slide the thrust washer and the pinion off the shaft **(see illustrations 32.28c, b and a)**.

Output shaft inspection

26 Refer to Steps 7 to 14 above.

Output shaft reassembly

27 During reassembly, apply molybdenum disulphide oil (a 50/50 mixture of molybdenum disulphide grease and clean engine oil) to the mating surfaces of the shaft, pinions and bushes. When installing the circlips, do not expand the ends any further than is necessary and locate them as shown, i.e. against a spline wall, not in the spline trenches. Install

the stamped circlips so that their chamfered side faces the pinion it secures, i.e. so that its sharp edge faces the direction of thrust load (see *correct fitting of a stamped circlip* illustration in Tools and Workshop Tips of the Reference section). Use new needle bearings and do not expand their ends any more than necessary when installing them.
28 Slide the 2nd gear pinion onto the shaft with its dog holes facing away from the shaft shoulder **(see illustration)**. Slide the thrust washer onto the shaft **(see illustration)**. Secure them in place with the circlip, making sure it is properly seated in its groove **(see illustrations)**.
29 Slide the 6th gear pinion onto the shaft with its selector fork groove facing away from the 2nd gear pinion, and secure it in place with the circlip, making sure it is properly seated in its groove **(see illustrations)**.

32.28b . . . followed by the thrust washer . . .

32.28c . . . then fit the circlip . . .

32.28d . . . locating it in its groove

32.29a Slide the 6th gear pinion onto the shaft . . .

32.29b . . . then fit the circlip . . .

32.29c . . . locating it in its groove

32.30a Slide the splined washer onto the shaft . . .

32.30b . . . then fit the needle bearings

32.30c Slide the 4th gear pinion onto its bearing . . .

30 Slide the splined thrust washer onto the shaft, followed by the 4th and 3rd gear pinion needle bearings **(see illustrations)**. Now slide the 4th and 3rd gear pinions onto the bearings **(see illustrations)**.

31 Slide the splined washer onto the shaft,

then fit the circlip, making sure it is properly seated in its groove **(see illustrations)**.

32 Slide the 5th gear pinion onto the shaft with its selector fork groove facing the 3rd gear pinion, followed by the thrust washer **(see illustrations)**.

33 Slide the 1st gear pinion needle bearing onto the shaft then slide the pinion, with the dog holes facing the 5th gear pinion, onto the bearing **(see illustrations)**. Slide the thrust washer against the 1st gear pinion **(see illustration)**.

32.30d . . . followed by the 3rd gear pinion

32.31a Slide the splined washer onto the shaft . . .

32.31b . . . then fit the circlip . . .

32.31c . . . locating it in its groove

32.32a Slide the 5th gear pinion onto the shaft . . .

32.32b . . . followed by the thrust washer

32.33a Fit the 1st gear pinion needle bearing . . .

32.33b . . . then fit the pinion onto the bearing

32.33c Slide the thrust washer against the pinion

32.34 The assembled output shaft

34 Check that all components have been correctly installed **(see illustration).**

33 Running-in procedure

1 Make sure the engine oil and coolant levels are correct (see *Daily (pre-ride) checks*). Make sure there is fuel in the tank.
2 Disconnect the wiring connector from each injector. Turn the ignition ON. If necessary turn the engine kill switch to the ON position and place the transmission in neutral. Turn the

engine over on the starter motor until the oil pressure warning light goes out.
3 Start the engine in the normal way – set the fast idle lever enough to encourage the bike to start, but not so much as to allow it to race. Allow the engine to run at a moderately fast idle until it reaches operating temperature. Check carefully that there are no oil or coolant leaks.

 Warning: If the oil pressure warning light doesn't go off, or it comes on while the engine is running, stop the engine immediately.

4 Check the oil and coolant levels, then perform an oil pressure check (see Chapter 1). Also check throttle body synchronisation and idle speed (see Chapter 1).
5 Make sure the transmission and controls, especially the brakes, function properly before road testing the machine.
6 If a lubrication failure is suspected, stop the engine immediately and try to find the cause. If an engine is run without oil, even for a short period of time, severe damage will occur.

7 Treat the machine gently for the first few miles to make sure oil has circulated throughout the engine and any new parts installed have started to seat.
8 Even greater care is necessary if new cylinder/piston components or a new crankshaft have been fitted. This means greater use of the transmission and a restraining hand on the throttle until at least 625 miles (1000 km) have been covered. There's no point in keeping to any set speed limit – the main idea is to keep from labouring the engine and to gradually increase performance up to the 625 mile (1000 km) mark. Experience is the best guide, since it's easy to tell when an engine is running freely. The following maximum engine speed limitations, which Aprilia provide for new motorcycles, can be used as a guide.
9 Upon completion of the road test, and after the engine has cooled down completely, recheck the valve clearances (see Chapter 1) and check the engine oil and coolant levels (see *Daily (pre-ride) checks*).

Up to 625 miles (1000 km)	6000 rpm max	Vary throttle position/speed
625 to 950 miles (1000 to 1500 km)	7500 rpm max	Vary throttle position/speed. Use full throttle for short bursts
Over 950 miles (1500 km)	10,500 rpm max	Do not exceed tachometer red line

Notes

Chapter 3
Cooling system

Contents

Degrees of difficulty

Easy, suitable for novice with little experience	Fairly easy, suitable for beginner with some experience	Fairly difficult, suitable for competent DIY mechanic	Difficult, suitable for experienced DIY mechanic	Very difficult, suitable for expert DIY or professional

Specifications

Coolant
Mixture type and capacity .... see Chapter 1

Cooling fan switch
Switch closes (fan ON) .... approx. 100°C
Switch opens (fan OFF) .... approx. 85°C

Engine coolant temperature (ECT) sensors
Resistance@ 20°C .... 1960 to 2940 ohms
Resistance@ 40°C .... 800 to 1200 ohms
Resistance @ 60°C .... 400 to 700 ohms
Resistance @ 80°C .... 200 to 400 ohms
Resistance @ 100°C .... 120 to 250 ohms

Thermostat
Opening temperature .... 63 to 67°C
Fully open .... 80°C
Valve
   Actual lift .... 7 mm (min)
   Depth when measured from top .... 39 mm

Water pump
Pump drive shaft bore diameter in clutch cover (max) .... 10.10 mm
Pump drive shaft bore diameter in driven gear (max) .... 10.20 mm
Drive pin slot width in driven gear (max) .... 3.70 mm

Torque settings
Clutch diaphragm plate nut .... 30 Nm
Clutch inner cover bolts
   6 mm bolts .... 11 Nm
   8 mm bolts .... 19 Nm
Clutch outer cover bolts .... 5 Nm
Engine coolant temperature (ECT) sensors .... 30 Nm
Fan switch .... 30 Nm
Water pump cover bolts .... 11 Nm

1 General information

The cooling system uses a water/antifreeze coolant to carry away excess heat from the engine and maintain as constant a temperature as possible. The cylinders are surrounded by a water jacket from which the heated coolant is circulated by thermo-syphonic action in conjunction with a water pump, which is driven by gear off the front balancer shaft. The hot coolant passes from the engine via a three-way manifold and into the radiators, then onto the water pump and back to the engine where the cycle is repeated.

A thermostat is fitted in the system to prevent the coolant flowing through the radiators when the engine is cold, therefore accelerating the speed at which the engine reaches normal operating temperature. Two coolant temperature sensors are fitted, one in each cylinder head. A cooling fan fitted to the back of each radiator aids cooling in extreme conditions by drawing extra air through. A cooling fan thermal switch in the three-way manifold opens and closes the circuit to the cooling fans at pre-set temperatures.

The complete cooling system is partially sealed and pressurised. By pressurising the coolant the boiling point is raised, preventing premature boiling in adverse conditions. The overflow pipe from the system is connected to a reservoir into which excess coolant is expelled under pressure. The discharged coolant automatically returns to the radiator by the vacuum created when the engine cools.

 Warning: Do not remove the cap from the filler neck when the engine is hot. Scalding hot coolant and steam may be blown out under pressure, which could cause serious injury. When the engine has cooled, place a thick rag, like a towel, over the cap; slowly rotate the cap anti-clockwise and allow any residual pressure to escape. When the steam has stopped escaping, remove the cap.

Caution: Do not allow antifreeze to come in contact with your skin or painted surfaces

of the motorcycle. Rinse off any spills immediately with plenty of water. Antifreeze is highly toxic if ingested. Never leave antifreeze lying around in an open container or in puddles on the floor; children and pets are attracted by its sweet smell and may drink it. Check with the local authorities about disposing of used antifreeze. Many communities will have collection centres which will see that antifreeze is disposed of safely.

Caution: At all times use the specified type of antifreeze, and always mix it with distilled water in the correct proportion. The antifreeze contains corrosion inhibitors which are essential to avoid damage to the cooling system. A lack of these inhibitors could lead to a build-up of corrosion which would block the coolant passages, resulting in overheating and severe engine damage. Distilled water must be used as opposed to tap water to avoid a build-up of scale which would also block the passages.

2 Cooling fans, fan switch and relay

1 If the engine is overheating and neither cooling fan is coming on, first check the cooling fan circuit fuse (C) (see Chapter 9). If the fuse is blown, check the fan circuit for a short to earth (see the wiring diagrams at the end of Chapter 9). If the fuse is good, check the fan switch and relay as described below before checking the fans themselves. If only one fan is coming on the fault will be confined to the fan motor itself or the wiring.

Cooling fan

Check

2 To access the fan wiring connector, remove the relevant fairing side panel (see Chapter 8). Trace the wiring from the fan and disconnect it at the connector **(see illustration)**.
3 Using a 12 volt battery and two jumper wires with suitable connectors, connect the battery positive (+) lead to the yellow/black wire terminal on the fan side of the wiring connector,

and the battery negative (–) lead to the blue wire terminal. Once connected the fan should operate. If it doesn't, and the wiring and terminals between the connector and the motor are all good, then the fan motor is faulty – replace the fan with a new one. If it does come on, check the yellow/black wire and terminals between the fan connector and the relay, and the blue wire to earth, referring to the wiring diagram for your model at the end of Chapter 9.

Replacement

 Warning: The engine must be completely cool before carrying out this procedure.

4 Remove the radiators (see Section 5).
5 Unscrew the bolts securing the fan to the radiator and remove it **(see illustration)**. Note how the nuts are captive in the mounting brackets. Check the condition of the rubber grommet for the locating peg and replace it with a new one if it is damaged, deformed or deteriorated.
6 Installation is the reverse of removal.

Fan switch

Check

7 Raise the fuel tank (see Chapter 4).
8 Disconnect the wiring connectors from the fan switch, noting which fits where **(see illustration)**. Check that there is battery voltage at the yellow/grey wire terminal on the loom side of the connector with the ignition ON. If not, check the wiring for continuity and the connections as described in Chapter 9, following the relevant Wiring Diagram. Turn the ignition OFF.
9 If the voltage is good, connect across the fan switch wiring connector terminals using a jumper wire. Turn the ignition switch ON. If the fans come on the fan switch is proven defective and must be replaced with a new one. If the fans do not come on, test the fan motor itself (see above). If the fan is good, check for continuity to earth in the blue wire from the fan switch connector.
10 If the fans are on the whole time, disconnect the switch wiring connectors, noting which fits where **(see illustration 2.8)**. The fan should stop. If it does, the switch is defective and must be replaced with a new one.
11 If the fan works but is suspected of

2.2 Left-hand fan motor wiring connector

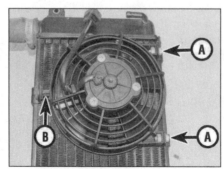

2.5 Unscrew the bolts (A), and note how the peg (B) locates

2.8 Disconnect the fan switch wiring connectors (arrowed)

cutting in at the wrong temperature, a more comprehensive test of the switch can be made as follows.

12 Remove the switch (see Steps 14 and 15). Fill a small heatproof container with coolant and place it on a stove. Connect the positive (+) probe of an ohmmeter or continuity tester to one terminal on the switch and the negative (–) probe to the other terminal, and using some wire or other support suspend the switch in the coolant so that just the sensing portion and the threads are submerged **(see illustration)**. Also place a thermometer capable of reading temperatures up to 150°C in the coolant so that its bulb is close to the switch. **Note:** *None of the components should be allowed to directly touch the container.*

13 Initially the meter reading should be very high or show no continuity indicating that the switch is open (OFF). Heat the coolant, stirring it gently.

 Warning: This must be done very carefully to avoid the risk of personal injury.

When the temperature reaches around 100°C the meter reading should drop to around zero ohms or show continuity, indicating that the switch has closed (ON). Now turn the heat off. As the temperature falls to around 85°C the meter reading should again show infinite (very high) resistance or no continuity, indicating that the switch has opened (OFF). If the meter readings obtained are different, or they are obtained at different temperatures, then the switch is faulty and must be replaced with a new one. On completion, fit the switch as described in Steps 16 and 17.

Replacement

 Warning: The engine must be completely cool before carrying out this procedure.

14 Place a rag around and below the three-way manifold to catch any spilt coolant. Alternatively drain the cooling system (see Chapter 1).

15 Disconnect the wiring connectors from the fan switch, noting which fits where **(see illustration 2.8)**. Unscrew the switch and withdraw it from the manifold. Discard the washer as a new one should be used.

16 Apply a suitable thread sealant (such as Loctite 572) to the threads of the switch. Install the switch using a new sealing washer and tighten it to the torque setting specified at the beginning of the Chapter.

17 Reconnect the switch wiring and top up (if necessary) or refill the cooling system (see Chapter 1).

Relay

18 Unclip the relay box lid (the box is on the left-hand end of the instrument cluster) and remove the cooling fan relay – identify it from the label on the box **(see illustrations)**.

19 Set a multimeter to the ohms x 1 scale and connect it across the relay's 30 and 87 terminals **(see illustration)**. Using a fully-charged 12 volt battery and two insulated

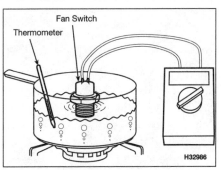

2.12 Cooling fan switch test set-up

2.18b . . . then unclip the lid . . .

jumper wires, connect the positive (+) terminal of the battery to the 85 terminal on the relay, and the negative (-) terminal of the battery to the 86 terminal on the relay. At this point the relay should be heard to click and the multimeter read 0 ohms (continuity). If this is the case the relay is proved good. If the relay does not click when battery voltage is applied and indicates no continuity (infinite resistance) across its terminals, it is faulty and must be replaced with a new one.

20 If the relay is good, check for battery voltage at the green wire terminal on the relay connector with the ignition ON. If no voltage is

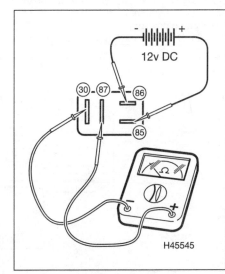

2.19 Relay test set-up

2.18a Locate the relay box (arrowed) . . .

2.18c . . . and remove the fan relay

present check the fuse (D), and the wiring between (see Chapter 9). If voltage is present, check the yellow/grey wire between the relay and the switch, and the switch itself (see above). Similarly check for voltage at the red/brown wire terminal on the relay connector with the ignition ON. If no voltage is present check the fuse (C) and the wiring to the ignition switch (see Chapter 9). If voltage is present, check the yellow/black wire between the relay and the fans, and the fans themselves (see above).

3 Engine coolant temperature (ECT) sensors

1 An engine coolant temperature (ECT) sensor is mounted in the side of each cylinder head. The sensor in the right-hand side of the front head transmits to the temperature display on the instrument cluster. The sensor in the left-hand side of the rear head transmits to the engine control unit (ECU).

Check

2 To check the sensor resistance remove it from the cylinder (see Steps 5 to 7).

3 Fill a small heatproof container with coolant and place it on a stove. Using an ohmmeter set initially to the K-ohms scale, connect the meter probes to the sensor terminals, and using some wire or other support, suspend the sensor in the coolant so that just the sensing portion and the threads are submerged **(see illustration 2.12)**. Also place a thermometer capable of reading temperatures up to 150ºC in the coolant so that its bulb is close to the switch. **Note:** *None of the components should be allowed to touch the container directly.*

4 Check the meter reading and compare the result with the specifications at the beginning of this Chapter, then heat the coolant slowly, stirring it gently.

 Warning: This must be done very carefully to avoid the risk of personal injury.

As the temperature of the coolant rises, the sensor resistance should fall (depending on your meter you may need to change scale to get an accurate reading). Check that the specified resistance is obtained at the correct temperature (see Specifications at the beginning of this Chapter). If the readings obtained are widely different, or are obtained at different temperatures, the sensor is faulty and must be replaced with a new one. If the readings are as specified for the front head sensor, the fault could lie in the coolant temperature display circuit in the instrument cluster (see Chapter 9). Also check the wiring to and from the sensors and the connectors, using the wiring diagrams at the end of Chapter 9.

Removal and installation

 Warning: The engine must be completely cool before carrying out this procedure.
Caution: Handle the sensor with care as it could be damaged if dropped.

5 Place a rag around and below the sensor to catch any spilt coolant. Alternatively drain the cooling system (see Chapter 1).

6 Raise the fuel tank (see Chapter 4).

7 Disconnect the wiring connector from the sensor **(see illustration)**. Unscrew the sensor and withdraw it from the head. Discard the washer as a new one should be used.

8 Apply a suitable thread sealant (such as Loctite 574) to the threads of the sensor. Install the sensor using a new sealing washer and tighten it to the torque setting specified at the beginning of the Chapter.

9 Reconnect the switch wiring and lower the

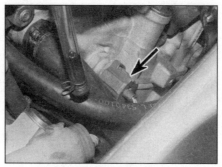

3.7 Coolant temperature sensor wiring connector (arrowed)

fuel tank (see Chapter 4). Top up (if necessary) or refill the cooling system (see Chapter 1).

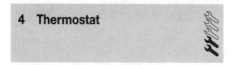
4 Thermostat

Removal

 Warning: The engine must be completely cool before carrying out this procedure.
Note: *Where the clip-type (as opposed to the screw-type) hose clamps are used on the coolant hoses, a flat-bladed screwdriver is the best way of releasing them, but note that to rejoin this type of clamp a special pair of pliers makes the job much easier. Also note that these clamps should only be used once, and so new ones should be obtained for the installation procedure.*

1 The thermostat is automatic in operation and should give many years service without requiring attention. In the event of a failure, the valve will probably jam open, in which case the engine will take much longer than normal to warm up. Conversely, if the valve jams shut, the coolant will be unable to circulate and the engine will overheat. Neither condition is acceptable, and the fault must be investigated promptly.

2 Drain the cooling system (see Chapter 1).

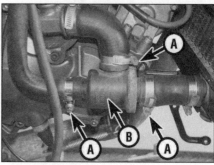

4.3 Release the clamps (A) and detach the hoses to free the thermostat (B)

The thermostat housing is on the right-hand side of the engine behind the radiator.

3 Release the clamps securing the hoses to the thermostat **(see illustration)**. Detach the hoses and remove the thermostat.

Check

4 Examine the thermostat visually before carrying out the test. If it remains in the open position at room temperature, it should be replaced with a new one. Check the wax expansion unit for cracks and other damage.

5 Suspend the thermostat by a piece of wire in a container of coolant water. Place a thermometer capable of reading temperatures up to 150°C in the coolant so that the bulb is close to the thermostat **(see illustration)**. Heat the coolant, noting the temperature when the thermostat opens, and compare the result with the specifications given at the beginning of the Chapter.

6 Also check the amount the valve opens after it has been heated for a few minutes and compare the measurement to the specifications – measure the depth of the valve in the body from the top as shown, using a Vernier caliper **(see illustration)**. If the readings obtained differ from those given, or if the thermostat doesn't open, the thermostat is faulty and must be replaced with a new one.

Installation

7 Attach the hoses to the thermostat and

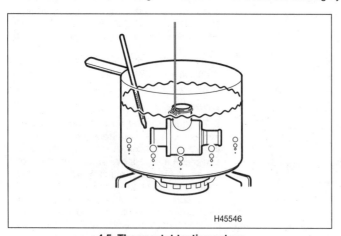

4.5 Thermostat testing set-up

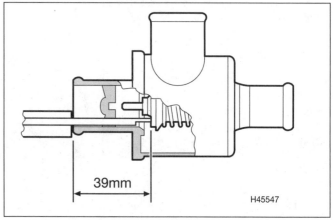

39mm

4.6 Measure the amount the thermostat has opened as shown

5.2a Undo the screw (arrowed) at the bottom . . .

5.2b . . . and the two screws (arrowed) at the top and remove the shroud

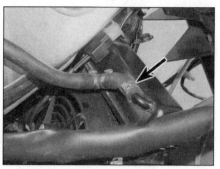

5.4a Disconnect the top . . .

5.4b . . . and bottom hoses (arrowed) from the right-hand radiator . . .

5.4c . . . and the bottom hose (arrowed) from the left-hand radiator

5.5 Radiator mounting bolt (arrowed)

secure them with their clamps, using new ones where necessary (see **Note** at start of Section).

8 Refill the cooling system (see Chapter 1).

5 Radiators

Removal

> ⚠️ **Warning: The engine must be completely cool before carrying out this procedure.**

Note: *Where the clip-type (as opposed to the screw-type) hose clamps are used on the coolant hoses, a flat-bladed screwdriver is the best way of releasing them, but note that to rejoin this type of clamp a special pair of pliers makes the job much easier. Also note that these clamps should only be used once, and so new ones should be obtained for the installation procedure.*

1 Drain the cooling system (see Chapter 1).

2 Undo the three screws securing the central shroud and manoeuvre it out **(see illustrations)**.

3 Refer to Section 2, Step 2 and disconnect the cooling fan wiring connector(s).

4 Release the clamps securing the hoses to the radiator and detach them, noting which fits where – you may find it easier to disconnect the top interconnecting hose as you are removing the radiator **(see**

illustrations). Keep the overflow hose to the reservoir above the level of the reservoir or it will drain itself.

5 Unscrew the top mounting bolt, then tip the radiator forwards and lift it to release the bottom pegs from the grommets in the bracket **(see illustration)**.

6 If necessary, remove the cooling fan from the radiator (see Section 2). Check the radiator for signs of damage and clear any dirt or debris that might obstruct air flow and inhibit cooling. If the radiator fins are badly damaged or broken the radiator must be replaced with a new one. Also check the rubber mounting grommets, and replace them with new ones if they are damaged deformed or deteriorated, noting the spacers that fit inside them.

Installation

7 Installation is the reverse of removal, noting the following.

● Make sure the rubber grommets are correctly located in their mounts.

● Make sure that the spacers are fitted in the grommets.

● Make sure that the wiring is correctly routed and connected.

● Ensure the coolant hoses are in good condition (see Chapter 1), and are securely retained by their clamps, using new ones if necessary.

● On completion refill the cooling system as described in Chapter 1.

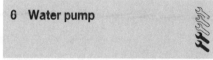

6 Water pump

Check

1 The water pump is located on the lower right-hand side of the engine at the front. Visually check the area around the pump cover for signs of leakage.

2 To prevent leakage of coolant from the cooling system to the lubrication system and vice versa, two seals are fitted on the pump shaft. Below the pump housing in the clutch cover there is a drain hole **(see illustration)**. If either seal fails, the drain allows the coolant or oil to escape and prevents them mixing. If the

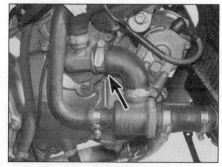

6.2 Check the drain hole (arrowed) for signs of leakage

6.4a Disconnect the wiring connector (arrowed) . . .

6.4b . . . then unscrew the bolts (arrowed) and remove the bracket

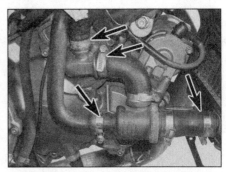

6.5 Release the clamps (arrowed) and detach the hoses from the cover

oil and coolant mix a white emulsion is produced. The seal on the water pump side is of the mechanical type which bears on the rear face of the impeller. The second seal, which is mounted behind the mechanical seal is of the normal feathered lip type. Both seals are available separately. If on inspection there is evidence of leakage from the drain hole, remove the water pump and replace both seals with new ones.

Removal

Note: *Where the clip-type (as opposed to the*

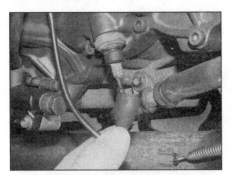

6.7 Disconnect the wire from the oil pressure switch

screw-type) hose clamps are used on the coolant hoses, a flat-bladed screwdriver is the best way of releasing them, but note that to rejoin this type of clamp a special pair of pliers makes the job much easier. Also note that these clamps should only be used once, and so new ones should be obtained for the installation procedure.

3 Drain the engine oil, and the coolant (see Chapter 1). Remove the coolant reservoir (see Section 8).

4 Remove the rear brake pedal – there is no need to detach the master cylinder pushrod, but take care when drawing it out of the cylinder (see Chapter 6). Displace the rear brake master cylinder and reservoir from the right-hand side of the engine and secure it clear, making sure no strain is placed on the hoses and the reservoir is kept upright (see Chapter 7). Trace the wiring from the rear brake switch and disconnect it at the connector – feed the wiring down to the switch, noting its routing **(see illustration)**. Unscrew the bolts securing the pedal bracket and remove it along with the switch **(see illustration)**.

5 Remove the starter motor (see Chapter 9). Remove the thermostat along with the large

bore hoses that attach to it, detaching the hoses from the water pump cover and the right-hand radiator **(see illustration)**. Also detach the filler neck hose from the pump cover. Secure the small-bore thermostat hose and the filler neck hose clear of the cover.

6 Release the clamp securing the vacuum hose to the clutch outer cover and detach the hose.

7 Pull the rubber boot off the oil pressure switch, then pull the wiring connector off the terminal **(see illustration)**.

8 Unscrew the clutch outer cover bolts and remove the cover **(see illustration)**.

9 Release the clutch diaphragm tabs from the raised sections around the bolt holes and rotate the clutch so the tabs are clear – this will prevent the diaphragm catching and tearing if the clutch turns while unscrewing the diaphragm plate nut. Counter-hold the clutch using a hex key in the centre of the shaft and unscrew the nut **(see illustration)**. Remove the outer washer, outer diaphragm plate, diaphragm, inner plate and inner washer, noting which way round they all fit **(see illustrations 6.33e, d, c, b and a)**.

10 Unscrew the water pump cover bolts, noting which fits where, and remove the cover

6.8 Clutch outer cover bolts (arrowed)

6.9 Offset the diaphragm tabs, then hold the hex and unscrew the nut

6.10 Unscrew the bolts (arrowed) and remove the pump cover

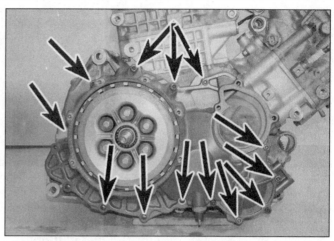

6.11 Unscrew the bolts (arrowed) and remove the clutch cover

(see illustration). Remove the O-ring and discard it as a new one must be used. Note the sealing washer on the bottom bolt – this must also be replaced with a new one.

11 Unscrew the remaining clutch inner cover bolts, then draw the cover off the engine (see illustration). Remove the gasket and discard it. Remove the dowels if they are loose. Note the sealing washer on the bolt to the rear of the oil pressure switch – a new one must be used on installation. Note the master cylinder reservoir bracket secured by the two bottom bolts.

12 The water pump and its seals are all housed in the clutch inner cover.

Inspection

13 Check for corrosion or a build-up of scale in the pump cover and clean it or replace it with a new one if necessary.

14 Check the impeller fins for signs of damage and replace it with a new one if necessary (see Step 17).

15 Check the driven gear on the inside of the cover and the idle gear on the crankcase, looking for broken or worn teeth. To remove the driven gear see Step 18). To remove the idle gear and to access the pump drive gear

refer to Chapter 2 and first remove the primary drive and balancer shaft gears.

16 If there was any evidence of leakage (see Step 2), disassemble the pump and replace the seals with new ones (see below).

Disassembly

17 Grasp the driven gear using a cloth and unscrew the impeller from the shaft (see illustration).

18 Press down on the top of the shaft with your thumbs and lift the driven gear with your fingers to release it from the drive pin (see illustration). Withdraw the pin from the shaft and remove the washer (see illustration 6.27b and a). Make sure the pin is a good fit in its slot in the gear. Measure the width of the slot and compare the result to the limit specified at the beginning of the Chapter. Replace the gear with a new one if necessary.

19 Draw the shaft out of the seals from the inner (gear) side.

20 Check the shaft for signs of wear, and check the shaft bore in the cover and the driven gear. Measure the internal diameters of the bores in the cover and gear and compare the results to the limits specified at the beginning of the Chapter.

Seal renewal

21 Disassemble the pump (see Steps 17 to 19).

22 Using a suitably sized drift inserted first in one of the holes on the inside of the cover, then in the other hole, drive the seals out of the cover one tap at a time so they are driven out squarely (see illustration). Discard the seals as new ones must be used.

23 Drive the new oil seal in from the outside using a suitable socket, making sure its marked side faces out towards the mechanical seal and impeller. Drive it all the way in until it seats.

24 Drive the new mechanical seal into the housing from the outside using a suitable socket or tube that bears only on the outer rim of the seal body, until the rim seats on the hub.

25 Reassemble the pump (see Steps 26 to 29).

Reassembly

26 Thread the impeller onto the outer end of the shaft. Slide the shaft through the seals from the outside of the cover.

27 Fit the washer onto the shaft and

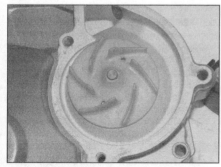

6.17 The impeller threads onto the end of the shaft

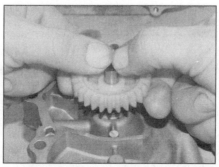

6.18 Release the gear from the drive pin as described

6.22 Drive the seals out using a punch inserted in the holes (arrowed)

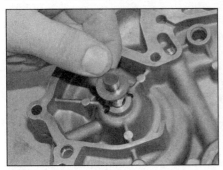

6.27a Fit the washer . . .

6.27b . . . and the drive pin . . .

6.28 . . . then press the gear onto the pin until the pin clicks into the slot

slide the drive pin into its hole (see illustrations).

28 Support the threaded end of the shaft on something solid and press the driven gear onto the drive pin, making sure it is felt to click into place (see illustration).

29 Grasp the driven gear using a cloth and tighten the impeller.

Installation

30 If removed, fit the dowels into the crankcase. Lubricate the ends of the crankshaft, balancer shaft and water pump shaft with molybdenum oil (a 50/50 mixture of molybdenum grease and engine oil). Lay a new gasket onto the crankcase, locating it over the dowels (see illustration).

31 Install the clutch cover, making sure the crankshaft and balancer shaft ends locate in their end bearings, and the water pump shaft locates in its bore and the driven gear engages correctly with the idle gear – turn the impeller as required until they engage (see illustrations).

32 Fit the inner cover bolts, not forgetting the brake master cylinder bracket and the pedal bracket, and using a new sealing washer on the bolt to the rear of the oil pressure switch, and tighten them finger-tight (see illustrations and 6.4b). Fit a new O-ring into the groove in the water pump cover, then install the cover and tighten the bolts finger-tight, using a new sealing washer on the bottom bolt (see illustrations). Now tighten

6.30 Fit the dowels (arrowed) then lay a new gasket over them

6.31a Install the cover . . .

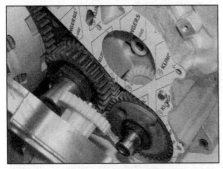

6.31b . . . making sure everything locates and engages correctly

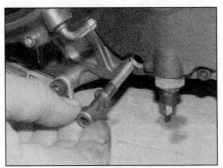

6.32a Use a new sealing washer on this bolt

6.32b Fit the master cylinder bracket with the bottom bolts

6.32c Fit a new O-ring into the groove . . .

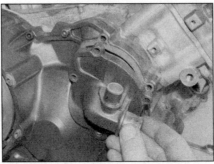

6.32d . . . then install the cover

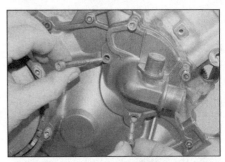

6.32e The long bolt goes in the rear hole – use a new sealing washer on the bottom (drain) bolt

6.33a Fit the inner washer . . .

6.33b . . . and the inner diaphragm plate . . .

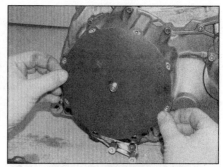

6.33c . . . then fit the diaphragm, offsetting the tabs as described

6.33d Fit the outer diaphragm plate . . .

6.33e . . . and the outer washer . . .

6.33f . . . then fit the nut . . .

6.33g . . . and tighten it as described

6.33h Locate the tabs over the raised sections . . .

6.34 . . . then fit the cover

all the bolts evenly and in a criss-cross pattern to the torque setting specified at the beginning of the Chapter.

33 Slide the inner washer and diaphragm plate onto the end of the shaft, with the curved rim of the plate located on the pressure plate **(see illustrations)**. Fit the diaphragm onto the shaft, aligning it so the holed tabs in its rim are away from the raised ends of the cover bolt holes **(see illustration)**. Fit the outer diaphragm plate with its curved rim facing away from the diaphragm **(see illustration)**. Fit the outer washer **(see illustration)**. Apply a suitable thread locking compound (such as Loctite 648) to the diaphragm nut threads and tighten it to the specified torque setting, counter-holding the shaft using a hex key located in the end as on removal **(see illustrations)**. Turn the clutch to align the holed tabs in its rim with the cover

bolt holes, then locate the holes over the raised sections **(see illustration)**.

34 Fit the outer cover and tighten its bolts in a criss-cross sequence to the specified torque setting **(see illustration)**.

35 Install all remaining components (see Steps 7 to 4).

36 Refill the engine with oil and coolant (see Chapter 1).

7 Coolant hoses

Removal

Note: Where the clip-type (as opposed to the screw-type) hose clamps are used on the coolant hoses, a flat-bladed screwdriver is the

best way of releasing them, but note that to rejoin this type of clamp a special pair of pliers makes the job much easier. Also note that these clamps should only be used once, and so new ones should be obtained for the installation procedure.

1 Before removing a hose, drain the coolant (see Chapter 1).

2 Use a screwdriver to slacken or release the hose clamps, then slide them back along the hose and clear of the union spigot. Note the orientation of the hose and clamp before removal – some have alignment marks which correspond to a mark on their union, and these ensure clamps are easy to access and shaped hoses do not become twisted.

Caution: The radiator unions are fragile. Do not use excessive force when attempting to remove the hoses.

3 If a hose proves stubborn, release it by

8.2a Release the clamp and detach the hose . . .

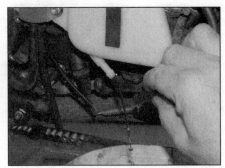

8.2b . . . and allow the coolant to drain

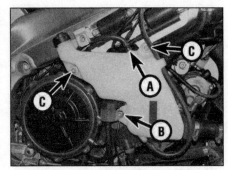

8.3 Detach the hose (A) and the master cylinder (B), then unscrew the bolts (C) and remove the reservoir

rotating it on its union before working it off. If all else fails, cut the hose with a sharp knife. Whilst this means replacing the hose, it is preferable to buying a new radiator.

Installation

4 Slide the clamps onto the hose and then work the hose on to its union.

HAYNES HINT *If the hose is difficult to push on its union, soften it by soaking it in very hot water, or alternatively a little soapy water on the union can be used as a lubricant.*

5 Rotate the hose on its union to settle it in position before sliding the clamps into place and securing them – make sure the hoses and clamps are aligned as noted on removal, where relevant.

8 Coolant reservoir

Removal

1 Remove the lower fairing (see Chapter 8). Remove the filler cap from the reservoir.
2 Position a suitable container beneath the reservoir on the right-hand side of the engine.

Release the clamp and detach the hose from the bottom of the reservoir and allow the coolant to completely drain **(see illustrations)**.
3 Release the clamp and detach the hose from the top of the reservoir **(see illustration)**.
4 Unscrew the bolt securing the rear brake master cylinder reservoir and support it upright.
5 Unscrew the remaining bolts securing the coolant reservoir and remove it.

Installation

6 Installation is the reverse of removal. Top up the coolant reservoir (see *Daily (pre-ride) checks*).

Chapter 4
Fuel, engine management and exhaust systems

Contents

Degrees of difficulty

Easy, suitable for novice with little experience	**Fairly easy,** suitable for beginner with some experience	**Fairly difficult,** suitable for competent DIY mechanic	**Difficult,** suitable for experienced DIY mechanic	**Very difficult,** suitable for expert DIY or professional

Specifications

Fuel
Grade
    European models .... Unleaded, minimum 95 RON (Research Octane Number)
    US models and Canada .... Unleaded, minimum 85 ((R+M) /2 method)
Fuel tank capacity
    Total (inc. reserve)
        1998 to 2000 models .... 20 litres
        2001 to 2003 models .... 18 litres
    Reserve .... 4.5 litres

Fuel supply system
Operating pressure .... 65.25 psi (4.5 Bar)
Test pressure .... 50.75 psi (3.5 Bar) minimum

Component test data

Camshaft position (CMP) sensor resistance	150 to 350 ohms
Crankshaft position (CKP) sensor resistance	150 to 350 ohms
Engine coolant temperature (ECT) sensor resistance	see Chapter 3
Injector resistance	11 to 17 ohms @ 20°C
Intake air pressure (IAP) sensor	
Input voltage (Test A)	4.5 to 5.5 V
Resistance	
Test B	10.8 13.2 K-ohms
Test C	10.0 to 13.0 K-ohms
Test D	3.6 to 4.4 K-ohms
Intake air temperature (IAT) sensor	
Resistance@ 20°C	1960 to 2940 ohms
Resistance@ 40°C	800 to 1200 ohms
Resistance @ 60°C	400 to 700 ohms
Resistance @ 80°C	200 to 400 ohms
Resistance @ 100°C	120 to 250 ohms
Throttle position (TP) sensor	
Input voltage (Test A)	4.5 to 5.5 V
Resistance	
Test B	2.87 5.33 K-ohms
Test C	
Closed	0.34 to 5.69 K-ohms
Open	2.87 to 8.41 K-ohms
Tip over (TO) sensor	
Upright	52 to 72 K-ohms
Angled	0 to 1 ohms

Torque settings

Cam chain top guide bolts	11 Nm
Camshaft holder bolt	11 Nm
Camshaft position sensor bolts	4 Nm
Exhaust system	
Header pipe nuts	25 Nm
Silencer mounting bolt nut	25 Nm
Fuel injector holder screws	9 Nm
Fuel pump mounting bolts	7 Nm
Fuel supply hose banjo bolts	22 Nm
Fuel tank mounting bolts	12 Nm

1 General information and precautions

General information

The fuel system consists of the fuel tank, incorporating the fuel pump and filter, the fuel hose to the fuel rail on the throttle bodies, the injectors that are located in the throttle bodies, the fuel pressure regulator and the return hose to the tank. All models have single valve throttle bodies with one injector per body.

The fuel pump is activated initially by the ignition switch and continues to deliver fuel so long as the engine is running. Fuel pressure is controlled within the system by a pressure regulator. In the event of the machine falling over, a tip-over sensor cuts power to the fuel pump, injectors and ignition coils.

The entire fuel injection system is controlled by the engine control unit (ECU) which monitors data sent from the various system sensors and adjusts fuel delivery to the engine accordingly. The ECU performs a check of the system and its components every time the ignition is switched on. If a fault develops in the injection system, the letters EFI illuminate on the instrument cluster LCD.

For running the engine from cold, a fast idle lever is incorporated in the left-handlebar switch housing and is connected to the throttle body assembly by a cable.

The exhaust system is a two-into-one design.

California models feature an EVAP emission control system that prevents fuel vapour escaping into the atmosphere from the fuel tank.

Precautions

 Warning: Petrol (gasoline) is extremely flammable, so take extra precautions when you work on any part of the fuel system. Don't smoke or allow open flames or bare light bulbs near the work area, and don't work in a garage where a natural gas-type appliance is present. If you spill any fuel on your skin, rinse it off immediately with soap and water. When you perform any kind of work on the fuel system, wear safety glasses and have a fire extinguisher suitable for a class B type fire (flammable liquids) on hand.

Always perform service procedures in a well-ventilated area to prevent a build-up of fumes.

Never work in a building containing a gas appliance with a pilot light, or any other form of naked flame. Ensure that there are no naked light bulbs or any sources of flame or sparks nearby.

Do not smoke (or allow anyone else to smoke) while in the vicinity of petrol (gasoline) or of components containing it. Remember the possible presence of vapour from these sources and move well clear before smoking.

Check all electrical equipment belonging to the house, garage or workshop where work is being undertaken (see the Safety first! section of this manual). Remember that certain electrical appliances such as drills, cutters etc. create sparks in the normal course of operation and must not be used near petrol (gasoline) or any component containing it. Again, remember the possible presence of fumes before using electrical equipment.

Always mop up any spilt fuel and safely dispose of the rag used.

2.2 Unscrew the bolts (arrowed) . . .

2.3 . . . then raise the front of the tank and support it with the prop

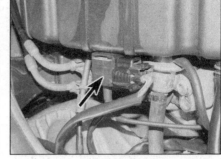

2.4 Displace the IAP sensor (arrowed) from its mount

Any stored fuel that is drained off during servicing work must be kept in sealed containers that are suitable for holding petrol (gasoline), and clearly marked as such; the containers themselves should be kept in a safe place. Note that this last point applies equally to the fuel tank if it is removed from the machine; also remember to keep its filler cap closed at all times.

Read the Safety first! section of this manual carefully before starting work.

Owners of machines used in the US, particularly California, should note that their machines must comply at all times with Federal or State legislation governing the permissible levels of noise and of pollutants such as unburnt hydrocarbons, carbon monoxide etc. that can be emitted by those machines. All vehicles offered for sale must comply with legislation in force at the date of manufacture and must not subsequently be altered in any way which will affect their emission of noise or of pollutants.

In practice, this means that adjustments may not be made to any part of the fuel, ignition or exhaust systems by anyone who is not authorised or mechanically qualified to do so, or who does not have the tools, equipment and data necessary to properly carry out the task. Also if any part of these systems is to be renewed it must be renewed with only genuine Aprilia components or by components which are approved under the relevant legislation. The machine must never be used with any part of these systems removed, modified or damaged.

2 Fuel tank

Warning: Refer to the precautions given in Section 1 before starting work.

Raising the tank

1 Make sure the fuel cap is secure. Remove both seats and the side trim panels (see Chapter 8). Remove the fuel tank prop from the storage space underneath the seat.
2 Unscrew the bolts securing the front of the tank **(see illustration)**.
3 Raise the front of the tank and support it with the prop, locating it between the hole in the steering stem nut and one of the fuel tank mounting bolt holes **(see illustration)** – take care not lose or damage the collars or rubbers.

Draining the tank

Note: If you need to drain the tank try to do so when it is nearly empty to minimise the volume and weight.
4 Make sure the fuel cap is secure. Raise the fuel tank (see Steps 1 to 3). Displace the intake air pressure (IAP) sensor from the left-hand side of the air filter housing **(see illustration)**.
5 Obtain a container suitable for storing the amount of fuel that is in the tank, and place it on a support so that it is below the level of the

tank but close enough to the throttle bodies for the fuel return hose to be placed in it once detached.
6 Place some rag around the left-hand side of the throttle bodies and rear valve cover to catch any fuel spillage. Press in the clip on the fuel return hose coupling and pull the sections apart – the coupling is self-sealing so do not worry about fuel coming out at this stage **(see illustrations)**.
7 Release the clamp securing the fuel return hose to its union on the fuel pressure regulator – a flat-bladed screwdriver is the best way of releasing the clamp, but note that to rejoin this type of clamp a special pair of pliers makes the job much easier **(see illustration)**. Discard the clamp as a new one should be used. Pull the hose off its union and place the end in the container.
8 Reconnect the return hose coupling, making sure it clips together properly **(see illustration 2.6b)** – as the connection is made fuel will flow out of the end of the return hose and into the container. Allow the tank to fully drain, opening the filler cap to aid breathing and speed the process once you are certain the level is below the cap if the tank was quite full.
9 When the tank has drained, reconnect the return hose to the pressure regulator using a new clamp **(see illustration 2.7)**. Aprilia specify that you should not use any other type of clamp than that fitted as original equipment at the factory. Close the fuel cap. Remount the IAP sensor **(see illustration 2.4)**.

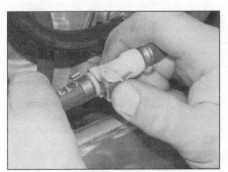

2.6a Press in the clip . . .

2.6b . . . and release the return hose coupling

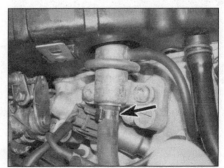

2.7 Release the clamp (arrowed) and detach the hose

2.10 Disconnect the pump assembly wiring connector

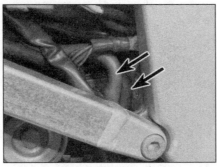

2.12 Detach the breather and overflow hoses (arrowed)

2.14a Unscrew the bolts (arrowed) . . .

2.14b . . . then lift the tank, turn it upside down and support it

Removal

10 Ensure the ignition switch is OFF. Raise the tank (see above). Disconnect the fuel pump assembly wiring connector **(see illustration)**.

11 Either drain the tank (see Steps 4 to 9), or alternatively obtain enough of the correct size copper sealing washers to make up the thickness of the banjo union so the bolt can be threaded back into the tank after detaching the hose. This must be done as the tank should not be stored upside down with fuel in it as it could leak out via the filler cap.

12 Pull the overflow and breather hoses off their unions **(see illustration)**.

13 Place a rag underneath the fuel return hose coupling to catch any residual fuel, then release the clip on the coupling and disconnect it – this coupling is self-sealing so

there should be little or no spillage **(see illustrations 2.6a and b)**.

14 Unscrew the bolts securing the rear tank bracket to the frame **(see illustration)**. Remove the prop, then lift the tank up, turn it upside down and support it – use plenty of rag to protect the tank from resting against other parts of the bike, but preferably get an assistant to hold it for you **(see illustration)**.

15 Slacken the supply hose banjo bolt and wait until any residual pressure has released, then unscrew the bolt and detach the hose, noting the sealing washers **(see illustration)**. If the tank has been drained remove it and store it on some rag. If the tank has fuel in it, fit your extra sealing washers onto the banjo bolt then thread it back into the tank and tighten it **(see illustration)**. Store the tank the correct way up on some rag and check for leakage past the washers – if there is any

tighten the bolt further, but not beyond the torque setting specified at the beginning of the Chapter. If it continues to leak, drain the tank.

Installation

16 Installation is the reverse of removal, noting the following:
● Refer to Chapter 1 and check the condition of the fuel system hoses before installing the tank.
● Align the fuel supply hose so its sits between the lugs on the tank **(see illustration 2.15a)**. Use new sealing washers on each side of the banjo union and tighten the bolt to the torque setting specified at the beginning of the Chapter **(see illustration)**.
● Make sure the return hose coupling is securely connected.
● Tighten the tank mounting bolts to the specified torque setting.
● Start the engine and check that there is no sign of fuel leakage.

Cleaning and repair

17 All repairs to the fuel tank should be carried out by a professional who has experience in this critical and potentially dangerous work. Even after cleaning and flushing the fuel system, explosive fumes can remain and ignite during repair of the tank.

18 If the fuel tank is removed from the bike, it should not be placed in an area where sparks or open flames could ignite the fumes coming out of the tank. Be especially careful inside garages where a natural gas-type appliance is located, because the pilot light could cause an explosion.

3 Fuel pressure check

 Warning: Refer to the precautions given in Section 1 before starting work.

1 The fuel pump is located inside the fuel tank. When the ignition is switched ON, it should be possible to hear the pump run for a few seconds until the system is up to

2.15a Slacken the banjo bolt to release any pressure, then fully unscrew it and detach the hose

2.15b If required fit copper sealing washers onto the bolt and fit it back into the tank to seal it

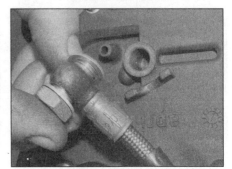

2.16 Use new sealing washers when reconnecting the hose

3.4a Unscrew the supply hose bolt (arrowed) . . .

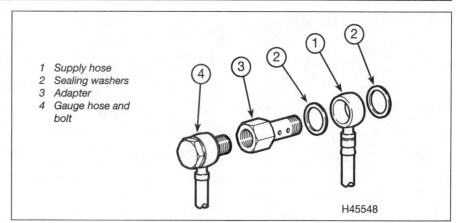

1 Supply hose
2 Sealing washers
3 Adapter
4 Gauge hose and bolt

H45548

3.4b . . . and fit the adapter and gauge with the supply hose as shown

pressure. If you can't hear anything, first check fuses B and E (see Chapter 9), then check the pump relay and the engine shut-off relay (see Section 4) and the tip-over (TO) sensor (see Section 11). If they are good, check the wiring and terminals for physical damage or loose or corroded connections and rectify as necessary (see the *Wiring Diagrams* at the end of Chapter 9). If the pump still will not run, remove it for a visual check (see Sections 5 and 6).

2 To check the fuel pressure, a suitable gauge, gauge hose with adapter and sealing washers are needed. Aprilia provides service tools (Pt. Nos. 8140197 and 8140181) for this purpose.

3 Raise the fuel tank (see Section 2). Disconnect the fuel pump wiring connector **(see illustration 2.10)**. It is best to perform the check with the tank nearly empty, so partially drain it if necessary (see Section 2).

4 Place some rag underneath the fuel supply hose union bolt on the right-hand side of the throttle bodies **(see illustration)**. Slacken the bolt slightly and allow any residual pressure to escape. Unscrew the bolt and hold it vertical while fitting the adapter bolt, gauge hose and washers as shown **(see illustration)**.

5 Using a fully-charged 12 V battery and connectors apply battery voltage to the green (+) and blue (-) wire terminal on the pump side of the wiring connector. The pump should start. Check the pressure reading on the gauge. The pressure should be as specified (test pressure) at the beginning of this Chapter.

6 Disconnect the battery from the connector.

Remove the gauge and adapter and reconnect the supply hose using the original bolt and two new sealing washers. Tighten the bolt to the torque setting specified at the beginning of the Chapter. Use a rag to catch any residual fuel as before.

7 If the pressure is too low, check for a leak in the fuel supply system, a blocked fuel filter (see Section 6), a faulty pressure regulator (see Section 7) or a faulty fuel pump.

8 If the pressure is too high, either the pressure regulator or the fuel pump check valve is faulty, or the return hose may be pinched.

9 Lower the fuel tank and connect the pump wiring connector (see Section 2). On completion run the engine and check that there are no leaks from the fuel hoses.

4 Fuel pump relay and engine shut-off relay

1 The fuel pump relay is mounted under the passenger seat and is the relay on the left-hand side **(see illustration)**. The engine shut-off relay is mounted under the passenger seat and is the relay in the middle **(see illustration)**. Both relays are tested in the same way.

2 Remove the passenger seat (see Chapter 8).

3 Pull the relay off its mounting and disconnect the wiring connector.

4 Using a multimeter or test light, check for continuity between terminals 3 and 5 on the relay **(see illustration)**. There should be no continuity. Now use jumper wires to connect the positive (+ve) terminal of a fully charged 12 volt battery to terminal 1 on the relay and the negative (-ve) battery terminal to relay terminal 2. There should now be continuity shown across terminals 3 and 5. If the relay fails either of the checks, replace it with a new one.

5 Fuel pump assembly removal and installation

⚠️ *Warning: Refer to the precautions given in Section 1 before starting work.*

Removal

Note: *The clip-type hose clamps used on the overflow and breather hoses on 1998 to 2000 models, and on the return hose on all models,*

4.1a Fuel pump relay

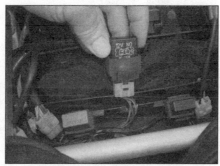

4.1b Engine shut-off relay

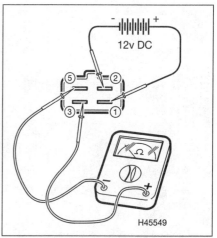

H45549

4.4 Relay terminal identification and test set-up

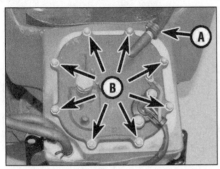

5.3 Detach the supply hose (A) if required. Unscrew the pump mounting bolts (B)

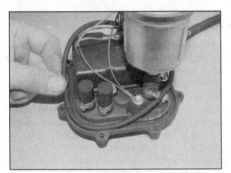

5.7 Fit a new O-ring into the groove

are best released using a flat-bladed screwdriver, but note that to rejoin this type of clamp a special pair of pliers makes the job much easier. Also note that these clamps should only be used once, and so new ones should be obtained for the installation procedure.

1 The fuel pump is located inside the fuel tank. Drain the tank and remove it (see Section 2).

2 Turn the tank upside down and rest it on some clean rag to protect the paintwork. If required, release the clamp securing the supply hose to its union on the base and detach it (see illustration 5.3).

5.5 Carefully withdraw the pump assembly from the tank

3 Undo the bolts securing the pump base to the underside of the tank (see illustration).

4 On 1998 to 2000 models, lift the pump slightly until the overflow and breather hose clamps are accessible, then release the clamps and detach the hoses from their unions on the pump base. Now carefully remove the pump (see illustration 5.5). Discard the O-ring as a new one must be fitted on reassembly.

5 On 2001 to 2003 models, carefully lift the pump out of the tank (see illustration). Discard the O-ring as a new one must be fitted on reassembly.

6 Refer to Section 6 for details on the individual components in the pump assembly (pump, filter, strainer and level sensor). Check that the wiring terminals for the fuel pump and the level sensor and the bolts for the pump cover are tight.

Installation

7 Fit a new O-ring into the groove in the fuel pump base, using a smear of Loctite 518 to seal it and keep it in place (see illustration). Install the pump with the return hose union at the front and the wiring at the back (see illustration 5.5).

8 On 1998 to 2000 models fit the overflow and breather hoses onto their unions and secure them using new clamps.

9 Install the bolts and tighten them finger-tight. Now tighten them evenly and a little at a time in the numerical sequence shown to the torque setting specified at the beginning of the Chapter (see illustration).

10 If detached, fit the return hose into its union and secure it using a new clamp.

11 Install the fuel tank (see Section 2) and refill it. Ensure there are no signs of fuel leakage around the pump base.

6 Fuel filter, pump, strainer and level sensor

⚠️ **Warning: Refer to the precautions given in Section 1 before starting work.**

Note 1: The clip-type hose clamps used on the pump assembly hoses are best released using a flat-bladed screwdriver, but note that to rejoin this type of clamp a special pair of pliers makes the job much easier. Also note that these clamps should only be used once, and so new ones should be obtained for the installation procedure.

Note 2: If the pump assembly is being completely dismantled for replacement of the base or pump cover, make a note of all wiring routing and terminals before doing so.

Fuel filter

1 Remove the fuel pump assembly from the tank (see Section 5).

2 Release the clamps securing the hoses to the filter, then detach the hoses and remove the filter (see illustration).

3 Fit the new filter into the hoses, making sure the rimmed end of the filter is at the top. Secure the hoses with new clamps.

4 Install the fuel pump (see Section 5).

Fuel pump

5 Remove the fuel pump assembly from the tank (see Section 5).

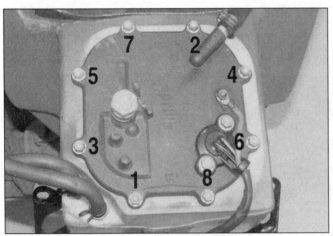

5.9 Fuel pump bolt tightening sequence

6.2 Release the clamps (arrowed), detach the hoses and remove the filter

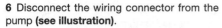

6.6 Disconnect the wiring connector (A), then release the clamp (B) and detach the hose

6.8a Unscrew the two bolts (arrowed) . . .

6.8b . . . and the one (arrowed) on the other side to release the base

6 Disconnect the wiring connector from the pump **(see illustration)**.

7 Release the clamp securing the hose to the pump, then detach the hose **(see illustration 6.6)**.

8 Unscrew the bolts securing the pump cover to the base **(see illustrations)**. Lift the pump cover enough to draw the pump out of it, taking care not to strain any of the wiring, and holding the filter aside. Discard the O-ring that sits between the top of the pump and the cover as a new one must be used. Check the condition of the pump seat in the base and replace it with a new one if it has deteriorated.

9 Reassemble the pump in reverse order, using a new O-ring and hose clamp, and seat if required.

Fuel strainer

10 Remove the fuel pump assembly from the tank (see Section 5), then remove the pump from the assembly (see Steps 6 to 8).

11 Clean any sediment off the strainer with a soft brush or low pressure compressed air. If the strainer is very clogged with dirt and/or rust (metal tank only) and cannot be cleaned, or if there is evidence that some has made its way through the gauze, or if the gauze is torn or damaged, a new pump must be fitted – the strainer is not available separately. If there

was a lot of sediment on the strainer fit a new filter (see Steps 2 and 3).

Low fuel level sensor

Note: *The low fuel warning symbol will come on when the volume of fuel in the tank drops to 4.5 litres.*

Check

12 If the low fuel warning symbol in the instrument cluster does not come on when there is less than 4.5 litres of fuel remaining, first check the bulb, then check the fuse (see Chapter 9). If they are both good, raise the fuel tank (see Section 2).

13 Disconnect the fuel pump assembly wiring connector **(see illustration 2.10)**.

14 Using a jumper wire bridge between the orange/black and blue wires on the loom side of the connector. Switch the ignition ON. The low fuel warning symbol in the instrument cluster should come on. If it doesn't, check the wiring between the connector and the instrument cluster (refer to the wiring diagrams at the end of Chapter 9), then check the instrument cluster (see Chapter 9).

15 If the low fuel warning symbol does come on, remove the fuel pump assembly from the tank (see Section 5), then check the wiring between the fuel pump assembly wiring connector and the terminals on the sensor

itself for continuity **(see illustration)**. If the wiring is good replace the sensor with a new one (see Steps 17 to 20).

Removal and installation

16 Remove the fuel pump assembly from the tank (see Section 5).

17 Cut the cable tie securing the wiring to the sensor **(see illustration)**.

18 Undo the screw securing the wires to the terminal on the pump cover and detach the wire to the sensor, then re-attach the wire from the base loosely.

19 Undo the screws securing the sensor and remove it, noting how it fits and how the bottom screw secures the earth wire.

20 Installation is the reverse of removal. Make sure the wiring is securely connected.

---

7 Fuel pressure regulator

Warning: **Refer** **to** **the** **precautions given in Section 1 before starting work.**

Check

1 To check the regulator, remove it as described below.

6.15 Check that all the wiring to the sensor is good (arrowed)

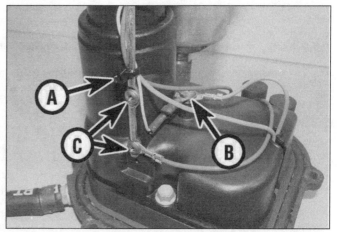

6.17 Cut the cable tie (A), release the wiring (B), then undo the sensor screws (C)

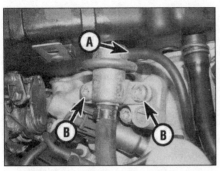

7.5 Detach the vacuum hose (A), then undo the screws (B)

8.2 Displace the IAP sensor wiring connector and detach the crankcase breather hose (arrowed)

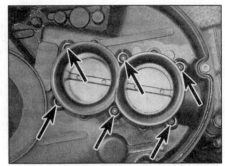

8.4a Undo the screws (arrowed) . . .

2 Aprilia provides no test procedure for the pressure regulator. However, if it is stuck open, it will be possible to blow through it with a low pressure air source. If it is stuck closed, then a high pressure air source with a gauge can be used to check the pressure at which it does open, if at all. Bear in mind that during normal operation a vacuum is acting on the diaphragm, so a static test will require a slightly higher pressure than specified to open the valve (no figures are available for the level of vacuum applied during operation). Make sure the vacuum hose from the throttle bodies to the regulator is in good condition and securely connected.

3 The definitive test is to substitute the suspect regulator with a known good one, repeat the fuel pressure check and assess any difference.

Removal and installation

Note: *The clip-type hose clamp used on the fuel return hose connected to the bottom of the regulator is best released using a flat-bladed screwdriver, but note that to rejoin this type of clamp a special pair of pliers makes the job much easier. Also note that these clamps should only be used once, and so a new one should be obtained for the installation procedure.*

4 Drain the fuel tank (see Section 2), and afterwards leave the return hose detached from the regulator. For best access remove the air filter housing (see Section 8).

5 Pull the vacuum hose off its union on the top of the regulator **(see illustration)**.

6 Undo the two screws securing the regulator to the throttle bodies, being prepared to catch residual fuel spillage with a rag, and remove it **(see illustration 7.5)**. Discard the O-ring as a new one must be used.

7 Install the regulator using a new O-ring. Fit the hoses back onto their unions using a new clamp on the return hose.

8 Install the air filter housing and tank as required – if the housing wasn't removed do not forget to fit the IAP sensor onto its mount.

8 Air filter housing

Removal

1 Remove the air filter (see Chapter 1). If required remove the fuel tank rather than just raising it to give more clearance and space in which to work.

2 Displace the intake air pressure (IAP) sensor from the left-hand side of the housing **(see illustration)**.

3 Release the clip and disconnect the crankcase breather hose from the housing **(see illustration 8.2)**.

4 Undo the screws securing the housing to the throttle bodies, then carefully lift the housing off and manoeuvre it away, noting how the intake ducts locate in or against (according to model) the holes in the frame beams **(see illustrations)**. Remove the small

O-ring from the air passage in the throttle bodies **(see illustration)**.

Installation

5 Installation is the reverse of removal.

● Do not forget to fit the air passage O-ring onto the throttle bodies, using a new one if necessary **(see illustration 8.4c)**.

● On models where the intake ducts locate against gaskets around the holes in the frame, make sure the gaskets are in good condition, otherwise replace them with new ones to ensure a good seal.

● On all other models make sure the intake ducts locate correctly in the holes in the frame and the rim seals are not distorted **(see illustration)**.

● Make sure the housing is flatly seated on the throttle bodies before installing and tightening the screws.

● Make sure the crankcase hose is in good condition and securely connected.

9 Fuel injection system description

1 The fuel injection system consists of two main component groups, the fuel supply circuit and the electronic control circuit.

2 The fuel supply circuit consists of the tank, pump and filter, pressure regulator and injectors. Fuel is pumped under pressure from the tank to the throttle bodies, from which the

8.4b . . . and remove the housing

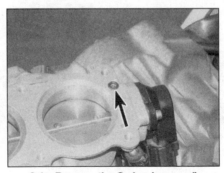

8.4c Remove the O-ring (arrowed)

8.5 Make sure the intake ducts locate correctly

individual injectors are fed. Operating pressure is maintained initially by the pump check valve (a one-way valve that maintains pressure in the system even when the pump has stopped), and, once the engine is running, by the pressure regulator. The injectors spray pressurised fuel into the throttle body where it mixes with air and vaporises, before entering the cylinder where it is compressed and ignited.

3 The electronic control circuit consists of the engine control unit (ECU), which operates and co-ordinates both the fuel injection and ignition systems, and the various sensors which provide the ECU with information on engine operating conditions.

4 The ECU monitors signals from the following sensors:
● *Intake air temperature (IAT) sensor*
● *Intake air pressure (IAP) sensor*
● *Throttle position (TP) sensor*
● *Camshaft position (CMP) sensor*
● *Crankshaft position (CKP) sensor*
● *Coolant temperature (ECT) sensor in rear cylinder head*
● *Atmospheric pressure (AP) sensor*
● *Tip over (TO) sensor*

5 Based on the information it receives, the ECU calculates the appropriate ignition and fuel requirements of the engine. By varying the length of the electronic pulse it sends to each injector, the ECU controls the length of time the injectors are held open and thereby the amount of fuel that is supplied to the engine. Fuel supply varies according to the engine's needs for starting, warming-up, idling, cruising and acceleration.

6 In the event of an abnormality in any of the sensor signals during use, the ECU will determine whether the engine can still be run safely. If it can, a back-up mode replaces the sensor signal with a fixed signal, restricting performance but allowing the bike to be ridden home or to a dealer. When this occurs, the right-hand LCD display in the instrument cluster will indicate the letters EFI. If the unit decides that the fault is too serious, the appropriate system will be shut down and the engine will not run. Note that the EFI letters show for three seconds every time the ignition is switched on – this is normal and does not indicate there is a fault. If the letters start to flash after three seconds, there is a fault in the system and the engine should not be started. If the letters go out, but come on again after the engine has been started, there is a fault in the system.

7 The system incorporates two safety circuits. When the ignition is switched ON, the fuel pump runs for three seconds and pressurises the system. Thereafter the pump automatically switches off until the engine is started. The second circuit incorporates a tip-over sensor, which automatically switches off the fuel pump and cuts the ignition and injection circuits if the motorcycle falls over.

10 Fuel injection system fault diagnosis

1 The system incorporates a self-diagnostic function whereby any faults are stored in the ECU memory. If the EFI letters appear during normal use, or are constantly flashing before the engine has been started (see Section 9, Step 6), the fault code must be accessed.

2 To access the fault code, remove the right-hand side trim panel (and if necessary the seat cowling, depending on access) (see Chapter 8) and locate the test wiring connectors (two single connectors, one with a green/white wire going to it, the other with two blue/green wires). Ensure the ignition is OFF. Using a piece of wire with suitable terminals fitted, connect between the sockets in the test connectors.

3 Turn the ignition switch ON. Start the engine, or if it will not start, crank the engine on the electric starter for at least four seconds. The letters DIAG along with the fault code will be displayed on the right-hand LCD panel on the instrument cluster. Note the fault code and identify the fault from the following table.

4 To check the fuel injection system components see Section 11.

5 If there is a fault in the system and there is no warning displayed and no code stored, check the fuses, the ignition and kill switches, and the neutral, clutch and sidestand switches (Chapter 9), and/or the fuel pump and the fuel pump and engine shut-off relays and the injectors, according to symptom. Also check that the wiring between the ECU and instrument cluster is good, and that the LCD display is working correctly.

6 Once the fault has been corrected, turn the ignition switch ON and check the fault has been cleared from the ECU. Remove the jumper wire from the test connectors.

Fault code	Faulty component – symptoms	Possible causes
11	Camshaft position sensor – engine may continue to run but will not restart once turned OFF	Faulty wiring or wiring connector Faulty sensor
12	Crankshaft position sensor – engine will not run	Faulty wiring or wiring connector Faulty sensor or damaged trigger on rotor
13	Intake air pressure sensor – engine will run	Faulty wiring or wiring connector Faulty sensor
14	Intake air pressure sensor – engine will run	Damaged or disconnected vacuum pipe(s)
15	Throttle position sensor – engine will run, throttle position signal fixed	Faulty wiring or wiring connector Faulty sensor
21	Engine coolant temperature sensor – engine will run, cold starting difficult	Faulty wiring or wiring connector Faulty sensor
22	Intake air temperature sensor – engine will run, air temperature signal fixed	Faulty wiring or wiring connector Faulty sensor
23	Atmospheric pressure sensor – engine will run, atmospheric pressure signal fixed	Faulty sensor (it is inside ECU and has no wiring)
33 and/or 34	Front cylinder ignition coil(s) – engine will run on other coil and/or cylinder	Faulty wiring or wiring connector Faulty ignition coil Faulty power supply to the coil *(see Chapter 5 for details)*
35 and/or 36	Rear cylinder ignition coil(s) – engine will run on other coil and/or cylinder	Faulty wiring or wiring connector Faulty ignition coil Faulty power supply to the coil *(see Chapter 5 for details)*
41	Tip-over sensor	Faulty wiring or wiring connector Faulty sensor

11.4 Camshaft position sensor wiring connector (arrowed)

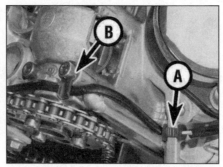

11.7a Free the wiring grommet (A) and slacken the clamp bolt (B)

11.7b Unscrew the bolts (arrowed) and remove the guide . . .

11 Fuel injection system components

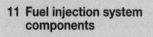

1 If a fault is indicated on any of the system components, first check the wiring and connectors between the appropriate component and the engine control unit (ECU); see *Wiring Diagrams* at the end of Chapter 9. A continuity test of all wires will locate a break or short in any circuit. Inspect the terminals inside the wiring connectors and ensure they are not loose or corroded. Spray the inside of the connectors with an electrical terminal cleaner before reconnection.

2 It is possible to undertake some checks on system components using a multimeter and comparing the results with the specifications at the beginning of this Chapter. **Note:** *Different meters may give slightly different results to those specified even though the component being tested is not faulty – do not consign a component to the bin before having it double-checked.*

3 If after a thorough check the source of a fault has not been identified, it is possible that the ECU itself is faulty. Aprilia provides no test specifications for the ECU. In order to determine conclusively that the unit is defective, it should be substituted with a known good one (see Chapter 5). If the problem is then rectified, the original unit is confirmed faulty.

Camshaft position (CMP) sensor

4 Make sure the ignition is OFF. Raise the fuel tank (see Section 2). The CMP sensor is under

the front valve cover. Trace the wiring from the cover and disconnect it at the connector **(see illustration)**.

5 Use an ohmmeter or multimeter set to the ohms x 100 scale and measure the resistance between the terminals on the sensor side of the connector. If the result is not as specified, remove the sensor (Step 7) and check that the wiring between the connector and the sensor itself is good. If it is replace the sensor with a new one.

6 If the result is good, remove the sensor (Step 7) and check that the fault is not caused by a build-up of dirt and/or debris on the sensor tip – clean the tip with solvent and recheck the resistance.

7 To remove the sensor first remove the valve cover (see Chapter 2). Free the wiring grommet from its cut-out in the head and slacken the rear camshaft holder bolt enough to allow the wiring past the clamp **(see illustration)**. Unscrew the bolts securing the cam chain top guide and remove it, noting how the camshaft position sensor wiring routes under the tab on the inner face of the guide **(see illustration)**. Unscrew the sensor bolts and remove the sensor, noting the routing of the wiring.

8 Install the sensor and tighten its bolts to the specified torque setting. Install the cam chain top guide, making sure the camshaft position sensor wiring routes under the tab on the inner face of the guide, and tighten the bolts to the torque setting specified at the beginning of the Chapter. Fit the wiring under the clamp and tighten the camshaft holder bolt to the specified torque. Fit the wiring

grommet into its cut-out in the head using a dab of sealant, then connect the wiring connector **(see illustration 11.4)**. Install the valve cover (see Chapter 2).

Crankshaft position (CKP) sensor

9 Make sure the ignition is OFF. To access the CKP sensor wiring connector raise the fuel tank (see Section 2). The sensor itself is in the alternator cover and is actuated by a trigger on the alternator rotor. Trace the wiring from the alternator cover and disconnect it at the wiring connector **(see illustration)**.

10 Using an ohmmeter or multimeter set to the ohms x 100 scale, measure the resistance between the terminals on the sensor side of the connector. If the result is not as specified, remove the sensor (see Chapter 9, Section 30) and check that the wiring between the connector and the sensor itself is good. If it is replace the sensor with a new one.

11 If the result is good, remove the sensor and check that the fault is not caused by a build-up of dirt and/or debris on the sensor tip – clean the tip with solvent and recheck the resistance.

12 To remove the sensor, see Chapter 9 – it is part of the alternator stator in the valve cover and is not available separately.

Intake air pressure (IAP) sensor

13 Make sure the ignition is OFF. Raise the fuel tank (see Section 2). The IAP sensor is on the left-hand side of the air filter housing **(see illustration)**. Check the condition of the vacuum hose between the sensor and the

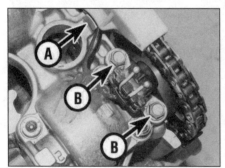

11.7c . . . noting the routing of the wiring (A). Sensor mounting bolts (B)

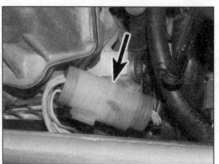

11.9 Crankshaft position sensor wiring connector (arrowed)

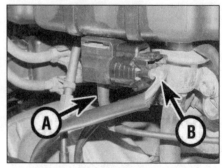

11.13 Intake air pressure sensor vacuum hose (A) and wiring connector (B)

throttle bodies. If the hose is cracked or perished replace it with a new one. Ensure the hose is a tight fit on the sensor union and the throttle bodies.

14 Disconnect the sensor wiring connector and turn the ignition ON. Connect the probes of a voltmeter to the outer terminals on the loom side of the wiring connector as shown (Test A) to check the input voltage **(see illustration)**. Turn the ignition OFF. If the input voltage is not as specified, check the wiring to the ECU and the ECU connector terminals.

15 If the input voltage is good, measure the resistance between the terminals shown for the three tests (B, C and D) on the sensor side of the wiring connector. Use an ohmmeter set to the K-ohms scale. If any of the readings are outside the values specified, replace the sensor with a new one.

16 To remove the IAP sensor, displace it from its mount then disconnect the vacuum hose and the wiring connector. On installation, ensure the wiring connector terminals are clean and that the vacuum hose is a tight fit on the sensor union.

Throttle position (TP) sensor

17 Make sure the ignition is OFF. Raise the fuel tank (see Section 2) – the TP sensor is located on the back of the throttle body assembly **(see illustration)**. Disconnect the sensor wiring connector. Turn the ignition ON. Connect the probes of a voltmeter to the outer terminals on the loom side of the wiring connector as shown (Test A) to check the input voltage **(see illustration)**. Turn the ignition OFF. If the input voltage is not as specified, check the wiring to the ECU and the ECU connector terminals.

18 If the input voltage is good, measure the resistance between the terminals shown for Test B on the TP sensor side of the connector using an ohmmeter set to the K-ohms scale. If the reading is outside the value specified, replace the sensor with a new one.

19 Now connect the ohmmeter probes as shown for Test C on the TP sensor side of the connector and take two resistance readings, one with the throttle closed, then one with the throttle fully open. If the results are not as specified replace the sensor with a new one.

20 To remove the TP sensor, first disconnect its wiring connector **(see illustration 11.17a)**. Mark the position of the sensor to aid installation. Undo the screws and remove the sensor; note that the screws are treated with Loctite 243 so may be difficult to slacken. Note the seal, and how the end of the throttle shaft engages in the sensor. Check to see if the sensor spring is broken.

21 Installation is the reverse of removal. Apply some Loctite 243 to the screw threads. Ensure that the throttle shaft engages correctly in the sensor and align any marks previously made before loosely fitting the screws. Ensure the wiring connector terminals are clean. Connect the connector then adjust the sensor (Step 22).

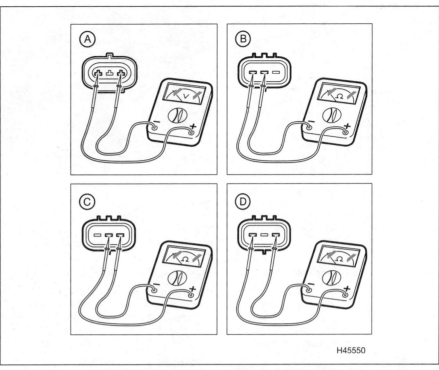

11.14 IAP sensor set-ups for tests A, B, C and D

22 To adjust the position of the TP sensor, first connect the test connectors (see Section 10, Step 2). Turn the ignition ON. Turn the TP sensor by hand until the top readout in the right-hand LCD display in the instrument cluster reads 0. When it does, tighten the sensor screws lightly, making sure the sensor does not move, and check that the display still reads 0 after tightening. If it does, turn the ignition OFF and remove the jumper wire from the test connectors.

Engine coolant temperature (ECT) sensor

23 Refer to Chapter 3.

Intake air temperature (IAT) sensor

24 To check the sensor resistance remove it from the left-hand air duct (see Step 28).
25 Fill a small heatproof container with water and place it on a stove. Using an ohmmeter

11.17a Throttle position sensor (arrowed)

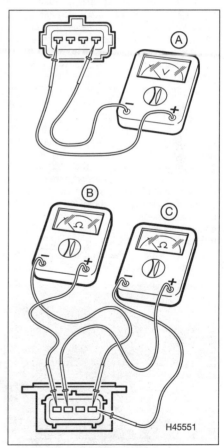

11.17b TP sensor set-ups for tests A, B, and C

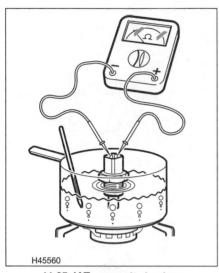

11.25 IAT sensor test set-up

set initially to the K-ohms scale, connect the meter probes to the sensor terminals, and using some wire or other support, suspend the sensor in the water so that just the sensing portion and the threads are submerged **(see illustration)**. Also place a thermometer capable of reading temperatures up to 150°C in the water so that its bulb is close to the switch. **Note:** *None of the components should be allowed to touch the container directly.*

26 Check the meter reading and compare the result with the specifications at the beginning of this Chapter, then heat the water slowly, stirring it gently.

 Warning: This must be done very carefully to avoid the risk of personal injury.

27 As the temperature of the water rises, the sensor resistance should fall (depending on your meter you may need to change scale to get an accurate reading). Check that the specified resistance is obtained at the correct temperature (see Specifications at the beginning of this Chapter). If the readings obtained are different, or are obtained at different temperatures, the sensor is faulty and must be replaced with a new one. Also check the wiring to and from the sensor and the connectors, using the wiring diagrams at the end of Chapter 9.

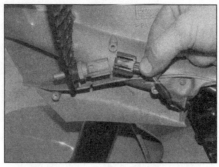

11.28 Disconnect the wiring connector and remove the IAT sensor

28 To remove the sensor, remove the left-hand air duct outer cover (see Chapter 8). Disconnect the wiring connector then release the sensor from the grill in the duct **(see illustration)**.

Atmospheric pressure (AP) sensor

29 The AP sensor is an internal and integral part of the ECU and cannot itself be checked. If the diagnostics indicate the AP sensor is faulty, substitute the ECU with one that is known to be good and recheck for the fault code.

Tip-over (TO) sensor

30 Make sure the ignition is OFF. Remove the rider's seat (see Chapter 8) – the TO sensor is mounted on the right-hand side **(see illustration)**. First make sure that the sensor is correctly mounted with its wiring on the right-hand side and the UPPER mark on the back of the rubber holder the correct way up **(see illustration 11.33)**.

31 Trace the wiring from the sensor and disconnect it at the connector. Using an ohmmeter or multimeter set to the K-ohms scale, measure the resistance between the terminals on the sensor side of the connector. Compare the upright result to that given in the Specifications at the beginning of this Chapter; if the result is good, reconnect the wiring connector. If not, replace the sensor with a new one.

32 If the result was good, carefully unclip the sensor from its bracket and check the resistance reading when the sensor is leaned 45° to one side and then to the other (this simulates the cut-off point reached if the motorcycle falls over). Compare the angled

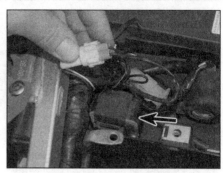

11.30 Tip-over sensor (arrowed) and its wiring connector

result to that given in the Specifications at the beginning of this Chapter. If the result is good, check the wiring and connectors between the sensor and the ECU, referring to the wiring diagrams at the end of Chapter 9. If not the sensor is faulty.

33 To remove the sensor, first disconnect the wiring connector. Unclip the sensor holder from its bracket and remove the sensor from the holder, noting which way round it fits. Installation is the reverse of removal, making sure it is fitted the correct way up **(see illustration)**.

---

12 Throttle bodies

 Warning: Refer to the precautions given in Section 1 before starting work.

Removal

Note: *The clip-type hose clamps used on the vacuum hoses for the clutch diaphragm are best released using a flat-bladed screwdriver, but note that to rejoin this type of clamp a special pair of pliers makes the job much easier. Also note that these clamps should only be used once, and so new ones should be obtained for the installation procedure.*

1 Remove the fuel tank (see Section 2) and the air filter housing (see Section 8).

2 On late models (from frame no. ZD4MEE009YS000293) release the idle speed adjuster from its holder **(see illustrations)**.

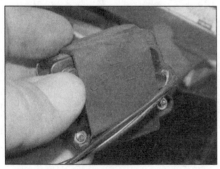

11.33 Make sure the sensor is correctly orientated

12.2a Remove the E-clip . . .

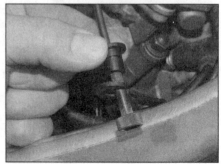

12.2b . . . and free the idle speed adjuster

3 Disconnect the throttle cables (see Section 14).

4 Disconnect the fast idle cable (see Section 15).

5 Disconnect the wiring connectors from the fuel injectors **(see illustration)**.

6 Disconnect the throttle position (TP) sensor wiring connector **(see illustration 11.17a)**.

7 Release the clamps securing the clutch diaphragm vacuum hoses and detach them from their unions **(see illustration)**.

8 Slacken the clamp screws securing the throttle bodies to the intake ducts **(see illustration)**. Ease the bodies up off the ducts and remove them, noting how the fuel supply hose routes under the throttle bodies and between the ducts **(see illustration)**.

Cleaning

Caution: Use only a petroleum based solvent or dedicated injector cleaner for throttle body cleaning. Don't use caustic cleaners.

9 Only use the cleaner on metal components and always follow manufacturers instructions. If a spray cleaner is used, direct the spray into all passages.

10 After the cleaner has loosened and dissolved most of the varnish and other deposits, use a nylon-bristled brush to remove the stubborn deposits. Rinse the throttle bodies again, then dry them with compressed air.

11 Use compressed air to blow out all of the fuel and air passages.

Caution: Never clean passages with a piece of wire or a drill bit, as they could be enlarged, causing the fuel/air metering rates to be upset.

Inspection

12 Check the throttle bodies for cracks or any other damage which may result in air getting in.

13 Check that all parts move smoothly and freely. Inspect the valve shafts and throttle bodies for wear. Check the condition of the valve shaft springs.

Disassembly

14 Disassembly of the throttle bodies is not advised, apart from removing the fuel injectors (which involves removing the pulley assembly) and pressure regulator – refer to the relevant Sections to do so. If a component on the throttle body assembly is worn or damaged and does need replacing, also refer to the exploded diagram and remove only the necessary parts, noting how they fit **(see illustration)**.

15 If the synchronizing screws have been disturbed, screw them in until they seat lightly then screw them out by one full turn. After installing the throttle bodies synchronize them (see Chapter 1).

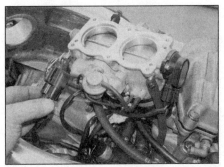

12.5 Disconnect the connector from each injector

12.7 Release the clamp and detach each hose from its union

12.8a Slacken the clamps (arrowed) . . .

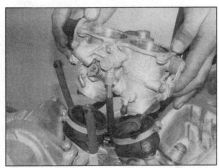

12.8b . . . and remove the throttle bodies

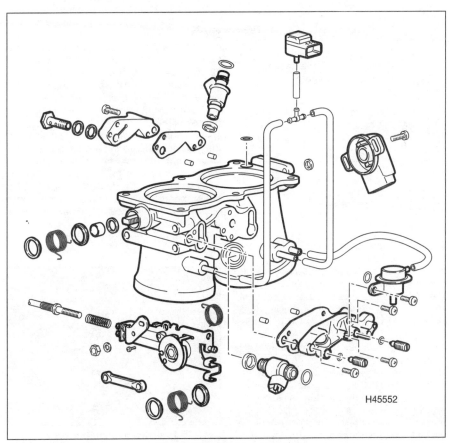

H45552

12.14 Throttle body assembly

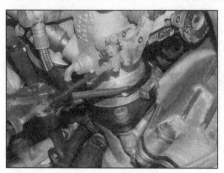

12.16 Use a screwdriver to persuade the bodies into the intake ducts

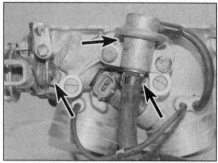

13.7a Unscrew the nut (A), then undo the screws (B) and remove the assembly

13.7b Undo the screws (arrowed, but hidden) and remove the injector holder

Installation

16 Installation is the reverse of removal, noting the following:

● Ensure the throttle bodies are fully engaged with the intake ducts on the cylinder heads before tightening the clamps – fit the rear body into the rear stub first, then push down on the front while carefully easing it into the stub using a flat-bladed screwdriver **(see illustration)**.

● Ensure the fuel injector, IAP and TP sensor wiring connectors are securely connected.

● Make sure all hoses are in good condition, correctly routed and not pinched.

● Check the operation of the fast idle and throttle cables and adjust them as necessary (see Chapter 1).

● Check the engine idle speed and adjust as necessary (see Chapter 1). If the throttle bodies have been disassembled or the synchronisation screws have been moved, synchronise them (see Chapter 1).

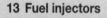

13 Fuel injectors

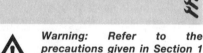

Warning: Refer to the precautions given in Section 1 before proceeding.

Check

1 Make sure the ignition is OFF. Raise the fuel tank (see Section 2).

2 If the engine runs, start it and allow it to idle. Check the operation of each injector using a stethoscope or sounding rod; an injector will emit a 'clicking' noise when functioning. If the injector is silent, either it or its wiring harness is faulty.

3 If the engine does not run, disconnect the wiring connector from the injector **(see illustration 12.5)**. Using an ohmmeter or multimeter set to the ohms scale, measure the resistance between the terminals on the injector. If the result is as specified, check that there is no continuity (infinite resistance) between each terminal and earth (ground). If the injector is proved faulty a new one must

be installed. Also check the wiring between the connector and the ECU, referring to the Wiring Diagrams at the end of Chapter 9.

Removal

Note: The fuel injectors can be removed with the throttle bodies in place. If the bodies have been removed, ignore the Steps which do not apply.

4 Make sure the ignition is OFF. Remove the air filter housing (see Section 8). If you haven't removed the fuel tank, drain it (see Section 2).

5 Place rag around the throttle bodies to catch any residual fuel.

6 Disconnect the wiring connector from the fuel injector **(see illustration 12.5)**.

7 To remove the rear cylinder injector, displace the fuel pressure regulator (see Section 7 – there is no need to detach the hoses). Unscrew the nut on the end of the throttle valve shaft **(see illustration and 12.14)**. Turn the throttle arm as required for access and undo the screws securing the cable bracket and pulley assembly and detach it from the throttle bodies, noting the bushes with the return spring and how the spring ends locate. Undo the screws securing the injector holder to the throttle bodies **(see illustration)**. Carefully detach the holder from the throttle bodies – the injector should come away with it, but if it doesn't carefully pull it out of the throttle bodies. Discard the holder gasket and injector sealing ring as new ones must be used.

8 To remove the front cylinder injector,

unscrew the fuel supply hose banjo bolt and detach the hose **(see illustration)**. Discard the sealing washers as new ones must be used. Undo the screws securing the injector holder to the throttle bodies **(see illustration)**. Carefully detach the holder from the throttle bodies – the injector should come away with it, but if it doesn't carefully pull it out of the throttle bodies. Discard the holder gasket and injector sealing ring as new ones should be used.

9 Pull the injector out of its holder. Discard the injector O-ring and spacer as new ones must be fitted on reassembly.

10 Modern fuels contain detergents which should keep the injectors clean and free of gum or varnish from fuel residue. If an injector is suspected of being blocked, clean it through with injector cleaner. If the injector is clean but its performance is suspect, take it to an Aprilia dealer for assessment.

Installation

Note: Apply a smear of clean engine oil to all new seals and O-rings before reassembly.

11 Fit a new spacer and O-ring onto the top of the injector, and smear them with clean oil **(see illustration 12.14)**. Carefully press the injector into its holder, aligning it so the wiring connector faces out. **Note:** Avoid twisting the injectors as this may damage the seals. Fit a new seal into the throttle body.

12 To install the front cylinder injector, fit a new holder gasket onto the throttle bodies, then fit the holder, making sure the injector

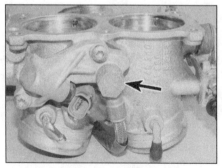

13.8a Unscrew the bolt (arrowed) and detach the hose

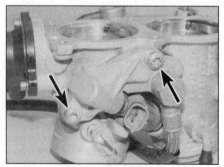

13.8b Undo the screws (arrowed) and remove the injector holder

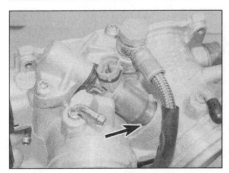

13.12 Make sure the injector locates correctly (arrowed)

14.2a Slacken the locknuts (arrowed)

14.2b Release the upper cable from the bracket . . .

nozzle locates in the seal **(see illustration)**. Install the screws and tighten them to the torque setting specified at the beginning of the chapter **(see illustration 13.8b)**. Connect the fuel supply hose union to the holder using new sealing washers and aligning it as noted on removal **(see illustration 13.8a)**. Tighten the banjo bolt to the torque setting specified at the beginning of the Chapter.

13 To install the rear cylinder injector, fit a new holder gasket onto the throttle bodies, then fit the holder, making sure the injector nozzle locates in the seal **(see illustration 13.12)**. Install the screws and tighten them to the torque setting specified at the beginning of the Chapter **(see illustration 13.7b)**. Fit the cable bracket and pulley assembly onto the throttle bodies, making sure the return spring and its bushes locate correctly **(see illustration 13.7a)**. Apply Loctite 243 to the

threads of the bracket screws and to the throttle valve shaft nut before installing and tightening them. Install the pressure regulator (see Section 7).

14 Connect the injector wiring connectors **(see illustration 12.5)**.

15 Install the remaining components in the reverse order of removal. On completion, start the engine and check carefully that there are no fuel leaks.

14 Throttle cables

Removal

1 Remove the air filter housing (see Section 8).
2 Slacken the locknuts securing the throttle

cable adjusters in the bracket, then slip them out of the bracket and detach them from the throttle pulley, noting how they fit – thread the lower cable nut off the end of the adjuster otherwise it is difficult to get it out of the bracket **(see illustrations)**. The upper cable is the throttle opening cable, the lower cable is the throttle closing cable. Draw the cables out to the handlebars, noting their routing.
3 Unscrew the locknuts securing the cables in the cable housing **(see illustration)**. Remove the cable housing bolts and remove the top cover **(see illustration)**. Detach the cable ends from the twistgrip pulley, noting how they fit, then thread the cables out of the lower half of the housing **(see illustration)**.

Installation

4 Thread the cables into the cable housing on the handlebar – the one with adjuster is the

14.2c . . . and then from the pulley

14.2d Thread the nut off the end of the lower cable and release it from the bracket . . .

14.2e . . . and then from the pulley

14.3a Unscrew the cable nuts (arrowed) . . .

14.3b . . . then unscrew the housing bolts and remove the top . . .

14.3c . . . and free the cables from the throttle pulley

14.4 Align the mating surfaces of the housing with the punch mark (arrowed)

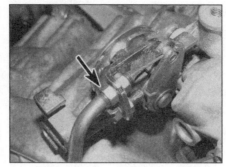

15.2a Slacken the locknut (arrowed) . . .

15.2b . . . then thread the nut off the end . . .

opening cable and fits into the front of the housing. Lubricate the cable ends with multi-purpose grease and attach them to the pulley **(see illustration 14.3c)**. Fit the top cover onto the housing, aligning the mating surfaces with the punch mark on the handlebar, and tighten the screws **(see illustration)**.

5 Feed the cables through to the throttle bodies, making sure they are correctly routed – they must not interfere with any other component and should not be kinked or bent sharply.

6 Check that the twistgrip pulley turns freely.

7 Lubricate the cable ends with multi-purpose grease. Fit the end of each cable onto the throttle pulley; the closing cable goes around the bottom of the pulley, the opening cable goes around the top **(see illustrations 14.2e and c)**. Locate the cable adjusters in their holders on the bracket, ensuring the

adjuster locknuts are located on each side of the holder **(see illustration 14.2d and b)**. Thread the nut onto the bottom cable **(see illustration 14.2a)**. Adjust the cables as described in Chapter 1.

8 Install the air filter housing (see Section 8).

9 Start the engine and check the action of throttle, and that the idle speed does not rise as the handlebars are turned. If it does, correct the problem before riding the motorcycle.

15 Fast idle system

Cable removal

1 Remove the air filter housing (see Section 8).

2 Loosen the outer locknut on the fast

idle cable adjuster, then thread the inner locknut off the end **(see illustrations)**. Disconnect the cable end from the arm and draw the cable out of its bracket **(see illustration)**.

3 Remove the two handlebar switch housing screws and separate the halves **(see illustrations)**. Note how the pin on the bottom half of the housing locates in the hole in the handlebar.

4 Undo the two cable housing screws and draw the housing away from the clutch master cylinder **(see illustration)**. Detach the housing cover by carefully releasing the two sets of tabs from the inner side **(see illustrations)**. Release the cable end from the lever and free the cable elbow from the housing **(see illustrations)**.

5 Remove the cable from the machine, noting its routing.

15.2c . . . and free the cable

15.3 Undo the screws on the underside of the housing and separate the halves

15.4a Undo the screws (arrowed) and draw the housing off

15.4b Release the tabs . . .

15.4c . . . and detach the cover

15.4d Detach the lever from the housing . . .

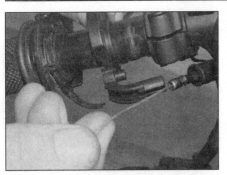

15.4e . . . and free the cable from both the lever and the housing

15.7 Fit the cable end into its socket in the lever

15.8 Locate the pin (arrowed) in the hole

Cable installation

6 Thread the cable through to the throttle bodies and up to the handlebars, making sure it is correctly routed – it must not interfere with any other component and should not be kinked or bent sharply.

7 Lubricate the end of the cable with multi-purpose grease. Fit the cable elbow into the housing **(see illustration 15.4e)**, then attach the cable end to the lever **(see illustration)**. Fit the lever onto the housing, then fit the cover, pressing it home until the tabs locate **(see illustrations 15.4d and c)**. Locate the cable housing against the master cylinder clamp and tighten its screws **(see illustration 15.4a)**. Check that the lever turns freely.

8 Fit the two halves of the switch housing onto the handlebar, locating the pin in the bottom half in the hole in the handlebar, and install the screws **(see illustration)**.

9 Fit the end of the cable onto the fast idle arm and fit the cable adjuster into the bracket **(see illustrations 15.2c and b)**. Thread the locknut onto the cable and secure the cable in the bracket, making sure there is a bit of slack in the inner cable **(see illustrations 15.2a)**. Check the action of the fast idle lever.

Fast idle adjustment

10 Remove the air filter housing (see Section 8).

11 Pull the fast idle cable arm back until it touches the stopper screw and hold it there **(see illustration)**. Check the gap between the idle adjuster screw and the throttle shaft arm – it should be 1.6 to 1.8 mm **(see illustration)**. If

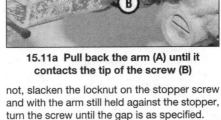

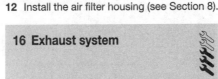

15.11a Pull back the arm (A) until it contacts the tip of the screw (B)

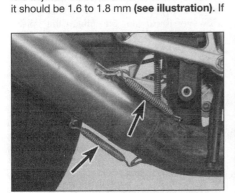

16.1 Carefully release the springs (arrowed)

not, slacken the locknut on the stopper screw and with the arm still held against the stopper, turn the screw until the gap is as specified.

12 Install the air filter housing (see Section 8).

16 Exhaust system

⚠ *Warning: If the engine has been running the exhaust system will be very hot. Allow the system to cool before carrying out any work.*

Silencer

Removal

1 To prevent the possibility of damage, remove the exhaust shroud from the lower fairing, and the lower fairing itself if required

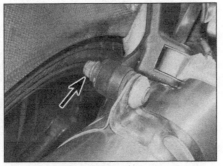

16.2a Unscrew the nut (arrowed) and remove the washer

15.11b With the arm held back check the gap (arrowed)

(see Chapter 8). Carefully unhook and remove the springs securing the silencer to the downpipe assembly **(see illustration)**.

2 Unscrew the nut from the bolt securing the silencer to the passenger footrest bracket and remove the washer **(see illustration)**. Support the silencer and withdraw the bolt with its bush. Remove the washer from between the silencer bracket and the rubber bush in the footrest bracket. Draw the silencer off the downpipe assembly **(see illustration)**. **Note:** *If the silencer is stuck and proves impossible to remove due to restricted movement, remove the downpipe assembly and silencer as one and separate them afterwards.*

3 Check the condition of the rubber bushes and collar in the footrest bracket and replace them with new ones if necessary.

Installation

4 Installation is the reverse of removal.

16.2b Remove the silencer as described

16.6a Undo the lower screw (arrowed) . . .

16.6b . . . then the upper screws (arrowed)

16.7 Unscrew the nuts and bolts and remove the bracket

Tighten the silencer mounting bolt nut to the specified torque.

5 Run the engine and check that there are no exhaust gas leaks.

Complete system

Removal

6 Remove the lower fairing (see Chapter 8). Undo the three screws securing the central shroud and manoeuvre it out **(see illustrations)**.

7 Displace the oil cooler and oil tank from the mounting bracket (see Chapter 2). Unscrew the nuts and bolts securing the mounting bracket to the engine and remove the bracket, noting how the radiator bottom pegs locate in the grommets **(see illustration)**.

8 Remove the silencer (see Steps 1 to 3).

9 Carefully unhook and remove the spring securing the downpipe assembly to the rear cylinder header pipe **(see illustration)**.

10 Unscrew the nuts securing the front cylinder header pipe to the cylinder head **(see illustration)**. Manoeuvre the assembly off the front cylinder head and out from under the bike **(see illustration)**.

11 If required carefully unhook and remove the spring securing the front cylinder header pipe in the downpipe assembly and pull the header pipe out.

12 Unscrew the nuts securing the rear cylinder header pipe to the cylinder head and manoeuvre it out – you will need a universal socket drive or extension bars with swivel joint to access the nuts fully **(see illustration)**.

13 Remove the gasket from each cylinder head exhaust port as new ones must be used.

Installation

14 Installation is the reverse of removal. Apply a smear of grease to the new cylinder exhaust port gaskets to keep them in place. Tighten the header pipe nuts to the specified torque.

15 Run the engine and check that there are no exhaust gas leaks.

17 EVAP system (California models)

General information

1 This system prevents the escape of fuel vapour into the atmosphere by storing it in a charcoal-filled canister.

2 When the engine is not running, excess fuel vapour from the tank passes into the canister. When the engine is started, intake manifold depression draws the vapour from the canister into the throttle bodies to be burned during the normal combustion process.

3 The canister has a one way valve which allows air to be drawn into the system as the volume of fuel decreases in the tank. A shut-off valve also prevents any fuel escaping through it in the event of the bike falling over.

4 The system is not adjustable and can only be properly tested by an Aprilia dealer. However the owner can check that all the hoses are in good condition and are securely connected at each end. Replace any hoses that are cracked, split or generally deteriorated with new ones.

Removal and installation

5 To access the canister remove the seat cowling (see Chapter 8). The canister and purge valve are mounted in front of the tail light. Label and disconnect the hoses, then remove the clamp screw and take the canister out. Make sure the hoses are correctly reconnected on installation.

16.9 Carefully release the spring (arrowed)

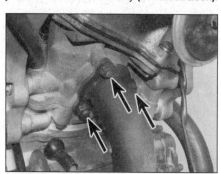

16.10a Unscrew the nuts (arrowed) . . .

16.10b . . . and remove the assembly

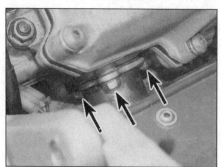

16.12 Rear cylinder header pipe nuts (arrowed)

Chapter 5
Ignition system

Contents

Degrees of difficulty

Easy, suitable for novice with little experience	**Fairly easy,** suitable for beginner with some experience	**Fairly difficult,** suitable for competent DIY mechanic	**Difficult,** suitable for experienced DIY mechanic	**Very difficult,** suitable for expert DIY or professional

Specifications

General information
Spark plugs . . . . see Chapter 1

Ignition HT coils
Primary winding resistance . . . . approx. 2.8 to 5.2 ohms @ 20°C
Secondary winding resistance (without plug caps) . . . . approx. 9.1 to 16.5 K-ohms @ 20°C
Spark plug cap resistance . . . . approx. 5 K-ohms @ 20°C

1 General information

All models are fitted with a fully transistorised electronic ignition system, which due to its lack of mechanical parts is totally maintenance free. The system comprises a trigger, crankshaft position sensor, engine control unit (ECU) and ignition HT coils (refer to the wiring diagrams at the end of Chapter 9 for details). All models are fitted with four HT coils, one for each spark plug (there are two plugs per cylinder).

The ignition trigger, which is on the alternator rotor on the left-hand end of the crankshaft, magnetically operates the crankshaft position sensor as the crankshaft rotates. The sensor sends a signal to the ECU which then supplies the ignition HT coils with the power necessary to produce a spark at the plugs.

The ignition timing is decided by the ECU, which compares the signals it receives from the sensors to stored data in the form of ignition maps in its ROM. Note that there is no provision for adjusting the ignition timing. On RSV-R models provision exists to change the EPROM chip in the ECU.

The system also incorporates a safety interlock circuit which will cut the ignition if the sidestand is extended whilst the engine is running and in gear, or if a gear is selected whilst the engine is running and the sidestand is extended. It also prevents the engine from being started unless the clutch lever is pulled in, and if the engine is in gear while the sidestand is down. The engine can be started in gear as long as the sidestand is up and the clutch is pulled in.

Because of their nature, the individual ignition system components can be checked but not repaired. If ignition system troubles occur, and the faulty component can be isolated, the only cure for the problem is to replace the part with a new one. Keep in mind that most electrical parts, once purchased, cannot be returned. To avoid unnecessary expense, make very sure the faulty component has been positively identified before buying a replacement part.

2 Ignition system check

⚠️ *Warning: The energy levels in electronic systems can be very high. On no account should the ignition be switched on whilst the plugs or plug caps are being held. Shocks from the*

HT circuit can be most unpleasant. Secondly, it is vital that the engine is not turned over or run with any of the plug caps removed, and that the plugs are soundly earthed (grounded) when the system is checked for sparking. The ignition system components can be seriously damaged if the HT circuit becomes isolated.

1 As no means of adjustment is available, any failure of the system can be traced to failure of a system component or a simple wiring fault. Of the two possibilities, the latter is by far the most likely. In the event of failure, check the system in a logical fashion, as described below.

2 Work on one cylinder at a time. Refer to Chapter 1 for access to the spark plugs and pull the cap off the plug. Fit a spare spark plug that is known to be good into the cap and lay the plug against the cylinder head with the threads contacting it. If necessary, hold the spark plug with an insulated tool.

⚠️ *Warning: Do not remove any of the spark plugs from the engine to perform this check – atomised fuel being pumped out of the open spark plug hole could ignite, causing severe injury! Make sure the plugs are securely held against the engine – if they are not earthed when the engine is turned over, the ECU could be damaged.*

3 Check that the kill switch is in the 'RUN'

position and the transmission is in neutral, then turn the ignition switch ON, and turn the engine over on the starter motor. If the system is in good condition a regular, fat blue spark should be evident at the plug electrodes. If the spark appears thin or yellowish, or is non-existent, further investigation will be necessary. Turn the ignition off and repeat the test for the other spark plug.

4 The ignition system must be able to produce a spark which is capable of jumping a particular size gap. A healthy system should produce a spark capable of jumping at least 8 mm. Simple ignition spark gap testing tools are commercially available – follow the manufacturer's instructions, and check each spark plug.

5 If the test results are good the entire ignition system can be considered good. If the spark appears thin or yellowish, or is non-existent, further investigation is necessary.

6 Ignition faults can be divided into two categories, namely those where the ignition system has failed completely, and those which are due to a partial failure. The likely faults are listed below, starting with the most probable source of failure. Work through the list systematically, referring to the subsequent sections for full details of the necessary checks and tests, and to the *Wiring Diagrams* at the end of Chapter 9. **Note:** *Before checking the following items ensure that the battery is fully charged and that all fuses are in good condition.*

● Loose, corroded or damaged wiring connections, broken or shorted wiring between any of the component parts of the ignition system (see Chapter 9).
● Faulty HT lead or spark plug cap, faulty spark plug, dirty, worn or corroded plug electrodes, or incorrect gap between electrodes.
● Faulty ignition (main) switch or engine kill switch (see Chapter 9).
● Faulty neutral, clutch or sidestand switch, or diodes (see Chapter 9).
● Faulty crankshaft position sensor or damaged trigger.
● Faulty ignition HT coil(s).
● Faulty ECU.

7 If the above checks don't reveal the cause of the problem, have the ignition system tested by an Aprilia dealer.

3   Ignition HT coils

Check

1 Make sure the ignition is switched OFF.

2 The coils are mounted on the outside of each main frame spar **(see illustration)**. The front cylinder coils are on the right-hand side – the front coil is for the upper spark plug and the rear coil for the lower. The rear cylinder coils are on the left-hand side – the front coil is for the lower plug and the rear is for the upper. Remove the fairing side panels for access (see Chapter 8). Check the coils visually for cracks, loose wiring connectors and leads, and other damage.

3 The coils can be tested in situ. Refer to Chapter 1 for access to the spark plugs and pull the cap off the plug. Unscrew the cap from the HT lead.

4 Measure the primary circuit resistance with an ohmmeter or multimeter as follows: disconnect the primary circuit wiring connectors for the coil being tested, noting which fits where **(see illustration)**. Set the meter to the ohms x 1 scale and measure the resistance between the terminals on the coil **(see illustration)**. If the reading obtained is not within the range shown in the Specifications, it is possible that the coil is defective.

5 Measure the secondary circuit resistance with a multimeter as follows: set the meter to the K-ohm scale. Connect the positive (+) meter probe to the HT lead end and the negative (-) probe to the primary circuit terminal on the side of the coil that the HT lead is on **(see illustration)**. If the reading obtained is not within the range shown in the Specifications, it is possible that the coil is defective.

6 Before buying a new coil, measure the resistance of the spark plug cap by connecting the meter probes between the HT

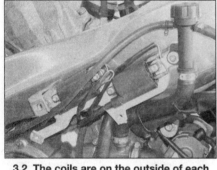

3.2 The coils are on the outside of each frame spar

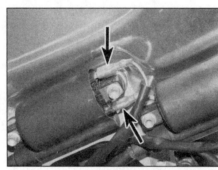

3.4a Disconnect the primary wiring connectors (arrowed)

3.4b To test the coil primary resistance, connect the multimeter leads between the primary circuit connector terminals

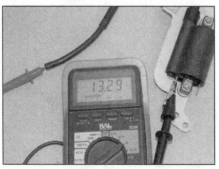

3.5 To test the coil secondary resistance, connect the probes to the spark plug cap socket and the connector terminal

3.6 Check the resistance of the plug cap as shown

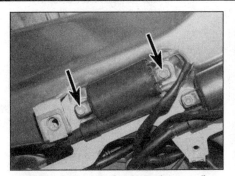

3.11a Coil mounting bolts (arrowed)

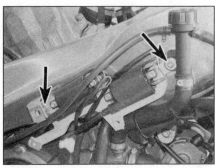

3.11b Coil plate mounting bolts (arrowed)

lead socket and the spark plug socket in the cap **(see illustration)**. If the reading obtained is not as specified, replace the spark plug cap with a new one. If the coil is still suspect, substitute it with one that is known to be good, (i.e. from the other cylinder), before condemning it. If the problem still exists, then the fault is probably in the primary wiring circuit – refer to Wiring Diagrams at the end of Chapter 9 and check the wiring and connectors in the circuit.

7 If a coil is confirmed to be faulty, it must be replaced with a new one; the coils are sealed units and cannot therefore be repaired.

Removal

8 Make sure the ignition is switched OFF.

9 The coils are mounted on the outside of each main frame spar **(see illustration 3.2)**.

10 Refer to Chapter 1 for access to the spark plugs and pull the cap off the plug. Feed it through to the coil, noting its routing.

11 Disconnect the primary circuit wiring connectors from the coil, making a careful note of which fits where **(see illustration 3.4a)**. Unscrew the bolts securing the coil – they have self-locking nuts on the inside, so if they turn with the bolt you will need to counter-hold them **(see illustration)**. If access is tricky, remove both coils on their mounting plate as an assembly, and separate the individual coil(s) from the plate afterwards **(see illustration)**. Note the collar and rubber bush on each coil mount. Replace the rubbers with new ones if they are damaged, deformed or deteriorated.

Installation

12 Installation is the reverse of removal. Make sure the wiring connectors and HT

leads are correctly routed and securely connected.

4 Engine control unit (ECU)

Check

1 If the tests shown in the preceding or following Sections have failed to isolate the cause of an ignition fault, it is possible that the ECU is faulty. No test details are available with which the unit can be tested. Take the bike to your dealer who with luck will substitute a test ECU for yours to analyse the problem.

Removal

2 Remove the seat cowling (see Chapter 8). Make sure the ignition is OFF.

3 Remove the rubber cover from the ECU **(see illustration)**. Lift it off its tray, then disconnect the wiring connectors and remove it **(see illustration)**.

4.3a Remove the rubber cover . . .

Installation

4 Installation is the reverse of removal. Make sure the wiring connectors are correctly and securely connected.

5 Ignition timing

Since it is not possible to adjust the ignition timing and since no component is subject to mechanical wear, there is no provision for any checks. While in theory it is possible to check the timing dynamically (engine running) using a stroboscopic lamp, the firing point at idle is not actually marked on the alternator rotor. If the timing is suspected of being out or not advancing properly, first check the crankshaft position sensor and its wiring and connectors (see Chapter 4), then if that is good substitute the ECU with a known good one to see if the problem is cured.

4.3b . . . then disconnect the wiring connectors and remove the ECU

Chapter 6
Frame, suspension and final drive

Contents

Degrees of difficulty

| Easy, suitable for novice with little experience | Fairly easy, suitable for beginner with some experience | Fairly difficult, suitable for competent DIY mechanic | Difficult, suitable for experienced DIY mechanic | Very difficult, suitable for expert DIY or professional |

Specifications

Front forks

Fork oil type . . . . 5W to 20W (see Section 7)
Fork oil capacity
    RSV models . . . . 517.5 to 522.5 cc
    RSV-R models . . . . 500 cc
Fork oil level*
    RSV models . . . . 116 to 120 mm
    RSV-R models . . . . 85 mm
Fork spring free length
    RSV models . . . . 284 mm min
    RSV-R models . . . . not available
Fork tube runout limit . . . . 0.2 mm
*Oil level is measured from the top of the tube with the fork spring removed and the leg fully compressed.

Rear suspension

Swingarm pivot bolt runout (max) . . . . 0.3 mm

Final drive

Drive chain slack, lubricant and stretch limit . . . . see Chapter 1
Drive chain
    Size 525
    Diameter of the master link staked ends . . . . 5.5 to 5.8 mm
Sprocket sizes
    Front (engine) sprocket 17T
    Rear (wheel) sprocket 42T

Torque settings

Brake pedal pivot bolt	15 Nm
Engine sprocket bolt	50 Nm
Engine sprocket cover bolts	12 Nm
Fork clamp bolts	
Top yoke	25 Nm
Bottom yoke	25 Nm
Fork cartridge bolt	35 Nm
Fork top bolt-to-damper rod locknut	35 Nm
Fork top bolt-to-fork tube	35 Nm
Handlebar clamp bolts	25 Nm
Handlebar positioning bolts	10 Nm
Rear sub-frame to main frame bolts	50 Nm
Rear suspension linkage and rear shock bolts/nuts	50 Nm
Sidestand bracket bolts	40 Nm
Sidestand pivot bolt	10 Nm
Sidestand pivot bolt nut	25 Nm
Steering damper mounting bolts	12 Nm
Steering head bearing adjuster nut (see text)	40 Nm
Steering stem nut	
1998 to 2000 models with plain nut	80 Nm
2001 to 2003 models with drilled nut	100 Nm
Shock absorber mounting bolt nuts	50 Nm
Swingarm adjuster bolt	12 Nm
Swingarm pivot bolt nut	90 Nm
Swingarm pivot bolt locknut	60 Nm
Rear sprocket nuts	50 Nm

1 General information

All models have an aluminium frame with the engine acting as a stressed member.

Front suspension is by a pair of oil-damped upside-down telescopic forks that are adjustable for spring pre-load and both rebound and compression damping. Showa forks are fitted to RSV models and Ohlins forks on RSV-R models.

At the rear, a box-section aluminium swingarm acts on a single shock absorber via a three-way linkage. The shock absorber is adjustable for spring pre-load and both rebound and compression damping. A Boge-Sachs shock is fitted to RSV models and an Ohlins shock on RSV-R models.

The drive to the rear wheel is by chain and sprockets.

2 Frame

1 The frame should not require attention unless accident damage has occurred. In most cases, frame renewal is the only satisfactory remedy for such damage. A few frame specialists have the jigs and other equipment necessary for straightening the frame to the required standard of accuracy, but even then there is no simple way of assessing to what extent the frame may have been over stressed.
2 After the machine has accumulated a lot of miles, the frame should be examined closely for signs of cracking or splitting at the welded joints. Loose engine mount bolts can cause ovaling or fracturing of the mounting tabs. Minor damage can often be repaired by welding, depending on the extent and nature of the damage.
3 Remember that a frame which is out of alignment will cause handling problems. If misalignment is suspected as the result of an accident, it will be necessary to strip the machine completely so the frame can be thoroughly checked.

3 Footrests, brake pedal and gearchange lever

Footrests

1 To remove the front footrests, remove the E-clip from the bottom of the pivot pin, then withdraw the pin and remove the footrest, noting how the return spring ends locate **(see illustration)**.
2 To remove the rear footrests, remove the E-clip from the bottom of the pivot pin, then withdraw the pin and remove the footrest, noting how the detent plates, ball and spring are fitted **(see illustration)**. Take care not to let the spring and ball ping out.
3 Installation is the reverse of removal. Apply some grease to the pivot pin, and to the mating surfaces of the footrest and its bracket, and to the rear footrest detent plates.

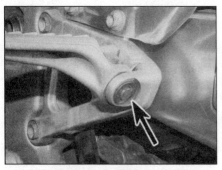

3.1 Remove the E-clip (arrowed) and withdraw the pivot pin

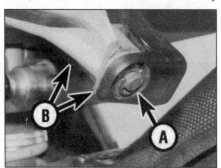

3.2 Remove the E-clip (A) and withdraw the pivot pin, noting the detent plates (B), ball and spring

3.4a Slide the O-ring off . . .

3.4b . . . then release clip . . .

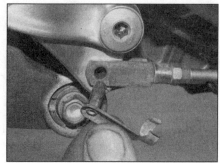

3.4c . . . and remove the pin

Brake pedal

Removal

4 Slide the O-ring off the clevis pin clip and onto the pushrod shank **(see illustration)**. Release the clip from the clevis and slide the pin out **(see illustrations)**. Withdraw the pushrod from the master cylinder **(see illustration)**.

5 Unhook the brake pedal return spring from the pedal **(see illustration)**.

6 Unscrew the footrest pivot bolt and remove the pedal, noting the O-rings and washer **(see illustrations)**. The toe rubber can be slid off the pin and replaced with a new one if necessary. The toe pin can be released by removing the E-clip and unscrewing the pinch bolt **(see illustration)** – new ones are available.

Installation

7 Installation is the reverse of removal, noting the following:

● Apply grease to the pivot section of the bolt and to the O-rings. Use new O-rings if the old ones are damaged, deformed or deteriorated **(see illustration 3.6b)**.

● Apply threadlock (Loctite 243) to the pivot bolt threads and tighten it to the torque setting specified at the beginning of the Chapter.

● Check the operation of the rear brake light switch (see Chapter 1).

Gearchange lever

8 Make an alignment mark between the gearchange shaft end and the slit in the lever clamp, then unscrew the pinch bolt and slide the lever off the shaft **(see illustration)**. The

toe rubber can be slid off the pin and replaced with a new one if necessary. The toe pin can be released by removing the E-clip and unscrewing the pinch bolt **(see illustration 3.6c)** – new ones are available.

9 Installation is the reverse of removal. Align the slit in the clamp with the mark made on the end of the gearchange shaft.

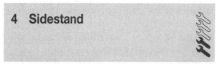

4 Sidestand

Removal

1 The sidestand is attached to a bracket on the frame. Two springs ensure the stand is held in the retracted or extended position.

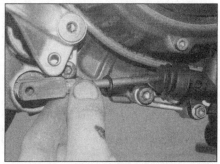

3.4d Remove the pushrod

3.5 Unhook the spring (arrowed)

3.6a Unscrew the pivot bolt (arrowed) and remove the pedal

3.6b Note the washer and O-rings

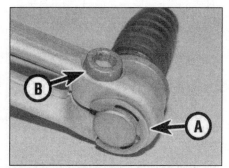

3.6c Remove the E-clip (A) and unscrew the bolt (B) to release the toe pin

3.8 Unscrew the pinch bolt (arrowed) and slide the lever off

4.3 Unscrew the bolt (arrowed) and displace the switch

4.4 Unhook the springs (arrowed)

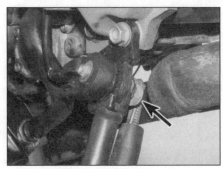

4.5 Unscrew the nut (arrowed) from the pivot bolt

2 Support the bike on an auxiliary stand. Remove the lower fairing (see Chapter 8).

3 Unscrew the bolt securing the sidestand switch and displace it from the stand, noting how it locates **(see illustration)**. If you are removing the stand because the bike is being used on a track, remove the switch completely (see Chapter 9), then plug the Aprilia tool (part No. 8124943) into the connector for the switch wiring.

4 Unhook the stand springs **(see illustration)**.

5 Unscrew the nut from the pivot bolt, noting the spring washer **(see illustration)**. Unscrew the pivot bolt and remove the stand.

6 If required unscrew the bolts securing the bracket to the frame.

Installation

7 Installation is the reverse of removal, noting the following:
● If removed, tighten the sidestand bracket

bolts to the torque setting specified at the beginning of the chapter.
● Apply grease to the pivot bolt shank.
● Reconnect the springs and check that they hold the stand securely up when not in use – an accident is almost certain to occur if the stand extends while the machine is in motion **(see illustration 4.4)**.
● Check the operation of the sidestand switch (see Chapter 1, Section 22).

5 Handlebars and levers

Handlebars

1 Remove the fairing (see Chapter 8) – although it is not essential, doing so improves access and negates the possibility of scratching the paint should a tool slip.

Right handlebar removal

2 Displace the front brake master cylinder and reservoir (see Chapter 7). Keep the master cylinder reservoir upright to prevent possible fluid leakage – wrap it in some rag just in case.

3 Displace the handlebar switch housing (see Chapter 9).

4 If required, remove the throttle cables (See Chapter 4). To avoid having to do this, just remove the cable housing cover, secured by two bolts, then slide the twistgrip and cable housing off the end of the handlebar with the cables still attached after the handlebar has been displaced from the fork.

5 Unscrew the handlebar end-weight retaining screw, counter-holding the weight using some grips padded with rag or tape, then remove the weight from the end of the handlebar **(see illustration)**. If the throttle cables have been detached, slide the twistgrip off the handlebar. If required, remove the pin from the end-weight shaft, then slide off the O-ring, unscrew the end-piece and remove the shaft and its rubber bush.

6 Unscrew the handlebar positioning bolt for each handlebar on the underside of the yoke **(see illustration)**. Slacken the fork clamp bolts in the top yoke **(see illustration)**. Unscrew the steering stem nut and remove the washer **(see illustration)**. Gently ease the top yoke up and off the forks and position it clear, using a rag to protect other components – take care not to strain the throttle cables which pass through a guide secured to the ignition switch base **(see illustration)**.

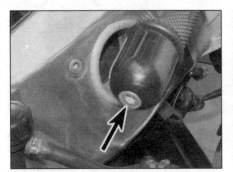

5.5 Handlebar end-weight screw (arrowed)

5.6a Unscrew the handlebar positioning bolt on each side . . .

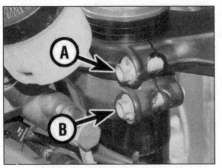

5.6b . . . then slacken the fork clamp bolt (A) on each side. Handlebar clamp bolt (B)

5.6c Unscrew the steering stem nut and remove the washer . . .

5.6d . . . then lift the yoke off the forks

7 Slacken the handlebar clamp bolt **(see illustration 5.6b)**, then ease the handlebar up and off the fork. If required, slide the throttle twistgrip off the handlebar.

Left handlebar removal

8 Displace the clutch master cylinder and reservoir (see Chapter 2) – this procedure incorporates detaching the handlebar switch housing and the fast idle cable from the lever. Keep the master cylinder reservoir upright to prevent possible fluid leakage – wrap it in some rag just in case.

9 Unscrew the handlebar end-weight retaining screw, counter-holding the weight using some grips padded with rag or tape, then remove the weight from the end of the handlebar **(see illustration)**. If required, remove the pin from the end-weight shaft, then slide off the O-ring, unscrew the end-piece and remove the shaft and its rubber bush.

10 Slide the grip off the handlebar – you will probably have to slide a screwdriver or inject compressed air between the grip and the handlebar to release it. If the grip has been glued on, you will probably have to slit it with a knife. Slide the fast idle lever assembly off the handlebar.

11 Unscrew the handlebar positioning bolt for each handlebar on the underside of the yoke **(see illustration 5.6a)**. Slacken the fork clamp bolts in the top yoke **(see illustration 5.6b)**. Unscrew the steering stem nut and remove the washer **(see illustration 5.6c)**. Gently ease the top yoke up and off the forks and position it clear, using a rag to protect other components – take care not to strain the throttle cables which pass through a guide secured to the ignition switch base **(see illustration 5.6d)**.

12 Slacken the handlebar clamp bolt **(see illustration 5.6b)**, then ease the handlebar up and off the fork.

Installation

13 Installation is the reverse of removal, noting the following.
● Do not forget to slide the fast idle lever assembly onto the left-hand bar before fitting the grip.

5.9 Handlebar end-weight screw (arrowed)

● If the throttle cables were not detached slide the twistgrip and cable housing onto the handlebar before fitting the bar onto the fork.
● Smear some engine oil onto the steering stem nut threads **(see illustration 5.6c)**.
● Tighten the steering stem nut first, then the fork clamp bolts in the top yoke, then the handlebar positioning bolts, then the handlebar clamp bolts, tightening them all to the torque settings specified at the beginning of the Chapter.
● Apply some grease to the throttle twistgrip section of the right handlebar.
● Align the master cylinder clamp mating surfaces with the mark on the handlebar, and fit the clamp with the triangular mark pointing forwards (see Chapter 6).
● Make sure the pin in the bottom half of each switch housing locates in its hole in the handlebar (see Chapter 9).
● Make sure the throttle opens freely and snaps shut when released.
● Check the operation of the throttle and fast idle cables, the front brake and the clutch before riding the bike on the road (see Chapter 1).

Handlebar levers

14 Unscrew the nut on the underside of the lever bracket **(see illustration)**. Unscrew the pivot bolt and remove the lever.

15 Installation of the levers is the reverse of removal. Apply grease to the pivot bolt shafts and the contact areas between the lever and

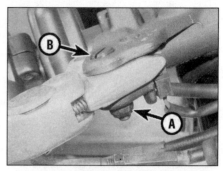

5.14 Unscrew the nut (A), then the pivot bolt (B) and remove the lever

its bracket. Apply silicone grease to the contact surfaces of the lever and master cylinder pushrod.

6 Fork removal and installation

Removal

1 Remove the fairing side panels (see Chapter 8). Also remove the fairing if required to prevent the possibility of damage should a tool slip.

2 Remove the front wheel (see Chapter 7). Tie the front brake calipers and hoses back so that they are out of the way.

3 Remove the front mudguard (see Chapter 8).

4 Slacken the handlebar clamp bolt for the fork being removed **(see illustration 5.6b)**.

5 Note the amount of protrusion of the fork tube above the top surface of the top yoke, either using the lines marked on the tube or by measuring the height. Record this information as a guide to refitting.

6 Working on one fork at a time, slacken the fork clamp bolt in the top yoke **(see illustration 5.6b)**. If the fork is to be disassembled, or if the fork oil is being changed, slacken the fork top bolt now **(see illustration)**.

7 Slacken the fork clamp bolts in the bottom yoke, and remove each fork by twisting it and pulling it downwards **(see illustrations)**.

6.6 Fork top bolt (arrowed)

6.7a Slacken the clamp bolts (arrowed) in the bottom yoke . . .

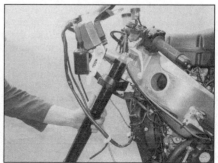

6.7b . . . and remove the fork

7.3 Unscrew the top bolt

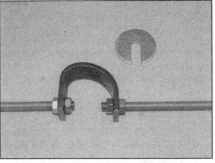

7.4a Holding tool and retaining plate

7.4b Locate the holding tool into the holes in the spacer, then grasp the handles of the tool and pull the spacer down to compress the spring and locate the retainer plate between the spacer and the nut

HAYNES HiNT *If the fork legs are seized in the yokes, spray the area with penetrating oil and allow time for it to soak in before trying again. If necessary lever the clamp open slightly by using a large flat-bladed screwdriver, taking care not to scratch anything.*

Installation

8 Remove all traces of corrosion from the fork tube and the yokes. Slide the fork up through the bottom yoke, through the handlebar clamp, and into the top yoke, making sure all cables, hoses and wiring are routed on the correct side of the fork **(see illustration 6.7b)**.

9 Set the amount of protrusion of the fork above the top yoke as noted on removal. Make sure it is the same for each fork.

10 Tighten the fork clamp bolts in the bottom yoke to the torque setting specified at the beginning of the Chapter **(see illustration 6.7a)**. If the fork has been dismantled or if the fork oil was changed, tighten the fork top bolt to the specified torque setting **(see illustration 6.6)**. Now tighten the fork clamp bolt in the top yoke to the specified torque **(see illustration 5.6b)**.

11 Tighten the handlebar clamp bolt to the specified torque setting **(see illustration 5.6b)**.

12 Adjust the suspension as required (see Section 14).

13 Install the front mudguard (see Chapter 8), and the front wheel (see Chapter 7). Install the fairing panels (see Chapter 8).

14 Check the operation of the front forks and brakes before taking the machine out on the road.

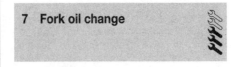

7 Fork oil change

RSV models

Note: *Aprilia do not specify a particular grade of fork oil, but say that the type used should be selected according to the feel required from the front suspension The lightest oil that should be used is a 5W, and the heaviest a 20W. A 10W fork oil is a good place to start if you are unsure as to which oil will perform best. Always make sure the same weight oil is used in each fork.*

1 Remove the forks (see Section 6). Always work on the fork legs separately to avoid interchanging parts and thus causing an accelerated rate of wear.

2 If the fork top bolt was not slackened with the fork in situ, re-locate it in the bottom yoke and tighten the clamp bolts, then slacken the top bolt.

3 Unscrew the top bolt from the top of the fork **(see illustration)**. The bolt will remain threaded on the damper cartridge rod.

4 Obtain either the Aprilia service tool set (part. No. 8140151), or construct home-made equivalents **(see illustration)**:

● *Holding tool - a piece of steel strap bent into a U-shape and some threaded rod and nuts.*

● *Retaining plate - a 40 mm diameter washer with a 10 mm wide slot cut into it to the middle.*

Either place the fork upright on the floor or carefully clamp the brake caliper lugs between the padded jaws of a vice. Slide the outer tube fully down onto the inner tube (wrap a rag around the top of the outer tube to minimise oil spillage) while, with the aid of an assistant if necessary, keeping the damper rod fully extended. Fit the holding tool onto the upper spacer, locating it into the holes **(see illustration)**. Push down on the spacer using the tool and have an assistant insert the retaining plate between the washer on the top of the upper spacer bush and the base of the locknut on the damper cartridge. This will keep the spacer and spring compressed while removing the top bolt assembly.

5 Using two spanners, one on the locknut and one on the flats on the inner section of the top bolt assembly, counter-hold the locknut and thread the top bolt assembly off the damper cartridge rod **(see illustration)**. Lift the assembly until the damping adjuster rod is clear of the damper cartridge rod **(see illustration)**.

6 Push down on the upper spacer using the holding tool and have an assistant remove the retaining tool **(see illustration)**, then slowly release the spring pressure.

7 Remove the washer and bush from the top of the upper spacer, then remove the upper

7.5a Counter-hold the locknut and unscrew the top bolt . . .

7.5b . . . and withdraw the damping adjuster rod with it

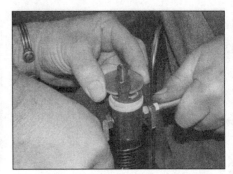

7.6 Compress the spring using the holding tool and remove the retaining tool

7.9 Invert the fork over a container and pump the fork as described to expel the oil

7.10a Pour the oil into the top of the tube

7.10b Measure the oil level and adjust if necessary

spacer, noting which way up it fits (you can leave the holding tool attached) **(see illustration 7.12c, b and a)**.

8 Using a piece of wire bent over at the end if necessary, remove the spring from the tube, noting which way up fits **(see illustration 7.11c)**.

9 Invert the fork over a suitable container and pump the tubes and damper rod vigorously to expel as much oil as possible **(see illustration)**. Support the fork upside down in the container for a while to allow as much oil as possible to drain, and pump the fork and damper rod again. The spring seat and lower spacer may well drop out when doing this **(see illustrations 7.11b and a)**.

10 Slowly pour in the specified quantity of the required grade of fork oil (see **Note** above) and pump the damper rod and the fork tubes at least ten times to distribute it evenly **(see illustration)**. Allow the fork to stand upright

for at least five minutes, then pump the damper rod and tubes some more and watch for any air bubbles in the oil. Do this until no bubbles can be seen – it is important that all air is expelled from the damper cartridge. Slide the outer tube fully down onto the inner tube. Measure the oil level, and make any adjustment by adding more or tipping some out until the oil is at the level specified at the beginning of the Chapter **(see illustration)**. Do not rely on the quantity of oil put in as an accurate gauge as it is impossible to tell how much old oil was left in the forks after draining – always measure the oil level as well.

11 If they came out when draining the oil, fit the lower spacer and spring seat into the fork **(see illustrations)**. Install the spring **(see illustration)**.

12 Withdraw the damper rod fully from the fork, using a pair of thin-nosed pliers to grab it if necessary. As the damper rod will have to

be kept extended out of the cartridge, tie a piece of wire around the threads on the top of the rod to use as a holder. Install the upper spacer with the spring stop on the bottom, sliding it over the wire **(see illustration)**. Fit the bush into the top of the spacer, then fit the washer onto the bush, sliding them both down the wire **(see illustrations)**.

13 If the holding tool used on disassembly was removed from the upper spacer, fit it back on. Keeping the damper rod fully extended (an assistant is useful) push down on the spacer using the holding tool and insert the retaining plate between the washer on the top of the spacer bush and the base of the locknut on the damper cartridge **(see illustration 7.6)**. This will keep the spacer and spring compressed while installing the top bolt assembly. You can now remove the piece of wire.

14 If required fit a new O-ring onto the top

7.11a Install the lower spacer . . .

7.11b . . . the spring seat . . .

7.11c . . . and the spring

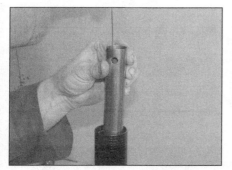

7.12a Install the upper spacer . . .

7.12b . . . the bush . . .

7.12c . . . and the washer

7.14 Thread the top bolt onto the damper cartridge rod

7.15 The washer locates against the pre-load adjuster tripod legs

7.16 Smear the O-ring (arrowed) with oil then thread the top bolt into the fork tube

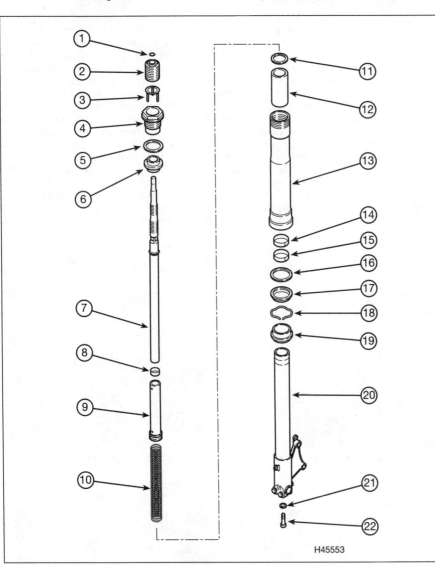

H45553

8.1 Front fork components

1 Retaining ring	7 Damper cartridge	12 Lower spacer	18 Retaining clip
2 Pre-load adjuster	with adjuster rod	13 Outer tube	19 Dust seal
3 Pre-load adjuster	8 Damper cartridge	14 Inner bush	20 Inner tube
tripod	seat	15 Outer bush	21 Sealing washer
4 Top bolt	9 Upper spacer	16 Oil seal washer	22 Damper cartridge
5 Washer	10 Spring	17 Oil seal	bolt
6 Bush	11 Spring seat		

bolt. Locate the tip of the damping adjuster rod into the damper cartridge rod and slide it all the way in **(see illustration 7.5b)**. Thread the top bolt assembly onto the damper cartridge rod until it seats against the locknut, holding the locknut to prevent the cartridge rod from turning **(see illustration)**. Counter-hold the locknut and tighten the top bolt assembly securely against it **(see illustration 7.5a)**.

15 Push down on the upper spacer using the holding tool and have an assistant remove the retaining tool, then slowly release the spring pressure and allow the spacer washer to settle against the pre-load adjuster legs **(see illustration)**. Remove the holding tool from the spacer.

16 Apply a smear of the specified clean oil to the top bolt O-ring. Fully extend the outer tube and carefully screw the top bolt into the tube making sure it is not cross-threaded **(see illustration)**. **Note:** *The top bolt can be tightened to the specified torque setting at this stage if the tube is held between the padded jaws of a vice, but do not risk distorting the tube by doing so. A better method is to tighten the top bolt when the fork leg has been installed and is securely held in the bottom yoke.*

17 Install the forks (see Section 6).

RSV-R models

18 Work on the forks fitted to R models should only be undertaken by an Ohlins service centre. Refer to your Aprilia dealer for further details. No procedures are given in this manual for these forks.

---

8   Fork overhaul

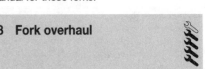

RSV models

Disassembly

1 Remove the forks (see Section 6). Always dismantle the fork legs separately to avoid interchanging parts and thus causing an accelerated rate of wear. Store all components in separate, clearly marked containers **(see illustration)**.

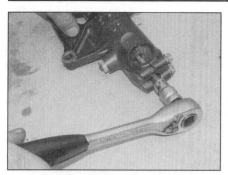

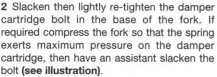

8.2 Slacken the damper cartridge bolt

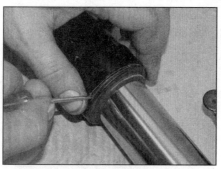

8.4 Prise out the dust seal using a flat-bladed screwdriver

8.5 Prise out the retaining clip using a flat-bladed screwdriver

2 Slacken then lightly re-tighten the damper cartridge bolt in the base of the fork. If required compress the fork so that the spring exerts maximum pressure on the damper cartridge, then have an assistant slacken the bolt **(see illustration)**.

3 Refer to Section 7, Steps 2 to 9, and drain the oil from the fork.

4 Carefully prise out the dust seal from the bottom of the outer tube to gain access to the oil seal retaining clip **(see illustration)**.

5 Carefully remove the retaining clip, taking care not to scratch the surface of the inner tube **(see illustration)**. It is advisable to fully compress the fork to keep any accidental damage above the seal area.

6 To separate the inner and outer tubes it is necessary to displace the oil seal and outer bush. The inner bush does not pass through the outer bush, and this can be used to good effect. Gently compress the fork – take care not to do this forcibly. Now pull the tubes sharply apart until the inner bush strikes the outer bush **(see illustration)**. Repeat this operation until the outer bush and seal are displaced, then draw the tubes fully apart.

7 Remove the inner bush from the inner tube by carefully levering its ends apart using a screwdriver **(see illustration)**. Slide the outer bush, the oil seal washer, the oil seal, the retaining clip and the dust seal off, noting which way up they fit. Discard the oil seal and the dust seal as new ones must be used.

8 Remove the previously slackened damper cartridge bolt and its copper sealing washer, manoeuvring them through the hole for the front axle **(see illustration 8.14c)**. Discard the sealing washer as a new one must be used on reassembly. Invert the fork and tip the damper cartridge out of the top **(see illustration 8.14b)**. Note the seat on the base of the cartridge – if it's not there tip it out of the fork **(see illustration 8.14a)**.

Inspection

9 Clean all parts in solvent and blow them dry with compressed air, if available. Check the outer surface of the inner tube and the inner surface of the outer tube for score marks, dents, scratches, pitting or flaking of the chrome finish, and excessive or abnormal

wear. Check the fork seal seat in the outer tube for nicks, gouges and scratches. If damage is evident, leaks will occur. Also check the oil seal washer for damage or distortion and replace it with a new one if necessary.

10 Check the inner tube for runout using V-blocks and a dial gauge. If the amount of runout exceeds the limit specified, replace the tube with a new one.

⚠️ **Warning: If the tube is bent or exceeds the runout limit, it should not be straightened; renew it.**

11 Check the spring for cracks and other damage. Measure the spring free length and compare the measurement to the

specifications at the beginning of the Chapter **(see illustration)**. If it is defective or sagged below the service limit, replace the springs in both forks with new ones – never replace only one spring.

12 Examine the working surfaces of the two bushes; if worn or scuffed they must be replaced with new ones – they are worn if the grey Teflon coating on the **sliding** surface (i.e. the inside of the outer bush and the outside of the inner bush) has rubbed off to reveal the copper surface **(see illustration)**. Note that it is advisable to fit new ones regardless of the condition of the old ones.

13 Check the damper cartridge for damage and wear. Holding the damper cartridge over the oil tray, pump the rod in and out **(see**

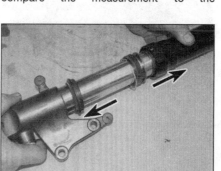

8.6 To separate the inner and outer tubes, pull them apart firmly several times – the slide-hammer effect will displace the oil seal and outer bush

8.7 Carefully lever the ends of the inner bush (arrowed) apart and slide it off, followed by the outer bush, washer, oil seal and dust seal off the inner tube

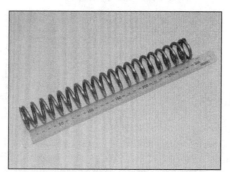

8.11 Check the spring free length

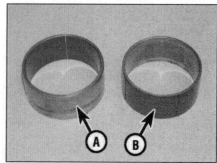

8.12 Check the bushes for wear – outer bush (A), inner bush (B)

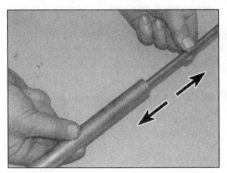

8.13 Check the action of the damper cartridge rod

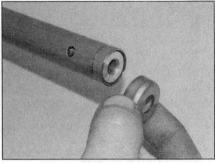

8.14a Fit the seat on the bottom of the damper cartridge

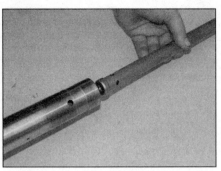

8.14b Slide the cartridge into the top of the fork

illustration). If the rod does not move smoothly in the cartridge the damper must be replaced with a new one.

Reassembly

14 Fit the seat onto the bottom of the damper cartridge **(see illustration)**. Lay the fork slider

8.14c Apply threadlock to the bolt and use a new sealing washer

flat and insert the damper cartridge in the top until it seats on the bottom **(see illustration)**. Fit a new sealing washer onto the damper cartridge bolt and apply a few drops of a suitable non-permanent thread locking compound, then fit the bolt into the bottom of the inner tube and tighten it to the torque setting

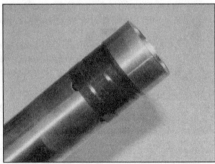

8.15 Protect the seal lips as described

specified at the beginning of the Chapter **(see illustration)**. If the damper cartridge rotates inside the tube, wait until the fork is fully reassembled before tightening the bolt.

15 Wrap some insulating tape or a plastic bag over the ridges on the top of the inner tube to protect the lips of the new oil seal as it is installed **(see illustration)**.

16 Apply a smear of the required clean fork oil to the lips of the oil seal and the inner surface of each bush. Slide the new dust seal, the retaining clip, the oil seal, the oil seal washer and the outer bush onto the inner tube, making sure that the dust seal is the correct way round and the marked side of the oil seal faces the dust seal **(see illustration 8.7)**. Remove the insulating tape and fit the inner bush into its recess in the tube.

17 Apply a smear of the required clean fork oil to the outer surface of each bush, then carefully insert the inner tube fully into the outer tube **(see illustration)**.

18 Support the fork upside down, then press the outer bush squarely into its recess in the outer tube as far as possible **(see illustration)**. Slide the oil seal washer on top of the bush, and keep the oil seal, the retaining clip and the dust seal out of the way by sliding them up the inner tube **(see illustration)**. If necessary, tape them to the tube to prevent them from falling down and interfering as the bush is driven into place.

19 Using either the special service tool set or a suitable drift covered in insulating tape, carefully drive the outer bush fully into its recess using the oil seal washer to prevent damaging the edges of the bush **(see illustrations)**. Make

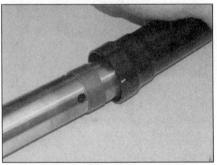

8.17 Slide the inner tube into the outer tube

8.18a Press the outer bush in . . .

8.18b . . . then lay the washer on top of it . . .

8.19a . . . to protect it as you drive the bush in . . .

8.19b . . . until its top rim is flush with the washer seat

sure the bush enters the recess squarely, and take care not to scratch or gouge the inner tube – it pays to wrap some insulating tape around it as well as the drift.

20 When the bush is seated fully and squarely in its recess in the tube (remove the washer to check, wipe the recess clean, then reinstall the washer), drive the new oil seal into place in the same way until the retaining clip groove is visible above the seal **(see illustrations)**.

21 Once the oil seal is correctly seated, fit the retaining clip, making sure it is correctly located in its groove, then press the dust seal into place **(see illustrations)**.

22 Refer to Section 7, Steps 10 to 17 to add the fork oil and finish rebuilding the fork.

RSV-R models

23 Work on the forks fitted to R models should only be undertaken by an Ohlins service centre. Refer to your Aprilia dealer for further details. No procedures are given in this manual for these forks.

8.20a Press the oil seal into the tube . . .

8.20b . . . and drive it fully into place until the groove for the retaining clip is fully exposed

---

9 Steering stem and head bearings

Removal

1 Remove the fairing side panels (See Chapter 8). Also remove the fairing if required to prevent the possibility of damage should a tool slip.

2 Remove the fuel tank (see Chapter 4) – this will prevent the possibility of damage should a tool slip.

3 Remove the front forks (see Section 6).

4 Where fitted unscrew the bolt securing the steering damper to the bottom yoke and remove the spacer.

5 Unscrew the bolts securing the plastic trim plate to the bottom yoke and remove the plate **(see illustration)**.

6 Unscrew the bolt securing the front brake hose splitter to the bottom yoke **(see illustration)**.

7 If required, unscrew the handlebar positioning bolts on the underside of the yoke and tie the handlebars aside – wrap them in rag and try to keep them upright **(see illustration 5.6a)**. Alternatively the handlebars can remain attached top the yoke and be lifted with it.

8 Unscrew the steering stem nut and remove the washer **(see illustration 5.6c)**. Ease the top yoke up and off the steering stem and position it clear, using a rag to protect other components – take care not to strain the throttle cables which pass through a guide secured to the ignition switch base **(see illustration)**.

9 Carefully bend down each of the lock washer tabs located in the notches in the adjuster locknut (the top nut) **(see illustration)**. Unscrew and remove the locknut – it may not be more than finger-tight, but use a drift located in one of the notches or a suitable C-spanner if necessary

8.21a Install the retaining clip . . .

8.21b . . . followed by the dust seal

9.5 Unscrew the bolts (arrowed) and remove the trim plate

9.6 Unscrew the bolt (arrowed) to release the brake hose

9.8 Lift the top yoke (and handlebars if attached) off the stem and place it aside

9.9a Bend the lockwasher tabs down

9.9b Unscrew the locknut . . .

9.9c . . . then remove the lockwasher

9.10a Unscrew the adjuster nut . . .

(see illustration). Remove the lock washer, noting how it's other tabs locate in the notches in the adjuster nut **(see illustration)**. Check the condition of the lock washer and replace it with a new one if any of the tabs look fatigued by the bending process – Aprilia recommend using a new one as a matter of course.

10 Support the bottom yoke, then unscrew the adjuster nut in the same way as the locknut **(see illustration)**. Remove the bearing cover and the seal **(see illustrations)**.
11 Gently lower the bottom yoke and steering stem out of the frame **(see illustration)**. Take care not to strain or knock the brake hoses.

12 Remove the inner race and bearing from the top of the steering head **(see illustrations 9.14b and a)**. Remove the bearing from the base of the steering stem **(see illustration 9.13)**. Remove all traces of old grease from the bearings and races and check them for wear or damage as described in Section 10. **Note:** *Do not attempt to remove the outer races from the steering head or the inner race from the steering stem unless they are to be replaced with new ones.*

Installation

13 Smear a liberal quantity of multi-purpose grease onto the bearing races, and work some grease well into both the upper and lower bearings. Also smear the grease seal. Fit the lower bearing onto the steering stem **(see illustration)**.
14 Carefully lift the steering stem/bottom yoke up through the steering head **(see illustration 9.11)**. Fit the upper bearing and its inner race into the top of the steering head **(see illustrations)**. Fit the grease seal and the bearing cover **(see illustrations 9.10c and b)**. Thread the adjuster nut onto the steering stem and tighten it finger-tight **(see illustration 9.10a)**.
15 If the Aprilia service tool (part No. 8140203) or a suitable peg spanner (which can be made by cutting castellations into an old socket) is available, tighten the adjuster nut to the torque setting specified at the beginning of the Chapter. Otherwise use a C-spanner to tighten the adjuster nut until all freeplay is removed, yet the steering is able to move freely **(see illustration)**. The object is to set the adjuster nut so that the bearings are under a very light loading, just enough to

9.10b . . . then remove the bearing cover . . .

9.10c . . . and the seal

9.11 Draw the bottom yoke/steering stem out of the steering head

9.13 Fit the lower bearing onto the inner race on the base of the stem

9.14a Fit the upper bearing . . .

9.14b . . . and the inner race

9.15 Using a C-spanner to tighten the adjuster nut

remove any freeplay, but not so much that the steering does not move freely from side to side as described in the check procedure in Chapter 1.

Caution: Take great care not to apply excessive pressure because this will cause premature failure of the bearings.

16 Now install all remaining components (except the top yoke, fuel tank and fairing panels). Re-check and finely adjust the amount of freeplay as described in Chapter 1.

17 With the bearings correctly adjusted, install the lock washer, using a new one if the tabs are weakened or cracked, onto the adjuster nut and fit two opposite tabs into the slots in the adjuster nut **(see illustration 9.9c)**.

18 Hold the adjuster nut to prevent it moving, then install the locknut and tighten it finger-tight **(see illustration 9.9b)**. Tighten the locknut further (but no more than 90°) until its notches align with the remaining lock washer tabs, making sure the adjuster nut does not turn as well (though that is unlikely). Secure the locknut in position by bending up the remaining lock washer tabs into its notches **(see illustration)**.

19 Install the top yoke and tighten the steering stem nut, the fork clamp bolts in the top yoke, the handlebar positioning bolts and then the clamp bolts to the torque settings specified at the beginning of the Chapter.

20 Install the remaining components in a reverse of the removal procedure.

21 Carry out a final check of the steering head bearing freeplay as described in Chapter 1, and if necessary re-adjust.

---

10 Steering head bearing inspection

Inspection

1 Remove the steering stem (see Section 9).

2 Remove all traces of old grease from the bearings and races and check them for wear or damage.

3 The inner and outer races should be polished and free from indentations. Inspect the bearing balls for signs of wear, damage or discoloration, and examine the ball retainer cage for signs of cracks or splits. If there are any signs of wear on any of the above components both upper and lower bearing assemblies must be replaced with new ones as a set. Only remove the outer races in the steering head and the lower bearing inner race on the steering stem if new ones are needed – do not re-use them once they have been removed.

Removal and installation

4 The outer races are an interference fit in the steering head and can be tapped from position with a suitable drift **(see illustration)**. Tap firmly and evenly around each race to

9.18 Bend the tabs up into the notches in the lockwasher

ensure that it is driven out squarely. It may prove advantageous to curve the end of the drift slightly to improve access.

5 Alternatively, the races can be removed using a slide-hammer type bearing extractor; these can often be hired from tool shops.

6 The new outer races can be pressed into the head using a drawbolt arrangement **(see illustration)**, or by using a large diameter tubular drift. Ensure that the drawbolt washer or drift (as applicable) bears only on the outer edge of the race and does not contact the working surface. Alternatively, have the races installed by an Aprilia dealer equipped with the bearing race installation tools.

> **HAYNES HiNT** *Installation of new bearing outer races is made much easier if the races are left overnight in the freezer. This causes them to contract slightly making them a looser fit. Alternatively, use a freeze spray.*

7 The lower bearing inner race should only be removed from the steering stem if a new one is being fitted **(see illustration)**. To remove the race, use two screwdrivers placed on opposite sides to work it free, using blocks of wood to improve leverage and protect the yoke, or tap under it using a cold chisel. If the steering stem is placed on its side on a hard surface, thread a suitable nut onto the top to prevent the threads being damaged. If the race is firmly in place it will be necessary to

10.7a Remove the lower bearing inner race (arrowed) as described . . .

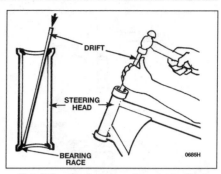

10.4 Drive the bearing races out with a brass drift locating it as shown

use a puller **(see illustration)**. Take the steering stem to an Aprilia dealer if required.

8 Remove the seal from the bottom of the stem and replace it with a new one. Smear the new one with grease.

9 Fit the new lower race onto the steering stem. A length of tubing with an internal diameter slightly larger than the steering stem will be needed to tap the new race into position – make sure the drift contacts the

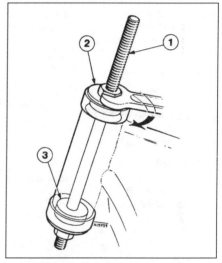

10.6 Drawbolt arrangement for fitting steering stem bearing races

1 *Long bolt or threaded bar*
2 *Thick washer*
3 *Guide for lower race*

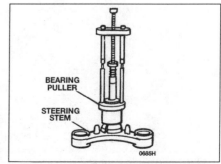

10.7b . . . or using a puller if necessary

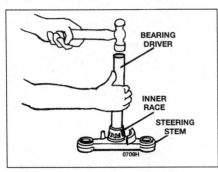

10.9 Drive the new race on using a suitable driver or a length of pipe

12.3 Unscrew the nut and withdraw the bolt joining the linkage plates to the shock absorber

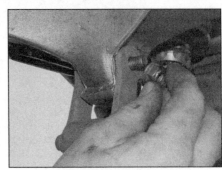

12.4 Unscrew the nut and withdraw the bolt joining the linkage plates to the swingarm

inner rim of the race only and not the bearing sliding surface **(see illustration)**.

10 Install the steering stem (see Section 9).

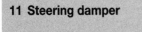

11 Steering damper

Note: *An adjustable steering damper is fitted as standard to RSV-R and a non-adjustable unit is available as optional equipment for RSV models.*

Removal

1 Remove the fairing (see Chapter 8).

2 Unscrew the damper mounting bolts, noting the spacer on the bottom yoke mount, and on standard models the bushes and O-rings with the frame mount.

Inspection

3 Inspect the damper for obvious physical damage. Check that the rod moves smoothly in and out of the body.

4 Inspect the damper rod for signs of bending, pitting and oil leakage.

5 Inspect the pivot hardware for wear or damage.

Installation

6 Installation is the reverse of removal, noting the following points.

● Apply multi-purpose grease to the mounting hardware and pivot points – clean off all old grease first.

● Tighten the mounting bolts to the torque setting specified at the beginning of the Chapter.

● Check the action of the steering and the damper after installation.

Adjustment

7 On RSV models the standard damper is not adjustable.

8 On RSV-R models and on RSV models fitted with the adjustable damper, adjustment is made by turning the knurled ring on the damper – turn the handlebars to full left lock to make the adjustment. There are approximately seventeen settings, each indicated by a click. Turn the adjuster anti-clockwise to slacken the steering and clockwise to stiffen it. The standard position is from twelve to fourteen clicks out from the stiffest setting.

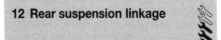

12 Rear suspension linkage

Removal

1 Support the motorcycle on an auxiliary stand that does not take the weight through

any part of the rear suspension, or by using a hoist. Position a support under the rear wheel or swingarm so that it does not drop when the spring unit and linkage is removed, but also making sure that the weight of the machine is off the rear suspension so that the spring is not compressed. Make a note of which side the bolts go in from, and make a note of which way round the spring unit fits.

2 Remove the lower fairing (see Chapter 8).

3 Unscrew the nut and withdraw the bolt securing the linkage plates to the bottom of the shock absorber **(see illustration)**.

4 Unscrew the nut and withdraw the bolt securing the linkage plates to the swingarm **(see illustration)**.

5 Unscrew the nut and withdraw the bolt securing the linkage plates to the linkage arm **(see illustration)**.

6 Unscrew the nut and withdraw the bolt securing the linkage arm to the frame **(see illustration)**. Retrieve the shouldered collar from the left-hand mount **(see illustration)**.

Inspection

Note: *Uncaged needle roller bearings are fitted in the suspension linkage pivots. When removing and inspecting the linkage components bear in mind that it is probable that the needles in uncaged bearings will drop out after removing the spacers, undoubtedly disappearing forever. New bearings come pre-*

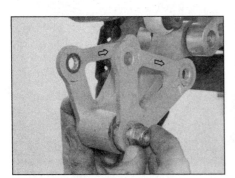

12.5 Unscrew the nut and withdraw the bolt joining the linkage plates to the linkage arm

12.6a Unscrew the nut and withdraw the bolt joining the linkage arm to the frame

12.6b Retrieve the collar from the mount

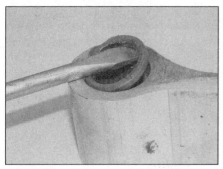

12.8 Lever the seal out from each side

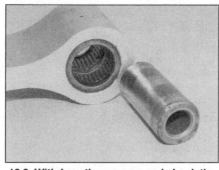

12.9 Withdraw the spacers and check the bearings

12.10a Fit a new bearing . . .

greased and are supplied with a nylon sleeve to keep the needles in place.

7 Inspect the linkage arm and plates, looking for signs of wear such as heavy scoring, or for damage such as cracks or distortion. Replace any worn or damaged components with new ones as required.

8 To remove the grease seals, push the spacer in until the seal is exposed, leaving the spacer to hold the bearing needles in place. Lever the seal out using a screwdriver **(see illustration)**. Discard the seals as new ones must be used. Check that there is not an excessive amount of freeplay between the spacers and the bearings.

9 Carefully withdraw the spacers from the linkage arm and from the swingarm **(see illustration)**. Check the condition of the needle roller bearings. Refer to *Tools and*

Workshop Tips (Section 5) in the Reference section for information on bearings. If you try to clean the bearings you will dislodge the needles, so take care. For the minimal cost, it is worth replacing old bearings with new ones even if they are in good condition and only require re-greasing, due to the hassle involved in cleaning the old grease off.

10 Worn bearings can be drifted out of their bores, but note that removal will destroy them. On the model photographed the bearings in the swingarm mount were corroded in place and needed to be pressed out using an hydraulic press. Obtain new bearings before you start. Do not remove the nylon sleeves fitted in the new bearings before installing them. Slide, press or draw the new bearings into their bores – do not drive them in **(see illustrations)**. In the absence of a

press, a suitable drawbolt tool can be made up as described in *Tools and Workshop Tips* in the Reference section. The new bearings are supplied pre-greased.

11 Lubricate the spacers with multi-purpose grease, then slide them into the bearings, using them to simultaneously push the nylon sleeves out – in this way there is no chance of dislodging any of the needles **(see illustration)**.

12 Fit new grease seals over the ends of the spacers and press them into place, making sure the lips do not turn inside out **(see illustration)**.

Installation

13 Installation is the reverse of removal, noting the following points.

● Do not forget to fit the collar into the left-hand frame mount for the linkage arm, fitting it with the shouldered end on the inside **(see illustration 12.6b)**.

● Make sure the arrow on each linkage plate points to the front of the bike **(see illustration 12.5)**.

● Leave all nuts and bolts loose until all are installed, then tighten them to the torque setting specified at the beginning of the Chapter.

12.10b . . . into each side

12.11a Slide the spacer in . . .

13 Rear shock absorber

1 Support the motorcycle on an auxiliary stand that does not take the weight through any part of the rear suspension, or by using a hoist. Position a support under the rear wheel or swingarm so that it does not drop when the shock absorber is removed, but also making sure that the weight of the machine is off the rear suspension so that the shock is not compressed. Make a note of which side the bolts go in from, and make a note of which way round the shock absorber fits.

2 Remove the seat and the side trim panels (see Chapter 8).

3 Unscrew the nut and withdraw the bolt securing the bottom of the shock absorber to the linkage plates **(see illustration 12.3)**.

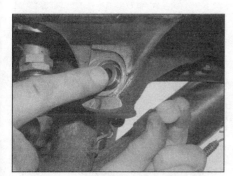

12.11b . . . using it to push the nylon sleeves out

12.12 Fit a new seal into each side

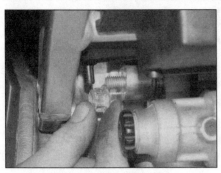

13.4a Unscrew the nut . . .

13.4b . . . withdraw the bolt . . .

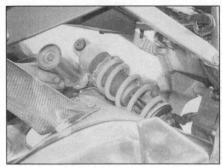

13.4c . . . and manoeuvre the shock out

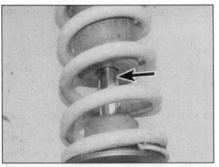

13.7 Check for pitting and oil on the rod (arrowed)

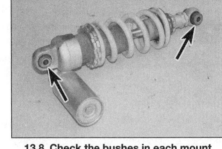

13.8 Check the bushes in each mount (arrowed)

14 Suspension adjustment

Note: *Refer to the suspension adjustment tables in machine's handbook in addition to that provided here. Settings are also given in the handbook for track use.*

Front suspension

Note: *The settings must the same on each fork to ensure even suspension performance.*

RSV models

1 Spring pre-load is adjusted using a suitable spanner on the adjuster flats on the top of the forks **(see illustration)**. The amount of pre-load is indicated by lines on the adjuster. Turn the adjuster clockwise to increase pre-load and anti-clockwise to decrease it.

2 Rebound damping is adjusted using a screwdriver in the slot in the adjuster protruding from the pre-load adjuster **(see illustration)**. The amount of damping is indicated by the number of turns anti-clockwise from the fully screwed-in position. The standard position is 1.5 turns out on 1998 to 2000 models and 1.25 turns out on 2001 models onward. Turn the adjuster clockwise to increase damping and anti-clockwise to decrease it.

3 Compression damping is adjusted using a screwdriver in the slot in the adjuster on the base of each fork **(see illustration)**. The

4 Unscrew the nut on the shock absorber upper mounting bolt **(see illustration)**. Support the shock absorber, then withdraw the bolt and manoeuvre the shock out of the top left-hand side **(see illustrations)**.
5 Note the bushes and O-rings fitted in the shock absorber mounts. On 1998 to 2000 models, note the shouldered collar in the upper mount and remove it for safekeeping if required.

Inspection

6 Inspect the shock absorber for obvious physical damage and the coil spring for looseness, cracks or signs of fatigue.
7 Inspect the rod for signs of bending, pitting and oil leakage **(see illustration)**.
8 Inspect the pivot bushes at the top and bottom for wear or damage **(see illustration)**.
9 With the exception of the mounting bushes,

O-rings, and nuts and bolts individual components are not available for DIY fitting. If the shock is worn, damaged or leaking return it to a Boge-Sachs (RSV) or Ohlins (RSV-R) service centre for rebuilding.

Installation

10 Installation is the reverse of removal, noting the following points.
● Apply multi-purpose grease to the spring unit/shock absorber and linkage pivot points.
● On 1998 to 2000 models do not forget to fit the shouldered collar.
● Fit the shock absorber with the reservoir at the back.
● Leave the nuts and bolts loose until all are installed, then tighten them to the torque setting specified at the beginning of the Chapter.

14.1 Spring pre-load adjuster (arrowed)

14.2 Rebound damping adjuster (arrowed)

14.3 Compression damping adjuster (arrowed)

amount of damping is indicated by the number of turns anti-clockwise from the fully screwed-in position. The standard position is 1.5 turns out on 1998 to 2000 models and 1 turn out on 2001 models onward. Turn the adjuster clockwise to increase damping and anti-clockwise to decrease it.

RSV-R models

4 Spring pre-load is adjusted using a suitable spanner on the adjuster flats on the top of the forks. Turn the adjuster clockwise to increase pre-load and anti-clockwise to decrease it.

5 Rebound damping is adjusted using a screwdriver in the slot in the adjuster protruding from the pre-load adjuster. The amount of damping is indicated by the number of clicks when turned anti-clockwise from the fully screwed-in position. The standard position is 8 clicks out on 1999 and 2000 models, and 12 clicks out on 2001 models onwarard. Turn the adjuster clockwise to increase damping and anti-clockwise to decrease it.

6 Compression damping is adjusted using a screwdriver in the slot in the adjuster on the base of each fork. The amount of damping is indicated by the number of clicks when turned anti-clockwise from the fully screwed-in position. The standard position is 12 clicks out. Turn the adjuster clockwise to increase damping and anti-clockwise to decrease it.

Rear suspension

⚠️ *Warning: The shock gas reservoir is nitrogen-charged. Do not disturb the screw, bolt or plug on the end of the reservoir opposite the compression damping adjuster knob.*

1998 to 2000 RSV models

7 Spring pre-load is adjusted by slackening the locknut on the top of the spring using a C-spanner, then turning the adjuster nut to alter the length of the spring **(see illustration 14.15)**. The standard pre-loaded spring length is 130 mm; this can be varied between 128 and 132 mm.

8 Rebound damping is adjusted using a screwdriver in the slot in the adjuster on the left-hand side of the unit. The amount of damping is indicated by the number of clicks when turned anti-clockwise from the fully screwed-in position. The standard position is around 14 clicks out. Turn the adjuster clockwise to increase damping and anti-clockwise to decrease it.

9 Compression damping is adjusted by turning the knob on the left-hand side of the reservoir on the back of the shock absorber. The amount of damping is indicated by the number of clicks when turned anti-clockwise from the fully screwed-in position. The standard position is 35 to 45 clicks out. Turn the adjuster clockwise to increase damping and anti-clockwise to decrease it.

10 Ride height can be altered by changing

the length of the shock absorber, i.e. the distance from the centre of its top mounting eye to the centre of the bottom mounting eye. The standard setting is 322 ± 1 mm, with an adjustment range between 320 and 327 mm. The adjuster nut is located just above the bottom mounting **(see illustration)**. Slacken the locknut (lower nut) and turn the adjuster nut as required. Tighten the locknut when adjustment is complete.

1999 and 2000 RSV-R models

11 Spring pre-load is adjusted by slackening the locknut on the top of the spring using a C-spanner, then turning the adjuster nut to alter the length of the spring **(see illustration 14.15)**. The standard pre-loaded spring length is 137 mm; this can be varied between 134 and 138 mm.

12 Rebound damping is adjusted by turning the knurled ring on the bottom of the shock absorber. The amount of damping is indicated by the number of clicks when turned anti-clockwise (looking down on it) from the fully screwed-in position. The standard position is around 14 clicks out. Turn the adjuster clockwise to increase damping and anti-clockwise to decrease it.

13 Compression damping is adjusted by turning the knob on the left-hand side of the reservoir on the back of the shock absorber. The amount of damping is indicated by the number of clicks when turned anti-clockwise from the fully screwed-in position. The standard position is 12 clicks out. Turn the adjuster clockwise to increase damping and anti-clockwise to decrease it.

14 Ride height can be altered by changing the length of the shock absorber, i.e. the distance from the centre of its top mounting eye to the centre of the bottom mounting eye. The standard setting is 322 ± 1 mm, with an adjustment range between 319 and 325 mm. The adjuster nut is located just above the bottom mounting. Slacken the locknut (lower nut) and turn the adjuster nut as required. Tighten the locknut when adjustment is complete.

2001 to 2003 RSV and RSV-R models

15 Spring pre-load is adjusted by slackening the locknut on the top of the spring using a C-spanner, then turning the adjuster

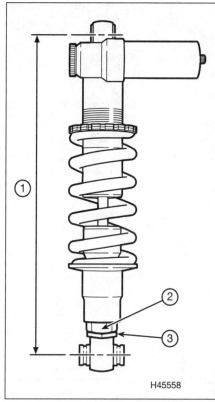

14.10 Rear shock ride height measurement and adjuster – 1998 to 2000 unit shown

1 Ride height   2 Adjuster   3 Locknut

nut to alter the length of the spring **(see illustration)**. The standard pre-loaded spring length is 147 mm; this can be varied between 145 and 149 mm.

16 Rebound damping is adjusted by turning the knurled ring on the bottom of the shock absorber **(see illustration)**. The amount of damping is indicated by the number of clicks when turned anti-clockwise (looking down on it) from the fully screwed-in position. The standard position is around 20 clicks out. Turn the adjuster clockwise to increase damping and anti-clockwise to decrease it.

17 Compression damping is adjusted by turning the knob on the left-hand side of the

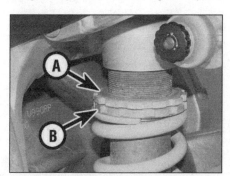

14.15 Slacken the locknut (A) and turn the adjuster nut (B)

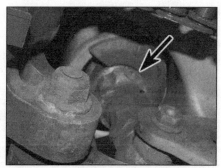

14.16 Rebound damping adjuster (arrowed)

14.17 Compression damping adjuster (arrowed)

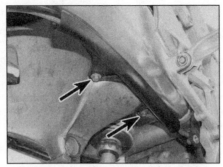

15.2 Unscrew the bolts (arrowed) and detach the guide

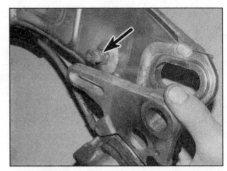

15.4 Displace the caliper bracket, noting how its slot locates over the pin (arrowed)

reservoir on the back of the shock absorber **(see illustration)**. The amount of damping is indicated by the number of clicks when turned anti-clockwise from the fully screwed-in position. The standard position is 12 clicks out. Turn the adjuster clockwise to increase damping and anti-clockwise to decrease it.

18 Ride height can be altered by changing the length of the shock absorber, i.e. the distance from the centre of its top mounting eye to the centre of the bottom mounting eye – the standard setting being 321 ± 1.5 mm. The adjuster nut is located just above the bottom mounting. Slacken the locknut (lower nut) and turn the adjuster nut as required. Tighten the locknut when adjustment is complete.

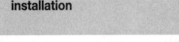

15 Swingarm removal and installation

Removal

1 Remove the complete exhaust system (see Chapter 4).
2 Unscrew the bolts securing the brake hose/speed sensor wiring guide to the underside of the swingarm and detach the guide **(see illustration)** – note that these bolts are prone to corrosion and should be liberally sprayed with penetrating fluid if seized, then tapped on their heads with a hammer, and even heated, otherwise they may shear off.
3 Either remove the front sprocket (see Section 18) and later remove the swingarm

with the chain looped through it, or split the drive chain (see Section 17) and remove the chain first, leaving the front sprocket in place, as required.
4 Remove the rear wheel (see Chapter 7). Lay the caliper down on some rag. Remove the brake caliper bracket from the swingarm **(see illustration)**.
5 Unscrew the nut and withdraw the bolt securing the linkage plates to the bottom of the shock absorber **(see illustration 12.3)**.
6 Unscrew the nut and withdraw the bolt securing the linkage plates to the swingarm and swing the linkage assembly down **(see illustration 12.4)**.
7 Unscrew the nut on the left-hand end of the pivot bolt and remove the washer **(see illustrations)**.
8 Unscrew the locknut on the swingarm adjuster bolt using a suitable peg spanner (see *Tool Tip*) **(see illustration)**.

> **TOOL TiP** *A peg spanner is required to slacken and tighten the adjuster bolt locknut on the right-hand end of the swingarm pivot. If the Aprilia service tool (Pt. No. 8140203) or an aftermarket version (see illustration 15.8) is not available, a suitable one can be fabricated by cutting an old socket of the correct size.*

9 Unscrew the adjuster bolt using a hex key in the end of the pivot bolt until it is flush with the inside of the frame, then support the swingarm and withdraw the pivot bolt from the right-hand side **(see illustrations)**. Manoeuvre the swingarm down until it clears the bottom of the shock absorber, then remove it, guiding the chain off the output shaft end if it wasn't split

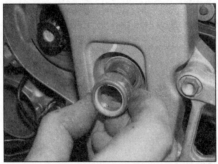

15.7a Unscrew the nut . . .

15.7b . . . and remove the washer

15.8 Unscrew the locknut on the right-hand side using a peg spanner

15.9a Unscrew the adjuster bolt using a hex bit

15.9b Withdraw the pivot bolt . . .

15.9c ... and guide the swingarm down and away

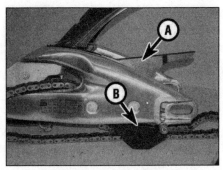

15.10 Remove the chainguard (A) and guide plate (B) if required

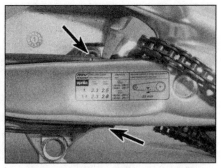

15.11 Chain slider bolts (arrowed)

(see illustration). If required fully unscrew and remove the adjuster bolt.

10 If required, undo the screws securing the chainguard and guide plate, bearing in mind the information in Step 2 regarding seized bolts/screws (see illustration).

11 If required, unscrew the bolts securing the chain slider and remove it, noting how it fits, again referring to Step 2 (see illustration). If badly worn or damaged the slider should be replaced with a new one.

12 Clean, inspect and re-grease all pivot components as described in Section 16.

Installation

13 If removed, install the chain slider, chainguard and guide plate, smearing the bolt and screw threads with copper grease (see illustrations 15.11 and 15.10).

14 Smear the pivot bolt with multi-purpose grease. If removed thread the adjuster bolt into the frame, leaving it flush with the inside. Offer up the swingarm and if available have an assistant hold it in place (see illustration 15.9c). If in place loop the chain over the output shaft. Slide the pivot bolt in from the right-hand side and push it all the way through, locating its head in the adjuster bolt so their hexagonal heads engage (see illustration 15.9b). Tighten the adjuster bolt using an Allen key in the end of the pivot bolt, to the torque setting specified at the beginning of the Chapter (see illustration).

15 Fit the locknut onto the adjuster bolt and tighten it to the specified torque setting, using the peg-spanner as on removal (see *Tool Tip*) (see illustration 15.8).

16 Fit the nut with its washer onto the left-hand end of the bolt (see illustrations 15.7b and a). Counter-hold the head of the bolt and tighten the nut to the specified torque setting. Move the swingarm up and down and check that it moves smoothly and freely. If it is tight slacken the nut, locknut and adjuster bolt and repeat the tightening procedure.

17 Fit the linkage plates to the swingarm and shock absorber, slide the bolts through and tighten the nuts to the specified torque setting (see illustrations 12.4 and 12.3).

18 Install the front sprocket or drive chain as required according to your removal procedure (see Section 18 or 17) – if the sprocket was removed, tighten the bolt after the rear wheel has been installed so the brake can be used to prevent the sprocket turning.

19 Smear the slot in the caliper bracket and the pin on the inside of the swingarm with some grease (see illustration 15.4). Locate the bracket on the swingarm.

20 Install the rear wheel (see Chapter 7).

21 Fit the brake hose/speed sensor wiring guide, smearing the bolt threads with copper grease (see illustration 15.2).

22 Install the exhaust system(see Chapter 4).

23 Check and adjust the drive chain slack (see Chapter 1). Check the operation of the

rear suspension and brake before taking the machine on the road.

16 Swingarm inspection and bearings

Inspection

1 Remove the swingarm (see Section 15).

2 Thoroughly clean the swingarm, removing all traces of dirt, corrosion and grease.

3 Inspect the swingarm closely, looking for obvious signs of wear such as heavy scoring, and cracks or distortion due to accident damage. Any damaged or worn component must be replaced with a new one.

4 Check the swingarm pivot bolt for straightness by rolling it on a flat surface such as a piece of plate glass (first wipe off all old grease and remove any corrosion using wire wool). If the equipment is available, place the axle in V-blocks and measure the runout using a dial gauge. If the axle is bent or the runout exceeds the limit specified, replace it with a new one.

Bearing check and renewal

5 Remove the shouldered collar from the left-hand pivot (see illustration). If required withdraw the bearing spacer from the left-hand side of the swingarm (see illustration).

6 Lever the grease seal out of each side,

15.14 Tighten the adjuster bolt to the specified torque

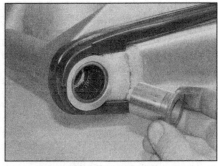

16.5a Withdraw the collar ...

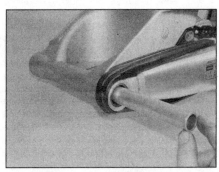

16.5b ... and the bearing spacer

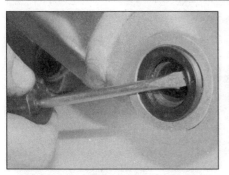

16.6 Lever out the grease seals and discard them

16.7a The ball bearings are secured by a circlip (arrowed)

16.7b Needle roller bearing is located in left-hand pivot

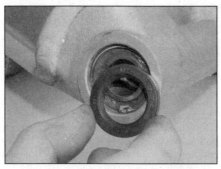

16.9 Removed grease seals must be replaced with new ones

noting which type fits where, and discard them as new ones must be used **(see illustration)**.

7 Clean off all old grease from the spacer and bearings. Check the condition of the bearings, noting that there are two caged ball bearings secured by a circlip in the right-hand side and a needle roller bearing in the left-hand side **(see illustrations)**. Slip the collar back into the needle bearing and the pivot bolt into the ball bearings and check that there is not an excessive amount of freeplay between the components. If the bearings do not run smoothly and freely or if there is excessive freeplay, they must be replaced with new ones. Refer to *Tools and Workshop Tips* (Section 5) in the Reference section for more information on bearings.

8 Worn bearings can be drifted out of their bores, but note that removal will destroy them; new bearings should be obtained before work commences. Do not forget to remove the circlip before trying to remove the ball bearings **(see illustration 16.7a)**. Remove the O-ring that fits between the inner end of each bearing and the bearing spacer and replace them with new ones. The new bearings should be pressed or drawn into their bores rather than driven into position. In the absence of a press, a suitable drawbolt tool can be made up as described in *Tools and Workshop Tips* in the Reference section. In all cases make sure the marked side of the bearing is on the outside.

9 Fit a new grease seal into each side of the swingarm **(see illustration)**.

10 Lubricate the bearings, collar and seals and all other pivot components with multi-purpose grease.

11 Slide the bearing spacer and collar into the left-hand side of the swingarm **(see illustrations 16.5b and a)**.

---

17 Drive chain

Removal

Note: *The original equipment drive chain has a riveted-type master (joining) link which can be disassembled using either Aprilia service tool, Pt. No. 8140192, or one of several commercially-available drive chain cutting/riveting tools. Such chains can be recognised by the master link side plate's identification marks (and usually its different colour), as well as by the staked ends of the link's two pins which look as if they have been deeply centre-punched, instead of peened over as with all the other pins.*

⚠️ **Warning: Use ONLY the correct service tools to disassemble the riveted-type of master link – if you do not have access to such tools or do not have the skill to operate them correctly, have the chain removed by a dealer.**

1 Remove the front sprocket cover (see Section 18). If the sprockets are being

replaced with new ones, slacken the front sprocket nut before splitting the chain so that the rear brake can be used to stop the sprocket turning (see Section 18).

2 Locate the joining link in a suitable position to work on by rotating the back wheel.

3 Slacken the drive chain as described in Chapter 1.

4 Split the chain at the joining link using the chain cutter, following carefully the manufacturer's operating instructions (see also Section 8 in *Tools and Workshop Tips* in the Reference Section). Remove the chain from the bike, noting its routing through the swingarm.

Installation

⚠️ **Warning: NEVER install a drive chain which uses a clip-type master (split) link. Use ONLY the correct service tools to secure the riveted-type of master link – if you do not have access to such tools or do not have the skill to operate them correctly, have the chain installed by a dealer service department or bike repair shop to be sure of having it securely installed.**

5 Slip the drive chain through the swingarm sections and around the front and rear sprockets, leaving the two ends in a convenient position to work on.

6 Refer to Section 8 in *Tools and Workshop Tips* in the Reference Section. Install the **new** joining link from the inside. Fit an O-ring onto each pin, then slide the link through and fit the other two O-rings. Install the new side plate with its identification marks facing out. Stake the new link using the drive chain cutting/staking tool, following carefully the instructions of both the chain manufacturer and the tool manufacturer. DO NOT re-use old joining link components.

7 After staking, check the joining link and staking for any signs of cracking. If there is any evidence of cracking, the joining link, O-rings and side plate must be replaced with new ones. Measure the diameter of the staked ends in two directions and check that it is evenly staked and within the measurements specified at the beginning of the Chapter.

8 Install the sprocket cover (see Section 18).

9 On completion, adjust and lubricate the chain following the procedures described in Chapter 1.

---

18 Sprocket cover and sprockets

Front sprocket cover

1 Remove the lower fairing (See Chapter 8).

2 Remove the gearchange lever (see Section 3). If you want to remove the drive chain guide plate displace the clutch release cylinder (see Chapter 2).

3 Unscrew the three front sprocket cover

18.3a Unscrew the bolts and remove the cover . . .

18.3b . . . and the guide plate

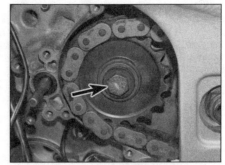

18.6 Unscrew the bolt (arrowed) and remove the washers

18.8 Slide the sprocket off the shaft and remove it

18.9 Make sure the sprocket is the correct way round

in or the marked side is facing out **(see illustration)**. Fit the chain onto the rear sprocket or install the rear wheel (see Chapter 7), then take up the slack in the chain.

10 Fit the plain washer and spring washer onto the bolt **(see illustration)**. Apply a suitable non-permanent thread locking compound on the bolt threads. Fit the bolt and tighten it to the specified torque setting, with the engine in gear and holding the rear brake on hard as before.

11 Install the sprocket cover. Adjust and lubricate the chain following the procedures described in Chapter 1.

> **HAYNES HINT** *Keep your old front sprocket as it can be used along with a holding tool to lock the transmission input shaft should you ever need to remove the clutch (see Chapter 2).*

Rear sprocket

12 Remove the rear wheel (see Chapter 7).
13 Lift the sprocket coupling off the wheel **(see illustration 19.3)**.
14 Counter-hold the studs using the hexes on the inner side of the sprocket and unscrew the nuts securing the sprocket – if available secure the sprocket in the padded jaws of a vice **(see illustration)**. Remove the sprocket

bolts and remove the cover **(see illustration)**. If you have displaced the clutch release cylinder remove the drive chain guide plate **(see illustration)**. Check the plate for wear and damage and replace it with a new one if necessary.
4 Installation is the reverse of removal.

Front sprocket

5 Remove the front sprocket cover (see above).
6 Engage a gear, then have an assistant hold the rear brake on hard. Unscrew the sprocket bolt and remove the washers **(see illustration)**.
7 Fully slacken the drive chain as described in Chapter 1. If the rear sprocket is being

removed as well, remove the rear wheel now to give full slack. Otherwise disengage the chain from the rear sprocket – if there is not enough slack to do this, either partially or completely remove the rear wheel (see Chapter 7) – partial removal means leaving it between the ends of the swingarm with the chain looped round its sprocket, but the axle needs to be removed and the wheel dropped to give enough slack in the chain to get the front sprocket off the shaft.
8 Slide the front sprocket off the shaft and disengage it from the chain **(see illustration)**.
9 Smear the shaft splines with grease. Fit the new sprocket into the chain and slide it onto the shaft, making sure the shouldered side is facing

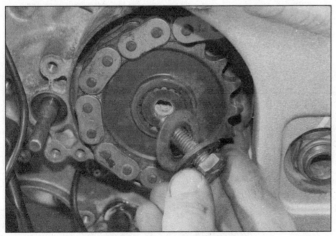

18.10 Fit the bolt with its washers

18.14 Counter-hold each stud using its hex (arrowed) while unscrewing the nuts

holder and withdraw the studs from the sprocket.

15 Fit the studs into the new sprocket from the inside, then fit the holder onto the outside. Counter-hold the studs using the hexes and tighten the nuts evenly and a little at a time in a criss-cross sequence to the torque setting specified at the beginning of the Chapter, again using a padded vice if possible.

16 Fit the sprocket coupling onto the wheel.

17 Install the rear wheel (see Chapter 7).

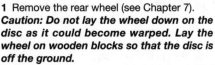

19 Rear sprocket coupling/rubber dampers

1 Remove the rear wheel (see Chapter 7).

Caution: Do not lay the wheel down on the disc as it could become warped. Lay the wheel on wooden blocks so that the disc is off the ground.

2 Grasp the sprocket and twist it back and forth to check for play between the sprocket

19.3 Lift the sprocket coupling out of the wheel

stud shafts and the rubber dampers. If there is any play new dampers must be installed.

3 Lift the sprocket coupling off the wheel leaving the rubber dampers in position **(see illustration)**. Check the coupling for cracks or any obvious signs of damage. Also check the sprocket studs for wear or damage.

4 Check the rubber damper segments for

19.4 Check the rubber dampers

cracks, hardening and general deterioration **(see illustration)**. Replace them as a set with new ones if necessary.

5 Procedures for the sprocket coupling bearings are described in Chapter 7.

6 Installation is the reverse of removal. Smear grease onto the sprocket stud shafts.

7 Install the rear wheel (see Chapter 7).

Chapter 7
Brakes, wheels and tyres

Contents

Degrees of difficulty

Easy, suitable for novice with little experience	**Fairly easy,** suitable for beginner with some experience	**Fairly difficult,** suitable for competent DIY mechanic	**Difficult,** suitable for experienced DIY mechanic	**Very difficult,** suitable for expert DIY or professional

Specifications

Brakes

Brake fluid type	DOT 5.1 glycol-based hydraulic fluid. DOT 5.1 is compatible with, and a later generation of, DOT 4. **Do not** use DOT 5 silicone fluid.
Disc minimum thickness	4.5 mm
Disc maximum runout	0.3 mm

Wheels

Size	Front 3.5 x 17 inch and rear 6.0 x 17 inch (RSV Mille cast alloy, RSV Mille R forged alloy)
Rim runout (max)	
Axial (side-to-side)	2.0 mm
Radial (out-of-round)	2.0 mm
Axle runout (max)	0.25 mm

Tyres

Tyre pressures and tread depth	see *Daily (pre-ride) checks*
Tyre sizes (standard – refer to owners handbook or Aprilia dealer for other fittings)	
Front	120/70-ZR17 (58W)
Rear	190/50-ZR17 (73W)

Torque wrench settings

Bleed valves	15 Nm
Brake disc bolts	30 Nm
Brake hose banjo bolts	20 Nm
Front brake caliper mounting bolts	50 Nm
Front wheel axle clamp bolts	22 Nm
Front wheel axle nut	80 Nm
Rear brake caliper mounting bolts	25 Nm
Rear brake master cylinder mounting bolts	12 Nm
Rear wheel axle nut	90 to 100 Nm

1 General information

All models are fitted with alloy wheels, cast on RSV models and forged on RSV-R models, designed for tubeless tyres only. Both front and rear brakes are hydraulically operated disc brakes.

The front brakes have twin 320 mm discs with twin opposed-piston calipers by Brembo. The rear brake has a single 220 mm disc with single opposed-piston caliper by Brembo.

Caution: *Disc brake components rarely require disassembly. Do not disassemble components unless absolutely necessary. If a hydraulic brake line is loosened, the entire system must be disassembled, drained, cleaned and then properly filled and bled upon reassembly. Do not use solvents on internal brake components. Solvents will cause the seals to swell and distort. Use only clean brake fluid for cleaning. Use care when working with brake fluid as it can injure your eyes and it will damage painted surfaces and plastic parts.*

2 Front brake pads

⚠ **Warning:** *The dust created by the brake system may contain asbestos, which is harmful to your health. Never blow it out with compressed air and don't inhale any of it. An approved filtering mask should be worn when working on the brakes. Do not, under any circumstances, use petroleum-based solvents to clean brake parts. Use clean brake fluid only.*

Note: *If the pad pins have not been previously greased and have not been removed for a while, they could well be very difficult to withdraw. If you apply penetrating fluid this will help, but make sure none gets on the pads or discs.*

2.2a Unscrew the bolts . . .

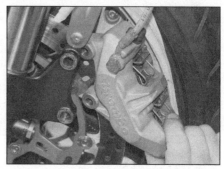

2.2b . . . and slide the caliper off the disc

1 As there is not much clearance between the caliper and the wheel, and it is easy to knock the caliper against the wheel, stick some protective tape on the wheel or place a rag around it. Where possible (according to model) it also helps to align the wheel so the caliper is between two spokes.

2 Unscrew the caliper mounting bolts and carefully slide the caliper off the disc, twisting it as it leaves the disc to clear the wheel **(see illustrations)**.

3 On 1998 to 2000 models two pads are fitted in each caliper, one for each side. Note how the pad spring and pins fit before removing them. Remove the retaining clips from the pad pins, then withdraw the pins using pliers. Remove the pad spring then remove the pads from the caliper.

4 On 2001 to 2003 models four pads are fitted in each caliper, one for each piston. Note how the pad springs and pins fit before removing them. Push down on the pad spring in one end of the caliper and withdraw the pad pin using pliers, then remove the spring, noting how it fits, and remove the two pads **(see illustrations)**. Remove the pads from the other end in the same way.

5 Inspect the surface of each pad for contamination and check whether the friction material has worn beyond its service limit (see Chapter 1, Section 2). If either pad is worn to or beyond the service limit, is fouled with oil or grease, or is heavily scored or damaged by dirt and debris, replace the pads in both calipers with new ones. Note that it is extremely difficult to effectively degrease

the friction material; if the pads are contaminated in any way new ones must be fitted.

6 If the pads are in good condition clean them carefully, using a fine wire brush which is completely free of oil and grease, to remove all traces of road dirt and corrosion. Using a pointed instrument, clean out the grooves in the friction material and dig out any embedded particles of foreign matter. Spray the inside of the caliper with a dedicated brake cleaner to remove any dust.

7 Check the condition of the brake disc (see Section 4).

8 Remove all traces of corrosion from the pad pins. If corrosion is excessive, or the pins are damaged in any way, replace them with new ones.

9 Clean around the exposed section of each piston to remove any dirt or debris that could cause the seals to be damaged. Now push the pistons back into the caliper – if new pads are being fitted you need to push them all the way in to create room for the new pads; if the old pads are still serviceable push them in a little way, not only because it makes installation easier, but also because it serves as a check that none of the pistons are seized in their bores. To push the pistons back first block the pair of pistons not being pushed in to prevent them being pushed out, then use finger pressure or a piece of wood as leverage, or place the old pads back in the caliper and use a metal bar or a screwdriver inserted between them, or use grips together with a piece of wood, rag or card to protect

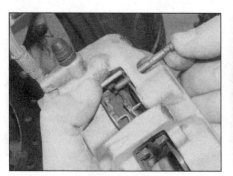

2.4a Press down on the spring and withdraw the pin . . .

2.4b . . . then remove the spring . . .

2.4c . . . and the pads

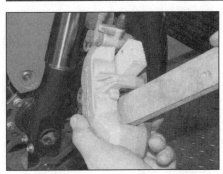

2.9 Using a piece of wood to push the pistons back

3.1a Unscrew the caliper mounting bolts (arrowed) . . .

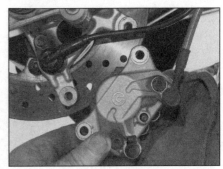

3.1b . . . and slide the caliper off the disc

the caliper body **(see illustration)**. Alternatively obtain a proper piston-pushing tool from a good tool supplier if you can find one that is narrow enough **(see illustration 3.7)**. It may be necessary to undo the master cylinder reservoir cap screws and remove the cap and diaphragm and siphon out some fluid (see *Daily (pre-ride) checks)*. If the pistons are difficult to push back, remove the bleed valve cap, then attach a length of clear hose to the bleed valve and place the open end in a suitable container, then open the valve and try again **(see illustration 10.7a)**. Take great care not to draw any air into the system. If in doubt, bleed the brakes afterwards (see Section 10). If any of the pistons appear seized, first apply the brake lever and check whether the piston in question moves at all. If it moves out but can't be pushed back in the chances are there is some hidden corrosion stopping it. If it is completely seized you will have to fit a new caliper – rebuild kits (pistons and seals) are not available (see Section 5).

10 Lightly smear the back and sides of the pad backing material (where it contacts the caliper body) with copper-based grease, making sure that none gets on the friction material. Also smear the pad pins.

11 On 1998 to 2000 models insert the pads into the caliper so that the friction material of each pad faces the other. Fit the pad spring with the arrow pointing to the top of the caliper (i.e. in direction of disc rotation), then install the pad pins, aligning the holes for the retaining clips correctly. Make sure the pins pass through the hole in each pad and the pad spring correctly. Secure the pins with the

retaining clips, using new ones if necessary.

12 On 2001 to 2003 models fit the pads into one end of the caliper so that the friction material of each pad faces the other **(see illustration 2.4c)**. Fit the pad spring onto the pads, then press the spring down and slide the pin over the tops of the pads and the spring and into the bore in the other side of the caliper, releasing the spring so its outer arm locates in the groove in the pin **(see illustrations 2.4b and a)**.

13 Slide the caliper onto the brake disc, making sure the pads sit squarely on each side of the disc. Clean the caliper mounting bolt threads and apply a suitable thread locking compound, then tighten the bolts to the torque setting specified at the beginning of the Chapter **(see illustration 2.2a)**.

14 Top up the master cylinder reservoir if necessary (see *Daily (pre-ride) checks)*, and refit the diaphragm and reservoir cap.

15 Operate the brake lever several times to bring the pads into contact with the disc. Check the operation of the brake before riding the motorcycle.

3 Rear brake pads

Warning: The dust created by the brake system may contain asbestos, which is harmful to your health. Never blow it out with compressed air and don't inhale any of it. An approved filtering mask should be

worn when working on the brakes. Do not, under any circumstances, use petroleum-based solvents to clean brake parts. Use clean brake fluid only.

Note: *If the pad pins have not been previously greased and have not been removed for a while, they could well be very difficult to withdraw. If this is the case, they will have to be driven out using a suitable drift or punch. To do this you will have to remove the caliper (see Section 5), as otherwise the shock could distort the disc. If you apply penetrating fluid this will help, but make sure none gets on the pads or disc.*

1 Unscrew the caliper mounting bolts and slide the caliper off the disc **(see illustrations)**.

2 Note how the pad spring and pin fit before removing them. Remove the E-clip from the inner end of the pad pin, then tap the pin out using a hammer and drift and withdraw it using pliers **(see illustrations)**. Remove the pad spring then remove the pads **(see illustrations 3.9b and a)**.

3 Inspect the surface of each pad for contamination and check whether the friction material has worn beyond its service limit (see Chapter 1, Section 2). If either pad is worn to or beyond the service limit, is fouled with oil or grease, or is heavily scored or damaged by dirt and debris, replace the pads with new ones. Note that it is extremely difficult to effectively degrease the friction material; if the pads are contaminated in any way new ones must be fitted.

4 If the pads are in good condition clean them carefully, using a fine wire brush which is

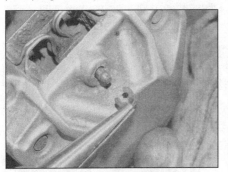

3.2a Remove the E-clip . . .

3.2b . . . then tap the pad pin out . . .

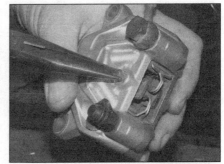

3.2c . . . and withdraw it using pliers

3.7 Using a dedicated tool to push the pistons back

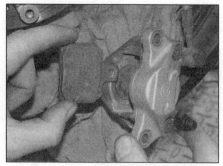

3.9a Insert the pads . . .

3.9b . . . then fit the spring

3.9c Slide the pin across . . .

3.9d . . . and tap it fully home

3.10 Apply threadlock and tighten the bolts to the specified torque

completely free of oil and grease to remove all traces of road dirt and corrosion. Using a pointed instrument, clean out the grooves in the friction material and dig out any embedded particles of foreign matter. Spray the inside of the caliper with a dedicated brake cleaner to remove any dust.

5 Check the condition of the brake disc (see Section 4).

6 Remove all traces of corrosion from the pad pin. If corrosion is excessive, or the pin is damaged in any way, replace it with a new one.

7 Clean around the exposed section of each piston to remove any dirt or debris that could cause the seals to be damaged. Now push the pistons back into the caliper – if new pads are being fitted you need to push them all the way in to create room for them; if the old pads are still serviceable push them in a little way, not only because it makes installation easier, but also because it serves as a check that neither of the pistons are seized in their bores. To push the pistons back use finger pressure or a piece of wood as leverage, or place the old pads back in the caliper and use a metal bar or a screwdriver inserted between them, or use grips and a piece of wood, rag or card to protect the caliper body **(see illustration 2.9)**. Alternatively obtain a proper piston-pushing tool from a good tool supplier **(see illustration)**. It may be necessary to remove the master cylinder reservoir cap, plate and diaphragm and siphon out some fluid (see *Daily (pre-ride) checks)*. If the pistons are difficult to push back, remove the bleed valve cap, then attach a length of clear hose to the bleed valve

and place the open end in a suitable container, then open the valve and try again **(see illustration 10.7b)**. Take great care not to draw any air into the system. If in doubt, bleed the brakes afterwards (see Section 10). If either piston appears seized, first apply the brake pedal and check whether the piston moves at all. If it moves out but can't be pushed back in the chances are there is some hidden corrosion stopping it. If it is completely seized you will have to fit a new caliper – rebuild kits (pistons and seals) are not available (see Section 6).

8 Lightly smear the back and the sides of the pad backing material (where it contacts the caliper body) with copper-based grease, making sure that none gets on the friction material. Also smear the pad pins.

9 Insert the pads into the caliper so that the friction material of each pad faces the other. Fit the pad spring onto the pads, then press down on the middle and slide the pad pin through the hole in the pads and over the middle section of the spring **(see illustrations)**. Tap the pin fully home **(see illustration)**, then secure it with the E-clip **(see illustration 3.2a)**.

10 Slide the caliper onto the brake disc, making sure the pads sit squarely on either side **(see illustration 3.1b)**. Clean the caliper mounting bolt threads and apply a suitable thread locking compound, then tighten the bolts to the torque setting specified at the beginning of the Chapter **(see illustration)**.

11 Top up the master cylinder reservoir if necessary (see *Daily (pre-ride) checks)*, and refit the diaphragm, plate and reservoir cover.

12 Operate the brake pedal several times to bring the pads into contact with the disc.

Check the operation of the brake before riding the motorcycle.

4 Brake discs

Warning: The dust created by the brake system may contain asbestos, which is harmful to your health. Never blow it out with compressed air and don't inhale any of it. An approved filtering mask should be worn when working on the brakes. Do not, under any circumstances, use petroleum-based solvents to clean brake parts. Use clean brake fluid only.

Inspection

1 Visually inspect the surface of the disc for score marks, pitting and other damage **(see illustration)**. Light scratches are normal after

4.1 This rear disc is quite badly pitted

4.3 The minimum disc thickness is marked on the front discs

4.5a Front disc bolts (arrowed)

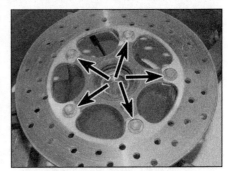

4.5b Rear disc bolts (arrowed)

use and won't affect brake operation, but deep grooves, pitting and heavy score marks will reduce braking efficiency and accelerate pad wear. If a disc is badly affected it must be replaced with a new one.

2 To check disc runout, position the bike on an auxiliary stand so that the wheel being checked is off the ground. Mount a dial gauge to a fork leg or on the swingarm, according to wheel, with the plunger on the gauge touching the surface of the disc about 10 mm (1/2 in) from the outer edge. Rotate the wheel and watch the gauge needle, comparing the reading with the limit listed in the Specifications at the beginning of the Chapter. If the runout is greater than the service limit, check the wheel bearings for play (see Chapter 1). If the bearings are worn, replace them with new ones (see Section 15) and repeat this check. It is also worth removing the disc (see below) and checking for built-up corrosion (see Step 6) as this will cause runout. If the runout is still excessive, the disc will have to be replaced with a new one, although machining by an engineer may be possible.

3 The disc must not be machined or allowed to wear down to a thickness less than the service limit as listed in this Chapter's Specifications and as marked on the front discs, but not on the rear **(see illustration)**. Check the thickness of the disc using a micrometer. If the thickness of the disc is less than the service limit, it must be replaced with a new one.

Removal

4 Remove the wheel (see Section 13 or 14).
Caution: Do not lay the wheel down and allow it to rest on the disc – the disc could become warped. Set the wheel on wood blocks so the disc doesn't support the weight of the wheel.

5 Mark the relationship of the disc to the wheel, so it can be installed in the same position. Unscrew the disc retaining bolts, using an impact driver if necessary and loosening them a little at a time in a criss-cross pattern to avoid distorting the disc, then remove the disc from the wheel **(see illustrations)**.

Installation

6 Before installing the disc, make sure there is no dirt or corrosion where the disc seats on

the hub, particularly right in the angle of the seat, as this will not allow the disc to sit flat when it is bolted down and it will appear to be warped when checked or when using the brake.

7 Install the disc on the wheel, making sure any directional arrow is on the outside and pointing in the direction of normal (i.e. forward) rotation. Also note any R or L marking on the front discs that denotes on which side of the wheel it must be mounted. Align the previously applied matchmarks (if you're reinstalling the original disc).

8 Apply a suitable non-permanent thread locking compound (Loctite 243) to the threads of the disc bolts, and tighten them evenly in a criss-cross pattern to the torque setting specified at the beginning of the Chapter **(see illustration 4.5a or b)**. Clean off all grease from the brake disc(s) using acetone or brake system cleaner. If a new brake disc has been installed, remove any protective coating from its working surfaces.

9 Install the wheel (see Section 13 or 14). Note that when installing a new disc you should also fit new brake pads (see Section 2 or 3).

10 Operate the brake lever and pedal several times to bring the pads into contact with the disc. Check the operation of the brakes carefully before riding the bike.

5 Front brake calipers

Warning: The dust created by the brake pads may contain asbestos, which is harmful to your health. Never blow it out with compressed air and don't inhale any of it. An approved filtering mask should be worn when working on the brakes. If a new caliper is being installed all old brake fluid should be flushed from the system. Do not, under any circumstances, use petroleum-based solvents to clean brake parts. Use a dedicated brake cleaner only. Use care when working with brake fluid as it can injure your eyes and it will damage painted surfaces and plastic parts – cover these with rag.

Note: *If the entire front brake system is being removed (i.e. master cylinder as well as calipers), or if you intend to change the brake fluid, drain the brake fluid completely from the system (see Section 10), as opposed to retaining the old fluid within it by blocking the hose as described (Step 4).*

1 If the caliper is leaking fluid, or if the brake pads are wearing unevenly, or the pistons do not move smoothly or are tight or stuck in their bores, then a new caliper is required – rebuild kits are not available and so overhaul is not possible.

2 If you are completely removing the caliper rather than just displacing it, you will need some new brake fluid (see Specifications) and some clean rags.

Removal

3 If the caliper is just being displaced and not completely removed, do not detach the brake hose.

4 If the caliper is being completely removed, unscrew the brake hose banjo bolt and detach the hose, noting its alignment with the caliper **(see illustration)**. Discard the sealing washers as new ones must be used on installation. Either clamp the hose, plug it using another suitable short piece of hose fitted through the eye of the banjo union (it must be a fairly tight fit to seal it properly), block it using a suitable bolt with sealing washers and a capped (domed) nut, or wrap some plastic foodwrap tightly around (a finger cut off a latex glove also works well), the object being to minimise fluid loss and prevent dirt entering the system. Whatever you do, also cover the end of the hose in rag,

5.4 Brake hose banjo bolt (arrowed)

just in case. Similarly block or cover the caliper where the hose connects.

5 As there is not much clearance between the caliper and the wheel, and it is easy to knock the caliper against the wheel, stick some protective tape on the wheel or place a rag around it. Where possible (according to model) it also helps to align the wheel so the caliper is between two spokes.

6 Unscrew the caliper mounting bolts and slide the caliper off the disc **(see illustration 2.2a and b)**.

7 If the required, remove the brake pads (see Section 2).

8 Clean the caliper with denatured alcohol or brake system cleaner.

Installation

9 If necessary, push the pistons a little way back into the caliper (see Section 2, Step 9). If removed, install the brake pads (see Section 2).

10 Slide the caliper onto the brake disc, making sure the pads sit squarely on either side. Clean the caliper mounting bolt threads and apply a suitable thread locking compound, then tighten the bolts to the torque setting specified at the beginning of the Chapter. Remove the rag or protective tape if used.

11 If removed, connect the brake hose to the caliper, using new sealing washers on each side of the union. Align the hose as noted on removal **(see illustration 5.4)**. Tighten the banjo bolt to the torque setting specified at the beginning of the Chapter. Top up the master cylinder reservoir (see *Daily (pre-ride) checks*) and bleed the system as described in Section 10.

12 Check for leaks and thoroughly test the operation of the brake before riding the motorcycle.

6 Rear brake caliper

> **Warning: The dust created by the brake pads may contain asbestos, which is harmful to your health. Never blow it out**

with compressed air and don't inhale any of it. An approved filtering mask should be worn when working on the brakes. If a new caliper is being installed all old brake fluid should be flushed from the system. Do not, under any circumstances, use petroleum-based solvents to clean brake parts. Use a dedicated brake cleaner only. Use care when working with brake fluid as it can injure your eyes and it will damage painted surfaces and plastic parts – cover these with rag.

Note: *If the entire rear brake system is being removed (i.e. master cyiinder as well as caliper), or if you intend to change the brake fluid, drain the brake fluid completely from the system (see Section 10), as opposed to retaining the old fluid within it by blocking the hose as described (Step 4).*

1 If the caliper is leaking fluid, or if the brake pads are wearing unevenly, or the pistons do not move smoothly or are tight or stuck in their bores, then a new caliper is required – rebuild kits are not available and so overhaul is not possible.

2 If you are completely removing the caliper rather than just displacing it, you will need some new brake fluid (see Specifications) and some clean rags.

Removal

3 If the caliper is just being displaced and not completely removed, do not detach the brake hose. If you need more flexibility for moving the caliper clear, cut the cable tie securing the hose to the speed sensor wiring, then if required unscrew the bolts securing the hose/speed sensor wire guide to the underside of the swingarm and detach the guide **(see illustrations)** – note that these bolts are prone to corrosion and should be liberally sprayed with penetrating fluid if seized, then tapped on their heads with a hammer, and even heated, otherwise they may shear off.

4 If the caliper is being completely removed, unscrew the brake hose banjo bolt and detach the hose, noting its alignment with the caliper **(see illustration)**. Discard the sealing washers as new ones must be used on installation. Either clamp the hose, plug it using another suitable short piece of hose

fitted through the eye of the banjo union (it must be a fairly tight fit to seal it properly), block it using a suitable bolt with sealing washers and a capped (domed) nut, or wrap some plastic foodwrap tightly around (a finger cut off a latex glove also works well), the object being to minimise fluid loss and prevent dirt entering the system. Whatever you do, also cover the end of the hose in rag, just in case. Similarly block or cover the caliper where the hose connects.

5 Unscrew the caliper mounting bolts and slide the caliper off the disc **(see illustrations 3.1a and b)**.

6 If required, remove the brake pads (see Section 3).

7 Clean the caliper with denatured alcohol or brake system cleaner.

Installation

8 If necessary, push the pistons a little way back into the caliper (see Section 3, Step 7). If removed, install the brake pads (see Section 3).

9 Slide the caliper onto the brake disc, making sure the pads sit squarely on either side **(see illustration 3.1b)**. Clean the caliper mounting bolt threads and apply a suitable thread locking compound, then tighten the bolts to the torque setting specified at the beginning of the Chapter **(see illustration 3.10)**.

10 If removed, connect the brake hose to the caliper, using new sealing washers on each side of the union. Align the hose as noted on removal **(see illustration 6.4)**. Tighten the banjo bolt to the torque setting specified at the beginning of the Chapter. Top up the master cylinder reservoir (see *Daily (pre-ride) checks*) and bleed the system as described in Section 10.

11 Check for leaks and thoroughly test the operation of the brake before riding the motorcycle.

7 Front brake master cylinder

> **Warning: Do not, under any circumstances, use petroleum-based solvents to clean brake parts. Use a dedicated brake**

6.3a Cut the cable tie (arrowed) . . .

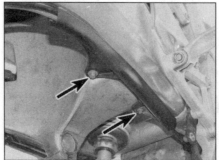

6.3b . . . . then unscrew the bolts (arrowed) and remove the guide

6.4 Brake hose banjo bolt (arrowed)

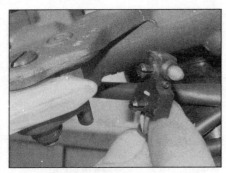

7.4 Carefully displace the front brake switch

7.5 Slacken the cap screws

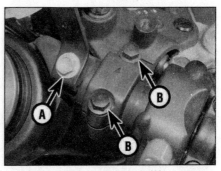

7.6 Reservoir bracket bolt (A), master cylinder clamp bolts (B)

cleaner only. Use care when working with brake fluid as it can injure your eyes and it will damage painted surfaces and plastic parts – cover surrounding components with rag and wipe up any spills immediately and wash the area with soap and water.

Note: *If the entire front brake system is being removed (i.e. calipers as well as master cylinder), or if you intend to change the brake fluid, drain the brake fluid completely from the system (see Section 10), as opposed to retaining the old fluid within it by blocking the hose as described (Step 8).*

1 If the master cylinder is leaking fluid, or if the lever does not produce a firm feel when the brake is applied, and bleeding the brake does not help (see Section 10), and the hydraulic hoses and unions are all in good condition, then a new master cylinder is required – rebuild kits are not available and so overhaul is not possible.

2 If you are completely removing the master cylinder rather than just displacing it, you will need some new brake fluid (see Specifications) and some clean rags.

Removal

Note: *If the master cylinder is being displaced from the handlebar and not being removed completely, follow Steps 6 and 9 only.*

3 Remove the front brake lever (see Chapter 6).

4 Carefully lever the brake light switch from its mount – it is a push fit with two expanding pegs locating in holes **(see illustration)**.

5 If you are draining the reservoir, slacken the

reservoir cap screws and lightly tighten them again **(see illustration)**.

6 Unscrew the bolt securing the reservoir bracket to the handlebar clamp **(see illustration)**.

7 If the master cylinder is just being displaced and not completely removed, do not detach the brake hose.

8 If the master cylinder is being completely removed, unscrew the brake hose banjo bolt and detach the hose from the master cylinder, noting its alignment **(see illustration)**. Discard the sealing washers as new ones must be used on installation. Either clamp the hose, plug it using another suitable short piece of hose fitted through the eye of the banjo union (it must be a fairly tight fit to seal it properly), block it using a suitable bolt with sealing washers and a capped (domed) nut, or wrap some plastic foodwrap tightly around (a finger cut off a latex glove also works well), the object being to minimise fluid loss and prevent dirt entering the system. Whatever you do, also cover the end of the hose in rag, just in case. Similarly block or cover the end of the master cylinder where the hose connects.

9 Check for an alignment mark between the handlebar and the master cylinder clamp mating surfaces and make one if not already there. Unscrew the master cylinder clamp bolts, then remove the clamp and lift the master cylinder and reservoir away from the handlebar **(see illustration 7.6)**.

10 Undo the reservoir cap screws and remove the cap and rubber diaphragm. If the system hasn't been drained, tip the brake fluid

from the reservoir into a suitable container. Wipe any remaining fluid out of the reservoir with a clean rag.

11 If required release the clamp securing the reservoir hose to the union on the master cylinder and detach the hose. Inspect the hose for cracks or splits and replace it with a new one if necessary.

Installation

12 Attach the master cylinder to the handlebar and fit the clamp with the triangular mark pointing forwards **(see illustration 7.6)**, aligning the mating surfaces with the mark on the handlebar **(see illustration)**. Tighten the bolts.

13 Locate the reservoir bracket on the handlebar and secure it with its bolt **(see illustration 7.6)**. If detached connect the reservoir hose to the union and secure it with the clamp.

14 If detached connect the brake hose to the master cylinder, using new sealing washers on each side of the union, and aligning the hose as noted on removal **(see illustration 7.8)**. Tighten the banjo bolt to the torque setting specified at the beginning of the Chapter.

15 Fit the brake light switch **(see illustration 7.4)** and install the brake lever (see Chapter 6).

16 Fill the fluid reservoir with brake fluid as described in *Daily (pre-ride) checks*. Refer to Section 10 of this Chapter and bleed the air from the system.

17 Fit the rubber diaphragm, making sure it is correctly seated, and the cap onto the reservoir. Install the cap screws.

18 Check the operation of the front brake and brake light before riding the motorcycle.

8 Rear brake master cylinder

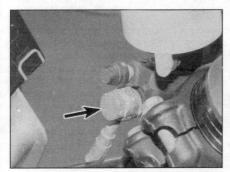

7.8 Brake hose banjo bolt (arrowed)

7.12 Align the mating surfaces with the mark (arrowed)

⚠️ *Warning: Do not, under any circumstances, use petroleum-based solvents to clean brake parts. Use a dedicated brake cleaner only. Use care when working with brake fluid as it can injure your eyes and it will damage painted surfaces and plastic*

parts – cover surrounding components with rag and wipe up any spills immediately and wash the area with soap and water.

Note: *If the entire front brake system is being removed (i.e. caliper as well as the master cylinder), or if you intend to change the brake fluid, drain the brake fluid completely from the system (see Section 10), as opposed to retaining the old fluid within it by blocking the hose as described (Step 6).*

1 If the master cylinder is leaking fluid, or if the pedal does not produce a firm feel when the brake is applied, and bleeding the brake does not help (see Section 10), and the hydraulic hose and unions are all in good condition, then a new master cylinder is required – rebuild kits are not available and so overhaul is not possible.

2 If you are completely removing the master cylinder rather than just displacing it, you will need some new brake fluid (see Specifications) and some clean rags.

Removal

Note: *If the master cylinder is being displaced from the handlebar and not being removed completely, follow Steps 3, 4 and 7 only.*

3 Remove the lower fairing (see Chapter 8).

4 Unscrew the bolt securing the reservoir **(see illustration)**.

5 Remove the reservoir cap and remove the diaphragm plate and diaphragm and tip the contents of the reservoir and hose into a suitable container. Wipe any remaining fluid out with a clean rag. Release the clamp and detach the reservoir hose from its union on the master cylinder, being prepared with a rag to catch any residual fluid, and remove the reservoir **(see illustration)**. Inspect the reservoir hose for cracks or splits and replace it with a new one if necessary.

6 If the master cylinder is just being displaced and not completely removed, do not disconnect the hose. If the master cylinder is being completely removed, unscrew the brake hose banjo bolt and detach the hose from the master cylinder, noting its alignment **(see illustration 8.5)**. Discard the sealing washers as new ones must be used on installation. Either clamp the hose, plug it using another suitable short piece of hose fitted through the eye of the banjo union (it must be a fairly tight fit to seal it properly), block it using a suitable bolt with sealing washers and a capped (domed) nut, or wrap some plastic foodwrap tightly around (a finger cut off a latex glove also works well), the object being to minimise fluid loss and prevent dirt entering the system. Whatever you do, also cover the end of the hose in rag, just in case. Similarly block or cover the end of the master cylinder where the hose connects.

7 Unscrew the two bolts securing the master cylinder and remove it, drawing it off the pushrod and noting how the rod locates **(see illustration 8.5)**.

Installation

8 Fit the master cylinder, locating the pushrod in its end, and tighten the bolts to the torque setting specified at the beginning of the Chapter.

9 Connect the brake hose to the master cylinder, using new sealing washers on each side of the union. Align the hose as noted on removal and tighten the banjo bolt to the specified torque setting **(see illustration 8.5)**.

10 Install the reservoir and tighten its bolt **(see illustration 8.4)**. Connect the reservoir hose to the union on the master cylinder and secure it with the clip **(see illustration 8.5)**. Check that the hose is secure at the reservoir end as well. If the clips have weakened, use new ones.

11 Fill the fluid reservoir with new brake fluid (see *Daily (pre-ride) checks*) and bleed the system following the procedure in Section 10.

12 Install the lower fairing (see Chapter 8).

13 Check the operation of the brake before riding the motorcycle.

9 Brake hoses and unions

Inspection

1 Brake hose condition should be checked regularly and the hoses replaced at the specified interval (see Chapter 1).

2 Twist and flex the hoses while looking for cracks, bulges and seeping fluid. Check extra carefully around the areas where the hoses connect with the banjo fittings, as these are common areas for hose failure.

3 Inspect the banjo union fittings connected to the brake hoses, and the hose splitter bolted to the bottom yoke for the front brake system. If the fittings are rusted, scratched or cracked, replace them with new ones.

Replacement

4 The brake hoses have banjo union fittings on each end. Cover the surrounding area with plenty of rags and unscrew the banjo bolt at each end of the hose, noting its alignment **(see illustrations 5.4, 6.4, 7.8 and 8.5)**. Free the hoses from any clips or guides and remove them. Discard the sealing washers as new ones must be used.

5 Position the new hose, making sure it isn't twisted or otherwise strained, and abut the tab on the hose union with the lug on the component casting, where present. Otherwise align the hose as noted on removal. Install the hose banjo bolts using new sealing washers on both sides of the unions. Tighten the banjo bolts to the torque setting specified at the beginning of this Chapter.

6 Make sure the hoses are correctly aligned and routed clear of all moving components. Flush the old brake fluid from the system, refill with new brake fluid (see *Daily (pre-ride) checks*) and bleed the air from the system (see Section 10). Check the operation of the brakes carefully before riding the motorcycle.

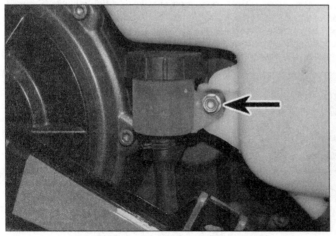

8.4 Reservoir mounting bolt (arrowed)

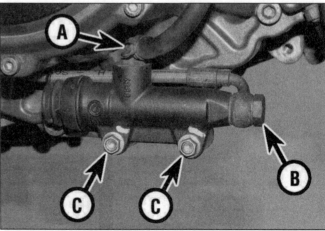

8.5 Reservoir hose union (A), brake hose banjo bolt (B), master cylinder mounting bolts (C)

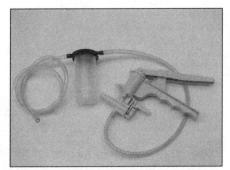

10.0 Vacuum type brake bleeding tool

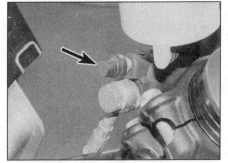

10.5 Remove the dust cap from the master cylinder bleed valve (arrowed)

10.7a Front brake caliper bleed valve (arrowed)

10 Brake system bleeding

Note: *If required use a commercially available vacuum-type brake bleeding tool. If bleeding the system using the conventional method does not work sufficiently well, it is advisable to obtain a bleeder and repeat the procedure detailed below, following the manufacturers instructions for using the tool* **(see illustration)**.

 Warning: Use care when working with brake fluid as it can injure your eyes and it will damage painted surfaces and plastic parts.

Bleeding

1 Bleeding the brakes is simply the process of removing all the air bubbles from the brake fluid reservoirs, the hoses and the brake calipers. Bleeding is necessary whenever a brake system hydraulic connection is loosened or when a component or hose is replaced with a new one. Leaks in the system may also allow air to enter, but leaking brake fluid will reveal their presence and warn you of the need for repair.
2 To bleed the brakes, you will need some new brake fluid (see Specifications), a length of clear vinyl or plastic tubing, a small container partially filled with clean brake fluid, some rags and a ring spanner to fit the brake caliper bleed valves.
3 Cover any body panels and other painted components as required to prevent damage in the event that brake fluid is spilled.

Front brake

4 Remove the reservoir cap and rubber diaphragm (see *Daily (pre-ride) checks*) and slowly pump the brake lever a few times, until no air bubbles can be seen floating up from the holes in the bottom of the reservoir. Loosely refit the reservoir cap.
5 First pull the dust cap off the bleed valve on the master cylinder **(see illustration)**. Attach one end of the clear vinyl or plastic tubing to the bleed valve and submerge the other end in the brake fluid in the container. Follow Step 8

onwards and bleed any air trapped in the high spot of the system.
6 Now pull the dust cap off the bleed valve on one of the front calipers **(see illustration)**. Attach one end of the clear vinyl or plastic tubing to the bleed valve and submerge the other end in the brake fluid in the container **(see illustration)**.
7 Carefully pump the brake lever three or four times and hold it in while opening the caliper bleed valve. When the valve is opened, brake fluid will flow into the clear tubing and the lever will move toward the handlebar. Check the fluid level in the reservoir – do not allow it to drop below the lower mark during the bleeding process.
8 Retighten the bleed valve, then release the brake lever. Repeat the process until no air bubbles are visible in the brake fluid leaving the caliper and the lever is firm when applied. Now connect the tubing to the bleed nipple on the other front caliper and repeat the process.
9 On completion, disconnect the bleeding equipment, then tighten the bleed valves to the torque setting specified at the beginning of the chapter and install the dust caps.
10 Wipe any moisture out of the diaphragm using an absorbent lint-free rag. Install the diaphragm and cap. Wipe up any spilled brake fluid and check the entire system for leaks.

Rear brake

11 Remove the reservoir cap, diaphragm plate (where fitted), and diaphragm (see *Daily (pre-ride) checks*) and slowly pump the brake pedal a few times, until no air bubbles can be

10.13 Rear brake caliper bleed valve (arrowed)

10.7b To bleed the brakes you need a spanner to fit on the bleed valve, a short section of clear tubing, and a clear container half-filled with brake fluid

seen floating up from the holes in the bottom of the reservoir. Loosely refit the reservoir cap.
12 Before bleeding the rear brake unscrew the bolts securing the hose guide to the bottom of the swingarm and remove it, allowing the hose to be as level as possible **(see illustration 6.3b)**.
13 Pull the dust cap off the bleed valve on the caliper **(see illustration)**. Attach one end of the clear vinyl or plastic tubing to the bleed valve and submerge the other end in the brake fluid in the container.
14 Carefully pump the brake pedal three or four times and hold it down while opening the caliper bleed valve. When the valve is opened, brake fluid will flow into the clear tubing and the pedal will move down. Check the fluid level in the reservoir – do not allow it to drop below the lower mark during the bleeding process.
15 Retighten the bleed valve, then release the brake pedal gradually. Repeat the process until no air bubbles are visible in the brake fluid leaving the caliper and the pedal is firm when applied. On completion, disconnect the bleeding equipment, then tighten the bleed valve to the torque setting specified at the beginning of the chapter and install the dust cap.
16 Wipe any moisture out of the diaphragm using an absorbent lint-free rag. Install the diaphragm, plate and cap. Wipe up any spilled brake fluid and check the entire system for leaks.

Changing the fluid

17 Changing the brake fluid is a similar process to bleeding the brakes and requires the same materials, plus a suitable tool for siphoning the fluid out of the hydraulic reservoir (such as a syringe, though if one isn't available it is no problem to displace the reservoir and tip the fluid out as described in Section 7 or 8). Ensure that your container is large enough to take all the old fluid when it is flushed out of the system.

18 Remove the reservoir cap and siphon or tip out the old fluid. Fill the reservoir with new brake fluid, then follow Steps 5 to 10 for the front brake or Steps 12 to 16 for the rear brake. Keep the reservoir topped-up with new fluid to above the LOWER level at all times or air may enter the system and greatly increase the length of the task. Repeat the process until new fluid can be seen emerging from the bleed valve.

Draining the system for overhaul

19 Draining the brake fluid is again a similar process to bleeding the brakes. The quickest and easiest way is to use a commercially available vacuum-type brake bleeding tool (see **Note** at the start of this Section) – follow the manufacturer's instructions. Otherwise follow the procedure described above for changing the fluid, but quite simply do not put any new fluid into the reservoir.

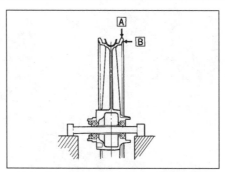

11.2 Check the wheel for radial (out-of-round) runout (A) and axial (side-to-side) runout (B)

11 Wheel inspection and repair

1 Position the motorcycle on an auxiliary stand so that the wheel being checked is raised off the ground. Clean the wheels thoroughly to remove mud and dirt that may interfere with the inspection procedure or mask defects. Make a general check of the wheels (see Chapter 1) and tyres (see *Daily (pre-ride) checks*).

2 To check axial (side-to-side) runout, attach a dial gauge to the fork slider or the swingarm and position its stem against the side of the rim **(see illustration)**. Spin the wheel slowly and check the amount of runout at the rim. To accurately check radial (out of round) runout with the dial gauge, remove the wheel from the machine, and the tyre from the wheel. With the axle clamped in a vice and the dial gauge positioned on the top of the rim, rotate the wheel and check the runout.

3 An easier, though slightly less accurate, method is to attach a stiff wire pointer to the fork slider or the swingarm and position the end a fraction of an inch from the wheel (where the wheel and tyre join). If the wheel is true, the distance from the pointer to the rim will be constant as the wheel is rotated. **Note:** *If wheel runout is excessive, check the wheel bearings and axle very carefully before replacing.*

4 Visually inspect the wheels for cracks, flat spots on the rim, and other damage. Look very closely for dents in the area where the tyre bead contacts the rim. Dents in this area may prevent complete sealing of the tyre against the rim, which leads to deflation of the tyre over a period of time.

5 If damage is evident, or if runout in either direction is excessive, the wheel will have to be replaced with a new one. Never attempt to repair a damaged cast alloy wheel.

12 Wheel alignment check

1 Misalignment of the wheels, which may be due to a bent frame or fork yokes, can cause strange and possibly serious handling problems. If the frame or yokes are at fault, repair by a frame specialist or replacement with new parts are the only alternatives.

2 To check the alignment you will need an assistant, a length of string or a perfectly straight piece of wood and a ruler. A plumb bob or other suitable weight will also be required.

3 Place the bike on an auxiliary stand on level ground, so the bike is upright. If possible measure the width of both tyres at their widest points. Subtract the smaller measurement from the larger measurement, then divide the difference by two. The result is the amount of offset that should exist between the front and rear tyres on both sides.

4 If a string is used, have your assistant hold one end of it about halfway between the floor and the rear axle, touching the rear sidewall of the tyre.

5 Run the other end of the string forward and pull it tight so that it is roughly parallel to the floor **(see illustration)**. Slowly bring the string into contact with the front sidewall of the rear tyre, then turn the front wheel until it is parallel with the string. Measure the distance from the front tyre sidewall to the string.

6 Repeat the procedure on the other side of the motorcycle. The distance from the front tyre sidewall to the string should be equal on both sides, and equal to the amount of offset if calculated earlier.

7 As previously mentioned, a perfectly straight length of wood or metal bar may be

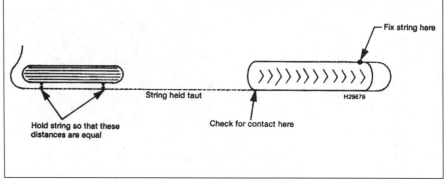

12.5 Wheel alignment check using string

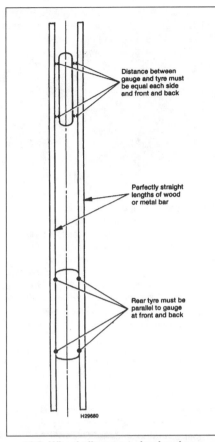

12.7 Wheel alignment check using a straight-edge

Distance between gauge and tyre must be equal each side and front and back

Perfectly straight lengths of wood or metal bar

Rear tyre must be parallel to gauge at front and back

H29680

substituted for the string (see illustration). The procedure is the same.

8 If the front-to-back alignment is correct, the wheels still may be out of alignment vertically.

9 Using a plumb bob, or other suitable weight, and a length of string, check the rear wheel to make sure it is vertical. To do this, hold the string against the tyre upper sidewall and allow the weight to settle just off the floor. When the string touches both the upper and lower tyre sidewalls and is perfectly straight, the wheel is vertical. If it is not, place thin spacers under one leg of the stand until it is.

10 Once the rear wheel is vertical, check the front wheel in the same manner. If both wheels are not perfectly vertical, the frame

13.3 Unscrew the axle nut (arrowed) and remove the washer

and/or major suspension components are bent.

13 Front wheel

Removal

1 Position the motorcycle on an auxiliary stand so that the wheel is raised off the ground. Always make sure the motorcycle is properly supported.

2 Displace the brake calipers (see Section 5). Support the calipers with a cable tie or a bungee cord so that no strain is placed on the hydraulic hoses. There is no need to disconnect the hoses from the calipers. **Note:** *Do not operate the front brake lever with the calipers removed.*

3 Unscrew the axle nut and remove the washer **(see illustration)**.

4 Slacken the axle clamp bolts on the bottom of each fork **(see illustration)**.

5 Support the wheel, then withdraw the axle from the left-hand side, using a soft-faced hammer to tap it out and a rod inserted through the holes in the end to draw it out if necessary, then lower the wheel and remove it from the front **(see illustration)**.

6 Remove the shouldered spacer from the right-hand side of the wheel if required (for example to access the bearing) **(see illustration 13.10b)**. On models up to frame number ZD4MEE009YS000292 also remove the plain spacer from the left-hand side.

Caution: Don't lay the wheel down and

13.4 Slacken the axle clamp bolts (arrowed) on each fork

allow it to rest on a disc – the disc could become warped. Set the wheel on wood blocks so the disc doesn't support the weight of the wheel.

7 Check that the axle is straight by rolling it on a flat surface such as a piece of plate glass (first wipe off all old grease and remove any corrosion using fine wire wool). If the equipment is available, place the axle in V-blocks and check for runout using a dial gauge. If the axle is bent, replace it with a new one.

8 Check the condition of the bearing seals and bearings (see Section 15).

Installation

9 Apply a smear of grease to the axle and the bearing seals. Also apply some to the inside of the wheel spacer, and to the outside where it fits into the wheel.

10 Manoeuvre the wheel into position between the forks, making sure the directional arrows on the tyre and wheel are pointing in the normal direction of rotation (check both to make sure they concur, especially if you have just had a new tyre fitted – the tyre could have been fitted the wrong way round) **(see illustration)**. Fit the shouldered spacer into the right-hand side of the wheel **(see illustration)**. On models up to frame number ZD4MEE009YS000292 also fit the plain spacer into the left-hand side.

11 Lift the wheel into place, making sure the spacer(s) remain(s) in position, and slide the axle in from the left-hand side, pushing it fully home **(see illustration 13.5)**. Tighten the axle clamp bolts on the bottom of the left-hand fork to the torque setting specified at the beginning of the Chapter **(see illustration 13.4)**.

12 Fit the axle nut with its washer and tighten

13.5 Withdraw the axle and remove the wheel

13.10a Make sure the wheel is the correct way round

13.10b Fit the spacer(s) into the wheel

the nut to the torque setting specified at the beginning of the Chapter **(see illustration)**. Check that the wheel spins freely.

13 Tighten the axle clamp bolts on the bottom of the right-hand fork to the torque setting specified at the beginning of the Chapter **(see illustration)**.

14 Slacken the axle clamp bolts on the bottom of the left-hand fork **(see illustration 13.4)**. Lower the front wheel to the ground, then install the brake calipers (see Section 5).

15 Apply the front brake a few times to bring the pads back into contact with the discs. Move the motorcycle off its stand, apply the front brake and pump the front forks a few times to settle all components in position.

16 Now tighten the axle clamp bolts on the bottom of the left-hand fork to the specified torque setting **(see illustration 13.4)**.

17 Check for correct operation of the brakes before riding the motorcycle.

14 Rear wheel

Removal

1 Position the motorcycle on an auxiliary stand or stands so that the wheel is off the ground. It is advisable to place a block in front of the front wheel, or better still to tie the front brake lever to the handlebar so that the front wheel is locked. Note that if the wheel is being removed as part of the swingarm removal

13.12 Fit the washer and nut and tighten the nut

procedure, do not use a paddock type stand that supports the bike via the swingarm.

2 Displace the rear caliper (see Section 6).

3 Fully slacken the chain (see Chapter 1, Section 1).

4 Unscrew the axle nut and remove the washer **(see illustration)**. Remove the chain adjuster block, noting how it fits.

5 Support the wheel (a good way to do this is to slide your foot part way under it) then tap the axle out from the right-hand end using a soft-faced hammer and withdraw it along with the adjuster block from the left-hand side, noting how it passes through the caliper bracket **(see illustration)**. Gently lower the wheel to the ground.

6 Disengage the chain from the sprocket and draw the wheel back and remove it **(see illustration)**. Displace the caliper bracket from the swingarm, noting how it locates **(see illustration)**.

13.13 Tighten the axle clamp bolts (arrowed)

7 Note the spacer in the seal in each side of the wheel and remove them for safekeeping if required (for example to access the bearings) **(see illustrations 14.11a and b)**.

Caution: Do not lay the wheel down and allow it to rest on the disc – it could become warped. Lay the tyre on blocks of wood or stand the wheel upright. Do not operate the brake pedal with the wheel removed.

8 Check that the axle is straight by rolling it on a flat surface such as a piece of plate glass (first wipe off all old grease and remove any corrosion using wire wool). If the equipment is available, place the axle in V-blocks and check for runout using a dial gauge. If the axle is bent, replace it with a new one.

9 Check the condition of the grease seals and wheel bearings, and of the rear sprocket coupling bearings (see Section 15) and dampers (see Chapter 6). Note that there have been instances of rear wheel bearing failure due to overtightening the axle nut, so check them carefully.

Installation

10 If you have had a new tyre fitted make sure the directional arrows point in the direction of normal rotation – you never know, it may have been fitted the wrong way round.

11 Apply a thin coat of grease to the lips of each bearing seal, to the inside and the inner faces of the spacers where they contact the seals, and to the axle. Slide the left-hand side adjuster block onto the axle, making sure its cut-out side faces the axle head. Fit the spacers into the wheel **(see illustrations)**.

12 Smear some grease onto the slot into the

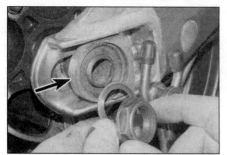
14.4 Unscrew the axle nut and remove the washer and the chain adjuster block (arrowed)

14.5 Withdraw the axle from the left and lower the wheel . . .

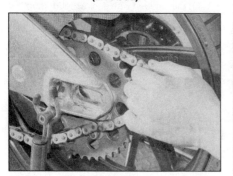
14.6a . . . then disengage the chain and manoeuvre the wheel out

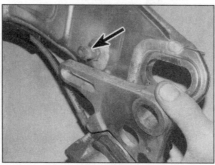
14.6b Displace the caliper bracket, noting how it locates on the peg (arrowed)

14.11a Fit the right-hand spacer . . .

14.11b . . . and the left-hand spacer

brake caliper bracket and the peg it locates on, then locate the bracket onto the swingarm, fitting the slot over the peg (see illustration 14.6b).
13 Manoeuvre the wheel into position between the ends of the swingarm. Make sure the brake caliper bracket is still correctly positioned against the swingarm.
14 Fit the drive chain around the sprocket (see illustration 14.6a).
15 Lift the wheel into position, making sure the spacers and caliper bracket remain correctly in place, and slide the axle in from the left (see illustration 14.5). Push the axle all the way through, locating the chain adjuster block in the swingarm with its flat end at the front, and locating the flats on the axle in the adjuster block (see illustration).
16 Check that everything is correctly aligned, then fit the right-hand side adjuster block, the washer and the axle nut, but do not tighten it yet (see illustration 14.4).
17 Adjust the chain slack as described in Chapter 1.
18 Tighten the axle nut to the torque setting specified at the beginning of the Chapter. Note that the torque setting specified is lower than that specified by Aprilia. The reason for this is that there have been a significant number of rear wheel bearing failures the cause of which has been identified as an overtight axle nut.
19 Install the rear caliper (see Section 6).
20 Operate the brake pedal several times to bring the pads into contact with the disc. Check the operation of the rear brake carefully before riding the bike.

15 Wheel bearing replacement

Note: *Before removing the bearings (but having removed the seals etc as required to access the bearings), refer to* Tools and Workshop Tips *in the Reference Section and check them to see if new ones are needed – however good their apparent condition, once the bearings have been extracted from the wheel they should be replaced with new ones rather than being reused, as the impact on the inner race when driving or pulling them out*

14.15 Locate the chain adjuster block and axle head as shown

could damage them. Always replace the wheel bearings in sets. Never replace the bearings individually. Avoid using a high pressure cleaner on the wheel bearing area.

Front wheel bearings
1 Remove the wheel (see Section 13).
2 Set the wheel on wood blocks so as not to allow the weight to rest on the brake disc.
3 Lever out the bearing seal on one side of the wheel using a seal hook or flat-bladed screwdriver, taking care not to damage the rim of the hub (see illustration). Turn the wheel over and remove the other seal. Discard the seals as new ones must be used.

HAYNES HiNT *Position a piece of wood against the wheel to prevent the screwdriver shaft damaging it when levering the grease seal out.*

15.3 Lever out the seal on each side

15.6 If necessary remove the bearings using a shaped drift as described

4 Refer to *Tools and Workshop Tips* (Section 5 in the Reference Section) and check the bearings as described.
5 If the bearings are being removed, remove the circlip from the right-hand side of the hub (see illustration).
6 To remove the bearings either the Aprilia extractor (part No. 8140180) or a bearing puller with a suitable attachment to locate in the notches in the end of the bearing spacer is required – note that if the spacer only has notches in one end the bearing from that end must be removed first (see illustration 5.17). With the tool correctly fitted, extract the bearing. Refer to *Tools and Workshop Tips* in the Reference Section for more details on using a bearing puller. Note that it may be possible to drive the first bearing out using a suitable drift inserted through the centre of the upper bearing and the spacer, with an end shaped to locate on the inner race of the bearing via the notch on the bottom end of the spacer (see illustration). Do not attempt to drive the first bearing out using a drift located on the top of the spacer itself as it is made of soft metal and will just distort.
7 Remove the bearing spacer. Lay the wheel on its other side and extract the other bearing.
8 Thoroughly clean the hub area of the wheel. First install the right-hand bearing into its recess in the hub, with the marked or sealed side facing outwards. Using the old bearing, a bearing driver or a socket large enough to contact the outer race of the bearing only, drive it in until it's completely seated (see illustration). Do not drive the bearing in using the inner race. When the bearing has seated on the hub fit the circlip into its groove.

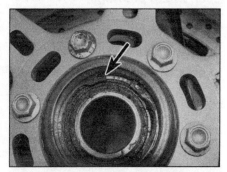

15.5 Release the circlip (arrowed) from the right-hand side

15.8 A socket can be used to drive in the bearing

15.10 Press or drive the seal into the wheel

15.13 Lift the sprocket coupling out of the wheel

15.14 Lever out the grease seal

9 Turn the wheel over and install the bearing spacer. Drive the left-hand side bearing into place as described above until it seats on the spacer. Do not force it or you may distort the circlip securing the right-hand bearing or damage the bearing itself.

10 Apply a smear of lithium based grease to the lips of the new seals, then press them into the wheel, using a seal or bearing driver or a suitable socket to drive it into place if necessary **(see illustration)**. As the seals sit flush with the top surface of their housing, using a piece of wood across the seals will automatically set them flush without the risk of setting them too deep and having to lever them out again.

11 Clean off all grease from the brake discs using acetone or brake system cleaner then install the wheel (see Section 13).

Rear wheel bearings

12 Remove the rear wheel (see Section 14). Set the wheel on wood blocks, disc side down, making sure the disc is off the work surface.

13 Lift the sprocket coupling out of the wheel, noting how it fits **(see illustration)**.

14 Turn the wheel over so the brake disc is facing up. Lever out the bearing seal using a seal hook or flat-bladed screwdriver, taking care not to damage the rim of the hub (see **Haynes Hint** above) **(see illustration)**. Discard the seal as a new one must be used.

15 Refer to *Tools and Workshop Tips* (Section 5 in the Reference Section) and check the bearings as described.

15.16 Release the circlip from the right-hand side

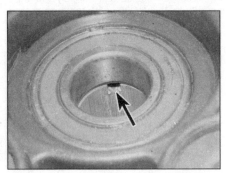

15.17 The tool locates in the notches (arrowed)

16 If the bearings are being removed, remove the circlip from the right-hand side of the hub **(see illustration)**.

17 To remove the bearings either the Aprilia extractor (part No. 8140180) or a bearing puller with a suitable attachment to locate in the notches in the end of the bearing spacer is required – note that if the spacer only has notches in one end the bearing from that end must be removed first **(see illustration)**. With the tool correctly fitted, extract the bearing. Refer to *Tools and Workshop Tips* in the Reference Section for more details on using a bearing puller. Note that it may be possible to drive the first bearing out using a suitable drift inserted through the centre of the upper bearing and the spacer, with an end shaped to locate on the inner race of the bearing via

the notch on the bottom end of the spacer. Do not attempt to drive the first bearing out using a drift located on the top of the spacer itself as it is made of soft metal and will just distort.

18 Remove the bearing spacer **(see illustration)**. Lay the wheel on its other side and extract the other bearing.

19 Thoroughly clean the hub area of the wheel. First install the right-hand bearing into its recess in the hub, with the marked side facing outwards **(see illustration)**. Using the old bearing, a bearing driver or a socket large enough to contact the outer race of the bearing only, drive it in until it's completely seated with the circlip groove visible **(see illustration)**. Do not drive the bearing in using the inner race. When the bearing has seated

15.18 Remove the bearing spacer

15.19a Fit the bearing with its marked side facing out . . .

15.19b . . . a socket can be used to drive the bearing in

15.19c Fit the circlip into its groove

15.20 Fit the bearing into the left-hand side

15.21a Fit the new seal . . .

15.21b . . . driving it into place if necessary

15.27 Lever out the grease seal

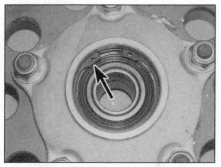

15.29 Release the circlip (arrowed)

on the hub fit the circlip into its groove **(see illustration)**.

20 Turn the wheel over and install the bearing spacer **(see illustration 15.18)**. Drive the left-hand side bearing into place as described above until it seats on the spacer **(see illustration)**. Do not force it or you may distort the circlip securing the right-hand bearing or damage the bearing itself.

21 Apply a smear of grease to the lips of the new grease seal, then press it into the right-hand side of the wheel, using a seal or bearing driver, a suitable socket or a flat piece of wood to drive it into place if necessary **(see illustrations)**.

22 Clean off all grease from the brake disc using acetone or brake system cleaner.

23 Smear some grease onto the sprocket stud shafts. Fit the sprocket coupling into the wheel **(see illustration 15.13)**.

24 Install the wheel (see Section 14).

Sprocket coupling bearings

25 Remove the rear wheel (see Section 14). Set the wheel on blocks, disc side down, making sure the disc is off the work surface.

26 Lift the sprocket coupling out of the wheel, noting how it fits **(see illustration 15.13)**.

27 Lever out the bearing seal on the outside of the coupling using a seal hook or flat-bladed screwdriver, taking care not to damage the rim of the coupling (see *Haynes Hint* above) **(see illustration)**. Discard the seal as a new one must be used.

28 Refer to *Tools and Workshop Tips*

(Section 5 in the Reference Section) and check the bearings as described.

29 If the bearings are being removed, remove the circlip from the outside of the coupling **(see illustration)**.

30 Support the coupling on blocks of wood and drive the bearings and the spacers out from the inside using a bearing driver or socket located on the inner bush flange **(see illustration)**. Remove the spacers from the bearings – if they are tight support the outer race of the bearing and drive the spacer out using a suitable socket.

31 Thoroughly clean the bearing recess. Fit the spacer into the inner bearing, supporting the inner race if you need to drive it in. Drive the bearing in from the outside of the coupling, making sure the spacer flange goes in first, using a bearing driver or a socket large enough to contact the outer race of the bearing only, and drive it in until it is

completely seated. Do not drive the bearing in using the inner race.

32 Fit the spacer into the outer bearing, supporting the inner race if you need to drive it in. Drive the bearing in from the outside of the coupling, making sure the spacer flange goes in first, until the flange contacts the inner bearing. Fit the circlip into its groove **(see illustration 15.29)**. Smear the spacer ends and insides with grease.

33 Apply a smear of grease to the lips of the new seal, then press it into the coupling, using a seal or bearing driver, a suitable socket or a flat piece of wood to drive it into place if necessary **(see illustration)**.

34 Check the sprocket coupling/rubber dampers (see Chapter 6).

35 Smear some grease onto the sprocket stud shafts. Fit the sprocket coupling into the wheel **(see illustration 15.13)**.

36 Install the wheel (see Section 14).

15.30 Drive the bearings out from the inside

15.33 Fit the new seal

16 Tyre fitting

General information

1 The wheels fitted to all models are designed to take tubeless tyres only. Tyre sizes are given in the Specifications at the beginning of this chapter.
2 Refer to the *Daily (pre-ride) checks* listed at the beginning of this manual for tyre maintenance.

Fitting new tyres

3 When selecting new tyres, refer to the tyre information label on the swingarm and the tyre options listed in the owners handbook. Ensure that front and rear tyre types are compatible, the correct size and correct speed rating; if necessary seek advice from a Aprilia dealer or tyre fitting specialist **(see illustration)**.
4 It is recommended that tyres are fitted by a motorcycle tyre specialist rather than attempted

in the home workshop. This is particularly relevant in the case of tubeless tyres because the force required to break the seal between the wheel rim and tyre bead is substantial, and is usually beyond the capabilities of an individual working with normal tyre levers. Additionally, the specialist will be able to balance the wheels after tyre fitting.
5 Note that punctured tubeless tyres can in some cases be repaired if the damage is small and confined to the tread area. Such repairs must only be carried out by a motorcycle tyre fitting specialist.

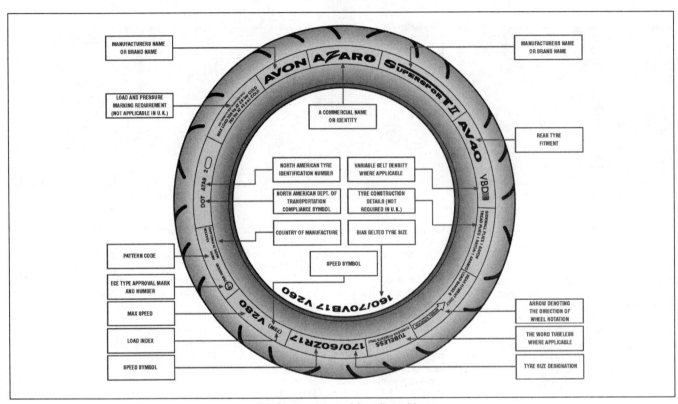

16.3 Common tyre sidewall markings

Chapter 8
Bodywork

Contents

Degrees of difficulty

Easy, suitable for novice with little experience		**Fairly easy,** suitable for beginner with some experience		**Fairly difficult,** suitable for competent DIY mechanic		**Difficult,** suitable for experienced DIY mechanic		**Very difficult,** suitable for expert DIY or professional	

1 General information

This Chapter covers the procedures necessary to remove and install the body parts. Since many service and repair operations on these motorcycles require the removal of body parts, the procedures are grouped here and referred to from other Chapters.

In the case of damage to the body parts, it is usually necessary to remove the broken component and replace it with a new (or used) one. The material that the body panels are composed of doesn't lend itself to conventional repair techniques. There are however some shops that specialise in 'plastic welding', so it may be worthwhile seeking the advice of one of these specialists before consigning an expensive component to the bin.

When attempting to remove any body panel, first study it closely, noting any fasteners and associated fittings, to be sure of returning everything to its correct place on installation. In some cases the aid of an assistant will be required when removing panels, to help avoid the risk of damage to paintwork. Once the evident fasteners have been removed, try to withdraw the panel as described but DO NOT FORCE IT – if it will not release, check that all fasteners have been removed and try again. Where a panel engages another by means of tabs, be careful not to break the tab or its mating slot or to damage the paintwork. Remember that a few moments of patience at this stage will save you a lot of money in replacing broken fairing panels!

When installing a body panel, first study it closely, noting any fasteners and associated fittings removed with it, to be sure of returning everything to its correct place. Check that all fasteners are in good condition, including all trim nuts or clips and damping/rubber mounts; any of these must be replaced if faulty before the panel is reassembled. Check also that all mounting brackets are straight and repair or replace them if necessary before attempting to install the panel. Where assistance was required to remove a panel, make sure your assistant is on hand to install it. Tighten the fasteners securely, but be careful not to overtighten any of them or the panel may break (not always immediately) due to the uneven stress.

 Note that a small amount of lubricant (liquid soap or similar) applied to the mounting rubber grommets will assist the lugs to engage without the need for undue pressure.

2.1a Unscrew the bolt on each side to release the seat . . .

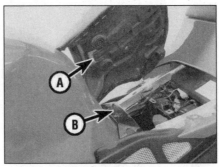

2.1b . . . noting how the tab (A) locates under the hook (B)

2.2a Turn the key to release the seat . . .

2 Seat(s)

Removal

Rider's seat

1 Lift the seat padding on each rear corner to access the bolts and unscrew them, noting the collars **(see illustration)**. Lift the seat up at the back and draw the tab at the front from under the hook on the fuel tank bracket **(see illustration)**.

Passenger seat

2 Insert the ignition key into the seat lock on the left-hand side of the seat cowling and turn it anti-clockwise to release the seat **(see illustration)**. Lift the seat up at the back and draw it out from under the passenger grab-strap, noting how the tabs on the front locate under the tabs on the seat cowling **(see illustration)**.

Passenger seat cover (optional accessory)

3 If fitted, the 'single seat look' rear cover is removed and installed in the same way as the seat itself, with the exception that the passenger grab-strap is folded away under the cover.

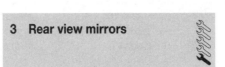

2.2b . . . noting how the tabs locate (arrowed)

Installation

4 Installation is the reverse of removal. When installing the passenger seat or seat cover make sure you do not leave the ignition key in the storage compartment, and push down on the passenger seat or seat cover to engage the latch!

3 Rear view mirrors

1 Unscrew the nut on the inside of the fairing stay and remove the washer, spring and bush **(see illustration)**. Withdraw the mirror from

3.1 Unscrew the nut (arrowed) to release the mirror

the fairing and remove the hemi-spherical cup if loose.
2 Installation is the reverse of removal. Align the mirror as required then tighten the nut.

4 Fairing and body panels

Fairing side panels

1 Turn the six quick-release fasteners 90° anticlockwise and remove the panel, noting how it fits **(see illustrations)**. If required undo the two screws securing the upper trim panel and remove it **(see illustration 4.13)**.

4.1a Release the fasteners as described . . .

4.1b . . . and remove the panel

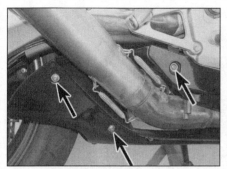

4.4a Undo the screws (arrowed) . . .

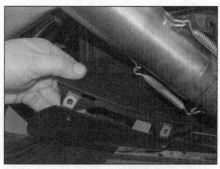

4.4b . . . and remove the exhaust shroud

4.5a Undo the bolt (arrowed) on the left-hand side . . .

2 Installation is the reverse of removal. Turn the quick-release fasteners 90° clockwise to lock them.

Lower fairing

3 Remove both fairing side panels (see Step 1).
4 Undo the three screws securing the exhaust shroud to the lower fairing on the right-hand side, then carefully manoeuvre the shroud out **(see illustrations)**.
5 Undo the bolt on the left-hand side and the two screws at the front, then carefully manoeuvre the lower fairing out from under the bike **(see illustrations)**.
6 Installation is the reverse of removal.

Fairing

7 Raise the rubber boot on the left-hand side of the fairing and disconnect the headlight

assembly wiring connector **(see illustrations)**.
8 Undo the screws securing the fairing to the air duct covers **(see illustrations)**.
9 Undo the screws securing the fairing to the fairing stay **(see illustration)**.

4.5b . . . and the two screws (arrowed) at the front . . .

10 Carefully draw the fairing forwards off its stay and remove it **(see illustration)**.
11 Installation is the reverse of removal. Make sure the rear view mirrors are correctly positioned.

4.5c . . . and remove the lower fairing

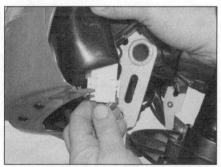

4.7a Raise the boot . . .

4.7b . . . and disconnect the headlight wiring connector

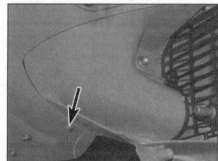

4.8a Undo the screw (arrowed) securing the underside of the fairing to each air duct

4.8b Undo the screw (arrowed) securing the topside of the fairing to each air duct

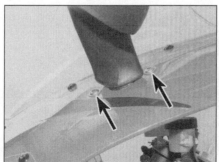

4.9 Undo the two screws (arrowed) on each side

4.10 Draw the fairing forwards off its stay

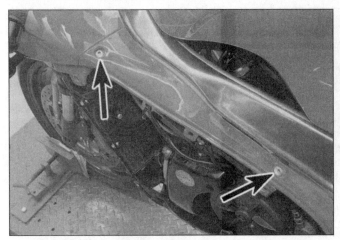

4.13 Undo the screws (arrowed) and remove the trim panel

4.14a Undo the screws (arrowed) . . .

4.14b . . . then displace the cover . . .

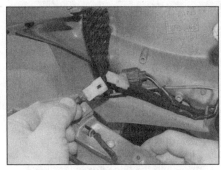

4.14c . . . and disconnect the wiring connector

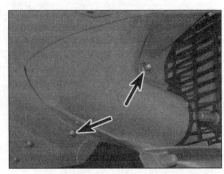

4.15 Undo the screw and the bolt (arrowed)

Air duct covers

12 Remove the fairing side panel (see Step 1).

13 Undo the two screws securing the upper trim panel and remove it **(see illustration)**.

14 Undo the seven screws securing the outer cover **(see illustration)**. Displace the cover and disconnect the turn signal wiring connector **(see illustrations)**.

15 Undo the screw and the bolt securing the front of the inner cover to the fairing and the frame **(see illustration)**.

16 If removing the left-hand cover disconnect the air sensor wiring connector **(see illustration)**.

17 Free the air sensor and/or turn signal wiring (according to side) from the cover, noting its routing.

18 Undo the screw securing the top of the inner cover to the fairing and the bolts securing the rear of the cover to the frame and remove the cover **(see illustrations)**.

19 Installation is the reverse of removal.

Seat cowling

20 Remove both seats (see Section 2).

21 Remove the tail light assembly (see Chapter 9).

22 Undo the two screws securing the underside of the cowl on each side **(see illustration)**.

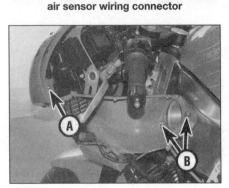

4.16 On the left-hand side disconnect the air sensor wiring connector

4.18a Undo the screw (A) and the bolts (B) . . .

4.18b . . . and remove the cover

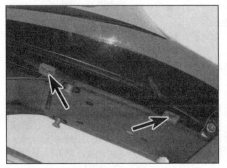

4.22 Undo the screws (arrowed) on the each underside . . .

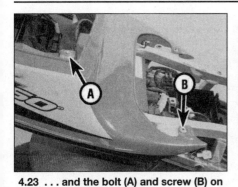

4.23 . . . and the bolt (A) and screw (B) on each top side . . .

4.24 . . . and carefully draw the cowling back and off

24 Carefully draw the cowling back off the bike **(see illustration)**.
25 Installation is the reverse of removal.

Side trim panels

26 Remove the rider's seat (see Section 2).
27 Undo the two screws and remove the panel, noting how it fits **(see illustrations)**.
28 Installation is the reverse of removal.

5 Front mudguard

1 Undo the two screws on each side of the mudguard, then draw it forwards, and remove it **(see illustration)**.
2 Installation is the reverse of removal.

23 Undo the screw and the bolt securing the topside of the cowl on each side, noting how

the bolts also hold the passenger grab-strap **(see illustration)**.

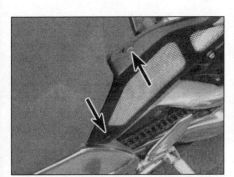

4.27a Undo the screws (arrowed) and remove the panel . . .

4.27b . . . noting how it locates (arrowed) – 2001-on model shown

5.1 Front mudguard screws (arrowed)

Chapter 9
Electrical system

Contents

Degrees of difficulty

Easy, suitable for novice with little experience	**Fairly easy,** suitable for beginner with some experience	**Fairly difficult,** suitable for competent DIY mechanic	**Difficult,** suitable for experienced DIY mechanic	**Very difficult,** suitable for expert DIY or professional

Specifications

Battery

Capacity	12 V, 12 Ah
Charging time	
Normal	8 to 10 hours @ 1.2 A
Quick	0.5 @ 12 A

Charging system

Current leakage	1 mA (max)
Alternator stator coil resistance	0.1 to 1.0 ohms
Alternator output (max)	approx. 400 W
Unregulated voltage output (no-load, cold engine)	min. 60 V (ac) @ 4000 rpm
Regulated (standard charging) voltage	13 to 15 V @ 4000 rpm

Starter motor

Brush length (min)	8 mm

Fuses

Main (under rider's seat)	30 A x 2
Secondary (in fusebox)	
A – Headlight	15 A
B – HT coils, fuel pump	15 A
C – Cooling fans, instruments	15 A
D – Parking light, brake light, turn signals, horn, instrument lights	15 A
E – ECU, fuel pump relay, engine shut-off relay	15 A

Bulbs

Headlight
   1998 to 2000 models
      LO beam
         European models .... 55 W H4
         US models .... 35 W H3
      HI beam
         European models .... 60 W H3 x 2
         US models .... 35 W H3 x 2
   2001 to 2003 models
      LO beam .... 55 W H7U
      HI beam .... 55 W H7U x 2
Sidelight .... 5 W
Brake/tail light .... 21/5 W x 2
Turn signal lights .... 10 W x 4

Torque settings

Alternator cover bolts .... 11 Nm
Alternator rotor bolt .... 130 Nm
Alternator stator bolts .... 11 Nm
Crankshaft position sensor bolts .... 11 Nm
Neutral switch .... 4 Nm
Oil pressure switch .... 15 Nm
Regulator/rectifier bolts .... 12 Nm
Sidestand switch bolt .... 10 Nm
Speed sensor bolt .... 12 Nm
Starter motor mounting bolts .... 11 Nm

1 General information

All models have a 12-volt electrical system charged by a three-phase alternator with a separate regulator/rectifier.

The regulator maintains the charging system output within the specified range to prevent overcharging, and the rectifier converts the ac (alternating current) output of the alternator to dc (direct current) to power the lights and other components and to charge the battery. The alternator rotor is mounted on the left-hand end of the crankshaft.

The starter motor is mounted on the front of the engine. The starting system includes the battery, the starter relay, the starter motor, and the various switches and wires. Some of the switches (sidestand switch, clutch switch and neutral switch) are part of the safety interlock circuit, which cuts the ignition if the sidestand is extended whilst the engine is running and in gear, or if a gear is selected whilst the engine is running and the sidestand is extended. It also prevents the engine from being started if the engine is in gear while the sidestand is down.

Note: *Keep in mind that electrical parts, once purchased, cannot be returned. To avoid unnecessary expense, make very sure the faulty component has been positively identified before buying a replacement part.*

2 Electrical system fault finding

 Warning: To prevent the risk of short circuits, the ignition (main) switch must always be OFF and the battery negative (–) terminal should be disconnected before any of the bike's other electrical components are disturbed. Don't forget to reconnect the terminal securely once work is finished or if battery power is needed for circuit testing.

1 A typical electrical circuit consists of an electrical component, the switches, relays, etc. related to that component and the wiring and connectors that link the component to the battery and the frame. To aid in locating a problem in any electrical circuit, and to guide you with the wiring colour codes and connectors, refer to the *Wiring Diagram* for you model at the end of this Chapter.

2 Before tackling any troublesome electrical circuit, first study the wiring diagram (see end of Chapter) thoroughly to get a complete picture of what makes up that individual circuit. Trouble spots, for instance, can often be narrowed down by noting if other components related to that circuit are operating properly or not. If several components or circuits fail at one time, chances are the fault lies in the fuse or earth (ground) connection, as several circuits often are routed through the same fuse and earth (ground) connections.

3 Electrical problems often stem from simple causes, such as loose or corroded connections or a blown fuse. Prior to any electrical fault finding, always visually check the condition of the fuse, wires and connections in the problem circuit. Intermittent failures can be especially frustrating, since you can't always duplicate the failure when it's convenient to test. In such situations, a good practice is to clean all connections in the affected circuit, whether or not they appear to be good. All of the connections and wires should also be wiggled to check for looseness which can cause intermittent failure.

4 If testing instruments are going to be used, use the wiring diagram to plan where you will make the necessary connections in order to accurately pinpoint the trouble spot.

5 The basic tools needed for electrical fault finding include a battery and bulb test circuit or a continuity tester, a test light, and a jumper wire. A multimeter capable of reading volts, ohms and amps is a very useful and inexpensive alternative and performs the functions of all of the above, and is necessary for performing more extensive tests and checks where specific voltage, current or resistance values are needed.

 Refer to Fault Finding Equipment in the Reference section for details of how to use electrical test equipment.

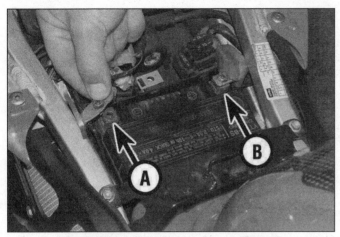

3.2 Negative terminal (A), positive terminal (B)

3.5 Carefully lift the battery out of the bike

3 Battery removal and maintenance

Caution: Be extremely careful when handling or working around the battery. The electrolyte is very caustic and an explosive gas (hydrogen) is given off when the battery is charging.

Removal and installation

1 Make sure the ignition is OFF. Remove the rider's seat (see Chapter 8).
2 Unscrew the negative (–) terminal bolt and disconnect the lead from the battery (see illustration).
3 Lift the insulating over off the positive (+) terminal, then unscrew the bolt and disconnect the lead.
4 Undo the battery clamp screw and remove the clamp.
5 Remove the battery from the bike (see illustration).
6 Before installing the battery, clean the terminals and lead ends with a wire brush or knife, and emery paper.
7 Installation is the reverse of removal. When you reconnect the leads, connect the positive (+) terminal first. Note that the clock and rev limiter will need resetting.

HAYNES HiNT *Battery corrosion can be kept to a minimum by applying a layer of petroleum jelly or battery terminal (dielectric) grease to the terminals after the cables have been connected. Do not use normal lubricating grease.*

Inspection and maintenance

8 All models are fitted with a sealed MF (maintenance free) battery. *Note: Do not attempt to remove the battery caps to check the electrolyte level or battery specific gravity. Removal will damage the caps, resulting in*

electrolyte leakage and battery damage. However the following checks should be regularly performed – remove the battery first (see above).
9 Check that the battery terminals and leads are clean. If corrosion is evident, clean the terminals and lead ends with a wire brush or knife, and emery paper. On installation apply a thin coat of petroleum jelly or battery terminal grease to the connections to slow further corrosion.
10 Keep the battery case clean to prevent current leakage, which can discharge the battery over a period of time (especially when it sits unused). Wash the outside of the case with a solution of baking soda and water. Rinse the battery thoroughly, then dry it.
11 Look for cracks in the case and replace the battery with a new one if any are found. If acid has been spilled on the frame or battery box, neutralise it with a baking soda and water solution, dry it thoroughly, then touch up any damaged paint.
12 If the motorcycle sits unused for long periods of time, refer to Section 4 and charge the battery once every month to six weeks.
13 Assess the condition of the battery by measuring the voltage across the battery

4.2 If the charger doesn't have an ammeter built in, connect one in series as shown. DO NOT connect the ammeter between the battery terminals or it will be ruined

terminals – connect the voltmeter positive (+) probe to the battery positive (+) terminal, and the negative (–) probe to the battery negative (–) terminal. When fully charged there should be 12.6 volts (or more) present. If the voltage falls below 12.0 volts remove the battery (see above) and recharge it as described in Section 4.

4 Battery charging

Caution: Be extremely careful when handling or working around the battery. The electrolyte is very caustic and an explosive gas (hydrogen) is given off when the battery is charging.

1 Your charger must be rated for 12 volts. Remove the battery (see Section 3). If not already done, refer to Section 3, Step 13, and check the voltage across its terminals (open-circuit voltage).
2 Connect the charger to the battery, making sure that the positive (+) lead on the charger is connected to the positive (+) terminal on the battery, and the negative (–) lead is connected to the negative (–) terminal. The battery should be charged at the rate and for the time specified at the beginning of the Chapter (or as marked on the battery case), or until the voltage across the terminals reaches 12.8V (allow the battery to stabilise for 30 minutes after charging before taking a voltage reading). Exceeding this can cause the battery to overheat, buckling the plates and rendering it useless. Few owners will have access to an expensive current controlled charger, so if a normal domestic charger is used check that after a possible initial peak, the charge rate falls to a reasonable level – if that level is more than specified, then reduce the charging time accordingly (see illustration). If the battery becomes hot during charging **stop**. Further charging will cause damage. *Note: In emergencies the battery can be charged at a higher rate of around 12 amps for a period of*

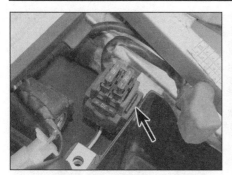

5.1a Main fuse holder (arrowed)

5.1b Fusebox (arrowed)

5.1c Slacken the bolt (arrowed) to release the lid clip

30 minutes. However, this is not recommended and the low amp charge is by far the safer method of charging the battery.
3 If the recharged battery discharges rapidly when left disconnected it is likely that an internal short caused by physical damage or sulphation has occurred. A new battery will be required. A sound item will tend to lose its charge at about 1% per day.
4 Install the battery (see Section 3).
5 If the motorcycle sits unused for long periods of time, charge the battery once every month to six weeks and leave it disconnected.

5 Fuses

1 The electrical system is protected by fuses of different ratings. The main fuses are housed in a holder behind the battery **(see illustration)** – remove the rider's seat for access (see Chapter 8). All the secondary fuses are housed in the fusebox, which is mounted on the right-hand end of the instrument cluster **(see illustration)**. Slacken the lid clip bolt and displace the clip to release the lid **(see illustration)**.
2 Each fuse is clearly marked with its rating and must only be replaced by a fuse of the same rating. The circuits relating to the secondary fuses are marked on a label in the fusebox lid, A to E **(see illustration)**. There is a spare main fuse in the holder, and three spare secondary fuses in the fusebox. If a

spare is used, always replace it with a new one.
3 The fuses can be removed and checked visually. If you can't pull the fuse out with your fingertips, use a suitable pair of pliers. A blown fuse is easily identified by a break in the element **(see illustration)**, or can be tested for continuity using an ohmmeter or continuity tester – if there is no continuity, it has blown.

 Warning: Never put in a fuse of a higher rating or bridge the terminals with any other substitute, however temporary it may be. Serious damage may be done to the circuit, or a fire may start.

4 If a fuse blows, be sure to check the wiring circuit very carefully for evidence of a short-circuit. Look for bare wires and chafed, melted or burned insulation. If the fuse is renewed before the cause is located, the new fuse will blow immediately.
5 Occasionally a fuse will blow or cause an open-circuit for no obvious reason. Corrosion of the fuse ends and fusebox terminals may occur and cause poor fuse contact. If this happens, remove the corrosion with a wire brush or emery paper, then spray the fuse end and terminals with electrical contact cleaner.

6 Lighting system check

1 The battery provides power for operation of the headlights, sidelight, tail lights, brake

lights, turn signals and instrument cluster lights. If none of the lights operate, always check battery voltage before proceeding. Low battery voltage indicates either a faulty battery or a defective charging system. Refer to Section 3 for battery checks and Section 29 for charging system tests. Also check the fuses (see Section 5). When checking for a blown filament in a bulb, it is advisable to back up a visual check with a continuity test of the filament as it is not always apparent that a bulb has blown. When testing for continuity, remember that on some bulbs it is the metal body of the bulb which is the ground or earth, and make sure when testing a dual filament tail light bulb that you are testing the correct filament, and if in doubt test them both. A definitive way of testing a bulb is to connect it directly to a fully charged 12 volt battery using suitable jumper wires, and to see whether it comes on or not. Note that if there is more than one problem at the same time, it is likely to be a fault relating to a multi-function component, such as one of the fuses governing more than one circuit, or the ignition switch.

Headlight

2 If a headlight fails to work, check the bulb, the bulb terminals and the wiring connector first (see Section 7), then the fuse (see Section 5), then the relay (Steps 3 and 4).
3 The relays, one for the HI beam circuit and one for the LO beam, are housed in the relay box on the left-hand end of the instrument cluster **(see illustration)**. Unclip the relay box

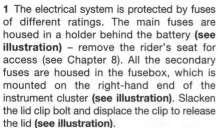

5.2 The fuse identity is marked on a label in the lid

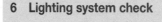

H28946

5.3 A blown fuse can be identified by a break in its element

6.3a Relay box (arrowed)

6.3b HI beam relay (A), LO beam relay (B)

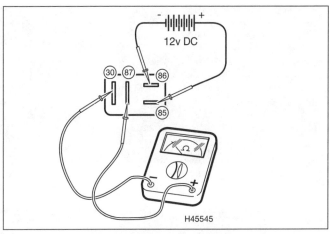

H45545

6.4 Headlight relay test set-up

lid to access them (see illustration). The easiest way of seeing whether a relay is faulty is to swap it for the other one – if the fault transfers from one beam to the other that relay is faulty and must be replaced with a new one. If the fault remains on the same beam the fault is in the wiring. The HI beam relay is the top one in the box and the LO beam relay is the middle one – simply pull them out of their socket.

4 To test a relay, set a multimeter to the ohms x 1 scale and connect it across the relay's 30 and 87 terminals (see illustration). Using a fully-charged 12 volt battery and two insulated jumper wires, connect the positive (+) terminal of the battery to the 85 terminal on the relay, and the negative (-) terminal of the battery to the 86 terminal on the relay. At this point the relay should be heard to click and the multimeter read 0 ohms (continuity). If this is the case the relay is proved good. If the relay does not click when battery voltage is applied and indicates no continuity (infinite resistance) across its terminals, it is faulty and must be replaced with a new one.

5 If the relay is good, check for battery voltage at the orange/light blue wire terminal on the relay connector with the ignition ON. If no voltage is present check the fuse (A), and the wiring between. If voltage is present, check the white/black (HI beam) or black/white (LO beam) wire between the relay and the bulb connector.

6 If they are all good, check for battery voltage at the white (HI beam) or black (LO beam) wire terminal on the relay wiring connector, with the ignition switch and light switch (where fitted) ON, and the dip switch set to the relevant position. If voltage is present, check the blue wire circuit to earth (ground) for an open or poor connection.

7 If no problem is found in the wiring and connectors, check the light switch (where fitted) and the ignition switch (see Sections 19 and 18).

Sidelight

8 If the sidelight fails to work, check the bulb, the bulb terminals and the wiring connector first (see Section 7), then check for battery voltage at the yellow wire terminal on the supply side of the sidelight wiring connector, with the ignition switch and light switch (where fitted) ON. If voltage is present, check for continuity between the wiring connector terminals on the sidelight side of the connector and the corresponding terminals in the bulbholder. If voltage and continuity are present, check for continuity between the red/blue wire terminal on the supply side of the sidelight wiring connector and earth (ground). If there is no continuity, check the earth (ground) circuit for an open or poor connection.

9 If no voltage is indicated, check the wiring and connectors between the sidelight, the light switch (where fitted) and the ignition switch, then check the switches themselves.

Tail light

10 If a tail light fails to work, check the bulb, the bulb terminals and the wiring connectors first (see Section 9), then the fuse (see Section 5), then check for battery voltage at the yellow wire terminal on the supply side of the tail light main wiring connector, with the ignition switch and light switch (where fitted) ON. If voltage is present, check for continuity in the wire between the wiring connector terminals on the tail light side of the connector and the corresponding terminals in the bulbholder. If voltage and continuity are present, check for continuity between the blue wire terminal on the supply side of the tail light wiring connector and earth (ground). If there is no continuity, check the earth (ground) circuit for an open or poor connection.

11 If no voltage is indicated, check the wiring and connectors between the tail light, the light switch (where fitted) and the ignition switch, then check the switches themselves.

Brake light

12 If a brake light fails to work, check the bulb, the bulb terminals and the wiring connector first (see Section 9), then fuse D, then check for battery voltage at the yellow/green wire terminal on the supply side of the main tail light wiring connector, with the ignition switch ON and the brake lever or pedal applied. If voltage is present, check for continuity in the wire between the wiring connector terminals on the tail light side of the connector and the corresponding terminals in the bulbholder. If voltage and continuity are present, check for continuity between the blue wire terminal on the supply side of the tail light wiring connector and earth (ground). If there is no continuity, check the earth (ground) circuit for an open or poor connection.

13 If no voltage is indicated, check the brake light switches (see Section 14), then the wiring and connectors between the tail light and the switches.

Instrument and warning lights

14 See Section 17.

Turn signal lights

15 If one light fails to work, check the bulb and the bulb terminals first, then the wiring connectors (see Section 12). If none of the turn signals work, first check the signal fuse (see Section 5).

16 If the fuse is good, see Section 11 for the turn signal circuit check.

---

7 Headlight bulb and sidelight bulb renewal

Note: *The headlight bulb is of the quartz-halogen type. Do not touch the bulb glass as skin acids will shorten the bulb's service life. If the bulb is accidentally touched, it should be wiped carefully when cold with a rag soaked in methylated spirit and dried before fitting.*

7.2a Remove the dust cover . . .

7.2b . . . then disconnect the headlight wiring connector

7.2c Release the retaining clip . . .

7.2d . . . and remove the bulb

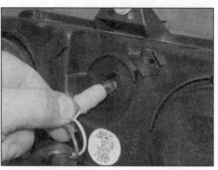

7.9a Pull the bulbholder out . . .

7.9b . . . then carefully pull the bulb out of the holder

 Warning: Allow the bulb time to cool before removing it if the headlight has just been on.

Headlight

1 To access the HI beam bulbs in the top of the headlight remove the fairing (see Chapter 8). The LO beam bulb in the bottom of the headlight can be accessed by reaching up under the fairing.

2 To remove the HI beam bulbs on 1998 to 2000 models and any bulb on 2001 to 2003 models, remove the rubber dust cover then disconnect the headlight wiring connector **(see illustrations)**. Release the bulb retaining clip(s) then remove the bulb **(see illustrations)**.

3 To remove the LO beam bulbs on 1998 to 2000 models, remove the rubber dust cover then disconnect the headlight wiring connector. Release the bulbholder by turning it anticlockwise, then pull the bulb off the holder.

4 Fit the new bulb in a reverse order, bearing in mind the information in the **Note** above. Make sure the bulb locates correctly.

5 Install the dust cover with the 'TOP' mark at the top.

6 Check the operation of the headlights.

7 Install the fairing if necessary (see Chapter 8).

HAYNES HINT *Always use a paper towel or dry cloth when handling new bulbs to prevent injury if the bulb should break and to increase bulb life.*

Sidelight

8 Remove the fairing (see Chapter 8).

9 Pull the bulbholder out of the headlight, then remove the bulb **(see illustrations)**. Fit the new bulb in the bulbholder, then fit the bulbholder into the headlight, making sure it correctly seated. Check the operation of the sidelight.

10 Install the fairing (see Chapter 8).

8 Headlight assembly

Removal

1 Remove the fairing (see Chapter 8).

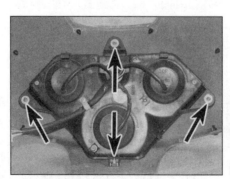

8.2 Headlight mounting screws (arrowed) – access the bottom one from the underside of the fairing

2 Undo screw the four screws securing the headlight and remove it **(see illustration)**.

3 If required remove the bulbs (see Section 7).

Installation

4 Installation is the reverse of removal. Check the operation of the headlight and sidelight. Check the headlight aim (see Chapter 1).

9 Brake/tail light bulb renewal

1 Undo the two lens screws and remove the lens **(see illustrations)**.

9.1a Undo the screws for the bulb being accessed . . .

9.1b ... and remove the lens ...

9.2 ... and the bulb

10.1 Tail light wiring connector (arrowed)

2 Push the bulb into the holder and twist it anti-clockwise to remove it **(see illustration)**.
3 Check the socket terminals for corrosion and clean them if necessary. Line up the pins of the new bulb with the slots in the socket, then push the bulb in and turn it clockwise until it locks into place. **Note:** *The pins on the bulb are offset so it can only be installed one way. It is a good idea to use a paper towel or dry cloth when handling the new bulb to prevent injury if the bulb should break and to increase bulb life.*
4 Install the lens – do not overtighten the screws as it is easy to crack the lens.

10 Tail light assembly

Removal

1 Remove the passenger seat (see Chapter 8). Trace the wiring from the tail light and disconnect it at the connector **(see illustration)**. Feed the wiring back to the light, noting its routing.
2 Undo the screws securing the tail light assembly and remove it from the back **(see illustrations)**.
3 To separate the light unit from the shroud unscrew the three nuts and remove the bolts securing them together **(see illustration)**. Note the collars in the rubber mounts. Check the rubber mounts for damage, deformation and deterioration and replace them with new ones if necessary.

10.2a Undo the screws (arrowed) on the underside ...

Installation

4 Installation is the reverse of removal. Check the operation of the tail light and the brake light.

11 Turn signal circuit check

1 Most turn signal problems are the result of a burned out bulb or a corroded socket. This is especially true when the turn signals function properly in one direction, but fail to flash in the other direction. Check the bulbs and the sockets (see Section 12) and the wiring connectors. Also, check the fuse D (see Section 5) and the switch (see Section 19).
2 The battery provides power for operation of the turn signal lights, so if they do not operate, also check the battery voltage. Low battery

10.2b ... and the screws (arrowed) on the back ...

voltage indicates either a faulty battery or a defective charging system. Refer to Section 3 for battery checks and Section 29 for charging system tests.
3 If the bulbs, sockets, connectors, fuse, switch and battery are good, the turn signal relay may be faulty – no test details are given for the relay so the best way to check it is to substitute it with one that is known to be good and to see if the fault is cured. To access the relay remove the fairing (see Chapter 8) – the relay is in front of the instrument cluster **(see illustration)**.
4 If a substitute relay is not available, or if the relay is not faulty, test the wiring to and from it as follows. Disconnect the wiring connector from the relay. Check for battery voltage at the green wire terminal on the connector with the ignition ON. Connect the positive (+) probe of the meter to the terminal and the negative (-) to the frame or engine.

10.2c ... and draw the unit out

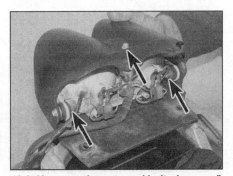

10.3 Unscrew the nuts and bolts (arrowed) and remove the shroud

11.3 Turn signal relay (arrowed)

13.2 Turn signal mounting nut (arrowed)

14.2 The front brake switch wiring connector is in the boot (arrowed)

14.3 Rear brake switch wiring connector (arrowed)

5 If no power was present at the relay, check the wiring from the relay to the fuse and then to the ignition switch for continuity.

6 If power was present at the relay, now check the wiring and connectors between the relay, turn signal switch, turn signal lights and earth (ground) for continuity. If the wiring and connectors are all good replace the relay with a new one.

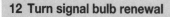

12 Turn signal bulb renewal

1 Undo the screw securing the lens to the housing and remove it.

2 Push the bulb into the holder and twist it anti-clockwise to remove it.

3 Check the socket terminals for corrosion and clean them if necessary.

4 Line up the pins of the new bulb with the slots in the socket, then push the bulb in and turn it clockwise until it locks into place.

5 Fit the lens, making sure it locates correctly, then install the screw.

13 Turn signal removal

Removal

Front

1 Remove the outer air duct cover (see Chapter 8).

2 Unscrew the nut, withdraw the bolt and remove the turn signal from the cover **(see illustration)**.

Rear

3 Remove the passenger seat, and if there is not enough access to the wiring connectors also remove the seat cowling (see Chapter 8).

4 Trace the wiring back from the turn signal and disconnect it at the connector.

5 Unscrew the nut securing the turn signal on the inside of the rear mudguard, then withdraw the bolt and remove the turn signal.

Installation

6 Installation is the reverse of removal. Make

sure the wiring is correctly routed and securely connected. Check the operation of the turn signals.

14 Brake light switches

Circuit check

1 Before checking the switches, check the brake light circuit (see Section 6, Step 12).

2 The front brake light switch is mounted on the brake master cylinder. Trace the wiring from the switch and disconnect it at the wiring connector inside the boot on the right-hand end of the instrument cluster **(see illustration)**.

3 The rear brake light switch is mounted above the brake pedal. Remove the rider's seat and if necessary the right-hand side trim panel to access the wiring connector (see Chapter 8). Trace the wiring from the switch and disconnect it at the connector **(see illustration)**.

4 Using a continuity tester, connect the probes to the terminals in the switch side of the wiring connector. With the brake lever or pedal at rest, there should be no continuity. With the brake lever or pedal applied, there should be continuity. If the switch does not behave as described, replace it with a new one

5 If the switches are good, check for voltage at the green wire terminal on the loom side of

14.7 Carefully lever the switch off the master cylinder

the connector with the ignition switch ON – there should be battery voltage. If there's no voltage present, check the wiring between the switch and the ignition switch (see the *Wiring Diagrams* at the end of this Chapter). If there is voltage, check the wiring and connectors between the switch and the brake light bulbs.

Switch renewal

Front brake light switch

6 The switch is mounted on the brake master cylinder. Trace the wiring from the switch and disconnect it at the wiring connector inside the boot on the right-hand end of the instrument cluster **(see illustration 14.2)**. Feed the wiring up to the switch, releasing it from any ties and noting its routing.

7 Carefully lever the switch from its mount – it is a push fit with two expanding pegs locating in holes **(see illustration)**.

8 Installation is the reverse of removal. Check the operation of the switch.

Rear brake light switch

9 The rear brake light switch is mounted above the brake pedal. Remove the rider's seat and if necessary the right-hand side trim panel to access the wiring connector (see Chapter 8). Trace the wiring from the switch and disconnect it at the connector **(see illustration 14.3)**. Feed the wiring down to the switch, noting its routing.

10 Unscrew and remove the switch **(see illustration)**.

11 Installation is the reverse of removal. Check the operation of the switch.

14.10 Rear brake light switch (arrowed)

15 Instrument cluster removal and installation

Removal

1 Remove the fairing (see Chapter 8).
2 Unscrew the three nuts securing the instrument cluster and remove the washers **(see illustration)**. Displace the cluster forwards and disconnect the wiring connector, then remove the cluster **(see illustration)**.

Installation

3 Installation is the reverse of removal. Check the rubber mounting grommets for cracks and deterioration and replace them with new ones if necessary.

16 Instrument check and disassembly

Note: *This manual does not describe the function and display characteristics of the instrument cluster – refer to the Aprilia owners handbook for this.*

Check

Speedometer and speed sensor

1 If the speedometer/odometer/trip meter fail to work, and this is not due to a failure of the LCD itself, remove the rider's seat and if necessary the right-hand side trim panel to access the speed sensor wiring connector, and remove the fairing to access the instrument cluster wiring connector (see Chapter 8). Disconnect the connectors and check for loose or corroded terminals **(see illustration and 15.2b)**. Check for continuity in the wiring between the connectors and the sensor in the rear brake caliper bracket.
2 Using a feeler gauge check that the air gap between the sensor tip and the brake disc bolts is 1.4 to 1.6 mm **(see illustration)**. If not, check that the sensor is securely mounted. If it is the sensor tip may be damaged. Make sure all the brake disc bolts are installed.
3 Reconnect the sensor and instrument cluster wiring connectors. Turn the ignition ON and perform the following three tests:
Test 1 – using a multimeter with suitable probes, measure the voltage between the green/violet and blue/orange wire terminals in the speed sensor connector. There should be more than 9 volts.
Test 2 – using a multimeter with suitable probes, measure the voltage between the grey/white and blue/orange wire terminals in the speed sensor connector. There should be more than 6 volts. Keep the probes inserted.
Test 3 – raise the rear wheel off the ground using a suitable stand. Make sure the transmission is in neutral. With the probes

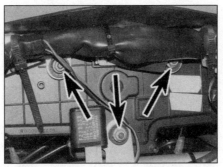

15.2a Unscrew the nuts (arrowed) . . .

connected as for test 2, slowly spin the rear wheel. When the brake disc bolts pass the sensor the voltage should drop to zero, then rise again to more than 6 volts.
4 If the reading obtained in test one was incorrect, remove the sensor and test again. If the value is still incorrect replace the instrument cluster with a new one. If test one was correct and test two reading was incorrect, replace the sensor with a new one (see Step 5). If tests one and two were correct yet the test three reading was incorrect, replace the sensor with a new one (see Step 8). If all three tests were correct replace the instrument cluster with a new one.
5 To remove the speed sensor, first remove the rider's seat and if necessary the right-hand side trim panel to access the speed sensor wiring connector. Trace the wiring from the sensor in the rear brake caliper bracket and disconnect it at the connector **(see illustration 16.1)**. Unscrew the bolt securing the sensor to the bracket and remove it **(see illustration 16.2)**. On installation check the sensor air gap (see Step 2).

Tachometer

6 Remove the fairing (see Chapter 8). Turn the ignition ON. Using a multimeter with suitable probes, measure the voltage between the green and blue/green wire terminals in the instrument cluster connector (with it still connected). There should be battery voltage. Turn the ignition OFF.
7 Remove the rider's seat (see Chapter 8).

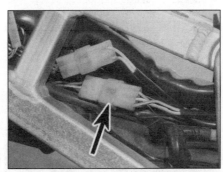

16.1 Speed sensor wiring connector (arrowed)

Remove the rubber cover from the ECU. Check for continuity in the grey/violet wire between the instrument cluster wiring connector and ECU wiring connector. If the wiring is good, substitute the instrument cluster with one that is known to be good; if that works OK, then the original unit is faulty. If the substitute does not work the ECU is faulty (see Chapter 5).

LCD displays

8 If the LCD displays fail completely a new instrument cluster should be installed. If there is a partial failure first check the engine coolant temperature (ECT) sensor and fuel level sensor (see Chapters 3 and 4), and the speed sensor (see above), according to the failure. All other LCD functions are controlled internally.

Oil pressure warning LED

9 When the ignition is first turned ON and before the engine is started, the oil warning LED should come on. When the engine is started it should extinguish.
10 If the LED does not come on remove the lower fairing (see Chapter 8). Disconnect the wiring connector from the oil pressure switch **(see illustration 24.3)**. Turn the ignition ON and earth (ground) the wiring connector on the crankcase – the warning LED should come on. If the LED does not come on, first check the wire between the oil pressure switch and instrument cluster wiring connector for continuity. If that is good the instrument cluster should be replaced with a new one.
11 If the warning LED comes on when the

15.2b . . . then displace the instruments and disconnect the wiring connector

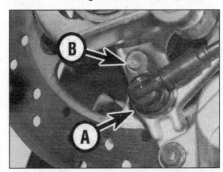

16.2 Check the air gap (A) between the speed sensor tip and the disc mounting bolt. Sensor mounting bolt (B)

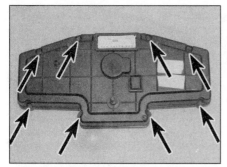

16.16a Undo the screws (arrowed) . . .

16.16b . . . and remove the rear cover . . .

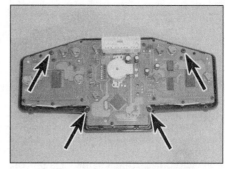

16.17a . . . then undo the screws (arrowed) . . .

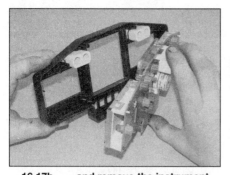

16.17b . . . and remove the instrument panel

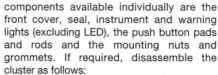
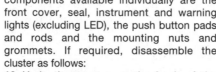
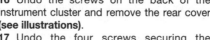

16.18a Check the push buttons and their rods . . .

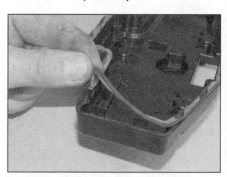

16.18b . . . and the cover seal

engine is running, and this is not due to low oil level or low oil pressure (see Chapter 1), disconnect the oil pressure switch wiring connector **(see illustration 24.3)**, then turn the ignition ON; the display and light should be out. If they are on, the wire between the switch and instrument cluster must be earthed (grounded) at some point.

12 If the LED is faulty replace the instrument cluster with a new one (see Section 15).

13 If the LED and the wiring are good check the oil pressure switch (see Section 24).

Disassembly

14 Remove the instrument cluster (see Section 15).

15 The instrument panel/PCB is not available individually – if a fault has occurred a new instrument cluster must be installed. The only

components available individually are the front cover, seal, instrument and warning lights (excluding LED), the push button pads and rods and the mounting nuts and grommets. If required, disassemble the cluster as follows:

16 Undo the screws on the back of the instrument cluster and remove the rear cover **(see illustrations)**.

17 Undo the four screws securing the instrument panel/PCB in the front cover and carefully lift the panel out **(see illustrations)**.

18 Check the rubber push button pad and the button rods for wear and damage and replace them with new ones if necessary **(see illustration)**. Check the condition of the rubber seal for the covers and replace it with a new one if necessary **(see illustration)**.

19 Installation is the reverse of removal. Make sure the seal is correctly seated.

17.3a Twist the bulbholder . . .

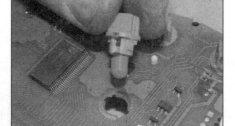

17.3b . . . and withdraw it from the panel

17 Instrument and warning light bulbs

1 Remove the instrument cluster (See Section 15).

2 Undo the screws on the back of the instrument cluster and remove the rear cover **(see illustrations 16.16a and b)**.

3 Twist the relevant bulbholder anticlockwise to release it, using pliers if required **(see illustration)**. The bulb and holder are one part **(see illustration)**.

4 Fit the new bulbholder, turning it clockwise to lock it in the PCB.

5 Fit the cover, making sure the seal is in good condition and correctly seated, then install the cluster.

18 Ignition (main) switch

⚠ **Warning: To prevent the risk of short circuits, remove the rider's seat and disconnect the battery negative (–) lead before making any ignition (main) switch checks.**

Check

1 Trace the wiring from the base of the ignition switch and disconnect it at the connector. The location of the connector may vary. On the model photographed it was

18.1 Ignition switch wiring connector (arrowed)

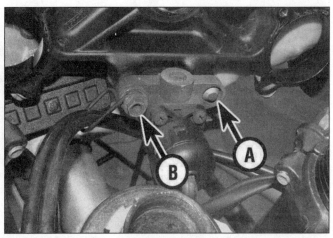

18.5 Shear-head bolt (A). Note how the conventional bolt (B) secures the cable guide

found to be in the top left-hand corner of the fairing stay **(see illustration)** and required fairing removal to access it. Another location is inside the rubber boot on the right-hand end of the instrument cluster **(see illustration 19.3a)**. Make the checks on the switch side of the connector.

2 Using an ohmmeter or a continuity tester, check the continuity of the connector terminal pairs (see the *Wiring Diagrams* at the end of this Chapter). Continuity should exist between the terminals connected by a solid line on the diagram when the switch key is turned to the indicated position.

3 If the switch fails any of the tests, replace it with a new one.

Removal

4 Trace the wiring from the base of the ignition switch and disconnect it at the connector (see Step 1). Release the wiring from any clips and ties and feed it through to the switch, noting its routing.

5 One security shear-head bolt and one normal bolt secure the ignition switch to the underside of the top yoke **(see illustration)**. Turn the handlebars as required to provide best access for your tools. If access is too restricted, or if the shear-head bolt proves tight, refer to Chapter 6, Section 9 and displace the top yoke, then remove the conventional bolt first which will free the throttle cables, then remove the yoke and secure it in a vice with rag as protection to hold it while driving the shear-head bolt round.

6 To release the shear-head bolt tap it round in the normal unscrewing direction using a cold chisel until it releases, then unscrew and remove it by hand.

7 Unscrew the other bolt, noting how it secures the throttle cable guide and the collar that fits in the base of the switch **(see illustration 18.5)**, and withdraw the switch from the yoke.

Installation

8 Installation is the reverse of removal. Tighten the shear-head bolt until its head shears off. Refer to Chapter 6 for installation of the top yoke if removed. Make sure the throttle cables and wiring are correctly routed and the connector securely connected.

19 Handlebar switches

Check

1 Generally speaking, the handlebar switches are reliable and trouble-free. Most troubles, when they do occur, are caused by dirty or corroded contacts, but wear and breakage of internal parts is a possibility that should not be overlooked. If breakage does occur, the entire switch and related wiring harness will have to be replaced with a new one, as individual parts are not available.

2 The switches can be checked for continuity using an ohmmeter or a continuity test light. Make sure the ignition is switched OFF.

3 Trace the wiring from the switch housing being checked and disconnect it at the

connector(s) inside the rubber boot on the relevant end of the instrument cluster **(see illustrations)**. Make the checks on the switch side of the connectors.

4 Check for continuity between the terminals of the switch connector with the switch in the various positions (i.e. switch off – no continuity, switch on – continuity) – see the *wiring diagrams* at the end of this Chapter. Continuity should exist between the terminals connected by a solid line on the diagram when the switch is in the indicated position.

5 If the continuity check indicates a problem exists, displace the switch housing (see below) and spray the switch contacts with electrical contact cleaner (there is no need to remove the switch completely). If they are accessible, the contacts can be scraped clean with a knife or polished with crocus cloth. If switch components are damaged or broken, it should be obvious when the switch is disassembled.

Removal

6 If the switch is to be removed from the machine, rather than just displaced from the handlebar, trace the wiring from the switch housing and disconnect it at the connector(s) inside the rubber boot on the relevant end of the instrument cluster **(see illustration 19.3a**

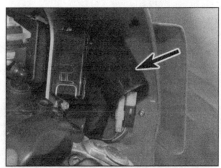

19.3a The right-hand handlebar switch wiring connectors are in the boot on the right-hand side (arrowed)

19.3b The left-hand handlebar switch wiring connectors are in the boot on the left-hand side (arrowed)

19.7 Undo the screws in the bottom half of the switch

19.8 Locate the pin (arrowed) in the hole in the handlebar

up to the connector and retained by any clips and ties. Reconnect the wiring connector.

11 Lower the fuel tank and install the fairing panel.

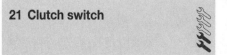

21 Clutch switch

Check

1 The clutch switch is mounted on the clutch master cylinder. The switch is part of the safety circuit which prevents or stops the engine running if the transmission is in gear whilst the sidestand is down, and prevents the engine from starting if the transmission is in gear unless the sidestand is up and the clutch lever is pulled in. The switch isn't adjustable.

2 To check the switch, trace the wiring from it and disconnect it at the wiring connector inside the boot on the left-hand end of the instrument cluster **(see illustration 19.3b)**. Connect the probes of an ohmmeter or a continuity test light to the two switch terminals. With the clutch lever pulled in, continuity should be indicated. With the clutch lever out, no continuity (infinite resistance) should be indicated.

3 If the switch is good, check the other components in the starter safety circuit (sidestand switch, neutral switch and diodes) as described in the relevant sections of this Chapter. If all components are good, check the wiring and connectors between the various components (see the *wiring diagrams* at the end of this book).

Renewal

4 The switch is mounted on the clutch master cylinder. Trace the wiring from the switch and disconnect it at the wiring connector inside the boot on the left-hand end of the instrument cluster **(see illustration 19.3b)**. Feed the wiring up to the switch, releasing it from any ties and noting its routing.

5 Carefully lever the switch from its mount – it is a push fit with two expanding pegs locating in holes **(see illustration)**.

6 Installation is the reverse of removal. Check the operation of the switch.

or b). Work back along the harness, freeing it from all clips and ties, and feed it to the switch, noting its routing.

7 Unscrew the handlebar switch screws and free the switch by separating the halves **(see illustration)**.

Installation

8 Installation is the reverse of removal. Make sure the wiring connectors are correctly routed and securely connected. When assembling the switch halves locate the pin on the housing in the hole in the handlebar **(see illustration)**.

20 Sidestand switch

Check

1 The sidestand switch is mounted on the sidestand pivot. The switch is part of the safety circuit which prevents or stops the engine running if the transmission is in gear whilst the sidestand is down, and prevents the engine from starting if the transmission is in gear unless the sidestand is up and the clutch lever is pulled in.

2 To access the wiring connector, raise the fuel tank (see Chapter 4). Trace the wiring from the switch and disconnect it at the connector **(see illustration)**.

3 Check the operation of the switch using an ohmmeter or continuity test light. Connect the meter between the black and green wire

terminals on the switch side of the connector. With the sidestand down there should be continuity (zero resistance) between the terminals, and with the stand up there should be no continuity (infinite resistance).

4 Now connect the meter between the black and brown wire terminals on the switch side of the connector. With the sidestand up there should be continuity (zero resistance) between the terminals, and with the stand down there should be no continuity (infinite resistance).

5 If the switch does not perform as expected, and the wiring and connectors are good, the switch is defective and must be replaced with a new one.

6 If the switch is good, check the other components in the starter safety circuit (clutch switch, neutral switch and diodes) as described in the relevant sections of this Chapter. If all components are good, check the wiring and connectors between the various components (see the *wiring diagrams* at the end of this book).

Removal and installation

7 Disconnect the switch wiring connector (see Step 2). Remove the lower fairing (See Chapter 8). Feed the wiring back to the switch noting its routing and freeing it from any clips or ties.

8 Unscrew the bolt securing the switch to the sidestand and remove the switch, noting how it locates **(see illustration)**.

9 Fit the new switch onto the sidestand and tighten the bolt.

10 Make sure the wiring is correctly routed

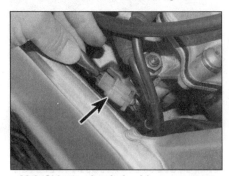

20.2 Sidestand switch wiring connector (arrowed)

20.8 Sidestand switch bolt (arrowed)

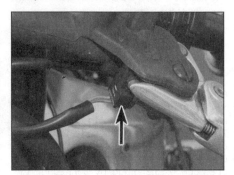

21.5 Carefully lever the clutch switch (arrowed) off the master cylinder

22.2 Diode unit (arrowed)

22 Diodes

Starter interlock circuit diode unit

1 The diodes are part of the safety circuit which prevents or stops the engine running if the transmission is in gear whilst the sidestand is down, and prevents the engine from starting if the transmission is in gear unless the sidestand is up and the clutch lever is pulled in. The diode block is located under the passenger seat – remove the seat to access it (see Chapter 8).

2 Pull the diode off its mount and unplug it from its connector **(see illustration)**.

3 Set up a 12 volt battery and a 2 watt bulb connected as shown, or alternatively use a continuity tester or diode tester **(see illustration)**. Check the operation of the diodes by connecting the battery leads to the various terminals in turn as shown in the table. If the bulb and tester do not produce the expected results the diode unit is faulty and must be replaced with a new one.

4 If the diodes are good, check the other components in the starter safety circuit (clutch switch, neutral switch, sidestand switch) as described in the relevant sections of this Chapter. If all components are good, check the wiring between the various components (see the *wiring diagrams* at the end of this book).

Lap timer diode

5 This diode is part of the circuit which allows the light flash button on the left-hand switch gear to be used as a lap timer when on a track (see owners handbook). If there is a problem with the function of the button in either mode, check the diode as follows:

6 Unplug the diode from its connector in the rubber boot on the left-hand end of the instrument cluster **(see illustration)**.

7 Set up a 12 volt battery and a 2 watt bulb connected as shown, or alternatively use a continuity tester or diode tester. Check the operation of the diode by connecting the battery leads to the outer terminals of the diode connector as shown in the two tests. If

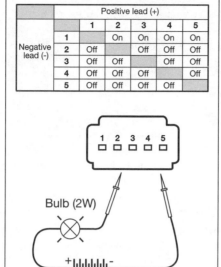

		Positive lead (+)				
		1	2	3	4	5
Negative lead (-)	1		On	On	On	On
	2	Off		Off	Off	Off
	3	Off	Off		Off	Off
	4	Off	Off	Off		Off
	5	Off	Off	Off	Off	

Bulb (2W)

12v Battery

H45559

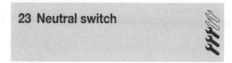

22.3 Starter interlock circuit diode test

the bulb comes on or shows continuity when connected as in test A, or does not come on or shows no continuity when connected as in test B, the diode is faulty and must be replaced with a new one.

23 Neutral switch

Check

1 The switch is part of the safety circuit which prevents or stops the engine running if the transmission is in gear whilst the sidestand is down, and prevents the engine from starting if the transmission is in gear unless the sidestand is up and the clutch lever is pulled in. Before checking the electrical circuit, check the bulb (see Section 17).

2 The switch is located in the left-hand side of the engine below the front sprocket cover. Remove the lower fairing to access it (see Chapter 8).

3 Undo the screw and detach the wiring connector from the switch **(see illustration)**. Make sure the transmission is in neutral.

4 With the connector disconnected and the ignition switch ON, the neutral light should be out. If not, the wire between the connector and instrument cluster must be earthed (grounded) at some point.

5 Check for continuity between the switch terminal and the crankcase. With the transmission in neutral, there should be continuity. With the transmission in gear, there should be no continuity. If the tests prove otherwise, then the switch is faulty.

6 If the switch is good, check the other components in the starter safety circuit

22.6 Lap marker diode (arrowed)

(sidestand switch, clutch switch and diodes) as described in the relevant sections of this Chapter. If all components are good, check the wiring and connectors between the various components (see the *wiring diagrams* at the end of this book).

Removal

7 The switch is located in the left-hand side of the engine below the front sprocket cover. Remove the lower fairing to access it (see Chapter 8).

8 Undo the screw and detach the wiring connector from the switch **(see illustration 23.3)**.

9 Clean the area around the switch, then unscrew it from the crankcase.

10 Check the tip of the plunger for wear and damage, and check whether the plunger moves in and out of the body without sticking.

Installation

11 Install the switch using a suitable threadlock (Loctite 574) and tighten it to the torque setting specified at the beginning of the Chapter.

12 Connect the wiring connector and check the operation of the neutral light.

24 Oil pressure switch

Check

1 When the ignition is first turned ON and before the engine is started, the oil warning

23.3 Neutral switch (arrowed) – undo the screw to release the wire

24.3 Oil pressure switch (arrowed) – pull the rubber boot off to access the wiring connector

25.2a Undo the screw (arrowed) on the bottom . . .

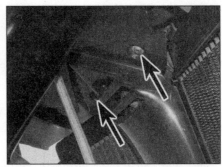

25.2b . . . and the screws (arrowed) on the top

LED should come on. When the engine is started it should extinguish. If it comes on whilst the engine is running, stop the engine immediately and carry out an oil level check, and if necessary a pressure check, as described in Chapter 1. If the oil pressure warning does not come on when the ignition is turned on, check the display (see Section 16).

2 The oil pressure switch is screwed into the right-hand side of the crankcase. Remove the lower fairing (see Chapter 8).

3 Pull back the rubber boot and detach the wiring connector from the switch **(see illustration)**. Turn the ignition ON and check for voltage at the wiring connector. If there is no voltage check the wiring to the switch (see *Wiring Diagrams* at the end of this Chapter). If there is voltage, earth (ground) the connector on the crankcase and check that the oil warning symbol and/or LED come on. If they do, the switch is faulty. If not, check the main earth connections between the engine and frame and back to the battery.

4 Now check for continuity between the switch terminal and the hex on the switch body – there should be continuity with the engine off and no continuity with the engine running. If the switch does not behave as described, and the oil pressure is good when checked with a gauge (see Step 1), the switch is faulty and a new one must be fitted.

Removal

5 Remove the lower fairing (see Chapter 8). Drain the engine oil (see Chapter 1).
6 Detach the wiring connector from the switch.

7 Unscrew the switch and withdraw it from the crankcase.

Installation

8 Apply a suitable threadlock (Loctite 243) to the threads near the switch body, then install it in the crankcase and tighten it to the torque setting specified at the beginning of the Chapter.
9 Attach the wiring connector and fit the rubber boot **(see illustration 24.3)**.
10 Fill the engine with the correct type and quantity of oil as described in Chapter 1. Start the engine and check for leaks around the switch. Check the operation of the switch.
11 Install the lower fairing (see Chapter 8).

25 Horn

Check

1 If the horn doesn't work, first check the fuse (see Section 5) and the battery (see Section 3).
2 The horn is mounted between the radiators at the top – remove the lower fairing (see Chapter 8). Undo the three screws securing the central shroud and manoeuvre it out **(see illustrations)**.
3 Unplug the wiring connectors from the horn **(see illustration)**. Using two jumper wires, apply battery voltage (12 volts) directly to the terminals on the horn. If the horn doesn't sound, replace it with a new one.
4 If the horn sounds, check for battery voltage at the grey wire terminal with the ignition ON

and the button pushed. If there is voltage check for continuity to earth in the blue wire from the horn (see *Wiring Diagrams* at the end of this Chapter). If there was no voltage check the grey wire between the horn and the horn button for continuity, then if the wiring is good check the button (see Section 19). If that is good check the wiring between the switch and the fusebox.

Renewal

5 The horn is mounted between the radiators at the top – remove the lower fairing (see Chapter 8). Undo the three screws securing the central shroud and manoeuvre it out **(see illustrations 25.2a and b)**.
6 Unplug the wiring connectors from the horn **(see illustration 25.3)**. Unscrew the bolt securing the horn and remove it from the bike.
7 Install the horn and tighten the bolt. Connect the wiring connectors then check that the horn works.

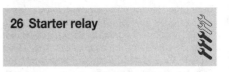

26 Starter relay

Check

1 If the starter circuit is faulty, first check the main fuses (see Section 5).
2 The starter relay is behind the battery **(see illustration)** – remove the rider's seat for access (see Chapter 8).
3 Disconnect the battery negative (-) lead (see Section 3). Displace the relay from its mount **(see illustration)**. Unscrew the nut securing

25.3 Horn wiring connectors (A) and mounting bolt (B)

26.2 Starter relay (arrowed) and its wiring connector

26.3 Displace the relay and lift the rubber boots to access the starter motor and battery leads (arrowed), each secured by a nut

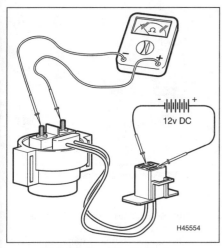

26.4 Starter relay test set-up

the starter motor lead to its terminal and disconnect the lead; position the lead away from the relay terminal. Reconnect the battery negative (-) lead. With the ignition switch ON, the engine kill switch in the RUN position, the transmission in neutral, press the starter switch. The relay should be heard to click. If not, switch off the ignition, then remove the relay as described below and test it as follows.

4 Using either a continuity tester or a multimeter set to the ohms x 1 scale, connect to the relay's starter motor and battery lead terminals **(see illustration)**. There should be no continuity (infinite resistance). Using a fully-charged 12 volt battery and two insulated jumper wires, connect the battery to the terminals of the relay wiring connector as shown. At this point the relay should be heard to click and the multimeter read 0 ohms (continuity). If this is the case the relay is proved good. If the relay does not click when battery voltage is applied and indicates no continuity (infinite resistance) across its terminals, it is faulty and must be replaced with a new one.

5 If the relay is good, check for battery voltage between the yellow/red and the violet/black wire terminals on the loom side of the connector with the ignition ON, the transmission in neutral, the kill switch in the

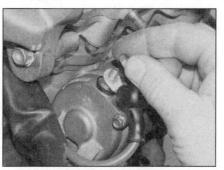

27.2 Pull back the rubber cover and unscrew the terminal nut

RUN position and the starter button pressed. If voltage is present, check the other components in the starter circuit as described in the relevant sections of this Chapter. If no voltage was present or if all components are good, check the wiring and connectors between the various components (see the *wiring diagrams* at the end of this book).

Removal and installation

6 The starter relay is behind the battery **(see illustration 26.2)** – remove the rider's seat for access (see Chapter 8).
7 Disconnect the battery negative (-) lead (see Section 3).
8 Disconnect the relay wiring connector. Displace the relay from its mount then unscrew the nuts securing the starter motor and battery leads to their terminals **(see illustration 26.3)**. Slip the relay out of its rubber sleeve.
9 Installation is the reverse of removal. Make sure the terminal nuts are tight. Connect the negative (-) lead.

27 Starter motor removal and installation

Removal

1 Disconnect the battery negative (–) lead (see Section 3). The starter motor is mounted on the front of the engine – remove the left-hand fairing side panel (see Chapter 8).
2 Peel back the rubber terminal cover **(see**

illustration). Unscrew the nut securing the lead and detach it.
3 Unscrew the two bolts securing the starter motor **(see illustration)**. Draw the starter motor out of the crankcase and remove it from the machine **(see illustration)**.
4 Remove the O-ring on the end of the starter motor and discard it as a new one must be used.

Installation

5 Fit a new O-ring onto the end of the starter motor, making sure it is seated in its groove, and smear it and the shaft splines with molybdenum grease **(see illustration)**.
6 Manoeuvre the motor into position and slide it into the crankcase. Ensure that the starter motor teeth mesh correctly with those of the starter reduction gear. Install the mounting bolts and tighten them to the torque setting specified at the beginning of the Chapter.
7 Connect the lead to the starter motor and secure it with the nut. Make sure the rubber cover is correctly seated over the terminal.
8 Connect the battery negative (–) lead. Install the fairing side panel (see Chapter 8).

28 Starter motor check and overhaul

Check

1 Remove the starter motor (see Section 27). Cover the body in some rag and clamp the motor in a soft-jawed vice – do not overtighten it.
2 Using a fully-charged 12 volt battery and two insulated jumper wires, connect the positive (+) terminal of the battery to the protruding terminal on the rear cover of the starter motor, and the negative (–) terminal to one of the motor's mounting lugs. At this point the starter motor should spin. If this is the case the motor is proved good, though it is worth disassembling it and checking it if you suspect it of not working properly under load. If the motor does not spin, disassemble it for inspection.
3 Check for continuity between the terminal

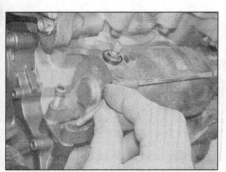

27.3a Unscrew the bolts . . .

27.3b . . . and remove the starter motor

27.5 Fit a new O-ring into the groove

28.5 Note any alignment markings between the main housing and end covers, or make your own if necessary

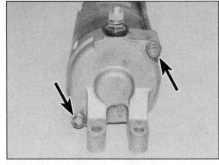

28.6 Unscrew and remove the two long bolts (arrowed)

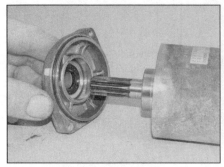

28.7 Remove the front cover

bolt and the rear cover – there should be no continuity (infinite resistance).

Disassembly

Note: *Before disassembling the motor, spray some penetrating fluid around the end cover bolt threads and holes – due to the position of the motor on the front of the engine it is possible that the threads will be seized in the cover.*

4 Remove the starter motor (see Section 27).

5 Note any alignment marks between the main housing and the front and rear covers, or make your own if they aren't clear **(see illustration)**.

6 Unscrew the two long bolts and withdraw them from the starter motor **(see illustration)**.

7 Wrap some insulating tape around the teeth on the end of the starter motor shaft – this will protect the oil seal from damage as the front cover is removed. Remove the front cover from the motor **(see illustration)**. Remove the sealing ring from the cover or main housing and discard it as a new one must be used **(see illustration 28.21)**.

8 Remove the rear cover from the motor, bringing the brushplate with it **(see illustration)**. Remove the shim(s) from the rear end of the armature shaft or from inside the rear cover **(see illustration 28.19b)**. Remove the sealing ring from the cover or main housing and discard it as a new one must be used.

9 Withdraw the armature from the main housing, noting that you will have to pull it out against the attraction of the magnets **(see illustration)**.

10 Unscrew the terminal nut and remove it

along with the insulator bush and the O-ring, which you may have to carefully dig out from around the base of the terminal bolt **(see illustrations 28.19g, f and d)**. Remove the brushplate from the rear cover, noting how it locates, drawing the terminal bolt out of the cover as you do **(see illustrations 28.19c)**. Remove the insulator piece from the terminal bolt if required **(see illustration 28.19a)**. Check the condition of the O-ring and replace it with a new one it if it is damaged, deformed or deteriorated.

Inspection

11 The parts of the starter motor that are most likely to require attention are the brushes. Check their length, and if they have worn to or below the minimum length specified at the beginning of the Chapter, or if they are cracked, chipped, or otherwise damaged, obtain the starter rebuild kit from a main dealer and fit all the new parts included **(see illustration)**.

12 Inspect the commutator bars on the armature for scoring, scratches and discoloration. The commutator can be cleaned and polished with crocus cloth, but do not use sandpaper or emery paper. After cleaning, wipe away any residue with a cloth soaked in electrical system cleaner or denatured alcohol. Check that the insulating Mica is below the surface of the commutator bars **(see illustration)**. If there is little or no

28.8 Remove the rear cover and brushplate

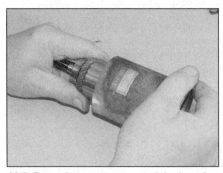

28.9 Draw the armature out of the housing

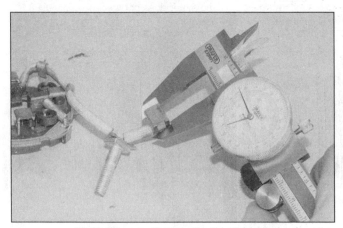

28.11 Measure the length of each brush

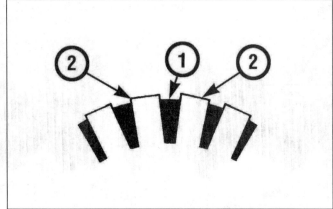

28.12 Check the Mica (1) is below the commutator bars (2)

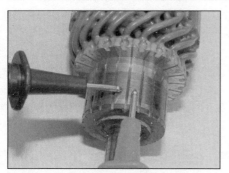

28.13a Continuity should exist between the commutator bars

28.13b There should be no continuity between the commutator bars and the armature shaft

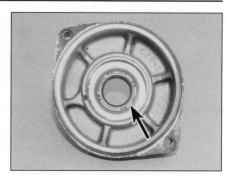

28.15a Check the oil seal (arrowed) . . .

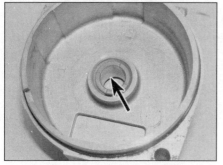

28.15b . . . the bush (arrowed) . . .

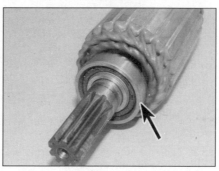

28.15c . . . and the bearing (arrowed)

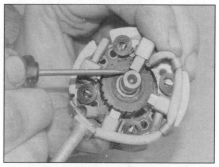

28.18 Slide the brushplate onto the commutator, locating the brush ends on the bars

undercut, scrape the Mica away until the undercut is as shown.

13 Using an ohmmeter or a continuity test light, check for continuity between the commutator bars (see illustration). Continuity should exist between each bar and all of the others. Also, check for continuity between the commutator bars and the armature shaft (see illustration). There should be no continuity (infinite resistance) between the commutator and the shaft. If the checks indicate otherwise, replace the starter motor with a new one (the armature is not available separately).

14 Check the front end of the armature shaft for worn, cracked, chipped and broken teeth.

15 Inspect the front and rear covers for signs of cracks or wear. Check the oil seal in the front cover and the bush in the rear cover for wear and damage (see illustrations). Also check the bearing on the shaft (see illustration). None of those components are available individually.

16 Inspect the magnets in the main housing and the housing itself for cracks.

17 Inspect the insulator bush, insulator piece and O-ring, and the sealing rings for signs of damage, deformation and deterioration and replace them with new ones if necessary – check with your dealer to see if these parts are available in the rebuild kit.

Reassembly

18 Slide the brushplate onto the commutator – you will need to press the brushes back into their housings as you do this so they do not snag (see illustration).

19 Fit the insulator piece onto the terminal bolt (see illustration). Fit the shim(s) onto the end of the shaft (see illustration). Smear the bush in the rear cover with some molybdenum grease (see illustration 28.15b). Fit the rear cover sealing ring. Insert the terminal bolt in the cover then locate the brushplate, making sure the shims stay in place, the shaft enters the bush, and the brushplate tab locates in its cut-out (see illustration). Fit the O-ring onto the terminal bolt and carefully feed it down so

28.19a Fit the insulator onto the bolt . . .

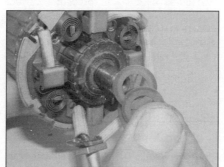

28.19b . . . and the shim(s) onto the shaft

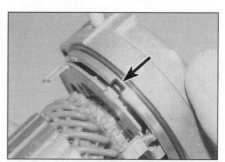

28.19c Fit the bolt through its hole and locate the shaft in its bush and the tab in its cut-out (arrowed)

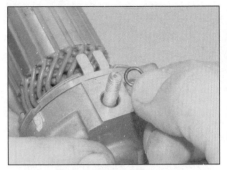

28.19d Fit the O-ring . . .

28.19e . . . and press it into place . . .

28.19f . . . then fit the bush . . .

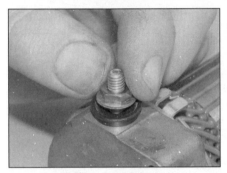

28.19g . . . and the nut

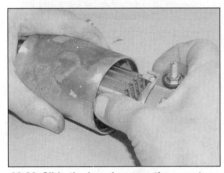

28.20 Slide the housing over the armature and onto the cover

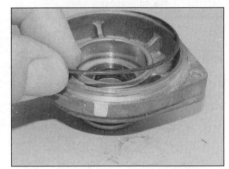

28.21 Fit a new sealing ring

it locates between the bolt and the cover **(see illustrations)**. Fit the bush and the nut **(see illustrations)**.

20 Slide the main housing over the armature and onto the cover, noting that the magnets will forcibly draw the cover on, or alternatively try to draw the armature out of the cover **(see illustration)**. Grasp each component securely and control the action, taking care not to get your fingers jammed between the housing and the cover.

21 Fit the front cover sealing ring **(see illustration)**. Apply a smear of grease to the lips of the front cover oil seal **(see illustration 27.15a)**. Install the cover, aligning the marks made on removal **(see illustration 28.7)**. Remove the protective tape from the shaft end.

22 Check the alignment marks made on removal are correctly aligned, then install the long bolts and tighten them **(see illustration)**.

23 Install the starter motor (see Section 27).

28.22 Install the two long bolts and tighten them

29 Charging system checks

General information and precautions

1 If the performance of the charging system is suspect, the system as a whole should be checked first, followed by testing of the individual components. **Note:** *Before beginning the checks, make sure the battery is fully charged and that all system connections are clean and tight.*

2 Checking the output of the charging system and the performance of the various components within the charging system requires the use of a multimeter (with voltage, current and resistance checking facilities).

3 When making the checks, follow the procedures carefully to prevent incorrect connections or short circuits, as irreparable damage to electrical system components may result if short circuits occur.

4 If a multimeter is not available, the job of checking the charging system should be left to an Aprilia dealer or automotive electrician.

5 If the charging system of the machine is thought to be faulty, perform the following checks.

Leakage test

Caution: Always connect an ammeter in series, never in parallel with the battery, otherwise it will be damaged. Do not turn the ignition ON or operate the starter

motor when the ammeter is connected – a sudden surge in current will blow the meter's fuse.

6 Remove the rider's seat (see Chapter 8).

7 Turn the ignition switch OFF and disconnect the lead from the battery negative (–) terminal **(see illustration 3.2)**.

8 Set the multimeter to the Amps function and connect its negative (–) probe to the battery negative (–) terminal, and positive (+) probe to the disconnected negative (–) lead **(see illustration)**. Always set the meter to a high amps range initially and then bring it down to the mA (milli Amps) range; if there is a high current flow in the circuit it may blow the meter's fuse.

9 No current flow should be indicated. If current leakage is indicated (generally greater than 1 mA*), there is a short circuit in the wiring. Using the wiring diagrams at the end of this Chapter, systematically disconnect individual electrical components, checking the meter each time until the source is identified. **Note*:** *If an alarm is fitted, remember to take its current draw into account.*

10 If no leakage is indicated, disconnect the meter and connect the negative (–) lead to the battery, tightening it securely.

Output test

11 Start the engine and warm it up to normal operating temperature. Remove the rider's seat (see Chapter 8).

12 To check the regulated voltage output, allow the engine to idle and connect a multimeter set to the 0 to 20 volts DC scale (voltmeter) across the terminals of the battery (positive (+) lead to battery positive (+) terminal,

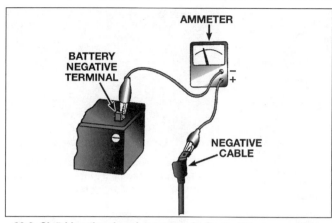

29.8 Checking the charging system leakage rate – connect the meter as shown

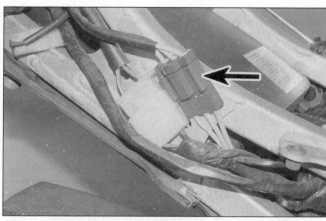

30.2 Alternator wiring connector (arrowed) to the regulator/rectifier

negative (–) lead to battery negative (–) terminal (see Section 3). Slowly increase the engine speed to 4000 rpm and note the reading obtained. The regulated voltage should be as specified at the beginning of the Chapter. If the voltage is outside these limits, check the unregulated no-load voltage output (see Step 13). If the voltage is good, then the charging system is fine, but if the battery may be faulty.

13 To check the unregulated no-load voltage output, raise the fuel tank (see Chapter 4) and disconnect the alternator wiring connector **(see illustration 30.3)**. Allow the engine to idle and connect a multimeter set to the 0 to 100 volts AC scale (voltmeter) across the yellow wire terminals in the alternator side of the connector – there are three wires, so connect between each pair in turn, taking a total of three readings. Slowly increase the engine speed to 4000 rpm and note the readings obtained. The unregulated voltage should be as specified at the beginning of the Chapter. If the voltage is outside these limits, check the alternator (see Section 30). If the readings are good, but the charging system is suspect, check the wiring and connectors to the regulator/rectifier (remove the seat cowling to expose them – see Chapter 8), and the regulator/rectifier itself (see Section 31).

> **HAYNES HINT** *Clues to a faulty regulator are constantly blowing bulbs, with brightness varying considerably with engine speed, and battery overheating.*

30 Alternator

Check

1 Remove the seat cowling (See Chapter 8).
2 Trace the wiring back from the regulator/rectifier mounted on the right-hand side of the rear sub-frame and disconnect it at the brown connector with three yellow wires **(see illustration)**.
3 Using a multimeter set to the ohms x 1 (ohmmeter) scale measure the stator coil winding resistance by connecting the probes between each of the yellow wire terminal pairs on the alternator side of the connector, taking a total of three readings. Also check for continuity between each terminal and ground (earth). If the stator coil windings are in good condition the three readings should be within the range shown in the Specifications at the start of this Chapter

and there should be no continuity (infinite resistance) between any of the terminals and ground (earth). If not, check the fault is not due to damaged wiring or connectors between the connector and stator, which is in the alternator cover on the left-hand side of the engine – raise the fuel tank (see Chapter 4) to access and check the round connector for the stator and crankshaft position (CKP) sensor wiring **(see illustration)**. If the wiring and connectors are good, the alternator stator coil assembly is at fault and must be replaced with a new one.

Removal

4 Drain the engine oil (see Chapter 1). Remove the oil tank (see Chapter 2).
5 Raise the fuel tank (see Chapter 4)
6 Trace the alternator and crankshaft position (CKP) sensor wiring back from the alternator cover on the left-hand side of the engine and disconnect it at the connector **(see illustration 30.3)**. Free the wiring from any ties and feed it through to the alternator cover, noting its routing.
7 Working in a criss-cross pattern, unscrew the alternator cover bolts **(see illustration)**. Remove the cover, noting that it will be restrained by the pull of the rotor magnets, and be prepared to catch any residual oil. Discard

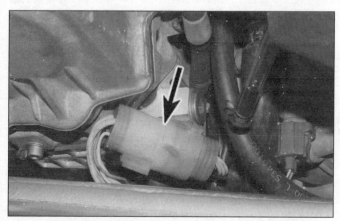

30.3 Combined alternator/CKP sensor wiring connector

30.7 Alternator cover bolts (arrowed)

30.8 Withdraw the starter idler gear shaft and remove the gear

30.9 Counter-hold the rotor using one of the methods described and unscrew the bolt (arrowed) in its centre

30.10a Thread the puller into the rotor and heat the boss until the rotor is displaced

30.10b Remove the Woodruff key (arrowed) if it is loose

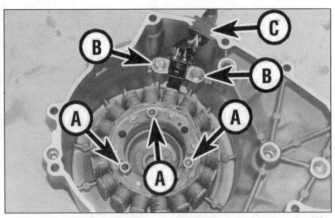

30.11 Stator bolts (A) CKP sensor bolts (B), wiring grommet (C)

the gasket as a new one must be used. Remove the dowel for safekeeping if it is loose.

8 Withdraw the starter idle gear shaft and remove the gear **(see illustration)**.

9 Counter-hold the alternator rotor using a rotor strap or a suitable holding tool on the flats on the rotor boss and unscrew the rotor bolt **(see illustration)**. Note that the bolt is very tight and is also threadlocked – if you have difficulty counter-holding the rotor, have an assistant do this for you, or have them engage a gear and apply the rear brake while you counter-hold it. Alternatively use an air wrench if available. If necessary (and it probably will be) refer to Chapter 2, Section 20 and lock the engine as described in **Note 2** and Steps 1, 4 and 5.

10 To remove the rotor from the shaft it is

necessary to use a rotor puller, either the Aprilia service tool (Pt. No. 0277730) or an aftermarket equivalent from a motorcycle dealer, and also to apply heat (from a hot air gun, not a naked flame) to the rotor hub as the inner section is sealed to the end of the crankshaft using Loctite 648 which requires heat to release it. Thread the rotor puller into the centre of the rotor and turn it to apply force, then heat the hub and turn the puller until the rotor is displaced from the shaft, holding the rotor as described above to prevent the engine turning **(see illustration)**. Remove the Woodruff key from its slot in the crankcase if it is loose **(see illustration)**. If required remove the starter driven gear and the starter clutch from the rotor (see Chapter 2).

11 To remove the stator from the cover, unscrew the bolts securing the stator and the

bolts securing the crankshaft position sensor, then free the wiring grommet from its cut-out and remove the stator assembly **(see illustration)**.

Installation

12 Fit the stator and crankshaft position sensor into the cover, then route the wiring to the cut-out **(see illustrations 30.11)**. Apply a suitable non-permanent thread locking compound to the threads of the stator and sensor bolts, and tighten them to the torque setting specified at the beginning of the Chapter. Apply a suitable sealant to the wiring grommet, then press it into the cut-out in the cover.

13 If removed fit the starter clutch and starter driven gear onto the rotor (see Chapter 2). Clean the tapered end of the crankshaft and the corresponding mating surface on the inside of the rotor with a suitable solvent. Fit the Woodruff key into its slot in the crankshaft if removed **(see illustration 30.10b)**. Apply a smear of Loctite 648 to the tapered end of the crankshaft – make sure none gets on or near the flat section for the starter driven gear **(see illustration)**. Make sure that no metal objects have attached themselves to the magnets on the inside of the rotor. Slide the rotor onto the shaft, making sure the groove on the inside is aligned with and fits over the Woodruff key **(see illustration)**. Make sure the Woodruff key does not become dislodged.

14 Apply some Loctite 648 to the rotor bolt threads. Install the rotor bolt with its washer and tighten it to the torque setting specified at

30.13a Smear some Loctite 648 onto the tapered section

30.13b Slide the rotor onto the shaft, aligning the cut-out with the Woodruff key

30.14 Install the bolt with its washer and tighten it to the specified torque

30.16a Locate the new gasket onto the dowel (arrowed) . . .

30.16b . . . then install the cover, making sure the shaft ends locate correctly

the beginning of the Chapter, using the method employed on removal to prevent the rotor from turning **(see illustration)**.

15 Lubricate the idle gear shaft with clean engine oil, then locate the gear, making sure its teeth engage correctly with both the reduction gear and the driven gear, and slide the shaft through and into the crankcase **(see illustration 30.8)**.

16 Fit the dowel into the crankcase if removed **(see illustration)**. Install the alternator cover using a new gasket, making sure it locates onto the dowel, and that the bores in the cover locate onto the reduction and idle gear shafts **(see illustration)** – take care not to trap your fingers as the cover is drawn into place by the pull of the magnets. Tighten the cover bolts evenly in a criss-cross sequence to the specified torque setting **(see illustration 30.7)**.

17 If the special holding tool was used to counter-hold the alternator rotor, remove the tool and reinstall the clutch cover bolt, then install the valve cover (see Chapter 2). Install the spark plugs (see Chapter 1).

18 Reconnect the wiring at the connector and secure it with any ties previously released **(see illustration 30.3)**. Lower the fuel tank (see Chapter 4).

19 Install the oil tank (see Chapter 2). Replenish the engine oil (see Chapter 1).

31 Regulator/rectifier

Check

1 Disconnect the battery negative (-) lead (see Section 3).

2 Remove the seat cowling (see Chapter 8) – the regulator/rectifier is mounted on the right-hand side of the rear sub-frame **(see illustration 31.8)**.

3 Disconnect the regulator/rectifier wiring connectors **(see illustration)**. Using a multimeter set to the M-ohm scale, measure the resistance between the various terminals on the regulator/rectifier side of the wiring connectors as shown in the table **(see illustrations)**. *Note: This testing method is approximate. If the readings do not compare closely with those shown in the table, have the regulator/rectifier tested by an Aprilia dealer, or better still substitute your unit for one that is known to be good and see if the problem is cured.*

4 If the regulator/rectifier appears to be good,

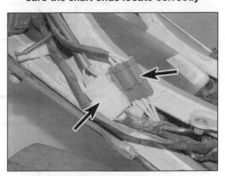

31.3a Regulator/rectifier wiring connectors (arrowed)

check the wiring between the battery, regulator/rectifier and alternator, and the wiring connectors (see *Wiring Diagrams* at the end of this book), and check the alternator and its output if not already done (see Section 29).

Removal and installation

5 Disconnect the battery negative (-) lead (see Section 3).

6 Remove the seat cowling (see Chapter 8) – the regulator/rectifier is mounted on the right-hand side of the rear sub-frame.

7 Disconnect the regulator/rectifier wiring connectors **(see illustration 31.3a)**.

8 Unscrew the two bolts securing the regulator/rectifier and remove it **(see illustration)**.

9 Install the new unit and tighten the bolts. Connect the wiring connectors.

10 Install the seat cowling (see Chapter 8). Reconnect the battery negative lead (-) (see Chapter 3).

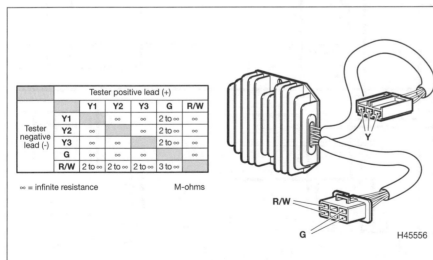

Tester negative lead (-)	Tester positive lead (+)				
		Y1	Y2	Y3	G	R/W
	Y1		∞	∞	2 to ∞	∞
	Y2	∞		∞	2 to ∞	∞
	Y3	∞	∞		2 to ∞	∞
	G	∞	∞	∞		∞
	R/W	2 to ∞	2 to ∞	2 to ∞	3 to ∞	

∞ = infinite resistance   M-ohms

R/W

G   H45556

31.3b Regulator/rectifier connector terminal identification and test details
Y Yellow   G Green   R/W Red and white

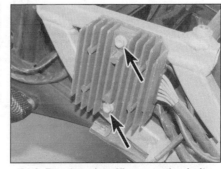

31.8 Regulator/rectifier mounting bolts (arrowed)

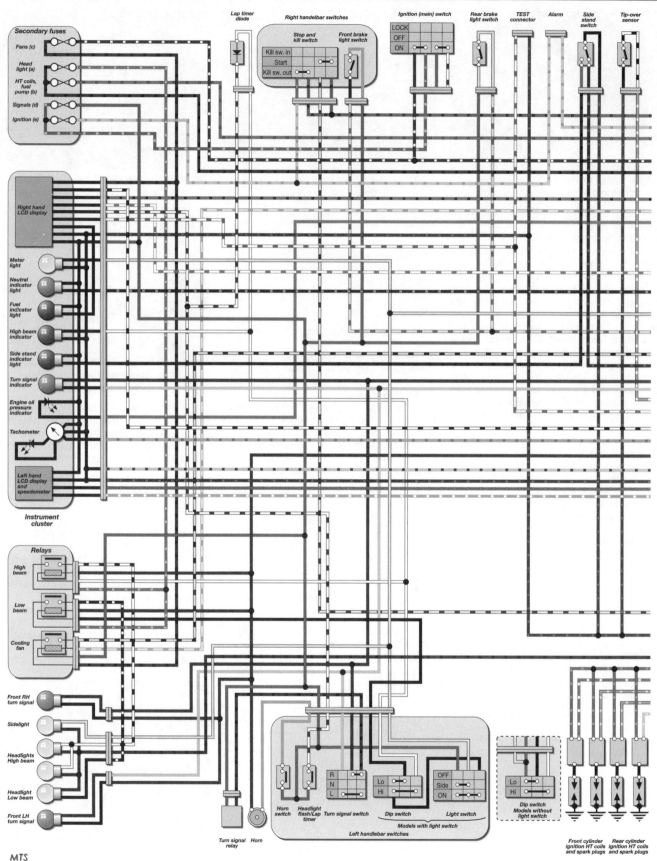

MTS
H33133

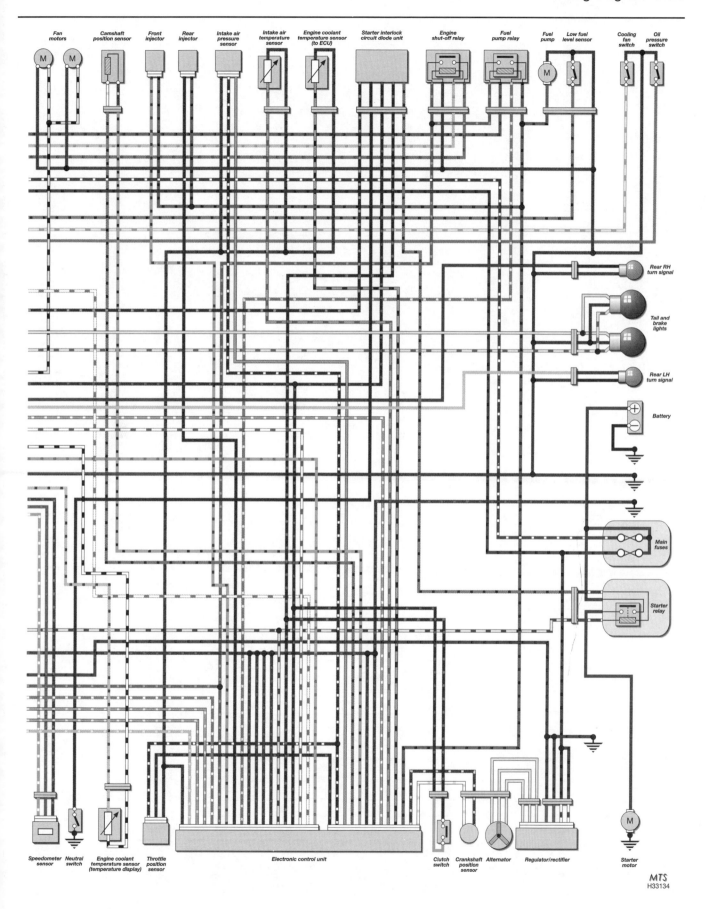

Fan motors · Camshaft position sensor · Front injector · Rear injector · Intake air pressure sensor · Intake air temperature sensor · Engine coolant temperature sensor (to ECU) · Starter interlock circuit diode unit · Engine shut-off relay · Fuel pump relay · Fuel pump · Low fuel level sensor · Cooling fan switch · Oil pressure switch

Rear RH turn signal

Tail and brake lights

Rear LH turn signal

Battery

Main fuses

Starter relay

Speedometer sensor · Neutral switch · Engine coolant temperature sensor (temperature display) · Throttle position sensor · Electronic control unit · Clutch switch · Crankshaft position sensor · Alternator · Regulator/rectifier · Starter motor

MTS
H33134

Reference

Tools and Workshop Tips

- Building up a tool kit and equipping your workshop ● Using tools ● Understanding bearing, seal, fastener and chain sizes and markings ● Repair techniques

Security

- Locks and chains
- U-locks ● Disc locks
- Alarms and immobilisers
- Security marking systems ● Tips on how to prevent bike theft

Lubricants and fluids

- Engine oils
- Transmission (gear) oils
- Coolant/anti-freeze
- Fork oils and suspension fluids ● Brake/clutch fluids
- Spray lubes, degreasers and solvents

Conversion Factors

34 Nm x 0.738

= 25 lbf ft

- Formulae for conversion of the metric (SI) units used throughout the manual into Imperial measures

MOT Test Checks

- A guide to the UK MOT test ● Which items are tested ● How to prepare your motorcycle for the test and perform a pre-test check

Storage

- How to prepare your motorcycle for going into storage and protect essential systems ● How to get the motorcycle back on the road

Fault Finding

- Common faults and their likely causes ● How to check engine cylinder compression ● How to make electrical tests and use test meters

Technical Terms Explained

- Component names, technical terms and common abbreviations explained

Index

Buying tools

A toolkit is a fundamental requirement for servicing and repairing a motorcycle. Although there will be an initial expense in building up enough tools for servicing, this will soon be offset by the savings made by doing the job yourself. As experience and confidence grow, additional tools can be added to enable the repair and overhaul of the motorcycle. Many of the specialist tools are expensive and not often used so it may be preferable to hire them, or for a group of friends or motorcycle club to join in the purchase.

As a rule, it is better to buy more expensive, good quality tools. Cheaper tools are likely to wear out faster and need to be renewed more often, nullifying the original saving.

> **Warning: To avoid the risk of a poor quality tool breaking in use, causing injury or damage to the component being worked on, always aim to purchase tools which meet the relevant national safety standards.**

The following lists of tools do not represent the manufacturer's service tools, but serve as a guide to help the owner decide which tools are needed for this level of work. In addition, items such as an electric drill, hacksaw, files, soldering iron and a workbench equipped with a vice, may be needed. Although not classed as tools, a selection of bolts, screws, nuts, washers and pieces of tubing always come in useful.

For more information about tools, refer to the Haynes *Motorcycle Workshop Practice TechBook* (Bk. No. 3470).

Manufacturer's service tools

Inevitably certain tasks require the use of a service tool. Where possible an alternative tool or method of approach is recommended, but sometimes there is no option if personal injury or damage to the component is to be avoided. Where required, service tools are referred to in the relevant procedure.

Service tools can usually only be purchased from a motorcycle dealer and are identified by a part number. Some of the commonly-used tools, such as rotor pullers, are available in aftermarket form from mail-order motorcycle tool and accessory suppliers.

Maintenance and minor repair tools

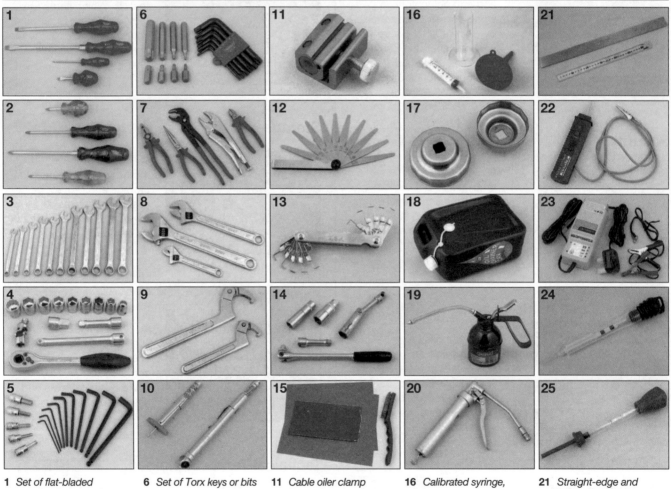

1   Set of flat-bladed
    screwdrivers
2   Set of Phillips head
    screwdrivers
3   Combination open-end
    and ring spanners
4   Socket set (3/8 inch
    or 1/2 inch drive)
5   Set of Allen keys or bits

6   Set of Torx keys or bits
7   Pliers, cutters and
    self-locking grips
    (Mole grips)
8   Adjustable spanners
9   C-spanners
10 Tread depth gauge and
    tyre pressure gauge

11 Cable oiler clamp
12 Feeler gauges
13 Spark plug gap
    measuring tool
14 Spark plug spanner or
    deep plug sockets
15 Wire brush and
    emery paper

16 Calibrated syringe,
    measuring vessel and
    funnel
17 Oil filter adapters
18 Oil drainer can or
    tray
19 Pump type oil can
20 Grease gun

21 Straight-edge and
    steel rule
22 Continuity tester
23 Battery charger
24 Hydrometer (for battery
    specific gravity check)
25 Anti-freeze tester (for
    liquid-cooled engines)

Repair and overhaul tools

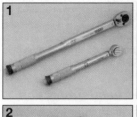

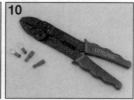

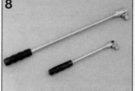

1 Torque wrench
   (small and mid-ranges)
2 Conventional, plastic or
   soft-faced hammers
3 Impact driver set

4 Vernier gauge
5 Circlip pliers (internal and
   external, or combination)
6 Set of cold chisels
   and punches

7 Selection of pullers
8 Breaker bars
9 Chain breaking/
   riveting tool set

10 Wire stripper and
    crimper tool
11 Multimeter (measures
    amps, volts and ohms)
12 Stroboscope (for
    dynamic timing checks)

13 Hose clamp
    (wingnut type shown)
14 Clutch holding tool
15 One-man brake/clutch
    bleeder kit

Specialist tools

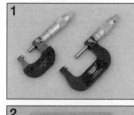

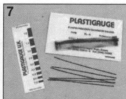

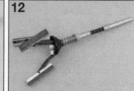
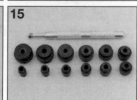

1 Micrometers
   (external type)
2 Telescoping gauges
3 Dial gauge

4 Cylinder
   compression gauge
5 Vacuum gauges (left) or
   manometer (right)
6 Oil pressure gauge

7 Plastigauge kit
8 Valve spring compressor
   (4-stroke engines)
9 Piston pin drawbolt tool

10 Piston ring removal and
    installation tool
11 Piston ring clamp
12 Cylinder bore hone
    (stone type shown)

13 Stud extractor
14 Screw extractor set
15 Bearing driver set

1 Workshop equipment and facilities

The workbench

● Work is made much easier by raising the bike up on a ramp - components are much more accessible if raised to waist level. The hydraulic or pneumatic types seen in the dealer's workshop are a sound investment if you undertake a lot of repairs or overhauls **(see illustration 1.1)**.

1.1 Hydraulic motorcycle ramp

● If raised off ground level, the bike must be supported on the ramp to avoid it falling. Most ramps incorporate a front wheel locating clamp which can be adjusted to suit different diameter wheels. When tightening the clamp, take care not to mark the wheel rim or damage the tyre - use wood blocks on each side to prevent this.
● Secure the bike to the ramp using tie-downs **(see illustration 1.2)**. If the bike has only a sidestand, and hence leans at a dangerous angle when raised, support the bike on an auxiliary stand.

1.2 Tie-downs are used around the passenger footrests to secure the bike

● Auxiliary (paddock) stands are widely available from mail order companies or motorcycle dealers and attach either to the wheel axle or swingarm pivot **(see illustration 1.3)**. If the motorcycle has a centrestand, you can support it under the crankcase to prevent it toppling whilst either wheel is removed **(see illustration 1.4)**.

1.3 This auxiliary stand attaches to the swingarm pivot

1.4 Always use a block of wood between the engine and jack head when supporting the engine in this way

Fumes and fire

● Refer to the Safety first! page at the beginning of the manual for full details. Make sure your workshop is equipped with a fire extinguisher suitable for fuel-related fires (Class B fire - flammable liquids) - it is not sufficient to have a water-filled extinguisher.
● Always ensure adequate ventilation is available. Unless an exhaust gas extraction system is available for use, ensure that the engine is run outside of the workshop.
● If working on the fuel system, make sure the workshop is ventilated to avoid a build-up of fumes. This applies equally to fume build-up when charging a battery. Do not smoke or allow anyone else to smoke in the workshop.

Fluids

● If you need to drain fuel from the tank, store it in an approved container marked as suitable for the storage of petrol (gasoline) **(see illustration 1.5)**. Do not store fuel in glass jars or bottles.

1.5 Use an approved can only for storing petrol (gasoline)

● Use proprietary engine degreasers or solvents which have a high flash-point, such as paraffin (kerosene), for cleaning off oil, grease and dirt - never use petrol (gasoline) for cleaning. Wear rubber gloves when handling solvent and engine degreaser. The fumes from certain solvents can be dangerous - always work in a well-ventilated area.

Dust, eye and hand protection

● Protect your lungs from inhalation of dust particles by wearing a filtering mask over the nose and mouth. Many frictional materials still contain asbestos which is dangerous to your health. Protect your eyes from spouts of liquid and sprung components by wearing a pair of protective goggles **(see illustration 1.6)**.

1.6 A fire extinguisher, goggles, mask and protective gloves should be at hand in the workshop

● Protect your hands from contact with solvents, fuel and oils by wearing rubber gloves. Alternatively apply a barrier cream to your hands before starting work. If handling hot components or fluids, wear suitable gloves to protect your hands from scalding and burns.

What to do with old fluids

● Old cleaning solvent, fuel, coolant and oils should not be poured down domestic drains or onto the ground. Package the fluid up in old oil containers, label it accordingly, and take it to a garage or disposal facility. Contact your local authority for location of such sites or ring the oil care hotline.

OIL CARE
FOLLOW THE CODE
OIL BANK LINE
0800 66 33 66
www.oilbankline.org.uk

Note: It is antisocial and illegal to dump oil down the drain. To find the location of your local oil recycling bank, call this number free.

In the USA, note that any oil supplier must accept used oil for recycling.

2 Fasteners -
screws, bolts and nuts

Fastener types and applications

Bolts and screws

● Fastener head types are either of hexagonal, Torx or splined design, with internal and external versions of each type **(see illustrations 2.1 and 2.2)**; splined head fasteners are not in common use on motorcycles. The conventional slotted or Phillips head design is used for certain screws. Bolt or screw length is always measured from the underside of the head to the end of the item **(see illustration 2.11)**.

2.1 Internal hexagon/Allen (A), Torx (B) and splined (C) fasteners, with corresponding bits

2.2 External Torx (A), splined (B) and hexagon (C) fasteners, with corresponding sockets

● Certain fasteners on the motorcycle have a tensile marking on their heads, the higher the marking the stronger the fastener. High tensile fasteners generally carry a 10 or higher marking. Never replace a high tensile fastener with one of a lower tensile strength.

Washers (see illustration 2.3)

● Plain washers are used between a fastener head and a component to prevent damage to the component or to spread the load when torque is applied. Plain washers can also be used as spacers or shims in certain assemblies. Copper or aluminium plain washers are often used as sealing washers on drain plugs.

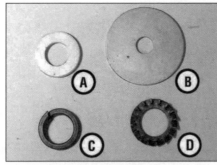

2.3 Plain washer (A), penny washer (B), spring washer (C) and serrated washer (D)

● The split-ring spring washer works by applying axial tension between the fastener head and component. If flattened, it is fatigued and must be renewed. If a plain (flat) washer is used on the fastener, position the spring washer between the fastener and the plain washer.

● Serrated star type washers dig into the fastener and component faces, preventing loosening. They are often used on electrical earth (ground) connections to the frame.

● Cone type washers (sometimes called Belleville) are conical and when tightened apply axial tension between the fastener head and component. They must be installed with the dished side against the component and often carry an OUTSIDE marking on their outer face. If flattened, they are fatigued and must be renewed.

● Tab washers are used to lock plain nuts or bolts on a shaft. A portion of the tab washer is bent up hard against one flat of the nut or bolt to prevent it loosening. Due to the tab washer being deformed in use, a new tab washer should be used every time it is disturbed.

● Wave washers are used to take up endfloat on a shaft. They provide light springing and prevent excessive side-to-side play of a component. Can be found on rocker arm shafts.

Nuts and split pins

● Conventional plain nuts are usually six-sided **(see illustration 2.4)**. They are sized by thread diameter and pitch. High tensile nuts carry a number on one end to denote their tensile strength.

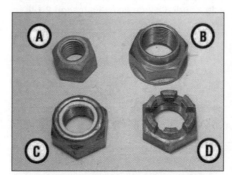

2.4 Plain nut (A), shouldered locknut (B), nylon insert nut (C) and castellated nut (D)

● Self-locking nuts either have a nylon insert, or two spring metal tabs, or a shoulder which is staked into a groove in the shaft - their advantage over conventional plain nuts is a resistance to loosening due to vibration. The nylon insert type can be used a number of times, but must be renewed when the friction of the nylon insert is reduced, ie when the nut spins freely on the shaft. The spring tab type can be reused unless the tabs are damaged. The shouldered type must be renewed every time it is disturbed.

● Split pins (cotter pins) are used to lock a castellated nut to a shaft or to prevent slackening of a plain nut. Common applications are wheel axles and brake torque arms. Because the split pin arms are deformed to lock around the nut a new split pin must always be used on installation - always fit the correct size split pin which will fit snugly in the shaft hole. Make sure the split pin arms are correctly located around the nut **(see illustrations 2.5 and 2.6)**.

2.5 Bend split pin (cotter pin) arms as shown (arrows) to secure a castellated nut

2.6 Bend split pin (cotter pin) arms as shown to secure a plain nut

Caution: If the castellated nut slots do not align with the shaft hole after tightening to the torque setting, tighten the nut until the next slot aligns with the hole - never slacken the nut to align its slot.

● R-pins (shaped like the letter R), or slip pins as they are sometimes called, are sprung and can be reused if they are otherwise in good condition. Always install R-pins with their closed end facing forwards **(see illustration 2.7)**.

2.7 Correct fitting of R-pin. Arrow indicates forward direction

Circlips (see illustration 2.8)

● Circlips (sometimes called snap-rings) are used to retain components on a shaft or in a housing and have corresponding external or internal ears to permit removal. Parallel-sided (machined) circlips can be installed either way round in their groove, whereas stamped circlips (which have a chamfered edge on one face) must be installed with the chamfer facing away from the direction of thrust load **(see illustration 2.9)**.

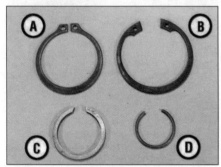

2.8 External stamped circlip (A), internal stamped circlip (B), machined circlip (C) and wire circlip (D)

● Always use circlip pliers to remove and install circlips; expand or compress them just enough to remove them. After installation, rotate the circlip in its groove to ensure it is securely seated. If installing a circlip on a splined shaft, always align its opening with a shaft channel to ensure the circlip ends are well supported and unlikely to catch **(see illustration 2.10)**.

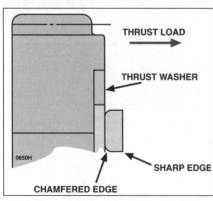

2.9 Correct fitting of a stamped circlip

THRUST LOAD

THRUST WASHER

SHARP EDGE

CHAMFERED EDGE

0650H

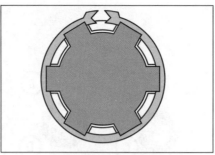

2.10 Align circlip opening with shaft channel

● Circlips can wear due to the thrust of components and become loose in their grooves, with the subsequent danger of becoming dislodged in operation. For this reason, renewal is advised every time a circlip is disturbed.

● Wire circlips are commonly used as piston pin retaining clips. If a removal tang is provided, long-nosed pliers can be used to dislodge them, otherwise careful use of a small flat-bladed screwdriver is necessary. Wire circlips should be renewed every time they are disturbed.

Thread diameter and pitch

● Diameter of a male thread (screw, bolt or stud) is the outside diameter of the threaded portion **(see illustration 2.11)**. Most motorcycle manufacturers use the ISO (International Standards Organisation) metric system expressed in millimetres, eg M6 refers to a 6 mm diameter thread. Sizing is the same for nuts, except that the thread diameter is measured across the valleys of the nut.

● Pitch is the distance between the peaks of the thread **(see illustration 2.11)**. It is expressed in millimetres, thus a common bolt size may be expressed as 6.0 x 1.0 mm (6 mm thread diameter and 1 mm pitch). Generally pitch increases in proportion to thread diameter, although there are always exceptions.

● Thread diameter and pitch are related for conventional fastener applications and the accompanying table can be used as a guide. Additionally, the AF (Across Flats), spanner or socket size dimension of the bolt or nut **(see illustration 2.11)** is linked to thread and pitch specification. Thread pitch can be measured with a thread gauge **(see illustration 2.12)**.

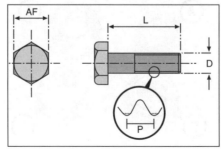

2.11 Fastener length (L), thread diameter (D), thread pitch (P) and head size (AF)

2.12 Using a thread gauge to measure pitch

AF size	Thread diameter x pitch (mm)
8 mm	M5 x 0.8
8 mm	M6 x 1.0
10 mm	M6 x 1.0
12 mm	M8 x 1.25
14 mm	M10 x 1.25
17 mm	M12 x 1.25

● The threads of most fasteners are of the right-hand type, ie they are turned clockwise to tighten and anti-clockwise to loosen. The reverse situation applies to left-hand thread fasteners, which are turned anti-clockwise to tighten and clockwise to loosen. Left-hand threads are used where rotation of a component might loosen a conventional right-hand thread fastener.

Seized fasteners

● Corrosion of external fasteners due to water or reaction between two dissimilar metals can occur over a period of time. It will build up sooner in wet conditions or in countries where salt is used on the roads during the winter. If a fastener is severely corroded it is likely that normal methods of removal will fail and result in its head being ruined. When you attempt removal, the fastener thread should be heard to crack free and unscrew easily - if it doesn't, stop there before damaging something.

● A smart tap on the head of the fastener will often succeed in breaking free corrosion which has occurred in the threads **(see illustration 2.13)**.

● An aerosol penetrating fluid (such as WD-40) applied the night beforehand may work its way down into the thread and ease removal. Depending on the location, you may be able to make up a Plasticine well around the fastener head and fill it with penetrating fluid.

2.13 A sharp tap on the head of a fastener will often break free a corroded thread

● If you are working on an engine internal component, corrosion will most likely not be a problem due to the well lubricated environment. However, components can be very tight and an impact driver is a useful tool in freeing them **(see illustration 2.14)**.

2.14 Using an impact driver to free a fastener

● Where corrosion has occurred between dissimilar metals (eg steel and aluminium alloy), the application of heat to the fastener head will create a disproportionate expansion rate between the two metals and break the seizure caused by the corrosion. Whether heat can be applied depends on the location of the fastener - any surrounding components likely to be damaged must first be removed **(see illustration 2.15)**. Heat can be applied using a paint stripper heat gun or clothes iron, or by immersing the component in boiling water - wear protective gloves to prevent scalding or burns to the hands.

2.15 Using heat to free a seized fastener

● As a last resort, it is possible to use a hammer and cold chisel to work the fastener head unscrewed **(see illustration 2.16)**. This will damage the fastener, but more importantly extreme care must be taken not to damage the surrounding component.

Caution: Remember that the component being secured is generally of more value than the bolt, nut or screw - when the fastener is freed, do not unscrew it with force, instead work the fastener back and forth when resistance is felt to prevent thread damage.

2.16 Using a hammer and chisel to free a seized fastener

Broken fasteners and damaged heads

● If the shank of a broken bolt or screw is accessible you can grip it with self-locking grips. The knurled wheel type stud extractor tool or self-gripping stud puller tool is particularly useful for removing the long studs which screw into the cylinder mouth surface of the crankcase or bolts and screws from which the head has broken off **(see illustration 2.17)**. Studs can also be removed by locking two nuts together on the threaded end of the stud and using a spanner on the lower nut **(see illustration 2.18)**.

2.17 Using a stud extractor tool to remove a broken crankcase stud

2.18 Two nuts can be locked together to unscrew a stud from a component

● A bolt or screw which has broken off below or level with the casing must be extracted using a screw extractor set. Centre punch the fastener to centralise the drill bit, then drill a hole in the fastener **(see illustration 2.19)**. Select a drill bit which is approximately half to three-quarters the

2.19 When using a screw extractor, first drill a hole in the fastener . . .

diameter of the fastener and drill to a depth which will accommodate the extractor. Use the largest size extractor possible, but avoid leaving too small a wall thickness otherwise the extractor will merely force the fastener walls outwards wedging it in the casing thread.

● If a spiral type extractor is used, thread it anti-clockwise into the fastener. As it is screwed in, it will grip the fastener and unscrew it from the casing **(see illustration 2.20)**.

2.20 . . . then thread the extractor anti-clockwise into the fastener

● If a taper type extractor is used, tap it into the fastener so that it is firmly wedged in place. Unscrew the extractor (anti-clockwise) to draw the fastener out.

> ⚠ *Warning: Stud extractors are very hard and may break off in the fastener if care is not taken - ask an engineer about spark erosion if this happens.*

● Alternatively, the broken bolt/screw can be drilled out and the hole retapped for an oversize bolt/screw or a diamond-section thread insert. It is essential that the drilling is carried out squarely and to the correct depth, otherwise the casing may be ruined - if in doubt, entrust the work to an engineer.

● Bolts and nuts with rounded corners cause the correct size spanner or socket to slip when force is applied. Of the types of spanner/socket available always use a six-point type rather than an eight or twelve-point type - better grip

2.21 Comparison of surface drive ring spanner (left) with 12-point type (right)

is obtained. Surface drive spanners grip the middle of the hex flats, rather than the corners, and are thus good in cases of damaged heads **(see illustration 2.21)**.

● Slotted-head or Phillips-head screws are often damaged by the use of the wrong size screwdriver. Allen-head and Torx-head screws are much less likely to sustain damage. If enough of the screw head is exposed you can use a hacksaw to cut a slot in its head and then use a conventional flat-bladed screwdriver to remove it. Alternatively use a hammer and cold chisel to tap the head of the fastener around to slacken it. Always replace damaged fasteners with new ones, preferably Torx or Allen-head type.

A dab of valve grinding compound between the screw head and screwdriver tip will often give a good grip.

Thread repair

● Threads (particularly those in aluminium alloy components) can be damaged by overtightening, being assembled with dirt in the threads, or from a component working loose and vibrating. Eventually the thread will fail completely, and it will be impossible to tighten the fastener.

● If a thread is damaged or clogged with old locking compound it can be renovated with a thread repair tool (thread chaser) **(see illustrations 2.22 and 2.23)**; special thread

2.22 A thread repair tool being used to correct an internal thread

2.23 A thread repair tool being used to correct an external thread

chasers are available for spark plug hole threads. The tool will not cut a new thread, but clean and true the original thread. Make sure that you use the correct diameter and pitch tool. Similarly, external threads can be cleaned up with a die or a thread restorer file **(see illustration 2.24)**.

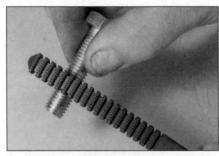

2.24 Using a thread restorer file

● It is possible to drill out the old thread and retap the component to the next thread size. This will work where there is enough surrounding material and a new bolt or screw can be obtained. Sometimes, however, this is not possible - such as where the bolt/screw passes through another component which must also be suitably modified, also in cases where a spark plug or oil drain plug cannot be obtained in a larger diameter thread size.

● The diamond-section thread insert (often known by its popular trade name of Heli-Coil) is a simple and effective method of renewing the thread and retaining the original size. A kit can be purchased which contains the tap, insert and installing tool **(see illustration 2.25)**. Drill out the damaged thread with the size drill specified **(see illustration 2.26)**. Carefully retap the thread **(see illustration 2.27)**. Install the

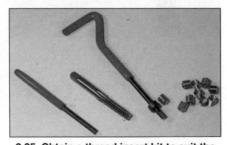

2.25 Obtain a thread insert kit to suit the thread diameter and pitch required

2.26 To install a thread insert, first drill out the original thread . . .

2.27 . . . tap a new thread . . .

2.28 . . . fit insert on the installing tool . . .

2.29 . . . and thread into the component . . .

2.30 . . . break off the tang when complete

insert on the installing tool and thread it slowly into place using a light downward pressure **(see illustrations 2.28 and 2.29)**. When positioned between a 1/4 and 1/2 turn below the surface withdraw the installing tool and use the break-off tool to press down on the tang, breaking it off **(see illustration 2.30)**.

● There are epoxy thread repair kits on the market which can rebuild stripped internal threads, although this repair should not be used on high load-bearing components.

Thread locking and sealing compounds

● Locking compounds are used in locations where the fastener is prone to loosening due to vibration or on important safety-related items which might cause loss of control of the motorcycle if they fail. It is also used where important fasteners cannot be secured by other means such as lockwashers or split pins.

● Before applying locking compound, make sure that the threads (internal and external) are clean and dry with all old compound removed. Select a compound to suit the component being secured - a non-permanent general locking and sealing type is suitable for most applications, but a high strength type is needed for permanent fixing of studs in castings. Apply a drop or two of the compound to the first few threads of the fastener, then thread it into place and tighten to the specified torque. Do not apply excessive thread locking compound otherwise the thread may be damaged on subsequent removal.

● Certain fasteners are impregnated with a dry film type coating of locking compound on their threads. Always renew this type of fastener if disturbed.

● Anti-seize compounds, such as copper-based greases, can be applied to protect threads from seizure due to extreme heat and corrosion. A common instance is spark plug threads and exhaust system fasteners.

3 Measuring tools and gauges

Feeler gauges

● Feeler gauges (or blades) are used for measuring small gaps and clearances (see illustration 3.1). They can also be used to measure endfloat (sideplay) of a component on a shaft where access is not possible with a dial gauge.

● Feeler gauge sets should be treated with care and not bent or damaged. They are etched with their size on one face. Keep them clean and very lightly oiled to prevent corrosion build-up.

3.1 Feeler gauges are used for measuring small gaps and clearances - thickness is marked on one face of gauge

● When measuring a clearance, select a gauge which is a light sliding fit between the two components. You may need to use two gauges together to measure the clearance accurately.

Micrometers

● A micrometer is a precision tool capable of measuring to 0.01 or 0.001 of a millimetre. It should always be stored in its case and not in the general toolbox. It must be kept clean and never dropped, otherwise its frame or measuring anvils could be distorted resulting in inaccurate readings.

● External micrometers are used for measuring outside diameters of components and have many more applications than internal micrometers. Micrometers are available in different size ranges, eg 0 to 25 mm, 25 to 50 mm, and upwards in 25 mm steps; some large micrometers have interchangeable anvils to allow a range of measurements to be taken. Generally the largest precision measurement you are likely to take on a motorcycle is the piston diameter.

● Internal micrometers (or bore micrometers) are used for measuring inside diameters, such as valve guides and cylinder bores. Telescoping gauges and small hole gauges are used in conjunction with an external micrometer, whereas the more expensive internal micrometers have their own measuring device.

External micrometer

Note: *The conventional analogue type instrument is described. Although much easier to read, digital micrometers are considerably more expensive.*

● Always check the calibration of the micrometer before use. With the anvils closed (0 to 25 mm type) or set over a test gauge (for

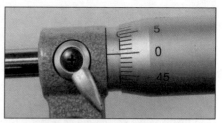

3.2 Check micrometer calibration before use

the larger types) the scale should read zero (see illustration 3.2); make sure that the anvils (and test piece) are clean first. Any discrepancy can be adjusted by referring to the instructions supplied with the tool. Remember that the micrometer is a precision measuring tool - don't force the anvils closed, use the ratchet (4) on the end of the micrometer to close it. In this way, a measured force is always applied.

● To use, first make sure that the item being measured is clean. Place the anvil of the micrometer (1) against the item and use the thimble (2) to bring the spindle (3) lightly into contact with the other side of the item (see illustration 3.3). Don't tighten the thimble down because this will damage the micrometer - instead use the ratchet (4) on the end of the micrometer. The ratchet mechanism applies a measured force preventing damage to the instrument.

● The micrometer is read by referring to the linear scale on the sleeve and the annular scale on the thimble. Read off the sleeve first to obtain the base measurement, then add the fine measurement from the thimble to obtain the overall reading. The linear scale on the sleeve represents the measuring range of the micrometer (eg 0 to 25 mm). The annular scale

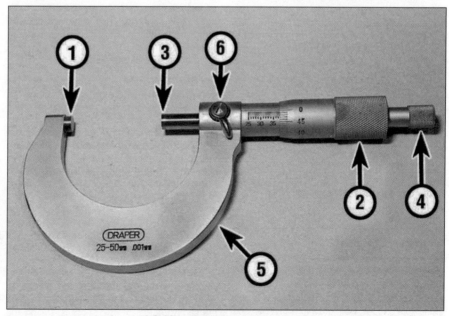

3.3 Micrometer component parts

1 Anvil	3 Spindle	5 Frame
2 Thimble	4 Ratchet	6 Locking lever

on the thimble will be in graduations of 0.01 mm (or as marked on the frame) - one full revolution of the thimble will move 0.5 mm on the linear scale. Take the reading where the datum line on the sleeve intersects the thimble's scale. Always position the eye directly above the scale otherwise an inaccurate reading will result.

In the example shown the item measures 2.95 mm **(see illustration 3.4)**:

Linear scale	2.00 mm
Linear scale	0.50 mm
Annular scale	0.45 mm
Total figure	**2.95 mm**

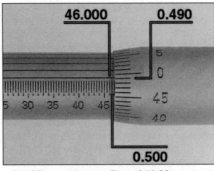

3.5 Micrometer reading of 46.99 mm on linear and annular scales . . .

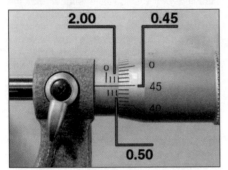

3.4 Micrometer reading of 2.95 mm

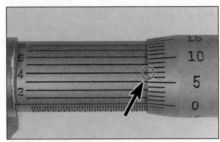

3.6 . . . and 0.004 mm on vernier scale

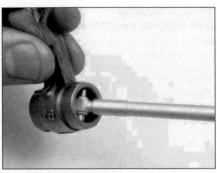

3.7 Expand the telescoping gauge in the bore, lock its position . . .

3.8 . . . then measure the gauge with a micrometer

Most micrometers have a locking lever (6) on the frame to hold the setting in place, allowing the item to be removed from the micrometer.
● Some micrometers have a vernier scale on their sleeve, providing an even finer measurement to be taken, in 0.001 increments of a millimetre. Take the sleeve and thimble measurement as described above, then check which graduation on the vernier scale aligns with that of the annular scale on the thimble **Note:** *The eye must be perpendicular to the scale when taking the vernier reading - if necessary rotate the body of the micrometer to ensure this.* Multiply the vernier scale figure by 0.001 and add it to the base and fine measurement figures.

In the example shown the item measures 46.994 mm **(see illustrations 3.5 and 3.6)**:

Linear scale (base)	46.000 mm
Linear scale (base)	00.500 mm
Annular scale (fine)	00.490 mm
Vernier scale	00.004 mm
Total figure	**46.994 mm**

Internal micrometer

● Internal micrometers are available for measuring bore diameters, but are expensive and unlikely to be available for home use. It is suggested that a set of telescoping gauges and small hole gauges, both of which must be used with an external micrometer, will suffice for taking internal measurements on a motorcycle.
● Telescoping gauges can be used to measure internal diameters of components. Select a gauge with the correct size range, make sure its ends are clean and insert it into the bore. Expand the gauge, then lock its position and withdraw it from the bore **(see illustration 3.7)**. Measure across the gauge ends with a micrometer **(see illustration 3.8)**.
● Very small diameter bores (such as valve guides) are measured with a small hole gauge. Once adjusted to a slip-fit inside the component, its position is locked and the gauge withdrawn for measurement with a micrometer **(see illustrations 3.9 and 3.10)**.

Vernier caliper

Note: *The conventional linear and dial gauge type instruments are described. Digital types are easier to read, but are far more expensive.*
● The vernier caliper does not provide the precision of a micrometer, but is versatile in being able to measure internal and external diameters. Some types also incorporate a depth gauge. It is ideal for measuring clutch plate friction material and spring free lengths.
● To use the conventional linear scale vernier, slacken off the vernier clamp screws (1) and set its jaws over (2), or inside (3), the item to be measured **(see illustration 3.11)**. Slide the jaw into contact, using the thumbwheel (4) for fine movement of the sliding scale (5) then tighten the clamp screws (1). Read off the main scale (6) where the zero on the sliding scale (5) intersects it, taking the whole number to the left of the zero; this provides the base measurement. View along the sliding scale and select the division which

3.9 Expand the small hole gauge in the bore, lock its position . . .

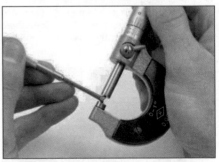

3.10 . . . then measure the gauge with a micrometer

lines up exactly with any of the divisions on the main scale, noting that the divisions usually represents 0.02 of a millimetre. Add this fine measurement to the base measurement to obtain the total reading.

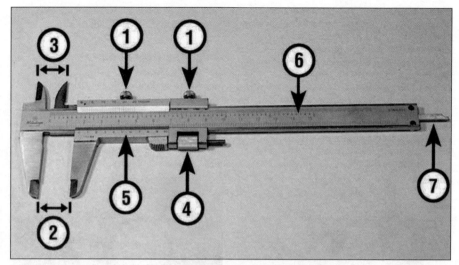

3.11 Vernier component parts (linear gauge)

1 Clamp screws	3 Internal jaws	5 Sliding scale	7 Depth gauge
2 External jaws	4 Thumbwheel	6 Main scale	

In the example shown the item measures 55.92 mm **(see illustration 3.12)**:

Base measurement	55.00 mm
Fine measurement	00.92 mm
Total figure	**55.92 mm**

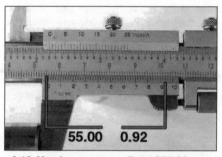

3.12 Vernier gauge reading of 55.92 mm

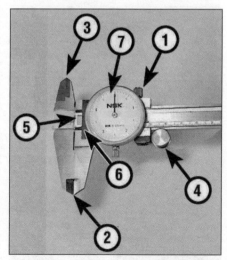

3.13 Vernier component parts (dial gauge)

1 Clamp screw	5 Main scale
2 External jaws	6 Sliding scale
3 Internal jaws	7 Dial gauge
4 Thumbwheel	

● Some vernier calipers are equipped with a dial gauge for fine measurement. Before use, check that the jaws are clean, then close them fully and check that the dial gauge reads zero. If necessary adjust the gauge ring accordingly. Slacken the vernier clamp screw (1) and set its jaws over (2), or inside (3), the item to be measured **(see illustration 3.13)**. Slide the jaws into contact, using the thumbwheel (4) for fine movement. Read off the main scale (5) where the edge of the sliding scale (6) intersects it, taking the whole number to the left of the zero; this provides the base measurement. Read off the needle position on the dial gauge (7) scale to provide the fine measurement; each division represents 0.05 of a millimetre. Add this fine measurement to the base measurement to obtain the total reading.

In the example shown the item measures 55.95 mm **(see illustration 3.14)**:

Base measurement	55.00 mm
Fine measurement	00.95 mm
Total figure	**55.95 mm**

3.14 Vernier gauge reading of 55.95 mm

Plastigauge

● Plastigauge is a plastic material which can be compressed between two surfaces to measure the oil clearance between them. The width of the compressed Plastigauge is measured against a calibrated scale to determine the clearance.

● Common uses of Plastigauge are for measuring the clearance between crankshaft journal and main bearing inserts, between crankshaft journal and big-end bearing inserts, and between camshaft and bearing surfaces. The following example describes big-end oil clearance measurement.

● Handle the Plastigauge material carefully to prevent distortion. Using a sharp knife, cut a length which corresponds with the width of the bearing being measured and place it carefully across the journal so that it is parallel with the shaft **(see illustration 3.15)**. Carefully install both bearing shells and the connecting rod. Without rotating the rod on the journal tighten its bolts or nuts (as applicable) to the specified torque. The connecting rod and bearings are then disassembled and the crushed Plastigauge examined.

3.15 Plastigauge placed across shaft journal

● Using the scale provided in the Plastigauge kit, measure the width of the material to determine the oil clearance **(see illustration 3.16)**. Always remove all traces of Plastigauge after use using your fingernails.

Caution: Arriving at the correct clearance demands that the assembly is torqued correctly, according to the settings and sequence (where applicable) provided by the motorcycle manufacturer.

3.16 Measuring the width of the crushed Plastigauge

Dial gauge or DTI (Dial Test Indicator)

● A dial gauge can be used to accurately measure small amounts of movement. Typical uses are measuring shaft runout or shaft endfloat (sideplay) and setting piston position for ignition timing on two-strokes. A dial gauge set usually comes with a range of different probes and adapters and mounting equipment.

● The gauge needle must point to zero when at rest. Rotate the ring around its periphery to zero the gauge.

● Check that the gauge is capable of reading the extent of movement in the work. Most gauges have a small dial set in the face which records whole millimetres of movement as well as the fine scale around the face periphery which is calibrated in 0.01 mm divisions. Read off the small dial first to obtain the base measurement, then add the measurement from the fine scale to obtain the total reading.

In the example shown the gauge reads 1.48 mm (see illustration 3.17):

Base measurement	1.00 mm
Fine measurement	0.48 mm
Total figure	**1.48 mm**

3.17 Dial gauge reading of 1.48 mm

● If measuring shaft runout, the shaft must be supported in vee-blocks and the gauge mounted on a stand perpendicular to the shaft. Rest the tip of the gauge against the centre of the shaft and rotate the shaft slowly whilst watching the gauge reading (see illustration 3.18). Take several measurements along the length of the shaft and record the

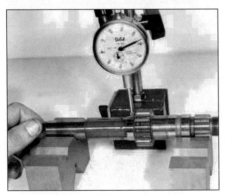

3.18 Using a dial gauge to measure shaft runout

maximum gauge reading as the amount of runout in the shaft. **Note:** *The reading obtained will be total runout at that point - some manufacturers specify that the runout figure is halved to compare with their specified runout limit.*

● Endfloat (sideplay) measurement requires that the gauge is mounted securely to the surrounding component with its probe touching the end of the shaft. Using hand pressure, push and pull on the shaft noting the maximum endfloat recorded on the gauge (see illustration 3.19).

3.19 Using a dial gauge to measure shaft endfloat

● A dial gauge with suitable adapters can be used to determine piston position BTDC on two-stroke engines for the purposes of ignition timing. The gauge, adapter and suitable length probe are installed in the place of the spark plug and the gauge zeroed at TDC. If the piston position is specified as 1.14 mm BTDC, rotate the engine back to 2.00 mm BTDC, then slowly forwards to 1.14 mm BTDC.

Cylinder compression gauges

● A compression gauge is used for measuring cylinder compression. Either the rubber-cone type or the threaded adapter type can be used. The latter is preferred to ensure a perfect seal against the cylinder head. A 0 to 300 psi (0 to 20 Bar) type gauge (for petrol/gasoline engines) will be suitable for motorcycles.

● The spark plug is removed and the gauge either held hard against the cylinder head (cone type) or the gauge adapter screwed into the cylinder head (threaded type) (see illustration 3.20). Cylinder compression is measured with the engine turning over, but not running - carry out the compression test as described in

3.20 Using a rubber-cone type cylinder compression gauge

Fault Finding Equipment. The gauge will hold the reading until manually released.

Oil pressure gauge

● An oil pressure gauge is used for measuring engine oil pressure. Most gauges come with a set of adapters to fit the thread of the take-off point (see illustration 3.21). If the take-off point specified by the motorcycle manufacturer is an external oil pipe union, make sure that the specified replacement union is used to prevent oil starvation.

3.21 Oil pressure gauge and take-off point adapter (arrow)

● Oil pressure is measured with the engine running (at a specific rpm) and often the manufacturer will specify pressure limits for a cold and hot engine.

Straight-edge and surface plate

● If checking the gasket face of a component for warpage, place a steel rule or precision straight-edge across the gasket face and measure any gap between the straight-edge and component with feeler gauges (see illustration 3.22). Check diagonally across the component and between mounting holes (see illustration 3.23).

3.22 Use a straight-edge and feeler gauges to check for warpage

3.23 Check for warpage in these directions

● Checking individual components for warpage, such as clutch plain (metal) plates, requires a perfectly flat plate or piece or plate glass and feeler gauges.

4 Torque and leverage

What is torque?

● Torque describes the twisting force about a shaft. The amount of torque applied is determined by the distance from the centre of the shaft to the end of the lever and the amount of force being applied to the end of the lever; distance multiplied by force equals torque.

● The manufacturer applies a measured torque to a bolt or nut to ensure that it will not slacken in use and to hold two components securely together without movement in the joint. The actual torque setting depends on the thread size, bolt or nut material and the composition of the components being held.

● Too little torque may cause the fastener to loosen due to vibration, whereas too much torque will distort the joint faces of the component or cause the fastener to shear off. Always stick to the specified torque setting.

Using a torque wrench

● Check the calibration of the torque wrench and make sure it has a suitable range for the job. Torque wrenches are available in Nm (Newton-metres), kgf m (kilograms-force metre), lbf ft (pounds-feet), lbf in (inch-pounds). Do not confuse lbf ft with lbf in.

● Adjust the tool to the desired torque on the scale (see illustration 4.1). If your torque wrench is not calibrated in the units specified, carefully convert the figure (see Conversion Factors). A manufacturer sometimes gives a torque setting as a range (8 to 10 Nm) rather than a single figure - in this case set the tool midway between the two settings. The same torque may be expressed as 9 Nm ± 1 Nm. Some torque wrenches have a method of locking the setting so that it isn't inadvertently altered during use.

4.1 Set the torque wrench index mark to the setting required, in this case 12 Nm

● Install the bolts/nuts in their correct location and secure them lightly. Their threads must be clean and free of any old locking compound. Unless specified the threads and flange should be dry - oiled threads are necessary in certain circumstances and the manufacturer will take this into account in the specified torque figure. Similarly, the manufacturer may also specify the application of thread-locking compound.

● Tighten the fasteners in the specified sequence until the torque wrench clicks, indicating that the torque setting has been reached. Apply the torque again to double-check the setting. Where different thread diameter fasteners secure the component, as a rule tighten the larger diameter ones first.

● When the torque wrench has been finished with, release the lock (where applicable) and fully back off its setting to zero - do not leave the torque wrench tensioned. Also, do not use a torque wrench for slackening a fastener.

Angle-tightening

● Manufacturers often specify a figure in degrees for final tightening of a fastener. This usually follows tightening to a specific torque setting.

● A degree disc can be set and attached to the socket (see illustration 4.2) or a protractor can be used to mark the angle of movement on the bolt/nut head and the surrounding casting (see illustration 4.3).

4.2 Angle tightening can be accomplished with a torque-angle gauge . . .

4.3 . . . or by marking the angle on the surrounding component

Loosening sequences

● Where more than one bolt/nut secures a component, loosen each fastener evenly a little at a time. In this way, not all the stress of the joint is held by one fastener and the components are not likely to distort.

● If a tightening sequence is provided, work in the REVERSE of this, but if not, work from the outside in, in a criss-cross sequence (see illustration 4.4).

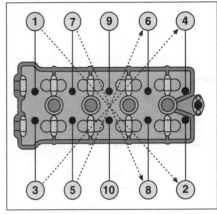

4.4 When slackening, work from the outside inwards

Tightening sequences

● If a component is held by more than one fastener it is important that the retaining bolts/nuts are tightened evenly to prevent uneven stress build-up and distortion of sealing faces. This is especially important on high-compression joints such as the cylinder head.

● A sequence is usually provided by the manufacturer, either in a diagram or actually marked in the casting. If not, always start in the centre and work outwards in a criss-cross pattern (see illustration 4.5). Start off by securing all bolts/nuts finger-tight, then set the torque wrench and tighten each fastener by a small amount in sequence until the final torque is reached. By following this practice,

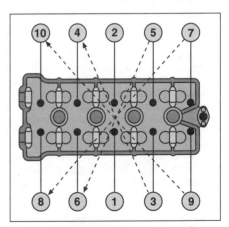

4.5 When tightening, work from the inside outwards

the joint will be held evenly and will not be distorted. Important joints, such as the cylinder head and big-end fasteners often have two- or three-stage torque settings.

Applying leverage

● Use tools at the correct angle. Position a socket wrench or spanner on the bolt/nut so that you pull it towards you when loosening. If this can't be done, push the spanner without curling your fingers around it **(see illustration 4.6)** - the spanner may slip or the fastener loosen suddenly, resulting in your fingers being crushed against a component.

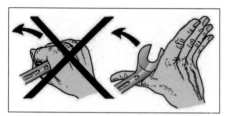

4.6 If you can't pull on the spanner to loosen a fastener, push with your hand open

● Additional leverage is gained by extending the length of the lever. The best way to do this is to use a breaker bar instead of the regular length tool, or to slip a length of tubing over the end of the spanner or socket wrench.
● If additional leverage will not work, the fastener head is either damaged or firmly corroded in place (see *Fasteners*).

5 Bearings

Bearing removal and installation

Drivers and sockets

● Before removing a bearing, always inspect the casing to see which way it must be driven out - some casings will have retaining plates or a cast step. Also check for any identifying markings on the bearing and if installed to a certain depth, measure this at this stage. Some roller bearings are sealed on one side - take note of the original fitted position.
● Bearings can be driven out of a casing using a bearing driver tool (with the correct size head) or a socket of the correct diameter. Select the driver head or socket so that it contacts the outer race of the bearing, not the balls/rollers or inner race. Always support the casing around the bearing housing with wood blocks, otherwise there is a risk of fracture. The bearing is driven out with a few blows on the driver or socket from a heavy mallet. Unless access is severely restricted (as with wheel bearings), a pin-punch is not recommended unless it is moved around the bearing to keep it square in its housing.

● The same equipment can be used to install bearings. Make sure the bearing housing is supported on wood blocks and line up the bearing in its housing. Fit the bearing as noted on removal - generally they are installed with their marked side facing outwards. Tap the bearing squarely into its housing using a driver or socket which bears only on the bearing's outer race - contact with the bearing balls/rollers or inner race will destroy it **(see illustrations 5.1 and 5.2)**.
● Check that the bearing inner race and balls/rollers rotate freely.

5.1 Using a bearing driver against the bearing's outer race

5.2 Using a large socket against the bearing's outer race

Pullers and slide-hammers

● Where a bearing is pressed on a shaft a puller will be required to extract it **(see illustration 5.3)**. Make sure that the puller clamp or legs fit securely behind the bearing and are unlikely to slip out. If pulling a bearing

5.3 This bearing puller clamps behind the bearing and pressure is applied to the shaft end to draw the bearing off

off a gear shaft for example, you may have to locate the puller behind a gear pinion if there is no access to the race and draw the gear pinion off the shaft as well **(see illustration 5.4)**.

> *Caution: Ensure that the puller's centre bolt locates securely against the end of the shaft and will not slip when pressure is applied. Also ensure that puller does not damage the shaft end.*

5.4 Where no access is available to the rear of the bearing, it is sometimes possible to draw off the adjacent component

● Operate the puller so that its centre bolt exerts pressure on the shaft end and draws the bearing off the shaft.
● When installing the bearing on the shaft, tap only on the bearing's inner race - contact with the balls/rollers or outer race with destroy the bearing. Use a socket or length of tubing as a drift which fits over the shaft end **(see illustration 5.5)**.

5.5 When installing a bearing on a shaft use a piece of tubing which bears only on the bearing's inner race

● Where a bearing locates in a blind hole in a casing, it cannot be driven or pulled out as described above. A slide-hammer with knife-edged bearing puller attachment will be required. The puller attachment passes through the bearing and when tightened expands to fit firmly behind the bearing **(see illustration 5.6)**. By operating the slide-hammer part of the tool the bearing is jarred out of its housing **(see illustration 5.7)**.
● It is possible, if the bearing is of reasonable weight, for it to drop out of its housing if the casing is heated as described opposite. If this

5.6 Expand the bearing puller so that it locks behind the bearing . . .

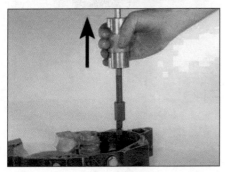

5.7 . . . attach the slide hammer to the bearing puller

method is attempted, first prepare a work surface which will enable the casing to be tapped face down to help dislodge the bearing - a wood surface is ideal since it will not damage the casing's gasket surface. Wearing protective gloves, tap the heated casing several times against the work surface to dislodge the bearing under its own weight **(see illustration 5.8)**.

5.8 Tapping a casing face down on wood blocks can often dislodge a bearing

● Bearings can be installed in blind holes using the driver or socket method described above.

Drawbolts

● Where a bearing or bush is set in the eye of a component, such as a suspension linkage arm or connecting rod small-end, removal by drift may damage the component. Furthermore, a rubber bushing in a shock absorber eye cannot successfully be driven out of position. If access is available to a engineering press, the task is straightforward. If not, a drawbolt can be fabricated to extract the bearing or bush.

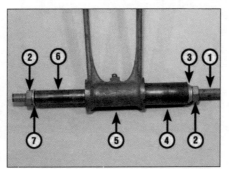

5.9 Drawbolt component parts assembled on a suspension arm

1   Bolt or length of threaded bar
2   Nuts
3   Washer (external diameter greater than tubing internal diameter)
4   Tubing (internal diameter sufficient to accommodate bearing)
5   Suspension arm with bearing
6   Tubing (external diameter slightly smaller than bearing)
7   Washer (external diameter slightly smaller than bearing)

5.10 Drawing the bearing out of the suspension arm

● To extract the bearing/bush you will need a long bolt with nut (or piece of threaded bar with two nuts), a piece of tubing which has an internal diameter larger than the bearing/bush, another piece of tubing which has an external diameter slightly smaller than the bearing/ bush, and a selection of washers **(see illustrations 5.9 and 5.10)**. Note that the pieces of tubing must be of the same length, or longer, than the bearing/bush.
● The same kit (without the pieces of tubing) can be used to draw the new bearing/bush back into place **(see illustration 5.11)**.

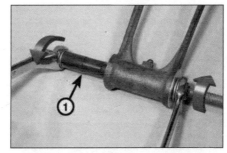

5.11 Installing a new bearing (1) in the suspension arm

Temperature change

● If the bearing's outer race is a tight fit in the casing, the aluminium casing can be heated to release its grip on the bearing. Aluminium will expand at a greater rate than the steel bearing outer race. There are several ways to do this, but avoid any localised extreme heat (such as a blow torch) - aluminium alloy has a low melting point.
● Approved methods of heating a casing are using a domestic oven (heated to 100°C) or immersing the casing in boiling water **(see illustration 5.12)**. Low temperature range localised heat sources such as a paint stripper heat gun or clothes iron can also be used **(see illustration 5.13)**. Alternatively, soak a rag in boiling water, wring it out and wrap it around the bearing housing.

> ⚠ **Warning: All of these methods require care in use to prevent scalding and burns to the hands. Wear protective gloves when handling hot components.**

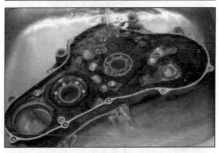

5.12 A casing can be immersed in a sink of boiling water to aid bearing removal

5.13 Using a localised heat source to aid bearing removal

● If heating the whole casing note that plastic components, such as the neutral switch, may suffer - remove them beforehand.
● After heating, remove the bearing as described above. You may find that the expansion is sufficient for the bearing to fall out of the casing under its own weight or with a light tap on the driver or socket.
● If necessary, the casing can be heated to aid bearing installation, and this is sometimes the recommended procedure if the motorcycle manufacturer has designed the housing and bearing fit with this intention.

● Installation of bearings can be eased by placing them in a freezer the night before installation. The steel bearing will contract slightly, allowing easy insertion in its housing. This is often useful when installing steering head outer races in the frame.

Bearing types and markings

● Plain shell bearings, ball bearings, needle roller bearings and tapered roller bearings will all be found on motorcycles **(see illustrations 5.14 and 5.15)**. The ball and roller types are usually caged between an inner and outer race, but uncaged variations may be found.

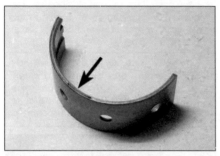

5.14 Shell bearings are either plain or grooved. They are usually identified by colour code (arrow)

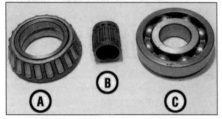

5.15 Tapered roller bearing (A), needle roller bearing (B) and ball journal bearing (C)

● Shell bearings (often called inserts) are usually found at the crankshaft main and connecting rod big-end where they are good at coping with high loads. They are made of a phosphor-bronze material and are impregnated with self-lubricating properties.
● Ball bearings and needle roller bearings consist of a steel inner and outer race with the balls or rollers between the races. They require constant lubrication by oil or grease and are good at coping with axial loads. Taper roller bearings consist of rollers set in a tapered cage set on the inner race; the outer race is separate. They are good at coping with axial loads and prevent movement along the shaft - a typical application is in the steering head.
● Bearing manufacturers produce bearings to ISO size standards and stamp one face of the bearing to indicate its internal and external diameter, load capacity and type **(see illustration 5.16)**.
● Metal bushes are usually of phosphor-bronze material. Rubber bushes are used in suspension mounting eyes. Fibre bushes have also been used in suspension pivots.

5.16 Typical bearing marking

Bearing fault finding

● If a bearing outer race has spun in its housing, the housing material will be damaged. You can use a bearing locking compound to bond the outer race in place if damage is not too severe.
● Shell bearings will fail due to damage of their working surface, as a result of lack of lubrication, corrosion or abrasive particles in the oil **(see illustration 5.17)**. Small particles of dirt in the oil may embed in the bearing material whereas larger particles will score the bearing and shaft journal. If a number of short journeys are made, insufficient heat will be generated to drive off condensation which has built up on the bearings.

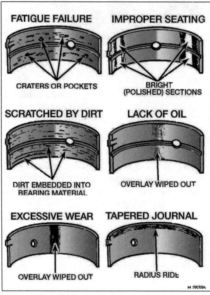

5.17 Typical bearing failures

● Ball and roller bearings will fail due to lack of lubrication or damage to the balls or rollers. Tapered-roller bearings can be damaged by overloading them. Unless the bearing is sealed on both sides, wash it in paraffin (kerosene) to remove all old grease then allow it to dry. Make a visual inspection looking to dented balls or rollers, damaged cages and worn or pitted races **(see illustration 5.18)**.
● A ball bearing can be checked for wear by listening to it when spun. Apply a film of light oil to the bearing and hold it close to the ear - hold the outer race with one hand and spin the inner

5.18 Example of ball journal bearing with damaged balls and cages

5.19 Hold outer race and listen to inner race when spun

race with the other hand **(see illustration 5.19)**. The bearing should be almost silent when spun; if it grates or rattles it is worn.

6 Oil seals

Oil seal removal and installation

● Oil seals should be renewed every time a component is dismantled. This is because the seal lips will become set to the sealing surface and will not necessarily reseal.
● Oil seals can be prised out of position using a large flat-bladed screwdriver **(see illustration 6.1)**. In the case of crankcase seals, check first that the seal is not lipped on the inside, preventing its removal with the crankcases joined.

6.1 Prise out oil seals with a large flat-bladed screwdriver

● New seals are usually installed with their marked face (containing the seal reference code) outwards and the spring side towards the fluid being retained. In certain cases, such as a two-stroke engine crankshaft seal, a double lipped seal may be used due to there being fluid or gas on each side of the joint.

● Use a bearing driver or socket which bears only on the outer hard edge of the seal to install it in the casing - tapping on the inner edge will damage the sealing lip.

Oil seal types and markings

● Oil seals are usually of the single-lipped type. Double-lipped seals are found where a liquid or gas is on both sides of the joint.
● Oil seals can harden and lose their sealing ability if the motorcycle has been in storage for a long period - renewal is the only solution.
● Oil seal manufacturers also conform to the ISO markings for seal size - these are moulded into the outer face of the seal (see illustration 6.2).

6.2 These oil seal markings indicate inside diameter, outside diameter and seal thickness

7 Gaskets and sealants

Types of gasket and sealant

● Gaskets are used to seal the mating surfaces between components and keep lubricants, fluids, vacuum or pressure contained within the assembly. Aluminium gaskets are sometimes found at the cylinder joints, but most gaskets are paper-based. If the mating surfaces of the components being joined are undamaged the gasket can be installed dry, although a dab of sealant or grease will be useful to hold it in place during assembly.
● RTV (Room Temperature Vulcanising) silicone rubber sealants cure when exposed to moisture in the atmosphere. These sealants are good at filling pits or irregular gasket faces, but will tend to be forced out of the joint under very high torque. They can be used to replace a paper gasket, but first make sure that the width of the paper gasket is not essential to the shimming of internal components. RTV sealants should not be used on components containing petrol (gasoline).
● Non-hardening, semi-hardening and hard setting liquid gasket compounds can be used with a gasket or between a metal-to-metal joint. Select the sealant to suit the application: universal non-hardening sealant can be used on virtually all joints; semi-hardening on joint faces which are rough or damaged; hard setting sealant on joints which require a permanent bond and are subjected to high temperature and pressure. **Note:** *Check first if the paper gasket has a bead of sealant*

impregnated in its surface before applying additional sealant.
● When choosing a sealant, make sure it is suitable for the application, particularly if being applied in a high-temperature area or in the vicinity of fuel. Certain manufacturers produce sealants in either clear, silver or black colours to match the finish of the engine. This has a particular application on motorcycles where much of the engine is exposed.
● Do not over-apply sealant. That which is squeezed out on the outside of the joint can be wiped off, whereas an excess of sealant on the inside can break off and clog oilways.

Breaking a sealed joint

● Age, heat, pressure and the use of hard setting sealant can cause two components to stick together so tightly that they are difficult to separate using finger pressure alone. Do not resort to using levers unless there is a pry point provided for this purpose (see illustration 7.1) or else the gasket surfaces will be damaged.
● Use a soft-faced hammer (see illustration 7.2) or a wood block and conventional hammer to strike the component near the mating surface. Avoid hammering against cast extremities since they may break off. If this method fails, try using a wood wedge between the two components.

> **Caution: If the joint will not separate, double-check that you have removed all the fasteners.**

7.1 If a pry point is provided, apply gently pressure with a flat-bladed screwdriver

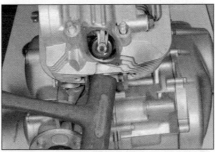

7.2 Tap around the joint with a soft-faced mallet if necessary - don't strike cooling fins

Removal of old gasket and sealant

● Paper gaskets will most likely come away complete, leaving only a few traces stuck on

Most components have one or two hollow locating dowels between the two gasket faces. If a dowel cannot be removed, do not resort to gripping it with pliers - it will almost certainly be distorted. Install a close-fitting socket or Phillips screwdriver into the dowel and then grip the outer edge of the dowel to free it.

the sealing faces of the components. It is imperative that all traces are removed to ensure correct sealing of the new gasket.
● Very carefully scrape all traces of gasket away making sure that the sealing surfaces are not gouged or scored by the scraper (see illustrations 7.3, 7.4 and 7.5). Stubborn deposits can be removed by spraying with an aerosol gasket remover. Final preparation of

7.3 Paper gaskets can be scraped off with a gasket scraper tool . . .

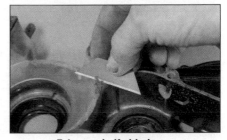

7.4 . . . a knife blade . . .

7.5 . . . or a household scraper

7.6 Fine abrasive paper is wrapped around a flat file to clean up the gasket face

7.7 A kitchen scourer can be used on stubborn deposits

8.1 Tighten the chain breaker to push the pin out of the link . . .

8.2 . . . withdraw the pin, remove the tool . . .

8.3 . . . and separate the chain link

8.4 Insert the new soft link, with O-rings, through the chain ends . . .

8.5 . . . install the O-rings over the pin ends . . .

8.6 . . . followed by the sideplate

the gasket surface can be made with very fine abrasive paper or a plastic kitchen scourer **(see illustrations 7.6 and 7.7)**.

● Old sealant can be scraped or peeled off components, depending on the type originally used. Note that gasket removal compounds are available to avoid scraping the components clean; make sure the gasket remover suits the type of sealant used.

8 Chains

Breaking and joining final drive chains

● Drive chains for all but small bikes are continuous and do not have a clip-type connecting link. The chain must be broken using a chain breaker tool and the new chain securely riveted together using a new soft rivet-type link. Never use a clip-type connecting link instead of a rivet-type link, except in an emergency. Various chain breaking and riveting tools are available, either as separate tools or combined as illustrated in the accompanying photographs - read the instructions supplied with the tool carefully.

> ⚠ **Warning: The need to rivet the new link pins correctly cannot be overstressed - loss of control of the motorcycle is very likely to result if the chain breaks in use.**

● Rotate the chain and look for the soft link. The soft link pins look like they have been deeply centre-punched instead of peened over like all the other pins **(see illustration 8.9)** and its sideplate may be a different colour. Position the soft link midway between the sprockets and assemble the chain breaker tool over one of the soft link pins **(see illustration 8.1)**. Operate the tool to push the pin out through the chain **(see illustration 8.2)**. On an O-ring chain, remove the O-rings **(see illustration 8.3)**. Carry out the same procedure on the other soft link pin.

> **Caution: Certain soft link pins (particularly on the larger chains) may require their ends to be filed or ground off before they can be pressed out using the tool.**

● Check that you have the correct size and strength (standard or heavy duty) new soft link - do not reuse the old link. Look for the size marking on the chain sideplates **(see illustration 8.10)**.

● Position the chain ends so that they are engaged over the rear sprocket. On an O-ring chain, install a new O-ring over each pin of the link and insert the link through the two chain ends **(see illustration 8.4)**. Install a new O-ring over the end of each pin, followed by the sideplate (with the chain manufacturer's marking facing outwards) **(see illustrations 8.5 and 8.6)**. On an unsealed chain, insert the link through the two chain ends, then install the sideplate with the chain manufacturer's marking facing outwards.

● Note that it may not be possible to install the sideplate using finger pressure alone. If using a joining tool, assemble it so that the plates of the tool clamp the link and press the sideplate over the pins **(see illustration 8.7)**. Otherwise, use two small sockets placed over

8.7 Push the sideplate into position using a clamp

8.8 Assemble the chain riveting tool over one pin at a time and tighten it fully

8.9 Pin end correctly riveted (A), pin end unriveted (B)

the rivet ends and two pieces of the wood between a G-clamp. Operate the clamp to press the sideplate over the pins.

● Assemble the joining tool over one pin (following the maker's instructions) and tighten the tool down to spread the pin end securely **(see illustrations 8.8 and 8.9)**. Do the same on the other pin.

 Warning: Check that the pin ends are secure and that there is no danger of the sideplate coming loose. If the pin ends are cracked the soft link must be renewed.

Final drive chain sizing

● Chains are sized using a three digit number, followed by a suffix to denote the chain type **(see illustration 8.10)**. Chain type is either standard or heavy duty (thicker sideplates), and also unsealed or O-ring/X-ring type.

● The first digit of the number relates to the pitch of the chain, ie the distance from the centre of one pin to the centre of the next pin **(see illustration 8.11)**. Pitch is expressed in eighths of an inch, as follows:

8.10 Typical chain size and type marking

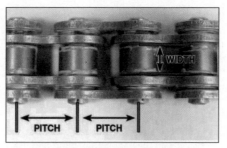

8.11 Chain dimensions

| Sizes commencing with a 4 (eg 428) have a pitch of 1/2 inch (12.7 mm) |
| Sizes commencing with a 5 (eg 520) have a pitch of 5/8 inch (15.9 mm) |
| Sizes commencing with a 6 (eg 630) have a pitch of 3/4 inch (19.1 mm) |

● The second and third digits of the chain size relate to the width of the rollers, again in imperial units, eg the 525 shown has 5/16 inch (7.94 mm) rollers **(see illustration 8.11)**.

9 Hoses

Clamping to prevent flow

● Small-bore flexible hoses can be clamped to prevent fluid flow whilst a component is worked on. Whichever method is used, ensure that the hose material is not permanently distorted or damaged by the clamp.

a) A brake hose clamp available from auto accessory shops **(see illustration 9.1)**.
b) A wingnut type hose clamp **(see illustration 9.2)**.

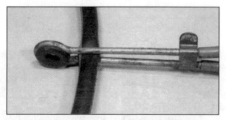

9.1 Hoses can be clamped with an automotive brake hose clamp . . .

9.2 . . . a wingnut type hose clamp . . .

c) Two sockets placed each side of the hose and held with straight-jawed self-locking grips **(see illustration 9.3)**.
d) Thick card each side of the hose held between straight-jawed self-locking grips **(see illustration 9.4)**.

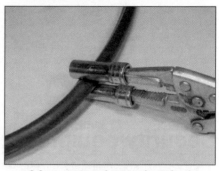

9.3 . . . two sockets and a pair of self-locking grips . . .

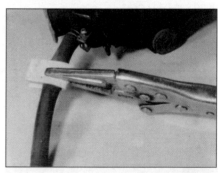

9.4 . . . or thick card and self-locking grips

Freeing and fitting hoses

● Always make sure the hose clamp is moved well clear of the hose end. Grip the hose with your hand and rotate it whilst pulling it off the union. If the hose has hardened due to age and will not move, slit it with a sharp knife and peel its ends off the union **(see illustration 9.5)**.

● Resist the temptation to use grease or soap on the unions to aid installation; although it helps the hose slip over the union it will equally aid the escape of fluid from the joint. It is preferable to soften the hose ends in hot water and wet the inside surface of the hose with water or a fluid which will evaporate.

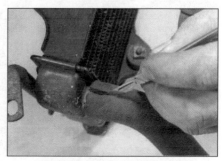

9.5 Cutting a coolant hose free with a sharp knife

Introduction

In less time than it takes to read this introduction, a thief could steal your motorcycle. Returning only to find your bike has gone is one of the worst feelings in the world. Even if the motorcycle is insured against theft, once you've got over the initial shock, you will have the inconvenience of dealing with the police and your insurance company.

The motorcycle is an easy target for the professional thief and the joyrider alike and the official figures on motorcycle theft make for depressing reading; on average a motorcycle is stolen every 16 minutes in the UK!

Motorcycle thefts fall into two categories, those stolen 'to order' and those taken by opportunists. The thief stealing to order will be on the look out for a specific make and model and will go to extraordinary lengths to obtain that motorcycle. The opportunist thief on the other hand will look for easy targets which can be stolen with the minimum of effort and risk.

Whilst it is never going to be possible to make your machine 100% secure, it is estimated that around half of all stolen motorcycles are taken by opportunist thieves. Remember that the opportunist thief is always on the look out for the easy option: if there are two similar motorcycles parked side-by-side, they will target the one with the lowest level of security. By taking a few precautions, you can reduce the chances of your motorcycle being stolen.

Security equipment

There are many specialised motorcycle security devices available and the following text summarises their applications and their good and bad points.

Once you have decided on the type of security equipment which best suits your needs, we recommended that you read one of the many equipment tests regularly carried out by the motorcycle press. These tests compare the products from all the major manufacturers and give impartial ratings on their effectiveness, value-for-money and ease of use.

No one item of security equipment can provide complete protection. It is highly recommended that two or more of the items described below are combined to increase the security of your motorcycle (a lock and chain plus an alarm system is just about ideal). The more security measures fitted to the bike, the less likely it is to be stolen.

Ensure the lock and chain you buy is of good quality and long enough to shackle your bike to a solid object

Lock and chain

Pros: *Very flexible to use; can be used to secure the motorcycle to almost any immovable object. On some locks and chains, the lock can be used on its own as a disc lock (see below).*

Cons: *Can be very heavy and awkward to carry on the motorcycle, although some types will be supplied with a carry bag which can be strapped to the pillion seat.*

● Heavy-duty chains and locks are an excellent security measure **(see illustration 1)**. Whenever the motorcycle is parked, use the lock and chain to secure the machine to a solid, immovable object such as a post or railings. This will prevent the machine from being ridden away or being lifted into the back of a van.

● When fitting the chain, always ensure the chain is routed around the motorcycle frame or swingarm **(see illustrations 2 and 3)**. Never merely pass the chain around one of the wheel rims; a thief may unbolt the wheel and lift the rest of the machine into a van, leaving you with just the wheel! Try to avoid having excess chain free, thus making it difficult to use cutting tools, and keep the chain and lock off the ground to prevent thieves attacking it with a cold chisel. Position the lock so that its lock barrel is facing downwards; this will make it harder for the thief to attack the lock mechanism.

Pass the chain through the bike's frame, rather than just through a wheel . . .

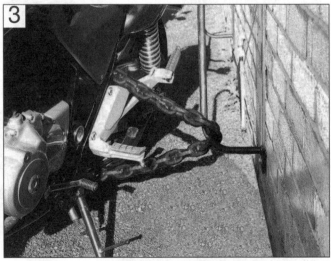

. . . and loop it around a solid object

U-locks

Pros: *Highly effective deterrent which can be used to secure the bike to a post or railings. Most U-locks come with a carrier which allows the lock to be easily carried on the bike.*

Cons: *Not as flexible to use as a lock and chain.*

● These are solid locks which are similar in use to a lock and chain. U-locks are lighter than a lock and chain but not so flexible to use. The length and shape of the lock shackle limit the objects to which the bike can be secured **(see illustration 4)**.

U-locks can be used to secure the bike to a solid object – ensure you purchase one which is long enough

Disc locks

Pros: *Small, light and very easy to carry; most can be stored underneath the seat.*

Cons: *Does not prevent the motorcycle being lifted into a van. Can be very embarrassing if you*

forget to remove the lock before attempting to ride off!

● Disc locks are designed to be attached to the front brake disc. The lock passes through one of the holes in the disc and prevents the wheel rotating by jamming against the fork/brake caliper **(see illustration 5)**. Some are equipped with an alarm siren which sounds if the disc lock is moved; this not only acts as a theft deterrent but also as a handy reminder if you try to move the bike with the lock still fitted.

● Combining the disc lock with a length of cable which can be looped around a post or railings provides an additional measure of security **(see illustration 6)**.

Alarms and immobilisers

Pros: *Once installed it is completely hassle-free to use. If the system is 'Thatcham' or 'Sold Secure-approved', insurance companies may give you a discount.*

Cons: *Can be expensive to buy and complex to install. No system will prevent the motorcycle from being lifted into a van and taken away.*

● Electronic alarms and immobilisers are available to suit a variety of budgets. There are three different types of system available: pure alarms, pure immobilisers, and the more expensive systems which are combined alarm/immobilisers **(see illustration 7)**.
● An alarm system is designed to emit an audible warning if the motorcycle is being tampered with.
● An immobiliser prevents the motorcycle being started and ridden away by disabling its electrical systems.
● When purchasing an alarm/immobiliser system, check the cost of installing the system unless you are able to do it yourself. If the motorcycle is not used regularly, another consideration is the current drain of the system. All alarm/immobiliser systems are powered by the motorcycle's battery; purchasing a system with a very low current drain could prevent the battery losing its charge whilst the motorcycle is not being used.

A typical disc lock attached through one of the holes in the disc

A disc lock combined with a security cable provides additional protection

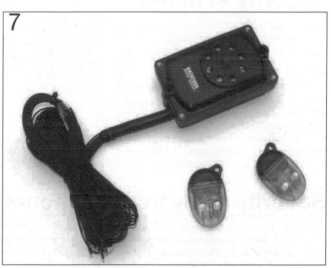

A typical alarm/immobiliser system

Indelible markings can be applied to most areas of the bike – always apply the manufacturer's sticker to warn off thieves

Chemically-etched code numbers can be applied to main body panels . . .

. . . again, always ensure that the kit manufacturer's sticker is applied in a prominent position

Security marking kits

Pros: *Very cheap and effective deterrent. Many insurance companies will give you a discount on your insurance premium if a recognised security marking kit is used on your motorcycle.*

Cons: *Does not prevent the motorcycle being stolen by joyriders.*

● There are many different types of security marking kits available. The idea is to mark as many parts of the motorcycle as possible with a unique security number **(see illustrations 8, 9 and 10)**. A form will be included with the kit to register your personal details and those of the motorcycle with the kit manufacturer. This register is made available to the police to help them trace the rightful owner of any motorcycle or components which they recover should all other forms of identification have been removed. Always apply the warning stickers provided with the kit to deter thieves.

Ground anchors, wheel clamps and security posts

Pros: *An excellent form of security which will deter all but the most determined of thieves.*

Cons: *Awkward to install and can be expensive.*

● Whilst the motorcycle is at home, it is a good idea to attach it securely to the floor or a solid wall, even if it is kept in a securely locked garage. Various types of ground anchors, security posts and wheel clamps are available for this purpose **(see illustration 11)**. These security devices are either bolted to a solid concrete or brick structure or can be cemented into the ground.

Permanent ground anchors provide an excellent level of security when the bike is at home

Security at home

A high percentage of motorcycle thefts are from the owner's home. Here are some things to consider whenever your motorcycle is at home:

✔ Where possible, always keep the motorcycle in a securely locked garage. Never rely solely on the standard lock on the garage door, these are usual hopelessly inadequate. Fit an additional locking mechanism to the door and consider having the garage alarmed. A security light, activated by a movement sensor, is also a good investment.

✔ Always secure the motorcycle to the ground or a wall, even if it is inside a securely locked garage.
✔ Do not regularly leave the motorcycle outside your home, try to keep it out of sight wherever possible. If a garage is not available, fit a motorcycle cover over the bike to disguise its true identity.
✔ It is not uncommon for thieves to follow a motorcyclist home to find out where the bike is kept. They will then return at a later date. Be aware of this whenever you are returning

home on your motorcycle. If you suspect you are being followed, do not return home, instead ride to a garage or shop and stop as a precaution.
✔ When selling a motorcycle, do not provide your home address or the location where the bike is normally kept. Arrange to meet the buyer at a location away from your home. Thieves have been known to pose as potential buyers to find out where motorcycles are kept and then return later to steal them.

Security away from the home

As well as fitting security equipment to your motorcycle here are a few general rules to follow whenever you park your motorcycle.
✔ Park in a busy, public place.
✔ Use car parks which incorporate security features, such as CCTV.

✔ At night, park in a well-lit area, preferably directly underneath a street light.
✔ Engage the steering lock.
✔ Secure the motorcycle to a solid, immovable object such as a post or railings with an additional lock. If this is not possible,

secure the bike to a friend's motorcycle. Some public parking places provide security loops for motorcycles.
✔ Never leave your helmet or luggage attached to the motorcycle. Take them with you at all times.

Lubricants and fluids

A wide range of lubricants, fluids and cleaning agents is available for motor-cycles. This is a guide as to what is available, its applications and properties.

Four-stroke engine oil

● Engine oil is without doubt the most important component of any four-stroke engine. Modern motorcycle engines place a lot of demands on their oil and choosing the right type is essential. Using an unsuitable oil will lead to an increased rate of engine wear and could result in serious engine damage. Before purchasing oil, always check the recommended oil specification given by the manufacturer. The manufacturer will state a recommended 'type or classification' and also a specific 'viscosity' range for engine oil.

● The oil 'type or classification' is identified by its API (American Petroleum Institute) rating. The API rating will be in the form of two letters, e.g. SG. The S identifies the oil as being suitable for use in a petrol (gasoline) engine (S stands for spark ignition) and the second letter, ranging from A to J, identifies the oil's performance rating. The later this letter, the higher the specification of the oil; for example API SG oil exceeds the requirements of API SF oil. **Note:** *On some oils there may also be a second rating consisting of another two letters, the first letter being C, e.g. API SF/CD. This rating indicates the oil is also suitable for use in a diesel engines (the C stands for compression ignition) and is thus of no relevance for motorcycle use.*

● The 'viscosity' of the oil is identified by its SAE (Society of Automotive Engineers) rating. All modern engines require multigrade oils and the SAE rating will consist of two numbers, the first followed by a W, e.g. 10W/40. The first number indicates the viscosity rating of the oil at low temperatures (W stands for winter – tested at –20ºC) and the second number represents the viscosity of the oil at high temperatures (tested at 100ºC). The lower the number, the thinner the oil. For example an oil with an SAE 10W/40 rating will give better cold starting and running than an SAE 15W/40 oil.

● As well as ensuring the 'type' and 'viscosity' of the oil match the recommendations, another consideration to make when buying engine oil is whether to purchase a standard mineral-based oil, a semi-synthetic oil (also known as a synthetic blend or synthetic-based oil) or a fully-synthetic oil. Although all oils will have a similar rating and viscosity, their cost will vary considerably; mineral-based oils are the cheapest, the fully-synthetic oils the most expensive with the semi-synthetic oils falling somewhere in-between. This decision is very much up to the owner, but it should be noted that modern synthetic oils have far better lubricating and cleaning qualities than traditional mineral-based oils and tend to retain these properties for far longer. Bearing in mind the operating conditions inside a modern, high-revving motorcycle engine it is highly recommended that a fully synthetic oil is used. The extra expense at each service could save you money in the long term by preventing premature engine wear.

● As a final note always ensure that the oil is specifically designed for use in motorcycle engines. Engine oils designed primarily for use in car engines sometimes contain additives or friction modifiers which could cause clutch slip on a motorcycle fitted with a wet-clutch.

Two-stroke engine oil

● Modern two-stroke engines, with their high power outputs, place high demands on their oil. If engine seizure is to be avoided it is essential that a high-quality oil is used. Two-stroke oils differ hugely from four-stroke oils. The oil lubricates only the crankshaft and piston(s) (the transmission has its own lubricating oil) and is used on a total-loss basis where it is burnt completely during the combustion process.

● The Japanese have recently introduced a classification system for two-stroke oils, the JASO rating. This rating is in the form of two letters, either FA, FB or FC – FA is the lowest classification and FC the highest. Ensure the oil being used meets or exceeds the recommended rating specified by the manufacturer.

● As well as ensuring the oil rating matches the recommendation, another consideration to make when buying engine oil is whether to purchase a standard mineral-based oil, a semi-synthetic oil (also known as a synthetic blend or synthetic-based oil) or a fully-synthetic oil. The cost of each type of oil varies considerably; mineral-based oils are the cheapest, the fully-synthetic oils the most expensive with the semi-synthetic oils falling somewhere in-between. This decision is very much up to the owner, but it should be noted that modern synthetic oils have far better lubricating properties and burn cleaner than traditional mineral-based oils. It is therefore recommended that a fully synthetic oil is used. The extra expense could save you money in the long term by preventing premature engine wear, engine performance will be improved, carbon deposits and exhaust smoke will be reduced.

● Always ensure that the oil is specifically designed for use in an injector system. Many high quality two-stroke oils are designed for competition use and need to be pre-mixed with fuel. These oils are of a much higher viscosity and are not designed to flow through the injector pumps used on road-going two-stroke motorcycles.

Transmission (gear) oil

● On a two-stroke engine, the transmission and clutch are lubricated by their own separate oil bath which must be changed in accordance with the Maintenance Schedule.
● Although the engine and transmission units of most four-strokes use a common lubrication supply, there are some exceptions where the engine and gearbox have separate oil reservoirs and a dry clutch is used.
● Motorcycle manufacturers will either recommend a monograde transmission oil or a four-stroke multigrade engine oil to lubricate the transmission.
● Transmission oils, or gear oils as they are often called, are designed specifically for use in transmission systems. The viscosity of these oils is represented by an SAE number, but the scale of measurement applied is different to that used to grade engine oils. As a rough guide a SAE90 gear oil will be of the same viscosity as an SAE50 engine oil.

Shaft drive oil

● On models equipped with shaft final drive, the shaft drive gears are will have their own oil supply. The manufacturer will state a recommended 'type or classification' and also a specific 'viscosity' range in the same manner as for four-stroke engine oil.
● Gear oil classification is given by the number which follows the API GL (GL standing for gear lubricant) rating, the higher the number, the higher the specification of the oil, e.g. API GL5 oil is a higher specification than API GL4 oil. Ensure the oil meets or

exceeds the classification specified and is of the correct viscosity. The viscosity of gear oils is also represented by an SAE number but the scale of measurement used is different to that used to grade engine oils. As a rough guide an SAE90 gear oil will be of the same viscosity as an SAE50 engine oil.
● If the use of an EP (Extreme Pressure) gear oil is specified, ensure the oil purchased is suitable.

Fork oil and suspension fluid

● Conventional telescopic front forks are hydraulic and require fork oil to work. To ensure the forks function correctly, the fork oil must be changed in accordance with the Maintenance Schedule.
● Fork oil is available in a variety of viscosities, identified by their SAE rating; fork oil ratings vary from light (SAE 5) to heavy (SAE 30). When purchasing fork oil, ensure the viscosity rating matches that specified by the manufacturer.
● Some lubricant manufacturers also produce a range of high-quality suspension fluids which are very similar to fork oil but are designed mainly for competition use. These fluids may have a different viscosity rating system which is not to be confused with the SAE rating of normal fork oil. Refer to the manufacturer's instructions if in any doubt.

Brake and clutch fluid

● All disc brake systems and some clutch systems are hydraulically operated. To ensure correct operation, the hydraulic fluid must be changed in accordance with the Maintenance Schedule.
● Brake and clutch fluid is classified by its DOT rating with most motorcycle manufacturers specifying DOT 3 or 4 fluid. Both fluid types are glycol-based and can be mixed together without adverse effect; DOT 4 fluid exceeds the requirements of DOT 3

fluid. Although it is safe to use DOT 4 fluid in a system designed for use with DOT 3 fluid, never use DOT 3 fluid in a system which specifies the use of DOT 4 as this will adversely affect the system's performance. The type required for the system will be marked on the fluid reservoir cap.
● Some manufacturers also produce a DOT 5 hydraulic fluid. DOT 5 hydraulic fluid is silicone-based and is not compatible with the glycol-based DOT 3 and 4 fluids. Never mix DOT 5 fluid with DOT 3 or 4 fluid as this will seriously affect the performance of the hydraulic system.

Coolant/antifreeze

● When purchasing coolant/antifreeze, always ensure it is suitable for use in an aluminium engine and contains corrosion inhibitors to prevent possible blockages of the internal coolant passages of the system. As a general rule, most coolants are designed to be used neat and should not be diluted whereas antifreeze can be mixed with distilled water to provide a coolant solution of the required strength. Refer to the manufacturer's instructions on the bottle.
● Ensure the coolant is changed in accordance with the Maintenance Schedule.

Chain lube

● Chain lube is an aerosol-type spray lubricant specifically designed for use on motorcycle final drive chains. Chain lube has two functions, to minimise friction between the final drive chain and sprockets and to prevent corrosion of the chain. Regular use of a good-quality chain lube will extend the life of the drive chain and sprockets and thus maximise the power being transmitted from the transmission to the rear wheel.
● When using chain lube, always allow some time for the solvents in the lube to evaporate before riding the motorcycle. This will minimise the amount of lube which will

'fling' off from the chain when the motorcycle is used. If the motorcycle is equipped with an 'O-ring' chain, ensure the chain lube is labelled as being suitable for use on 'O-ring' chains.

Degreasers and solvents

● There are many different types of solvents and degreasers available to remove the grime and grease which accumulate around the motorcycle during normal use. Degreasers and solvents are usually available as an aerosol-type spray or as a liquid which you apply with a brush. Always closely follow the manufacturer's instructions and wear eye protection during use. Be aware that many solvents are flammable and may give off noxious fumes; take adequate precautions when using them (see Safety First!).

● For general cleaning, use one of the many solvents or degreasers available from most motorcycle accessory shops. These solvents are usually applied then left for a certain time before being washed off with water.

Brake cleaner is a solvent specifically designed to remove all traces of oil, grease and dust from braking system components. Brake cleaner is designed to evaporate quickly and leaves behind no residue.

Carburettor cleaner is an aerosol-type solvent specifically designed to clear carburettor blockages and break down the hard deposits and gum often found inside carburettors during overhaul.

Contact cleaner is an aerosol-type solvent designed for cleaning electrical components. The cleaner will remove all traces of oil and dirt from components such as switch contacts or fouled spark plugs and then dry, leaving behind no residue.

Gasket remover is an aerosol-type solvent designed for removing stubborn gaskets from engine components during overhaul. Gasket remover will minimise the amount of scraping required to remove the gasket and therefore reduce the risk of damage to the mating surface.

Spray lubricants

● Aerosol-based spray lubricants are widely available and are excellent for lubricating lever pivots and exposed cables and switches. Try to use a lubricant which is of the dry-film type as the fluid evaporates, leaving behind a dry-film of lubricant. Lubricants which leave behind an oily residue will attract dust and dirt which will increase the rate of wear of the cable/lever.

● Most lubricants also act as a moisture dispersant and a penetrating fluid. This means they can also be used to 'dry out' electrical components such as wiring connectors or switches as well as helping to free seized fasteners.

Greases

● Grease is used to lubricate many of the pivot-points. A good-quality multi-purpose grease is suitable for most applications but some manufacturers will specify the use of specialist greases for use on components such as swingarm and suspension linkage bushes. These specialist greases can be purchased from most motorcycle (or car) accessory shops; commonly specified types include molybdenum disulphide grease, lithium-based grease, graphite-based grease, silicone-based grease and high-temperature copper-based grease.

Gasket sealing compounds

● Gasket sealing compounds can be used in conjunction with gaskets, to improve their sealing capabilities, or on their own to seal metal-to-metal joints. Depending on their type, sealing compounds either set hard or stay relatively soft and pliable.

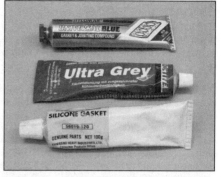

● When purchasing a gasket sealing compound, ensure that it is designed specifically for use on an internal combustion engine. General multi-purpose sealants available from DIY stores may appear visibly similar but they are not designed to withstand the extreme heat or contact with fuel and oil encountered when used on an engine (see 'Tools and Workshop Tips' for further information).

Thread locking compound

● Thread locking compounds are used to secure certain threaded fasteners in position to prevent them from loosening due to vibration. Thread locking compounds can be purchased from most motorcycle (and car) accessory shops. Ensure the threads of the both components are completely clean and dry before sparingly applying the locking compound (see 'Tools and Workshop Tips' for further information).

Fuel additives

● Fuel additives which protect and clean the fuel system components are widely available. These additives are designed to remove all traces of deposits that build up on the carburettors/injectors and prevent wear, helping the fuel system to operate more efficiently. If a fuel additive is being used, check that it is suitable for use with your motorcycle, especially if your motorcycle is equipped with a catalytic converter.

● Octane boosters are also available. These additives are designed to improve the performance of highly-tuned engines being run on normal pump-fuel and are of no real use on standard motorcycles.

Conversion Factors

Length (distance)

Inches (in)	x 25.4	= Millimetres (mm)	x 0.0394	= Inches (in)
Feet (ft)	x 0.305	= Metres (m)	x 3.281	= Feet (ft)
Miles	x 1.609	= Kilometres (km)	x 0.621	= Miles

Volume (capacity)

Cubic inches (cu in; in³)	x 16.387	= Cubic centimetres (cc; cm³)	x 0.061	= Cubic inches (cu in; in³)
Imperial pints (Imp pt)	x 0.568	= Litres (l)	x 1.76	= Imperial pints (Imp pt)
Imperial quarts (Imp qt)	x 1.137	= Litres (l)	x 0.88	= Imperial quarts (Imp qt)
Imperial quarts (Imp qt)	x 1.201	= US quarts (US qt)	x 0.833	= Imperial quarts (Imp qt)
US quarts (US qt)	x 0.946	= Litres (l)	x 1.057	= US quarts (US qt)
Imperial gallons (Imp gal)	x 4.546	= Litres (l)	x 0.22	= Imperial gallons (Imp gal)
Imperial gallons (Imp gal)	x 1.201	= US gallons (US gal)	x 0.833	= Imperial gallons (Imp gal)
US gallons (US gal)	x 3.785	= Litres (l)	x 0.264	= US gallons (US gal)

Mass (weight)

Ounces (oz)	x 28.35	= Grams (g)	x 0.035	= Ounces (oz)
Pounds (lb)	x 0.454	= Kilograms (kg)	x 2.205	= Pounds (lb)

Force

Ounces-force (ozf; oz)	x 0.278	= Newtons (N)	x 3.6	= Ounces-force (ozf; oz)
Pounds-force (lbf; lb)	x 4.448	= Newtons (N)	x 0.225	= Pounds-force (lbf; lb)
Newtons (N)	x 0.1	= Kilograms-force (kgf; kg)	x 9.81	= Newtons (N)

Pressure

Pounds-force per square inch (psi; lbf/in²; lb/in²)	x 0.070	= Kilograms-force per square centimetre (kgf/cm²; kg/cm²)	x 14.223	= Pounds-force per square inch (psi; lbf/in²; lb/in²)
Pounds-force per square inch (psi; lbf/in²; lb/in²)	x 0.068	= Atmospheres (atm)	x 14.696	= Pounds-force per square inch (psi; lbf/in²; lb/in²)
Pounds-force per square inch (psi; lbf/in²; lb/in²)	x 0.069	= Bars	x 14.5	= Pounds-force per square inch (psi; lbf/in²; lb/in²)
Pounds-force per square inch (psi; lbf/in²; lb/in²)	x 6.895	= Kilopascals (kPa)	x 0.145	= Pounds-force per square inch (psi; lbf/in²; lb/in²)
Kilopascals (kPa)	x 0.01	= Kilograms-force per square centimetre (kgf/cm²; kg/cm²)	x 98.1	= Kilopascals (kPa)
Millibar (mbar)	x 100	= Pascals (Pa)	x 0.01	= Millibar (mbar)
Millibar (mbar)	x 0.0145	= Pounds-force per square inch (psi; lbf/in²; lb/in²)	x 68.947	= Millibar (mbar)
Millibar (mbar)	x 0.75	= Millimetres of mercury (mmHg)	x 1.333	= Millibar (mbar)
Millibar (mbar)	x 0.401	= Inches of water (inH₂O)	x 2.491	= Millibar (mbar)
Millimetres of mercury (mmHg)	x 0.535	= Inches of water (inH₂O)	x 1.868	= Millimetres of mercury (mmHg)
Inches of water (inH₂O)	x 0.036	= Pounds-force per square inch (psi; lbf/in²; lb/in²)	x 27.68	= Inches of water (inH₂O)

Torque (moment of force)

Pounds-force inches (lbf in; lb in)	x 1.152	= Kilograms-force centimetre (kgf cm; kg cm)	x 0.868	= Pounds-force inches (lbf in; lb in)
Pounds-force inches (lbf in; lb in)	x 0.113	= Newton metres (Nm)	x 8.85	= Pounds-force inches (lbf in; lb in)
Pounds-force inches (lbf in; lb in)	x 0.083	= Pounds-force feet (lbf ft; lb ft)	x 12	= Pounds-force inches (lbf in; lb in)
Pounds-force feet (lbf ft; lb ft)	x 0.138	= Kilograms-force metres (kgf m; kg m)	x 7.233	= Pounds-force feet (lbf ft; lb ft)
Pounds-force feet (lbf ft; lb ft)	x 1.356	= Newton metres (Nm)	x 0.738	= Pounds-force feet (lbf ft; lb ft)
Newton metres (Nm)	x 0.102	= Kilograms-force metres (kgf m; kg m)	x 9.804	= Newton metres (Nm)

Power

Horsepower (hp)	x 745.7	= Watts (W)	x 0.0013	= Horsepower (hp)

Velocity (speed)

Miles per hour (miles/hr; mph)	x 1.609	= Kilometres per hour (km/hr; kph)	x 0.621	= Miles per hour (miles/hr; mph)

Fuel consumption*

Miles per gallon (mpg)	x 0.354	= Kilometres per litre (km/l)	x 2.825	= Miles per gallon (mpg)

Temperature

Degrees Fahrenheit = (°C x 1.8) + 32   Degrees Celsius (Degrees Centigrade; °C) = (°F - 32) x 0.56

It is common practice to convert from miles per gallon (mpg) to litres/100 kilometres (l/100km), where mpg x l/100 km = 282

About the MOT Test

In the UK, all vehicles more than three years old are subject to an annual test to ensure that they meet minimum safety requirements. A current test certificate must be issued before a machine can be used on public roads, and is required before a road fund licence can be issued. Riding without a current test certificate will also invalidate your insurance.

For most owners, the MOT test is an annual cause for anxiety, and this is largely due to owners not being sure what needs to be checked prior to submitting the motorcycle for testing. The simple answer is that a fully roadworthy motorcycle will have no difficulty in passing the test.

This is a guide to getting your motorcycle through the MOT test. Obviously it will not be possible to examine the motorcycle to the same standard as the professional MOT tester, particularly in view of the equipment required for some of the checks. However, working through the following procedures will enable you to identify any problem areas before submitting the motorcycle for the test.

It has only been possible to summarise the test requirements here, based on the regulations in force at the time of printing. Test standards are becoming increasingly stringent, although there are some exemptions for older vehicles. More information about the MOT test can be obtained from the TSO publications, *How Safe is your Motorcycle* and *The MOT Inspection Manual for Motorcycle Testing*.

Many of the checks require that one of the wheels is raised off the ground. If the motorcycle doesn't have a centre stand, note that an auxiliary stand will be required. Additionally, the help of an assistant may prove useful.

Certain exceptions apply to machines under 50 cc, machines without a lighting system, and Classic bikes - if in doubt about any of the requirements listed below seek confirmation from an MOT tester prior to submitting the motorcycle for the test.

Check that the frame number is clearly visible.

> **HAYNES HiNT**
> *If a component is in borderline condition, the tester has discretion in deciding whether to pass or fail it. If the motorcycle presented is clean and evidently well cared for, the tester may be more inclined to pass a borderline component than if the motorcycle is scruffy and apparently neglected.*

Electrical System

Lights, turn signals, horn and reflector

✔ With the ignition on, check the operation of the following electrical components. **Note:** *The electrical components on certain small-capacity machines are powered by the generator, requiring that the engine is run for this check.*

a) *Headlight and tail light. Check that both illuminate in the low and high beam switch positions.*

b) *Position lights. Check that the front position (or sidelight) and tail light illuminate in this switch position.*

c) *Turn signals. Check that all flash at the correct rate, and that the warning light(s) function correctly. Check that the turn signal switch works correctly.*

d) *Hazard warning system (where fitted). Check that all four turn signals flash in this switch position.*

e) *Brake stop light. Check that the light comes on when the front and rear brakes are independently applied. Models first used on or after 1st April 1986 must have a brake light switch on each brake.*

f) *Horn. Check that the sound is continuous and of reasonable volume.*

✔ Check that there is a red reflector on the rear of the machine, either mounted separately or as part of the tail light lens.

✔ Check the condition of the headlight, tail light and turn signal lenses.

Headlight beam height

✔ The MOT tester will perform a headlight beam height check using specialised beam setting equipment **(see illustration 1)**. This equipment will not be available to the home mechanic, but if you suspect that the headlight is incorrectly set or may have been maladjusted in the past, you can perform a rough test as follows.

✔ Position the bike in a straight line facing a brick wall. The bike must be off its stand, upright and with a rider seated. Measure the height from the ground to the centre of the headlight and mark a horizontal line on the wall at this height. Position the motorcycle 3.8 metres from the wall and draw a vertical

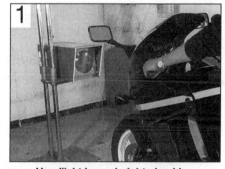

Headlight beam height checking equipment

line up the wall central to the centreline of the motorcycle. Switch to dipped beam and check that the beam pattern falls slightly lower than the horizontal line and to the left of the vertical line **(see illustration 2)**.

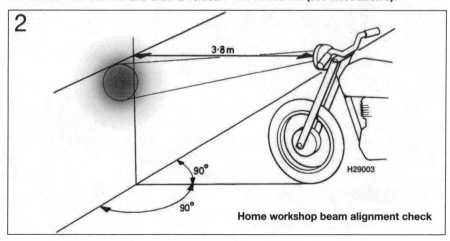

3·8 m

90°

90°

H29003

Home workshop beam alignment check

Exhaust System and Final Drive

Exhaust

✔ Check that the exhaust mountings are secure and that the system does not foul any of the rear suspension components.

✔ Start the motorcycle. When the revs are increased, check that the exhaust is neither holed nor leaking from any of its joints. On a linked system, check that the collector box is not leaking due to corrosion.

✔ Note that the exhaust decibel level ("loudness" of the exhaust) is assessed at the discretion of the tester. If the motorcycle was first used on or after 1st January 1985 the silencer must carry the BSAU 193 stamp, or a marking relating to its make and model, or be of OE (original equipment) manufacture. If the silencer is marked NOT FOR ROAD USE, RACING USE ONLY or similar, it will fail the MOT.

Final drive

✔ On chain or belt drive machines, check that the chain/belt is in good condition and does not have excessive slack. Also check that the sprocket is securely mounted on the rear wheel hub. Check that the chain/belt guard is in place.

✔ On shaft drive bikes, check for oil leaking from the drive unit and fouling the rear tyre.

Steering and Suspension

Steering

✔ With the front wheel raised off the ground, rotate the steering from lock to lock. The handlebar or switches must not contact the fuel tank or be close enough to trap the rider's hand. Problems can be caused by damaged lock stops on the lower yoke and frame, or by the fitting of non-standard handlebars.

✔ When performing the lock to lock check, also ensure that the steering moves freely without drag or notchiness. Steering movement can be impaired by poorly routed cables, or by overtight head bearings or worn bearings. The tester will perform a check of the steering head bearing lower race by mounting the front wheel on a surface plate, then performing a lock to

lock check with the weight of the machine on the lower bearing (see illustration 3).

✔ Grasp the fork sliders (lower legs) and attempt to push and pull on the forks (see

Front wheel mounted on a surface plate for steering head bearing lower race check

illustration 4). Any play in the steering head bearings will be felt. Note that in extreme cases, wear of the front fork bushes can be misinterpreted for head bearing play.

✔ Check that the handlebars are securely mounted.

✔ Check that the handlebar grip rubbers are secure. They should by bonded to the bar left end and to the throttle cable pulley on the right end.

Front suspension

✔ With the motorcycle off the stand, hold the front brake on and pump the front forks up and down (see illustration 5). Check that they are adequately damped.

Checking the steering head bearings for freeplay

Hold the front brake on and pump the front forks up and down to check operation

Inspect the area around the fork dust seal for oil leakage (arrow)

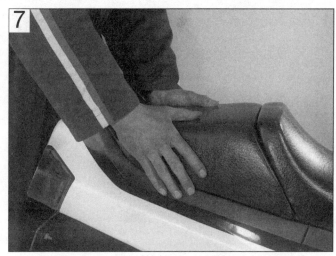

Bounce the rear of the motorcycle to check rear suspension operation

Checking for rear suspension linkage play

✔ Inspect the area above and around the front fork oil seals **(see illustration 6)**. There should be no sign of oil on the fork tube (stanchion) nor leaking down the slider (lower leg). On models so equipped, check that there is no oil leaking from the anti-dive units.

✔ On models with swingarm front suspension, check that there is no freeplay in the linkage when moved from side to side.

Rear suspension

✔ With the motorcycle off the stand and an assistant supporting the motorcycle by its handlebars, bounce the rear suspension **(see illustration 7)**. Check that the suspension components do not foul on any of the cycle parts and check that the shock absorber(s) provide adequate damping.

✔ Visually inspect the shock absorber(s) and check that there is no sign of oil leakage from its damper. This is somewhat restricted on certain single shock models due to the location of the shock absorber.

✔ With the rear wheel raised off the ground, grasp the wheel at the highest point and attempt to pull it up **(see illustration 8)**. Any play in the swingarm pivot or suspension linkage bearings will be felt as movement. **Note:** *Do not confuse play with actual suspension movement.* Failure to lubricate suspension linkage bearings can lead to bearing failure **(see illustration 9)**.

✔ With the rear wheel raised off the ground, grasp the swingarm ends and attempt to move the swingarm from side to side and forwards and backwards - any play indicates wear of the swingarm pivot bearings **(see illustration 10)**.

Worn suspension linkage pivots (arrows) are usually the cause of play in the rear suspension

Grasp the swingarm at the ends to check for play in its pivot bearings

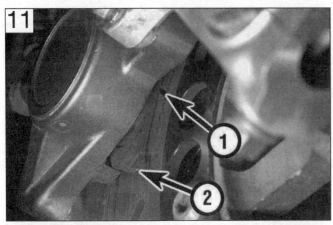

Brake pad wear can usually be viewed without removing the caliper. Most pads have wear indicator grooves (1) and some also have indicator tangs (2)

On drum brakes, check the angle of the operating lever with the brake fully applied. Most drum brakes have a wear indicator pointer and scale.

Brakes, Wheels and Tyres

Brakes

✔ With the wheel raised off the ground, apply the brake then free it off, and check that the wheel is about to revolve freely without brake drag.

✔ On disc brakes, examine the disc itself. Check that it is securely mounted and not cracked.

✔ On disc brakes, view the pad material through the caliper mouth and check that the pads are not worn down beyond the limit (see illustration 11).

✔ On drum brakes, check that when the brake is applied the angle between the operating lever and cable or rod is not too great (see illustration 12). Check also that the operating lever doesn't foul any other components.

✔ On disc brakes, examine the flexible hoses from top to bottom. Have an assistant hold the brake on so that the fluid in the hose is under pressure, and check that there is no sign of fluid leakage, bulges or cracking. If there are any metal brake pipes or unions, check that these are free from corrosion and damage. Where a brake-linked anti-dive system is fitted, check the hoses to the anti-dive in a similar manner.

✔ Check that the rear brake torque arm is secure and that its fasteners are secured by self-locking nuts or castellated nuts with split-pins or R-pins (see illustration 13).

✔ On models with ABS, check that the self-check warning light in the instrument panel works.

✔ The MOT tester will perform a test of the motorcycle's braking efficiency based on a calculation of rider and motorcycle weight. Although this cannot be carried out at home, you can at least ensure that the braking systems are properly maintained. For hydraulic disc brakes, check the fluid level, lever/pedal feel (bleed of air if its spongy) and pad material. For drum brakes, check adjustment, cable or rod operation and shoe lining thickness.

Wheels and tyres

✔ Check the wheel condition. Cast wheels should be free from cracks and if of the built-up design, all fasteners should be secure. Spoked wheels should be checked for broken, corroded, loose or bent spokes.

✔ With the wheel raised off the ground, spin the wheel and visually check that the tyre and wheel run true. Check that the tyre does not foul the suspension or mudguards.

✔ With the wheel raised off the ground, grasp the wheel and attempt to move it about the axle (spindle) (see illustration 14). Any play felt here indicates wheel bearing failure.

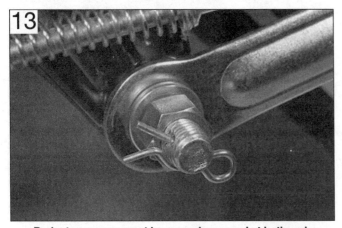

Brake torque arm must be properly secured at both ends

Check for wheel bearing play by trying to move the wheel about the axle (spindle)

Checking the tyre tread depth

Tyre direction of rotation arrow can be found on tyre sidewall

Castellated type wheel axle (spindle) nut must be secured by a split pin or R-pin

Two straightedges are used to check wheel alignment

✔ Check the tyre tread depth, tread condition and sidewall condition **(see illustration 15)**.
✔ Check the tyre type. Front and rear tyre types must be compatible and be suitable for road use. Tyres marked NOT FOR ROAD USE, COMPETITION USE ONLY or similar, will fail the MOT.

✔ If the tyre sidewall carries a direction of rotation arrow, this must be pointing in the direction of normal wheel rotation **(see illustration 16)**.
✔ Check that the wheel axle (spindle) nuts (where applicable) are properly secured. A self-locking nut or castellated nut with a split-pin or R-pin can be used **(see illustration 17)**.
✔ Wheel alignment is checked with the motorcycle off the stand and a rider seated. With the front wheel pointing straight ahead, two perfectly straight lengths of metal or wood and placed against the sidewalls of both tyres **(see illustration 18)**. The gap each side of the front tyre must be equidistant on both sides. Incorrect wheel alignment may be due to a cocked rear wheel (often as the result of poor chain adjustment) or in extreme cases, a bent frame.

General checks and condition

✔ Check the security of all major fasteners, bodypanels, seat, fairings (where fitted) and mudguards.

✔ Check that the rider and pillion footrests, handlebar levers and brake pedal are securely mounted.

✔ Check for corrosion on the frame or any load-bearing components. If severe, this may affect the structure, particularly under stress.

Sidecars

A motorcycle fitted with a sidecar requires additional checks relating to the stability of the machine and security of attachment and swivel joints, plus specific wheel alignment (toe-in) requirements. Additionally, tyre and lighting requirements differ from conventional motorcycle use. Owners are advised to check MOT test requirements with an official test centre.

Preparing for storage

Before you start

If repairs or an overhaul is needed, see that this is carried out now rather than left until you want to ride the bike again.

Give the bike a good wash and scrub all dirt from its underside. Make sure the bike dries completely before preparing for storage.

Engine

● Remove the spark plug(s) and lubricate the cylinder bores with approximately a teaspoon of motor oil using a spout-type oil can **(see illustration 1)**. Reinstall the spark plug(s). Crank the engine over a couple of times to coat the piston rings and bores with oil. If the bike has a kickstart, use this to turn the engine over. If not, flick the kill switch to the OFF position and crank the engine over on the starter **(see illustration 2)**. If the nature on the ignition system prevents the starter operating with the kill switch in the OFF position,

remove the spark plugs and fit them back in their caps; ensure that the plugs are earthed (grounded) against the cylinder head when the starter is operated **(see illustration 3)**.

⚠ *Warning: It is important that the plugs are earthed (grounded) away from the spark plug holes otherwise there is a risk of atomised fuel from the cylinders igniting.*

HAYNES HiNT *On a single cylinder four-stroke engine, you can seal the combustion chamber completely by positioning the piston at TDC on the compression stroke.*

● Drain the carburettor(s) otherwise there is a risk of jets becoming blocked by gum deposits from the fuel **(see illustration 4)**.

● If the bike is going into long-term storage, consider adding a fuel stabiliser to the fuel in the tank. If the tank is drained completely, corrosion of its internal surfaces may occur if left unprotected for a long period. The tank can be treated with a rust preventative especially for this purpose. Alternatively, remove the tank and pour half a litre of motor oil into it, install the filler cap and shake the tank to coat its internals with oil before draining off the excess. The same effect can also be achieved by spraying WD40 or a similar water-dispersant around the inside of the tank via its flexible nozzle.

● Make sure the cooling system contains the correct mix of antifreeze. Antifreeze also contains important corrosion inhibitors.

● The air intakes and exhaust can be sealed off by covering or plugging the openings. Ensure that you do not seal in any condensation; run the engine until it is hot,

Squirt a drop of motor oil into each cylinder

Flick the kill switch to OFF . . .

. . . and ensure that the metal bodies of the plugs (arrows) are earthed against the cylinder head

Connect a hose to the carburettor float chamber drain stub (arrow) and unscrew the drain screw

Exhausts can be sealed off with a plastic bag

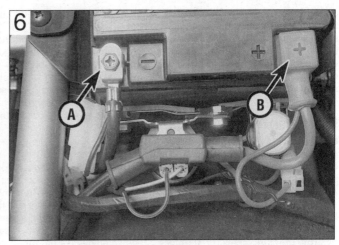

Disconnect the negative lead (A) first, followed by the positive lead (B)

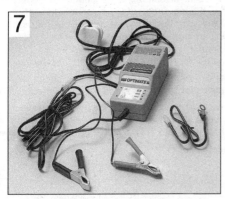

Use a suitable battery charger - this kit also assess battery condition

then switch off and allow to cool. Tape a piece of thick plastic over the silencer end(s) **(see illustration 5)**. Note that some advocate pouring a tablespoon of motor oil into the silencer(s) before sealing them off.

Battery

● Remove it from the bike - in extreme cases of cold the battery may freeze and crack its case **(see illustration 6)**.

● Check the electrolyte level and top up if necessary (conventional refillable batteries). Clean the terminals.
● Store the battery off the motorcycle and away from any sources of fire. Position a wooden block under the battery if it is to sit on the ground.
● Give the battery a trickle charge for a few hours every month **(see illustration 7)**.

Tyres

● Place the bike on its centrestand or an auxiliary stand which will support the motorcycle in an upright position. Position wood blocks under the tyres to keep them off the ground and to provide insulation from damp. If the bike is being put into long-term storage, ideally both tyres should be off the ground; not only will this protect the tyres, but will also ensure that no load is placed on the steering head or wheel bearings.
● Deflate each tyre by 5 to 10 psi, no more or the beads may unseat from the rim, making subsequent inflation difficult on tubeless tyres.

Pivots and controls

● Lubricate all lever, pedal, stand and

footrest pivot points. If grease nipples are fitted to the rear suspension components, apply lubricant to the pivots.
● Lubricate all control cables.

Cycle components

● Apply a wax protectant to all painted and plastic components. Wipe off any excess, but don't polish to a shine. Where fitted, clean the screen with soap and water.
● Coat metal parts with Vaseline (petroleum jelly). When applying this to the fork tubes, do not compress the forks otherwise the seals will rot from contact with the Vaseline.
● Apply a vinyl cleaner to the seat.

Storage conditions

● Aim to store the bike in a shed or garage which does not leak and is free from damp.
● Drape an old blanket or bedspread over the bike to protect it from dust and direct contact with sunlight (which will fade paint). This also hides the bike from prying eyes. Beware of tight-fitting plastic covers which may allow condensation to form and settle on the bike.

Getting back on the road

Engine and transmission

● Change the oil and replace the oil filter. If this was done prior to storage, check that the oil hasn't emulsified - a thick whitish substance which occurs through condensation.
● Remove the spark plugs. Using a spout-type oil can, squirt a few drops of oil into the cylinder(s). This will provide initial lubrication as the piston rings and bores comes back into contact. Service the spark plugs, or fit new ones, and install them in the engine.

● Check that the clutch isn't stuck on. The plates can stick together if left standing for some time, preventing clutch operation. Engage a gear and try rocking the bike back and forth with the clutch lever held against the handlebar. If this doesn't work on cable-operated clutches, hold the clutch lever back against the handlebar with a strong elastic band or cable tie for a couple of hours **(see illustration 8)**.
● If the air intakes or silencer end(s) were blocked off, remove the bung or cover used.
● If the fuel tank was coated with a rust

Hold clutch lever back against the handlebar with elastic bands or a cable tie

preventative, oil or a stabiliser added to the fuel, drain and flush the tank and dispose of the fuel sensibly. If no action was taken with the fuel tank prior to storage, it is advised that the old fuel is disposed of since it will go off over a period of time. Refill the fuel tank with fresh fuel.

Frame and running gear

● Oil all pivot points and cables.
● Check the tyre pressures. They will definitely need inflating if pressures were reduced for storage.
● Lubricate the final drive chain (where applicable).
● Remove any protective coating applied to the fork tubes (stanchions) since this may well destroy the fork seals. If the fork tubes weren't protected and have picked up rust spots, remove them with very fine abrasive paper and refinish with metal polish.
● Check that both brakes operate correctly. Apply each brake hard and check that it's not possible to move the motorcycle forwards, then check that the brake frees off again once released. Brake caliper pistons can stick due to corrosion around the piston head, or on the sliding caliper types, due to corrosion of the slider pins. If the brake doesn't free after repeated operation, take the caliper off for examination. Similarly drum brakes can stick

due to a seized operating cam, cable or rod linkage.
● If the motorcycle has been in long-term storage, renew the brake fluid and clutch fluid (where applicable).
● Depending on where the bike has been stored, the wiring, cables and hoses may have been nibbled by rodents. Make a visual check and investigate disturbed wiring loom tape.

Battery

● If the battery has been previously removal and given top up charges it can simply be reconnected. Remember to connect the positive cable first and the negative cable last.
● On conventional refillable batteries, if the battery has not received any attention, remove it from the motorcycle and check its electrolyte level. Top up if necessary then charge the battery. If the battery fails to hold a charge and a visual checks show heavy white sulphation of the plates, the battery is probably defective and must be renewed. This is particularly likely if the battery is old. Confirm battery condition with a specific gravity check.
● On sealed (MF) batteries, if the battery has not received any attention, remove it from the motorcycle and charge it according to the information on the battery case - if the battery fails to hold a charge it must be renewed.

Starting procedure

● If a kickstart is fitted, turn the engine over a couple of times with the ignition OFF to distribute oil around the engine. If no kickstart is fitted, flick the engine kill switch OFF and the ignition ON and crank the engine over a couple of times to work oil around the upper cylinder components. If the nature of the ignition system is such that the starter won't work with the kill switch OFF, remove the spark plugs, fit them back into their caps and earth (ground) their bodies on the cylinder head. Reinstall the spark plugs afterwards.
● Switch the kill switch to RUN, operate the choke and start the engine. If the engine won't start don't continue cranking the engine - not only will this flatten the battery, but the starter motor will overheat. Switch the ignition off and try again later. If the engine refuses to start, go through the fault finding procedures in this manual. **Note:** *If the bike has been in storage for a long time, old fuel or a carburettor blockage may be the problem. Gum deposits in carburettors can block jets - if a carburettor cleaner doesn't prove successful the carburettors must be dismantled for cleaning.*

● Once the engine has started, check that the lights, turn signals and horn work properly.

● Treat the bike gently for the first ride and check all fluid levels on completion. Settle the bike back into the maintenance schedule.

This Section provides an easy reference-guide to the more common faults that are likely to afflict your machine. Obviously, the opportunities are almost limitless for faults to occur as a result of obscure failures, and to try and cover all eventualities would require a book. Indeed, a number have been written on the subject.

Successful troubleshooting is not a mysterious 'black art' but the application of a bit of knowledge combined with a systematic and logical approach to the problem. Approach any troubleshooting by first accurately identifying the symptom and then checking through the list of possible causes, starting with the simplest or most obvious and progressing in stages to the most complex.

Take nothing for granted, but above all apply liberal quantities of common sense.

The main symptom of a fault is given in the text as a major heading below which are listed the various systems or areas which may contain the fault. Details of each possible cause for a fault and the remedial action to be taken are given, in brief, in the paragraphs below each heading. Further information should be sought in the relevant Chapter.

1 Engine doesn't start or is difficult to start

- ☐ Starter motor doesn't rotate
- ☐ Starter motor rotates but engine does not turn over
- ☐ No fuel flow
- ☐ Engine flooded
- ☐ No spark or weak spark
- ☐ Compression low
- ☐ Stalls after starting
- ☐ Rough idle

2 Poor running at low speed

- ☐ Spark weak
- ☐ Fuel/air mixture incorrect
- ☐ Compression low
- ☐ Poor acceleration

3 Poor running or no power at high speed

- ☐ Firing incorrect
- ☐ Fuel/air mixture incorrect
- ☐ Compression low
- ☐ Knocking or pinking
- ☐ Miscellaneous causes

4 Overheating

- ☐ Engine overheats
- ☐ Firing incorrect
- ☐ Fuel/air mixture incorrect
- ☐ Compression too high
- ☐ Engine load excessive
- ☐ Lubrication inadequate
- ☐ Miscellaneous causes

5 Clutch problems

- ☐ Clutch slipping
- ☐ Clutch not disengaging completely

6 Gearchange problems

- ☐ Doesn't go into gear, or lever doesn't return
- ☐ Jumps out of gear
- ☐ Overselects

7 Abnormal engine noise

- ☐ Knocking or pinking
- ☐ Piston slap or rattling
- ☐ Valve noise
- ☐ Other noise

8 Abnormal driveline noise

- ☐ Clutch noise
- ☐ Transmission noise
- ☐ Final drive noise

9 Abnormal frame and suspension noise

- ☐ Front end noise
- ☐ Rear suspension noise
- ☐ Brake noise

10 Oil pressure warning LED comes on

- ☐ Engine lubrication system
- ☐ Electrical system

11 Excessive exhaust smoke

- ☐ White smoke
- ☐ Black smoke
- ☐ Brown smoke

12 Poor handling or stability

- ☐ Handlebars hard to turn
- ☐ Handlebars shake or vibrates excessively
- ☐ Handlebars pull to one side
- ☐ Poor shock absorbing qualities

13 Braking problems

- ☐ Brakes are spongy or lack power
- ☐ Brake lever or pedal pulsates
- ☐ Brakes drag

14 Electrical problems

- ☐ Battery dead or weak
- ☐ Battery overcharged

1 Engine doesn't start or is difficult to start

Starter motor doesn't rotate

☐ Engine kill switch OFF.
☐ Fuse blown. Check main fuses (Chapter 9).
☐ Battery voltage low. Check and recharge battery (Chapter 9).
☐ Starter motor defective. Make sure the wiring to the starter is secure. Make sure the starter relay clicks when the start button is pushed. If the relay clicks, then the fault is in the wiring or motor.
☐ Starter relay faulty. Check it according to the procedure in Chapter 9.
☐ Starter button not contacting. The contacts could be wet, corroded or dirty. Disassemble and clean the switch housing (Chapter 9).
☐ Wiring open or shorted. Check all wiring connections and harnesses to make sure that they are dry, tight and not corroded. Also check for broken or frayed wires that can cause a short to ground (earth) (see wiring diagram, Chapter 9).
☐ Ignition (main) switch defective. Check the switch according to the procedure in Chapter 9. Replace the switch with a new one if it is defective.
☐ Engine kill switch defective. Check for wet, dirty or corroded contacts. Clean or replace the switch as necessary (Chapter 9).
☐ Faulty neutral switch, side stand switch or clutch switch, or diodes, or engine shut-off relay. Check the wiring to each switch and the switch itself according to the procedures in Chapter 9. Similarly check the diodes (see Chapter 9) and the relay (see Chapter 4).

Starter motor rotates but engine does not turn over

☐ Starter clutch defective. Inspect and repair or replace (Chapter 2).
☐ Damaged idle/reduction or starter gears. Inspect and renew the damaged parts (Chapter 2).
☐ Seized engine caused by one or more internally damaged components. Failure due to wear, abuse or lack of lubrication. Damage can include seized valves, followers, camshafts, pistons, crankshaft, connecting rod bearings, or transmission gears or bearings. Refer to Chapter 2 for engine disassembly.

No fuel flow

☐ No fuel in tank.
☐ Fuel tank breather hose obstructed.
☐ Fuel pump assembly filter clogged. Remove the pump and clean or renew the filter (Chapter 1 and 4).
☐ Fuel hose clogged. Remove the fuel tank and check the hoses.
☐ Faulty fuel pump relay. Check the relay (see Chapter 4).
☐ Fuel pump faulty. Check the fuel pressure (Chapter 4).

Engine flooded

☐ Faulty pressure regulator – if it is stuck closed there could be excessive pressure in the throttle bodies. Check as described in Chapter 4.
☐ Injector(s) stuck open, allowing a constant flow of fuel into the engine. Check as described in Chapter 4.
☐ Starting technique incorrect. When the engine is cold, use the fast idle lever on the handlebar and no throttle. When the engine is warm use a small amount of throttle.

No spark or weak spark

☐ Engine kill switch turned to the OFF position.
☐ Battery voltage low. Check and recharge the battery as necessary (Chapter 9).

☐ Spark plugs dirty, defective or worn out. Locate reason for fouled plugs using spark plug condition chart and follow the plug maintenance procedures (Chapter 1).
☐ Spark plug leads or caps faulty or not making good contact over the spark plugs. Check condition. Replace if cracks or deterioration are evident (Chapter 5).
☐ Faulty ignition HT coils or wiring connectors (see Chapter 5).
☐ ECU defective. Check the ignition system referring to Chapter 5 for details.
☐ Crankshaft position sensor defective. Check the unit, referring to Chapter 4 for details.
☐ Ignition or kill switch shorted. This is usually caused by water, corrosion, damage or excessive wear. The switches can be disassembled and cleaned with electrical contact cleaner. If cleaning does not help, renew the switches (Chapter 9).
☐ Wiring shorted or broken between:
    a)   Ignition (main) switch and engine kill switch (or blown fuse)
    b)   ECU and engine kill switch
    c)   ECU and ignition HT coils
    d)   ECU and crankshaft position sensor
☐ Make sure that all wiring connections are clean, dry and tight. Look for chafed and broken wires (Chapters 4, 5 and 9).

Compression low

☐ Spark plugs loose. Remove the plugs and inspect their threads. Reinstall and tighten to the specified torque (Chapter 1).
☐ Cylinder head not sufficiently tightened down. If a cylinder head is suspected of being loose, then there's a chance that the gasket or head is damaged if the problem has persisted for any length of time. The head nuts/bolts should be tightened to the proper torque in the correct sequence (Chapter 2).
☐ Incorrect valve clearance. This means that the valve is not closing completely and compression pressure is leaking past the valve. Check and adjust the valve clearances (Chapter 1).
☐ Cylinder and/or piston worn. Excessive wear will cause compression pressure to leak past the rings. This is usually accompanied by worn rings as well. A top-end overhaul is necessary (Chapter 2).
☐ Piston rings worn, weak, broken, or sticking. Broken or sticking piston rings usually indicate a lubrication or fuelling problem that causes excess carbon deposits or seizures to form on the pistons and rings. Top-end overhaul is necessary (Chapter 2).
☐ Piston ring-to-groove clearance excessive. This is caused by excessive wear of the piston ring lands. Piston replacement is necessary (Chapter 2).
☐ Cylinder head gasket damaged. If a head is allowed to become loose, or if excessive carbon build-up on the piston crown and combustion chamber causes extremely high compression, the head gasket may leak. Re-torquing the head is not always sufficient to restore the seal, so gasket renewal is necessary (Chapter 2).
☐ Cylinder head warped. This is caused by overheating or improperly tightened head nuts/bolts. Machine shop resurfacing or head replacement is necessary (Chapter 2).
☐ Valve spring broken or weak. Caused by component failure or wear; the springs must be renewed (Chapter 2).
☐ Valve not seating properly. This is caused by a bent valve (from over-revving or improper valve adjustment), burned valve or seat (improper fuelling) or an accumulation of carbon deposits on the seat (from fuelling or lubrication problems). The valves must be cleaned and/or renewed and the seats serviced if possible (Chapter 2).

1 Engine doesn't start or is difficult to start (continued)

Stalls after starting

- ☐ Ignition malfunction. See Chapter 5.
- ☐ Fuel injection system malfunction. See Chapter 4.
- ☐ Fuel contaminated. The fuel can be contaminated with either dirt or water, or can change chemically if the machine is allowed to sit for several months or more. Drain the tank (Chapter 4). Also check that the fuel flows freely and is not being restricted.
- ☐ Fuel pump faulty – perform a pressure check (see Chapter 4).
- ☐ Intake air leak. Check for loose throttle body-to-intake manifold connections, loose or missing vacuum gauge adapter caps or hoses (Chapter 4).
- ☐ Engine idle speed incorrect (see Chapter 1). Also check the fast idle cable adjustment (See Chapter 4).

Rough idle

- ☐ Ignition malfunction. See Chapter 5.
- ☐ Idle speed incorrect. See Chapter 1.
- ☐ Throttle bodies not synchronised. Adjust with vacuum gauge or manometer set as described in Chapter 1.
- ☐ Throttle body or fuel injection system malfunction. See Chapter 4.
- ☐ Fuel contaminated. The fuel can be contaminated with either dirt or water, or can change chemically if the machine is allowed to sit for several months or more. Drain the tank (Chapter 4).
- ☐ Intake air leak. Check for loose throttle body-to-intake manifold connections, loose or missing vacuum take-off point blanking caps or hoses (Chapter 4).
- ☐ Air filter clogged. Clean or renew the air filter element (Chapter 1).

2 Poor running at low speed

Spark weak

- ☐ Battery voltage low. Check and recharge battery (Chapter 9).
- ☐ Spark plugs fouled, defective or worn out. Refer to Chapter 1 for spark plug maintenance.
- ☐ Incorrect spark plugs. Wrong type, heat range or cap configuration. Check and install correct plugs listed in Chapter 1.
- ☐ ECU defective. Check the ignition system referring to Chapter 5 for details.
- ☐ Crankshaft position sensor defective. See Chapter 4.
- ☐ Ignition HT coils or spark plug leads or caps defective, or caps not making good contact with spark plugs. See Chapter 1.

Fuel/air mixture incorrect

- ☐ Fuel injection system malfunction (see Chapter 4).
- ☐ Fuel injector clogged (see Chapter 4).
- ☐ Fuel pump or pressure regulator faulty (see Chapter 4).
- ☐ Throttle body intake manifolds loose. Check for cracks, breaks, tears or loose clamps. Renew the rubber intake manifold joints if split or perished.
- ☐ Air filter clogged, poorly sealed or missing (Chapter 1).
- ☐ Air filter housing poorly sealed. Look for cracks, holes or loose clamps and renew or repair defective parts.
- ☐ Fuel tank breather hose obstructed.

Compression low

- ☐ Spark plugs loose. Remove the plugs and inspect their threads. Reinstall and tighten to the specified torque (Chapter 1).
- ☐ Cylinder head not sufficiently tightened down. If a cylinder head is suspected of being loose, then there's a chance that the gasket and head are damaged if the problem has persisted for any length of time. The head nuts/bolts should be tightened to the proper torque in the correct sequence (Chapter 2).
- ☐ Incorrect valve clearance. This means that the valve is not closing completely and compression pressure is leaking past the valve. Check and adjust the valve clearances (Chapter 1).
- ☐ Cylinder and/or piston worn. Excessive wear will cause compression pressure to leak past the rings. This is usually accompanied by worn rings as well. A top-end overhaul is necessary (Chapter 2).

- ☐ Piston rings worn, weak, broken, or sticking. Broken or sticking piston rings usually indicate a lubrication or fuelling problem that causes excess carbon deposits or seizures to form on the pistons and rings. Top-end overhaul is necessary (Chapter 2).
- ☐ Piston ring-to-groove clearance excessive. This is caused by excessive wear of the piston ring lands. Piston renewal is necessary (Chapter 2).
- ☐ Cylinder head gasket damaged. If a head is allowed to become loose, or if excessive carbon build-up on the piston crown and combustion chamber causes extremely high compression, the head gasket may leak. Retorquing the head is not always sufficient to restore the seal, so gasket renewal is necessary (Chapter 2).
- ☐ Cylinder head warped. This is caused by overheating or improperly tightened head nuts/bolts. Machine shop resurfacing or head renewal is necessary (Chapter 2).
- ☐ Valve spring broken or weak. Caused by component failure or wear; the springs must be renewed (Chapter 2).
- ☐ Valve not seating properly. This is caused by a bent valve (from over-revving or improper valve adjustment), burned valve or seat (improper fuelling) or an accumulation of carbon deposits on the seat (from fuelling, lubrication problems). The valves must be cleaned and/or renewed and the seats serviced if possible (Chapter 2).

Poor acceleration

- ☐ Throttle bodies leaking or dirty. Overhaul them (Chapter 4).
- ☐ Fuel injection system malfunction, faulty fuel pump, or pressure regulator – see Chapter 4.
- ☐ Timing not advancing. The CKP sensor or ECU may be defective. If so, they must be replaced with new ones, as they can't be repaired. Check them (see Chapters 4 and 5).
- ☐ Throttle bodies not synchronised. Adjust them with a vacuum gauge set or manometer as described in Chapter 1.
- ☐ Engine oil viscosity too high. Using a heavier oil than that recommended in Chapter 1 can damage the oil pump or lubrication system and cause drag on the engine.
- ☐ Brakes dragging. Usually caused by debris which has entered the brake piston seals, or from a warped disc or bent axle. Repair as necessary (Chapter 7).

3 Poor running or no power at high speed

Firing incorrect

☐ Air filter restricted. Clean or renew filter (Chapter 1).
☐ Spark plugs fouled, defective or worn out. See Chapter 1 for spark plug maintenance.
☐ Incorrect spark plugs. Wrong type, heat range or cap configuration. Check and install correct plugs listed in Chapter 1.
☐ ECU defective. See Chapter 4.
☐ Ignition HT coils or spark plug leads or caps defective or caps not making good contact with spark plugs. See Chapter 5.

Fuel/air mixture incorrect

☐ Fuel injection system malfunction (see Chapter 4).
☐ Fuel injector clogged (see Chapter 4).
☐ Fuel pump or pressure regulator faulty (see Chapter 4).
☐ Throttle body intake manifolds loose. Check for cracks, breaks, tears or loose clamps. Renew the rubber intake manifold joints if split or perished.
☐ Air filter clogged, poorly sealed or missing (Chapter 1).
☐ Air filter housing poorly sealed. Look for cracks, holes or loose clamps and renew or repair defective parts.
☐ Fuel tank breather hose obstructed.

Compression low

☐ Spark plugs loose. Remove the plugs and inspect their threads. Reinstall and tighten to the specified torque (Chapter 1).
☐ Cylinder head not sufficiently tightened down. If a cylinder head is suspected of being loose, then there's a chance that the gasket and head are damaged if the problem has persisted for any length of time. The head nuts/bolts should be tightened to the proper torque in the correct sequence (Chapter 2).
☐ Incorrect valve clearance. This means that the valve is not closing completely and compression pressure is leaking past the valve. Check and adjust the valve clearances (Chapter 1).
☐ Cylinder and/or piston worn. Excessive wear will cause compression pressure to leak past the rings. This is usually accompanied by worn rings as well. A top-end overhaul is necessary (Chapter 2).
☐ Piston rings worn, weak, broken, or sticking. Broken or sticking piston rings usually indicate a lubrication problem that causes excess carbon deposits or seizures to form on the pistons and rings. A top-end overhaul is necessary (Chapter 2).
☐ Piston ring-to-groove clearance excessive. This is caused by excessive wear of the piston ring lands. Piston renewal is necessary (Chapter 2).
☐ Cylinder head gasket damaged. If a head is allowed to become loose, or if excessive carbon build-up on the piston crown and combustion chamber causes extremely high compression, the head gasket may leak. Retorquing the head is not always sufficient to restore the seal, so gasket renewal is necessary (Chapter 2).
☐ Cylinder head warped. This is caused by overheating or improperly tightened head nuts/bolts. Machine shop resurfacing or head renewal is necessary (Chapter 2).
☐ Valve spring broken or weak. Caused by component failure or wear; the springs must be renewed (Chapter 2).
☐ Valve not seating properly. This is caused by a bent valve (from over-revving or improper valve adjustment), burned valve or seat (improper fuelling) or an accumulation of carbon deposits on the seat (from fuelling or lubrication problems). The valves must be cleaned and/or renewed and the seats serviced if possible (Chapter 2).

Knocking or pinking

☐ Carbon build-up in combustion chamber. Use of a fuel additive that will dissolve the adhesive bonding the carbon particles to the crown and chamber is the easiest way to remove the build-up. Otherwise, the cylinder heads will have to be removed and decarbonised (Chapter 2).
☐ Incorrect or poor quality fuel. Old or improper grades of fuel can cause detonation. This causes the piston to rattle, thus the knocking or pinking sound. Drain old fuel and always use the recommended fuel grade.
☐ Spark plug heat range incorrect. Uncontrolled detonation indicates the plug heat range is too hot. The plug in effect becomes a glow plug, raising cylinder temperatures. Install the proper heat range plug (Chapter 1).
☐ Improper air/fuel mixture. This will cause the cylinders to run hot, which leads to detonation. Clogged injectors or an air leak can cause this imbalance. See Chapter 4.

Miscellaneous causes

☐ Throttle valve doesn't open fully. Adjust the throttle grip freeplay (Chapter 1).
☐ Clutch slipping. May be caused by loose or worn clutch components. Refer to Chapter 2 for clutch overhaul procedures.
☐ Timing not advancing – faulty ECU.
☐ Engine oil viscosity too high. Using a heavier oil than the one recommended in Chapter 1 can damage the oil pump or lubrication system and cause drag on the engine.
☐ Brakes dragging. Usually caused by debris which has entered the brake piston seals, or from a warped disc or bent axle. Repair as necessary.

4 Overheating

Engine overheats

☐ Coolant level low. Check and add coolant (Chapter 1).
☐ Leak in cooling system. Check cooling system hoses and radiator for leaks and other damage. Repair or renew parts as necessary (Chapter 3).
☐ Thermostat sticking open or closed. Test as described in Chapter 3.
☐ Coolant passages clogged. Drain and flush the entire system, then refill with fresh coolant (Chapter 3).
☐ Water pump defective. Remove the pump and check the components (Chapter 3).
☐ Clogged radiator fins. Clean them by blowing compressed air through the fins from the rear side of the radiator.
☐ Cooling fan or fan switch fault (Chapter 3).

Firing incorrect

☐ Spark plugs fouled, defective or worn out. See Chapter 1 for spark plug maintenance.
☐ Incorrect spark plugs.
☐ ECU defective (Chapter 4).
☐ Crankshaft position sensor faulty (Chapter 4).
☐ Ignition HT coils or spark plug leads or caps defective or caps not making good contact with spark plugs. See Chapter 1.

Fuel/air mixture incorrect

☐ Fuel injection system malfunction (see Chapter 4).
☐ Fuel injector clogged (see Chapter 4).
☐ Fuel pump or pressure regulator faulty (see Chapter 4).
☐ Throttle body intake manifolds loose. Check for cracks, breaks, tears or loose clamps. Renew the rubber intake manifold joints if split or perished.
☐ Air filter clogged, poorly sealed or missing (Chapter 1).
☐ Air filter housing poorly sealed. Look for cracks, holes or loose clamps and renew or repair defective parts.
☐ Fuel tank breather hose obstructed.

Compression too high

☐ Carbon build-up in combustion chamber. Use of a fuel additive that will dissolve the adhesive bonding the carbon particles to the piston crown and chamber is the easiest way to remove the build-up. Otherwise, the cylinder heads will have to be removed and decarbonised (Chapter 2).

Engine load excessive

☐ Clutch slipping. Can be caused by damaged, loose or worn clutch components. Refer to Chapter 2 for overhaul procedures.
☐ Engine oil level too high. The addition of too much oil will cause pressurisation of the crankcase and inefficient engine operation. Check Specifications and drain to proper level (Chapter 1 and *Daily (pre-ride) checks*).
☐ Engine oil viscosity too high. Using a heavier oil than the one recommended in Chapter 1 can damage the oil pump or lubrication system as well as cause drag on the engine.
☐ Brakes dragging. Usually caused by debris which has entered the brake piston seals, or from a warped disc or bent axle. Repair as necessary.

Lubrication inadequate

☐ Engine oil level too low. Friction caused by intermittent lack of lubrication or from oil that is overworked can cause overheating. The oil provides a definite cooling function in the engine. Check the oil level (*Daily (pre-ride) checks*).
☐ Poor quality engine oil or incorrect viscosity or type. Oil is rated not only according to viscosity but also according to type. Some oils are not rated high enough for use in this engine. Check the Specifications section and change to the correct oil (Chapter 1).

Miscellaneous causes

☐ Modification to exhaust system. Most aftermarket exhaust systems cause the engine to run leaner, which make them run hotter.

5 Clutch problems

Clutch slipping

☐ Clutch master or release cylinder faulty (Chapter 2).
☐ Friction plates worn or warped. Overhaul the clutch assembly (Chapter 2).
☐ Plain plates warped (Chapter 2).
☐ Clutch springs broken or weak. Old or heat-damaged (from slipping clutch) springs should be replaced with new ones (Chapter 2).
☐ Clutch centre or housing unevenly worn. This causes improper engagement of the plates. Renew the damaged or worn parts (Chapter 2).

Clutch not disengaging completely

☐ Clutch master or release cylinder faulty, or system requires bleeding (Chapter 2).
☐ Clutch plates warped or damaged. This will cause clutch drag, which in turn will cause the machine to creep. Overhaul the clutch assembly (Chapter 2).

☐ Clutch spring tension uneven. Usually caused by a sagged or broken spring. Check and renew the springs as a set (Chapter 2).
☐ Engine oil deteriorated. Old, thin, worn out oil will not provide proper lubrication for the plates, causing the clutch to drag. Renew the oil and filter (Chapter 1).
☐ Engine oil viscosity too high. Using a heavier oil than recommended in Chapter 1 can cause the plates to stick together, putting a drag on the engine. Change to the correct weight oil (Chapter 1).
☐ Clutch housing seized on gearbox input shaft. Lack of lubrication, severe wear or damage can cause the guide to seize on the shaft. Overhaul of the clutch, and perhaps transmission, may be necessary to repair the damage (Chapter 2).
☐ Loose clutch centre nut. Causes housing and centre misalignment putting a drag on the engine. Engagement adjustment continually varies. Overhaul the clutch assembly (Chapter 2).

6 Gearchange problems

Doesn't go into gear or lever doesn't return

☐ Clutch not disengaging. See above.
☐ Selector fork(s) bent or seized. Often caused by dropping the machine or from lack of lubrication. Overhaul the transmission (Chapter 2).
☐ Gear(s) stuck on shaft. Most often caused by a lack of lubrication or excessive wear in transmission bearings and bushings. Overhaul the transmission (Chapter 2).
☐ Selector drum binding. Caused by lubrication failure or excessive wear. Renew the drum and bearing (Chapter 2).
☐ Gearchange lever return spring weak or broken (Chapter 2).
☐ Gearchange lever broken. Splines stripped out of lever or shaft, caused by allowing the lever to get loose or from accident damage. Renew necessary parts (Chapter 2).

☐ Gearchange mechanism stopper arm broken or worn. Full engagement and rotary movement of selector drum results. Renew the arm (Chapter 2).
☐ Stopper arm spring broken. Allows arm to float, causing sporadic selector operation. Renew spring (Chapter 2).

Jumps out of gear

☐ Selector fork(s) worn. Overhaul the transmission (Chapter 2).
☐ Gear groove(s) worn. Overhaul the transmission (Chapter 2).
☐ Gear dogs or dog slots worn or damaged. The gears should be inspected and renewed if necessary.

Overselects

☐ Stopper arm spring weak or broken (Chapter 2).
☐ Gearchange shaft return spring post broken or distorted (Chapter 2).

7 Abnormal engine noise

Knocking or pinking

☐ Carbon build-up in combustion chamber. Use of a fuel additive that will dissolve the adhesive bonding the carbon particles to the piston crown and chamber is the easiest way to remove the build-up. Otherwise, the cylinder heads will have to be removed and decarbonised (Chapter 2).
☐ Incorrect or poor quality fuel. Old or improper fuel can cause detonation. This causes the pistons to rattle, thus the knocking or pinking sound. Drain the old fuel and always use the recommended grade fuel (Chapter 4).
☐ Spark plug heat range incorrect. Uncontrolled detonation indicates that the plug heat range is too hot. The plug in effect becomes a glow plug, raising cylinder temperatures. Install the proper heat range plug (Chapter 1).
☐ Improper fuel/air mixture. This will cause the cylinders to run hot and lead to detonation. Clogged injectors or an air leak can cause this imbalance. See Chapter 4.

Piston slap or rattling

☐ Cylinder-to-piston clearance excessive. Caused by improper assembly. Inspect and overhaul top-end parts (Chapter 2).
☐ Connecting rod bent. Caused by over-revving, trying to start a badly flooded engine or from ingesting a foreign object into the combustion chamber. Renew the damaged parts (Chapter 2).
☐ Piston pin or piston pin bore worn or seized from wear or lack of lubrication. Renew damaged parts (Chapter 2).
☐ Piston ring(s) worn, broken or sticking. Overhaul the top-end (Chapter 2).
☐ Piston seizure damage. Usually from lack of lubrication or overheating. Renew the pistons and cylinders, as necessary (Chapter 2).

☐ Connecting rod small-end or big-end clearance excessive. Caused by excessive wear or lack of lubrication. Renew worn parts.

Valve noise

☐ Incorrect valve clearances. Adjust the clearances by referring to Chapter 1.
☐ Valve spring broken or weak. Check and renew weak valve springs (Chapter 2).
☐ Camshaft or cylinder head worn or damaged. Lack of lubrication at high rpm is usually the cause of damage. Insufficient oil or failure to change the oil at the recommended intervals are the chief causes. Since there are no replaceable bearings in the head, the head and camshaft holders will have to be renewed if there is excessive wear or damage (Chapter 2).

Other noise

☐ Cylinder head gasket leaking.
☐ Exhaust pipe leaking at cylinder head connection. Caused by improper fit of pipe or loose exhaust flange. All exhaust fasteners should be tightened evenly and carefully. Failure to do this will lead to a leak.
☐ Crankshaft runout excessive. Caused by a bent crankshaft (from over-revving) or damage from an upper cylinder component failure.
☐ Engine mounting bolts loose. Tighten all engine mount bolts (Chapter 2).
☐ Crankshaft bearings worn (Chapter 2).
☐ Cam chain tensioner defective, cam chain or guide blades worn. Check according to the procedure in Chapter 2.

8 Abnormal driveline noise

Clutch noise

☐ Clutch housing/friction plate clearance excessive (Chapter 2).
☐ Loose or damaged clutch pressure plate and/or bolts (Chapter 2).

Transmission noise

☐ Bearings worn. Also includes the possibility that the shafts are worn. Overhaul the transmission (Chapter 2).
☐ Gears worn or chipped (Chapter 2).
☐ Metal chips jammed in gear teeth. Probably pieces from a broken clutch, gear or selector mechanism that were picked up by the gears. This will cause early bearing failure (Chapter 2).

☐ Engine oil level too low. Causes a howl from transmission. Also affects engine power and clutch operation (Daily (pre-ride) checks).

Final drive noise

☐ Chain not adjusted properly (Chapter 1).
☐ Front or rear sprocket loose. Tighten fasteners (Chapter 6).
☐ Sprockets worn. Renew sprockets (Chapter 6).
☐ Rear sprocket warped. Renew sprockets (Chapter 6).
☐ Rubber dampers in rear wheel hub worn. Check and renew (Chapter 7).

9 Abnormal frame and suspension noise

Front end noise

- [ ] Low fluid level or improper viscosity oil in forks. This can sound like spurting and is usually accompanied by irregular fork action (Chapter 6).
- [ ] Spring weak or broken. Makes a clicking or scraping sound. Fork oil, when drained, will have a lot of metal particles in it (Chapter 6).
- [ ] Steering head bearings loose or damaged. Clicks when braking. Check and adjust or replace as necessary (Chapters 1 and 6).
- [ ] Fork yokes loose. Make sure all clamp pinch bolts are tightened to the specified torque (Chapter 6).
- [ ] Fork tube bent. Good possibility if machine has been dropped. Replace tube with a new one (Chapter 6).
- [ ] Front axle bolt or axle clamp bolts loose. Tighten them to the specified torque (Chapter 7).
- [ ] Loose or worn wheel bearings. Check and renew as necessary (Chapter 7).

Rear suspension noise

- [ ] Fluid level incorrect. Indicates a leak caused by defective seal. Shock will be covered with oil. Renew shock or seek advice on repair from an Aprilia dealer or suspension specialist (Chapter 6).

- [ ] Defective shock absorber with internal damage – this is in the body of the shock and can't be remedied. The shock must be replaced with a new one (Chapter 6).
- [ ] Bent or damaged shock body. Replace with a new one (Chapter 6).
- [ ] Loose or worn suspension linkage or swingarm components. Check and renew as necessary (Chapter 6). Pay particular attention to the needle bearings and their seals in the suspension linkage components and swingarm.

Brake noise

- [ ] Squeal caused by dust on brake pads. Usually found in combination with glazed pads. Clean using brake cleaning solvent (Chapter 7).
- [ ] Contamination of brake pads. Oil, brake fluid or dirt causing brake to chatter or squeal. Replace pads with new ones (Chapter 7).
- [ ] Pads glazed. Replace the pads with new ones (Chapter 7).
- [ ] Disc warped. Can cause a chattering, clicking or intermittent squeal. Usually accompanied by a pulsating lever or pedal and uneven braking. Renew the disc(s) (Chapter 7).
- [ ] Loose or worn wheel bearings. Check (Chapter 1) and replace with new ones (Chapter 7) as necessary.

10 Oil pressure warning LED comes on

Engine lubrication system

- [ ] Engine oil pump defective, blocked oil strainer gauze or failed relief valve. Carry out an oil pressure check (Chapter 1).
- [ ] Engine oil level low. Inspect for leak or other problem causing low oil level and add recommended oil (*Daily (pre-ride) checks*).
- [ ] Engine oil viscosity too low. Very old, thin oil or an improper weight of oil used in the engine. Change to correct oil (Chapter 1).
- [ ] Camshaft or journals worn. Excessive wear causing drop in oil pressure. Measure oil clearance (Chapter 2). Abnormal wear could

be caused by oil starvation at high rpm from low oil level or improper weight or type of oil (Chapter 1).
- [ ] Crankshaft and/or bearings worn. Same problems as above. Measure oil connecting rod and main bearing oil clearance (Chapter 2).

Electrical system

- [ ] Oil pressure switch defective. Check the switch according to the procedure in Chapter 9. Replace it if it is defective.
- [ ] Oil pressure warning LED circuit defective. Check for pinched, shorted, disconnected or damaged wiring (Chapter 9).

11 Excessive exhaust smoke

White smoke

- [ ] Piston oil ring worn. The ring may be broken or damaged, causing oil from the crankcase to be pulled past the piston into the combustion chamber. Replace the rings with new ones (Chapter 2).
- [ ] Cylinders worn, cracked, or scored. Caused by overheating or oil starvation. The cylinders will have to be renewed – reboring is not possible.
- [ ] Valve oil seal damaged or worn. Replace oil seals with new ones (Chapter 2).
- [ ] Valve guide worn. Perform a complete valve job (Chapter 2).
- [ ] Engine oil level too high, which causes the oil to be forced past the rings. Drain oil to the proper level (*Daily (pre-ride) checks*).

- [ ] Head gasket broken between oil return and cylinder. Causes oil to be pulled into the combustion chamber. Renew the head gasket and check the head for warpage (Chapter 2).
- [ ] Abnormal crankcase pressurisation, which forces oil past the rings. Clogged breather is usually the cause.

Black smoke

- [ ] Fuel injection system malfunction (see Chapter 4).
- [ ] Air filter clogged (Chapter 1).

Brown smoke

- [ ] Fuel injection system malfunction (see Chapter 4).
- [ ] Faulty fuel pump or pressure regulator (see Chapter 4).
- [ ] Air filter poorly sealed or not installed (Chapter 1).

12 Poor handling or stability

Handlebars hard to turn

- [ ] Steering head bearing adjuster nut too tight. Check adjustment as described in Chapter 1.
- [ ] Bearings damaged. Roughness can be felt as the bars are turned from side-to-side. Replace bearings and races with new ones (Chapter 6).
- [ ] Races dented or worn. Denting results from wear in only one position (e.g., straight ahead), from a collision or hitting a pothole or from dropping the machine. Replace bearings and races with new ones (Chapter 6).

- [ ] Steering stem lubrication inadequate. Causes are grease getting hard from age or being washed out by high pressure car washes. Disassemble steering head and repack bearings with fresh grease (Chapter 6).
- [ ] Steering stem bent. Caused by a collision, hitting a pothole or by dropping the machine. Renew damaged part. Don't try to straighten the steering stem (Chapter 6).
- [ ] Front tyre air pressure too low (*Daily (pre-ride) checks*).
- [ ] Faulty steering damper (where fitted) (Chapter 6).

12 Poor handling or stability (continued)

Handlebars shake or vibrates excessively

- [ ] Tyres worn or out of balance (Chapter 7).
- [ ] Swingarm bearings worn. Replace worn bearings with new ones (Chapter 6).
- [ ] Wheel rim(s) warped or damaged. Inspect wheels for runout (Chapter 7).
- [ ] Wheel bearings worn. Worn front or rear wheel bearings can cause poor tracking. Worn front bearings will cause wobble (Chapter 7).
- [ ] Handlebar clamp bolts loose (Chapter 6).
- [ ] Fork yoke bolts loose. Tighten them to the specified torque (Chapter 6).
- [ ] Engine mounting bolts loose. Will cause excessive vibration with increased engine rpm (Chapter 2).

Handlebars pull to one side

- [ ] Frame bent. Definitely suspect this if the machine has been dropped. May or may not be accompanied by cracking near the bend. Renew the frame (Chapter 6).
- [ ] Wheels out of alignment. Caused by improper location of axle spacers or from bent steering stem or frame (Chapter 6).
- [ ] Swingarm bent or twisted from accident damage. Renew the swingarm (Chapter 6).
- [ ] Steering stem bent. Caused by impact damage or by dropping the motorcycle. Renew the steering stem (Chapter 6).

- [ ] Fork tube bent. Disassemble the forks and renew the damaged parts (Chapter 6).
- [ ] Fork oil level uneven. Check and add or drain as necessary (Chapter 6).

Poor shock absorbing qualities

- [ ] Too hard:
  - a) Fork oil level excessive (Chapter 6).
  - b) Fork oil viscosity too high. Use a lighter oil (see the Specifications in Chapter 6).
  - c) Fork tube bent. Causes a harsh, sticking feeling (Chapter 6).
  - d) Rear shock absorber shaft or body bent or damaged (Chapter 6).
  - e) Fork internal damage (Chapter 6).
  - f) Shock absorber internal damage.
  - g) Tyre pressure too high (Chapter 1).
  - h) Incorrect adjustment settings (Chapter 6).

- [ ] Too soft:
  - a) Fork or shock oil insufficient and/or leaking (Chapter 6).
  - b) Fork oil level too low (Chapter 6).
  - c) Fork oil viscosity too light (Chapter 6).
  - d) Fork springs weak or broken (Chapter 6).
  - e) Shock absorber internal damage or leakage (Chapter 6).
  - f) Incorrect adjustment settings (Chapter 6).

13 Braking problems

Brakes are spongy, or lack power

- [ ] Air in brake line. Caused by inattention to master cylinder fluid level or by leakage. Locate problem and bleed brakes (Chapter 7).
- [ ] Pads or discs worn (Chapters 1 and 7).
- [ ] Brake fluid leak. See paragraph 1.
- [ ] Contaminated pads. Caused by contamination with oil, grease, brake fluid, etc. Replace pads with new ones (Chapter 7). Clean disc thoroughly with brake cleaner (Chapter 7).
- [ ] Brake fluid deteriorated. Fluid is old or contaminated. Drain system, replenish with new fluid and bleed the system (Chapter 7).
- [ ] Master cylinder internal parts worn or damaged causing fluid to bypass. Replace master cylinder with a new one (Chapter 7).
- [ ] Master cylinder bore scratched by foreign material or broken spring. Replace master cylinder with a new one (Chapter 7).
- [ ] Brake caliper piston seized in bore. Caused by wear or ingestion of dirt past deteriorated seal. Rebuild kits not available so fit a new caliper (Chapter 7).

Brake lever or pedal pulsates

- [ ] Disc warped. Replace disc with new one (Chapter 7).
- [ ] Wheel axle bent. Replace axle with a new one (Chapter 7).
- [ ] Brake caliper bolts loose (Chapter 7).
- [ ] Wheel warped or otherwise damaged (Chapter 7).
- [ ] Wheel bearings damaged or worn (Chapters 1 and 7).

Brakes drag

- [ ] Master cylinder piston seized. Caused by wear or damage to piston or cylinder bore (Chapter 7).
- [ ] Lever balky or stuck. Check pivot and lubricate (Chapter 7).
- [ ] Brake caliper piston seized in bore. Caused by wear or ingestion of dirt past deteriorated seal. Rebuild kits not available so fit a new caliper (Chapter 7).
- [ ] Brake pad damaged. Replace pads with new ones (Chapter 7).
- [ ] Pads improperly installed (Chapter 7).

14 Electrical problems

Battery dead or weak

- [ ] Battery faulty. Caused by sulphated plates which are shorted through sedimentation. Also, broken battery terminal making only occasional contact (Chapter 9).
- [ ] Battery cables making poor contact (Chapter 9).
- [ ] Load excessive. Caused by addition of high wattage lights or other electrical accessories.
- [ ] Ignition (main) switch defective. Switch either grounds (earths) internally or fails to shut off system. Renew the switch (Chapter 9).
- [ ] Regulator/rectifier defective (Chapter 9).

- [ ] Alternator stator coil open or shorted (Chapter 9).
- [ ] Wiring faulty. Wiring grounded (earthed) or connections loose in ignition, charging or lighting circuits (Chapter 9).

Battery overcharged

- [ ] Regulator/rectifier defective. Overcharging is noticed when battery gets excessively warm (Chapter 9).
- [ ] Battery defective. Replace battery with a new one (Chapter 9).
- [ ] Battery amperage too low, wrong type or size. Install manufacturer's specified amp-hour battery to handle charging load (Chapter 9).

Checking engine compression

● Low compression will result in exhaust smoke, heavy oil consumption, poor starting and poor performance. A compression test will provide useful information about an engine's condition and if performed regularly, can give warning of trouble before any other symptoms become apparent.

● A compression gauge will be required, along with an adapter to suit the spark plug hole thread size. Note that the screw-in type gauge/adapter set up is preferable to the rubber cone type.

● Before carrying out the test, first check the valve clearances as described in Chapter 1.

1 Run the engine until it reaches normal operating temperature, then stop it and remove the spark plug(s), taking care not to scald your hands on the hot components.

2 Install the gauge adapter and compression gauge in No. 1 cylinder spark plug hole (see illustration 1).

Screw the compression gauge adapter into the spark plug hole, then screw the gauge into the adapter

3 On kickstart-equipped motorcycles, make sure the ignition switch is OFF, then open the throttle fully and kick the engine over a couple of times until the gauge reading stabilises.

4 On motorcycles with electric start only, the procedure will differ depending on the nature of the ignition system. Flick the engine kill switch (engine stop switch) to OFF and turn the ignition switch ON; open the throttle fully and crank the engine over on the starter motor for a couple of revolutions until the gauge reading stabilises. If the starter will not operate with the kill switch OFF, turn the ignition switch OFF and refer to the next paragraph.

5 Install the plugs back in their caps and arrange the plug electrodes so that their metal bodies are earthed (grounded) against the cylinder head; this is essential to prevent damage to the ignition system (see illustration 2). Position the plugs well away from the plug holes otherwise there is a risk of

All spark plugs must be earthed (grounded) against the cylinder head

atomised fuel escaping from the plug holes and igniting. As a safety precaution, cover the cylinder head covers with rag and disconnect the fuel pump wiring connector (see Chapter 4). Turn the ignition switch and kill switch ON, open the throttle fully and crank the engine over on the starter motor for a couple of revolutions until the gauge reading stabilises.

6 After one or two revolutions the pressure should build up to a maximum figure and then stabilise. Take a note of this reading and on multi-cylinder engines repeat the test on the remaining cylinders.

7 The correct pressures are given in Chapter 1 Specifications. If the results fall within the specified range and on multi-cylinder engines all are relatively equal, the engine is in good condition. If there is a marked difference between the readings, or if the readings are lower than specified, inspection of the top-end components will be required.

8 Low compression pressure may be due to worn cylinder bores, pistons or rings, failure of the cylinder head gasket, worn valve seals, or poor valve seating.

9 To distinguish between cylinder/piston wear and valve leakage, pour a small quantity of oil into the bore to temporarily seal the piston rings, then repeat the compression

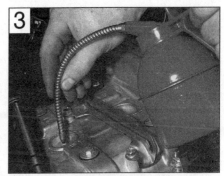

Bores can be temporarily sealed with a squirt of motor oil

tests (see illustration 3). If the readings show a noticeable increase in pressure this confirms that the cylinder bore, piston, or rings are worn. If, however, no change is indicated, the cylinder head gasket or valves should be examined.

10 High compression pressure indicates excessive carbon build-up in the combustion chamber and on the piston crown. If this is the case the cylinder head should be removed and the deposits removed. Note that excessive carbon build-up is less likely with the used on modern fuels.

Checking battery open-circuit voltage

⚠ *Warning: The gases produced by the battery are explosive - never smoke or create any sparks in the vicinity of the battery. Never allow the electrolyte to contact your skin or clothing - if it does, wash it off and seek immediate*

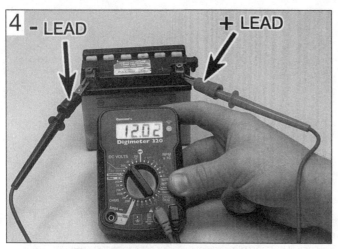

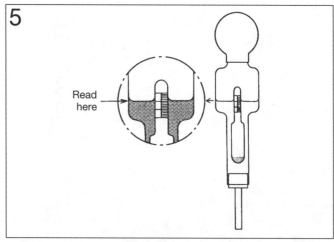

Measuring open-circuit battery voltage

Float-type hydrometer for measuring battery specific gravity

● Before any electrical fault is investigated the battery should be checked.
● You'll need a dc voltmeter or multimeter to check battery voltage. Check that the leads are inserted in the correct terminals on the meter, red lead to positive (+ve), black lead to negative (-ve). Incorrect connections can damage the meter.
● A sound fully-charged 12 volt battery should produce between 12.3 and 12.6 volts across its terminals (12.8 volts for a maintenance-free battery). On machines with a 6 volt battery, voltage should be between 6.1 and 6.3 volts.
1 Set a multimeter to the 0 to 20 volts dc range and connect its probes across the battery terminals. Connect the meter's positive (+ve) probe, usually red, to the battery positive (+ve) terminal, followed by the meter's negative (-ve) probe, usually black, to the battery negative terminal (-ve) **(see illustration 4)**.
2 If battery voltage is low (below 10 volts on a 12 volt battery or below 4 volts on a six volt battery), charge the battery and test the voltage again. If the battery repeatedly goes flat, investigate the motorcycle's charging system.

Checking battery specific gravity (SG)

⚠️ **Warning: The gases produced by the battery are explosive - never smoke or create any sparks in the vicinity of the battery. Never allow the electrolyte to contact your skin or clothing - if it does, wash it off and seek immediate medical attention.**

● The specific gravity check gives an indication of a battery's state of charge.
● A hydrometer is used for measuring specific gravity. Make sure you purchase one

which has a small enough hose to insert in the aperture of a motorcycle battery.
● Specific gravity is simply a measure of the electrolyte's density compared with that of water. Water has an SG of 1.000 and fully-charged battery electrolyte is about 26% heavier, at 1.260.
● Specific gravity checks are not possible on maintenance-free batteries. Testing the open-circuit voltage is the only means of determining their state of charge.
1 To measure SG, remove the battery from the motorcycle and remove the first cell cap. Draw

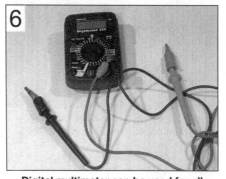

Digital multimeter can be used for all electrical tests

Battery-powered continuity tester

some electrolyte into the hydrometer and note the reading **(see illustration 5)**. Return the electrolyte to the cell and install the cap.
2 The reading should be in the region of 1.260 to 1.280. If SG is below 1.200 the battery needs charging. Note that SG will vary with temperature; it should be measured at 20°C (68°F). Add 0.007 to the reading for every 10°C above 20°C, and subtract 0.007 from the reading for every 10°C below 20°C. Add 0.004 to the reading for every 10°F above 68°F, and subtract 0.004 from the reading for every 10°F below 68°F.
3 When the check is complete, rinse the hydrometer thoroughly with clean water.

Checking for continuity

● The term continuity describes the uninterrupted flow of electricity through an electrical circuit. A continuity check will determine whether an **open-circuit** situation exists.
● Continuity can be checked with an ohmmeter, multimeter, continuity tester or battery and bulb test circuit **(see illustrations 6, 7 and 8)**.

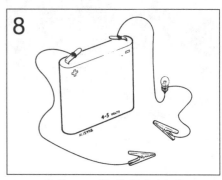

Battery and bulb test circuit

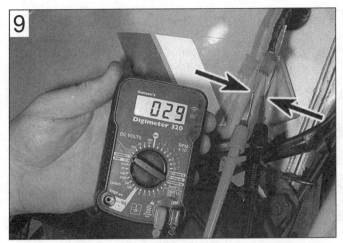

Continuity check of front brake light switch using a meter - note split pins used to access connector terminals

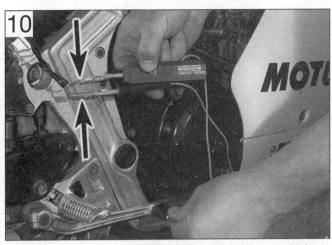

Continuity check of rear brake light switch using a continuity tester

● All of these instruments are self-powered by a battery, therefore the checks are made with the ignition OFF.

● As a safety precaution, always disconnect the battery negative (-ve) lead before making checks, particularly if ignition switch checks are being made.

● If using a meter, select the appropriate ohms scale and check that the meter reads infinity (∞). Touch the meter probes together and check that meter reads zero; where necessary adjust the meter so that it reads zero.

● After using a meter, always switch it OFF to conserve its battery.

Switch checks

1 If a switch is at fault, trace its wiring up to the wiring connectors. Separate the wire connectors and inspect them for security and condition. A build-up of dirt or corrosion here will most likely be the cause of the problem - clean up and apply a water dispersant such as WD40.

2 If using a test meter, set the meter to the ohms x 10 scale and connect its probes across the wires from the switch (see illustration 9). Simple ON/OFF type switches, such as brake light switches, only have two wires whereas combination switches, like the ignition switch, have many internal links. Study the wiring diagram to ensure that you are connecting across the correct pair of wires. Continuity (low or no measurable resistance - 0 ohms) should be indicated with the switch ON and no continuity (high resistance) with it OFF.

3 Note that the polarity of the test probes doesn't matter for continuity checks, although care should be taken to follow specific test procedures if a diode or solid-state component is being checked.

4 A continuity tester or battery and bulb circuit can be used in the same way. Connect its probes as described above (see illustration 10). The light should come on to indicate continuity in the ON switch position, but should extinguish in the OFF position.

Wiring checks

● Many electrical faults are caused by damaged wiring, often due to incorrect routing or chaffing on frame components.

● Loose, wet or corroded wire connectors can also be the cause of electrical problems, especially in exposed locations.

1 A continuity check can be made on a single length of wire by disconnecting it at each end and connecting a meter or continuity tester across both ends of the wire (see illustration 11).

2 Continuity (low or no resistance - 0 ohms) should be indicated if the wire is good. If no continuity (high resistance) is shown, suspect a broken wire.

Checking for voltage

● A voltage check can determine whether current is reaching a component.

● Voltage can be checked with a dc voltmeter, multimeter set on the dc volts scale, test light or buzzer (see illustrations 12 and 13). A meter has the advantage of being able to measure actual voltage.

● When using a meter, check that its leads are inserted in the correct terminals on the meter, red to positive (+ve), black to negative (-ve). Incorrect connections can damage the meter.

● A voltmeter (or multimeter set to the dc volts scale) should always be connected in parallel (across the load). Connecting it in series will not harm the meter, but the reading will not be meaningful.

● Voltage checks are made with the ignition ON.

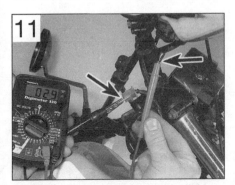

Continuity check of front brake light switch sub-harness

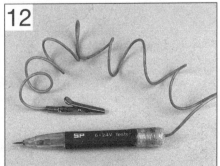

A simple test light can be used for voltage checks

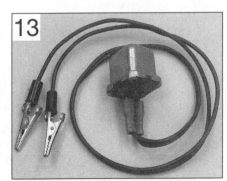

A buzzer is useful for voltage checks

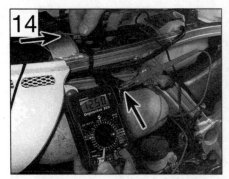

Checking for voltage at the rear brake light power supply wire using a meter . . .

1 First identify the relevant wiring circuit by referring to the wiring diagram at the end of this manual. If other electrical components share the same power supply (ie are fed from the same fuse), take note whether they are working correctly - this is useful information in deciding where to start checking the circuit.

2 If using a meter, check first that the meter leads are plugged into the correct terminals on the meter (see above). Set the meter to the dc volts function, at a range suitable for the battery voltage. Connect the meter red probe (+ve) to the power supply wire and the black probe to a good metal earth (ground) on the motorcycle's frame or directly to the battery negative (-ve) terminal **(see illustration 14)**. Battery voltage should be shown on the meter

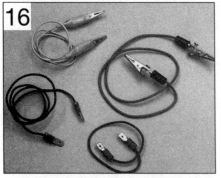

A selection of jumper wires for making earth (ground) checks

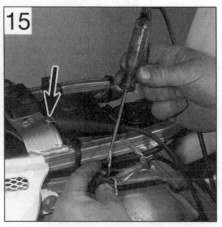

. . . or a test light - note the earth connection to the frame (arrow)

with the ignition switched ON.

3 If using a test light or buzzer, connect its positive (+ve) probe to the power supply terminal and its negative (-ve) probe to a good earth (ground) on the motorcycle's frame or directly to the battery negative (-ve) terminal **(see illustration 15)**. With the ignition ON, the test light should illuminate or the buzzer sound.

4 If no voltage is indicated, work back towards the fuse continuing to check for voltage. When you reach a point where there is voltage, you know the problem lies between that point and your last check point.

Checking the earth (ground)

● Earth connections are made either directly to the engine or frame (such as sensors, neutral switch etc. which only have a positive feed) or by a separate wire into the earth circuit of the wiring harness. Alternatively a short earth wire is sometimes run directly from the component to the motorcycle's frame.
● Corrosion is often the cause of a poor earth connection.
● If total failure is experienced, check the security of the main earth lead from the

negative (-ve) terminal of the battery and also the main earth (ground) point on the wiring harness. If corroded, dismantle the connection and clean all surfaces back to bare metal.

1 To check the earth on a component, use an insulated jumper wire to temporarily bypass its earth connection **(see illustration 16)**. Connect one end of the jumper wire between the earth terminal or metal body of the component and the other end to the motorcycle's frame.

2 If the circuit works with the jumper wire installed, the original earth circuit is faulty. Check the wiring for open-circuits or poor connections. Clean up direct earth connections, removing all traces of corrosion and remake the joint. Apply petroleum jelly to the joint to prevent future corrosion.

Tracing a short-circuit

● A short-circuit occurs where current shorts to earth (ground) bypassing the circuit components. This usually results in a blown fuse.

● A short-circuit is most likely to occur where the insulation has worn through due to wiring chafing on a component, allowing a direct path to earth (ground) on the frame.

1 Remove any bodypanels necessary to access the circuit wiring.

2 Check that all electrical switches in the circuit are OFF, then remove the circuit fuse and connect a test light, buzzer or voltmeter (set to the dc scale) across the fuse terminals. No voltage should be shown.

3 Move the wiring from side to side whilst observing the test light or meter. When the test light comes on, buzzer sounds or meter shows voltage, you have found the cause of the short. It will usually shown up as damaged or burned insulation.

4 Note that the same test can be performed on each component in the circuit, even the switch.

A

ABS (Anti-lock braking system) A system, usually electronically controlled, that senses incipient wheel lockup during braking and relieves hydraulic pressure at wheel which is about to skid.

Aftermarket Components suitable for the motorcycle, but not produced by the motorcycle manufacturer.

Allen key A hexagonal wrench which fits into a recessed hexagonal hole.

Alternating current (ac) Current produced by an alternator. Requires converting to direct current by a rectifier for charging purposes.

Alternator Converts mechanical energy from the engine into electrical energy to charge the battery and power the electrical system.

Ampere (amp) A unit of measurement for the flow of electrical current. Current = Volts ÷ Ohms.

Ampere-hour (Ah) Measure of battery capacity.

Angle-tightening A torque expressed in degrees. Often follows a conventional tightening torque for cylinder head or main bearing fasteners **(see illustration)**.

Angle-tightening cylinder head bolts

Antifreeze A substance (usually ethylene glycol) mixed with water, and added to the cooling system, to prevent freezing of the coolant in winter. Antifreeze also contains chemicals to inhibit corrosion and the formation of rust and other deposits that would tend to clog the radiator and coolant passages and reduce cooling efficiency.

Anti-dive System attached to the fork lower leg (slider) to prevent fork dive when braking hard.

Anti-seize compound A coating that reduces the risk of seizing on fasteners that are subjected to high temperatures, such as exhaust clamp bolts and nuts.

API American Petroleum Institute. A quality standard for 4-stroke motor oils.

Asbestos A natural fibrous mineral with great heat resistance, commonly used in the composition of brake friction materials. Asbestos is a health hazard and the dust created by brake systems should never be inhaled or ingested.

ATF Automatic Transmission Fluid. Often used in front forks.

ATU Automatic Timing Unit. Mechanical device for advancing the ignition timing on early engines.

ATV All Terrain Vehicle. Often called a Quad.

Axial play Side-to-side movement.

Axle A shaft on which a wheel revolves. Also known as a spindle.

B

Backlash The amount of movement between meshed components when one component is held still. Usually applies to gear teeth.

Ball bearing A bearing consisting of a hardened inner and outer race with hardened steel balls between the two races.

Bearings Used between two working surfaces to prevent wear of the components and a build-up of heat. Four types of bearing are commonly used on motorcycles: plain shell bearings, ball bearings, tapered roller bearings and needle roller bearings.

Bevel gears Used to turn the drive through 90°. Typical applications are shaft final drive and camshaft drive **(see illustration)**.

Bevel gears are used to turn the drive through 90°

BHP Brake Horsepower. The British measurement for engine power output. Power output is now usually expressed in kilowatts (kW).

Bias-belted tyre Similar construction to radial tyre, but with outer belt running at an angle to the wheel rim.

Big-end bearing The bearing in the end of the connecting rod that's attached to the crankshaft.

Bleeding The process of removing air from an hydraulic system via a bleed nipple or bleed screw.

Bottom-end A description of an engine's crankcase components and all components contained there-in.

BTDC Before Top Dead Centre in terms of piston position. Ignition timing is often expressed in terms of degrees or millimetres BTDC.

Bush A cylindrical metal or rubber component used between two moving parts.

Burr Rough edge left on a component after machining or as a result of excessive wear.

C

Cam chain The chain which takes drive from the crankshaft to the camshaft(s).

Canister The main component in an evaporative emission control system (California market only); contains activated charcoal granules to trap vapours from the fuel system rather than allowing them to vent to the atmosphere.

Castellated Resembling the parapets along the top of a castle wall. For example, a castellated wheel axle or spindle nut.

Catalytic converter A device in the exhaust system of some machines which converts certain pollutants in the exhaust gases into less harmful substances.

Charging system Description of the components which charge the battery, ie the alternator, rectifer and regulator.

Circlip A ring-shaped clip used to prevent endwise movement of cylindrical parts and shafts. An internal circlip is installed in a groove in a housing; an external circlip fits into a groove on the outside of a cylindrical piece such as a shaft. Also known as a snap-ring.

Clearance The amount of space between two parts. For example, between a piston and a cylinder, between a bearing and a journal, etc.

Coil spring A spiral of elastic steel found in various sizes throughout a vehicle, for example as a springing medium in the suspension and in the valve train.

Compression Reduction in volume, and increase in pressure and temperature, of a gas, caused by squeezing it into a smaller space.

Compression damping Controls the speed the suspension compresses when hitting a bump.

Compression ratio The relationship between cylinder volume when the piston is at top dead centre and cylinder volume when the piston is at bottom dead centre.

Continuity The uninterrupted path in the flow of electricity. Little or no measurable resistance.

Continuity tester Self-powered bleeper or test light which indicates continuity.

Cp Candlepower. Bulb rating commonly found on US motorcycles.

Crossply tyre Tyre plies arranged in a criss-cross pattern. Usually four or six plies used, hence 4PR or 6PR in tyre size codes.

Cush drive Rubber damper segments fitted between the rear wheel and final drive sprocket to absorb transmission shocks **(see illustration)**.

Cush drive rubbers dampen out transmission shocks

D

Degree disc Calibrated disc for measuring piston position. Expressed in degrees.

Dial gauge Clock-type gauge with adapters for measuring runout and piston position. Expressed in mm or inches.

Diaphragm The rubber membrane in a master cylinder or carburettor which seals the upper chamber.

Diaphragm spring A single sprung plate often used in clutches.

Direct current (dc) Current produced by a dc generator.

Decarbonisation The process of removing carbon deposits - typically from the combustion chamber, valves and exhaust port/system.

Detonation Destructive and damaging explosion of fuel/air mixture in combustion chamber instead of controlled burning.

Diode An electrical valve which only allows current to flow in one direction. Commonly used in rectifiers and starter interlock systems.

Disc valve (or rotary valve) A induction system used on some two-stroke engines.

Double-overhead camshaft (DOHC) An engine that uses two overhead camshafts, one for the intake valves and one for the exhaust valves.

Drivebelt A toothed belt used to transmit drive to the rear wheel on some motorcycles. A drivebelt has also been used to drive the camshafts. Drivebelts are usually made of Kevlar.

Driveshaft Any shaft used to transmit motion. Commonly used when referring to the final driveshaft on shaft drive motorcycles.

E

Earth return The return path of an electrical circuit, utilising the motorcycle's frame.

ECU (Electronic Control Unit) A computer which controls (for instance) an ignition system, or an anti-lock braking system.

EGO Exhaust Gas Oxygen sensor. Sometimes called a Lambda sensor.

Electrolyte The fluid in a lead-acid battery.

EMS (Engine Management System) A computer controlled system which manages the fuel injection and the ignition systems in an integrated fashion.

Endfloat The amount of lengthways movement between two parts. As applied to a crankshaft, the distance that the crankshaft can move side-to-side in the crankcase.

Endless chain A chain having no joining link. Common use for cam chains and final drive chains.

EP (Extreme Pressure) Oil type used in locations where high loads are applied, such as between gear teeth.

Evaporative emission control system Describes a charcoal filled canister which stores fuel vapours from the tank rather than allowing them to vent to the atmosphere. Usually only fitted to California models and referred to as an EVAP system.

Expansion chamber Section of two-stroke engine exhaust system so designed to improve engine efficiency and boost power.

F

Feeler blade or gauge A thin strip or blade of hardened steel, ground to an exact thickness, used to check or measure clearances between parts.

Final drive Description of the drive from the transmission to the rear wheel. Usually by chain or shaft, but sometimes by belt.

Firing order The order in which the engine cylinders fire, or deliver their power strokes, beginning with the number one cylinder.

Flooding Term used to describe a high fuel level in the carburettor float chambers, leading to fuel overflow. Also refers to excess fuel in the combustion chamber due to incorrect starting technique.

Free length The no-load state of a component when measured. Clutch, valve and fork spring lengths are measured at rest, without any preload.

Freeplay The amount of travel before any action takes place. The looseness in a linkage, or an assembly of parts, between the initial application of force and actual movement. For example, the distance the rear brake pedal moves before the rear brake is actuated.

Fuel injection The fuel/air mixture is metered electronically and directed into the engine intake ports (indirect injection) or into the cylinders (direct injection). Sensors supply information on engine speed and conditions.

Fuel/air mixture The charge of fuel and air going into the engine. See **Stoichiometric ratio**.

Fuse An electrical device which protects a circuit against accidental overload. The typical fuse contains a soft piece of metal which is calibrated to melt at a predetermined current flow (expressed as amps) and break the circuit.

G

Gap The distance the spark must travel in jumping from the centre electrode to the side electrode in a spark plug. Also refers to the distance between the ignition rotor and the pickup coil in an electronic ignition system.

Gasket Any thin, soft material - usually cork, cardboard, asbestos or soft metal - installed between two metal surfaces to ensure a good seal. For instance, the cylinder head gasket seals the joint between the block and the cylinder head.

Gauge An instrument panel display used to monitor engine conditions. A gauge with a movable pointer on a dial or a fixed scale is an analogue gauge. A gauge with a numerical readout is called a digital gauge.

Gear ratios The drive ratio of a pair of gears in a gearbox, calculated on their number of teeth.

Glaze-busting see **Honing**

Grinding Process for renovating the valve face and valve seat contact area in the cylinder head.

Gudgeon pin The shaft which connects the connecting rod small-end with the piston. Often called a piston pin or wrist pin.

H

Helical gears Gear teeth are slightly curved and produce less gear noise that straight-cut gears. Often used for primary drives.

Installing a Helicoil thread insert in a cylinder head

Helicoil A thread insert repair system. Commonly used as a repair for stripped spark plug threads **(see illustration)**.

Honing A process used to break down the glaze on a cylinder bore (also called glaze-busting). Can also be carried out to roughen a rebored cylinder to aid ring bedding-in.

HT (High Tension) Description of the electrical circuit from the secondary winding of the ignition coil to the spark plug.

Hydraulic A liquid filled system used to transmit pressure from one component to another. Common uses on motorcycles are brakes and clutches.

Hydrometer An instrument for measuring the specific gravity of a lead-acid battery.

Hygroscopic Water absorbing. In motorcycle applications, braking efficiency will be reduced if DOT 3 or 4 hydraulic fluid absorbs water from the air - care must be taken to keep new brake fluid in tightly sealed containers.

I

lbf ft Pounds-force feet. An imperial unit of torque. Sometimes written as ft-lbs.

lbf in Pound-force inch. An imperial unit of torque, applied to components where a very low torque is required. Sometimes written as in-lbs.

IC Abbreviation for Integrated Circuit.

Ignition advance Means of increasing the timing of the spark at higher engine speeds. Done by mechanical means (ATU) on early engines or electronically by the ignition control unit on later engines.

Ignition timing The moment at which the spark plug fires, expressed in the number of crankshaft degrees before the piston reaches the top of its stroke, or in the number of millimetres before the piston reaches the top of its stroke.

Infinity (∞) Description of an open-circuit electrical state, where no continuity exists.

Inverted forks (upside down forks) The sliders or lower legs are held in the yokes and the fork tubes or stanchions are connected to the wheel axle (spindle). Less unsprung weight and stiffer construction than conventional forks.

J

JASO Quality standard for 2-stroke oils.

Joule The unit of electrical energy.

Journal The bearing surface of a shaft.

K

Kickstart Mechanical means of turning the engine over for starting purposes. Only usually fitted to mopeds, small capacity motorcycles and off-road motorcycles.

Kill switch Handlebar-mounted switch for emergency ignition cut-out. Cuts the ignition circuit on all models, and additionally prevent starter motor operation on others.

km Symbol for kilometre.

kmh Abbreviation for kilometres per hour.

L

Lambda (λ) sensor A sensor fitted in the exhaust system to measure the exhaust gas oxygen content (excess air factor).

Lapping see **Grinding**.
LCD Abbreviation for Liquid Crystal Display.
LED Abbreviation for Light Emitting Diode.
Liner A steel cylinder liner inserted in a aluminium alloy cylinder block.
Locknut A nut used to lock an adjustment nut, or other threaded component, in place.
Lockstops The lugs on the lower triple clamp (yoke) which abut those on the frame, preventing handlebar-to-fuel tank contact.
Lockwasher A form of washer designed to prevent an attaching nut from working loose.
LT Low Tension Description of the electrical circuit from the power supply to the primary winding of the ignition coil.

M

Main bearings The bearings between the crankshaft and crankcase.
Maintenance-free (MF) battery A sealed battery which cannot be topped up.
Manometer Mercury-filled calibrated tubes used to measure intake tract vacuum. Used to synchronise carburettors on multi-cylinder engines.
Micrometer A precision measuring instrument that measures component outside diameters **(see illustration)**.

Tappet shims are measured with a micrometer

MON (Motor Octane Number) A measure of a fuel's resistance to knock.
Monograde oil An oil with a single viscosity, eg SAE80W.
Monoshock A single suspension unit linking the swingarm or suspension linkage to the frame.
mph Abbreviation for miles per hour.
Multigrade oil Having a wide viscosity range (eg 10W40). The W stands for Winter, thus the viscosity ranges from SAE10 when cold to SAE40 when hot.
Multimeter An electrical test instrument with the capability to measure voltage, current and resistance. Some meters also incorporate a continuity tester and buzzer.

N

Needle roller bearing Inner race of caged needle rollers and hardened outer race. Examples of uncaged needle rollers can be found on some engines. Commonly used in rear suspension applications and in two-stroke engines.
Nm Newton metres.
NOx Oxides of Nitrogen. A common toxic pollutant emitted by petrol engines at higher temperatures.

O

Octane The measure of a fuel's resistance to knock.
OE (Original Equipment) Relates to components fitted to a motorcycle as standard or replacement parts supplied by the motorcycle manufacturer.
Ohm The unit of electrical resistance. Ohms = Volts ÷ Current.
Ohmmeter An instrument for measuring electrical resistance.
Oil cooler System for diverting engine oil outside of the engine to a radiator for cooling purposes.
Oil injection A system of two-stroke engine lubrication where oil is pump-fed to the engine in accordance with throttle position.
Open-circuit An electrical condition where there is a break in the flow of electricity - no continuity (high resistance).
O-ring A type of sealing ring made of a special rubber-like material; in use, the O-ring is compressed into a groove to provide the sealing action.
Oversize (OS) Term used for piston and ring size options fitted to a rebored cylinder.
Overhead cam (sohc) engine An engine with single camshaft located on top of the cylinder head.
Overhead valve (ohv) engine An engine with the valves located in the cylinder head, but with the camshaft located in the engine block or crankcase.
Oxygen sensor A device installed in the exhaust system which senses the oxygen content in the exhaust and converts this information into an electric current. Also called a Lambda sensor.

P

Plastigauge A thin strip of plastic thread, available in different sizes, used for measuring clearances. For example, a strip of Plastigauge is laid across a bearing journal. The parts are assembled and dismantled; the width of the crushed strip indicates the clearance between journal and bearing.
Polarity Either negative or positive earth (ground), determined by which battery lead is connected to the frame (earth return). Modern motorcycles are usually negative earth.
Pre-ignition A situation where the fuel/air mixture ignites before the spark plug fires. Often due to a hot spot in the combustion chamber caused by carbon build-up. Engine has a tendency to 'run-on'.
Pre-load (suspension) The amount a spring is compressed when in the unloaded state. Preload can be applied by gas, spacer or mechanical adjuster.
Premix The method of engine lubrication on older two-stroke engines. Engine oil is mixed with the petrol in the fuel tank in a specific ratio. The fuel/oil mix is sometimes referred to as "petroil".
Primary drive Description of the drive from the crankshaft to the clutch. Usually by gear or chain.
PS Pfedestärke - a German interpretation of BHP.
PSI Pounds-force per square inch. Imperial measurement of tyre pressure and cylinder pressure measurement.
PTFE Polytetrafluoroethylene. A low friction substance.

Pulse secondary air injection system A process of promoting the burning of excess fuel present in the exhaust gases by routing fresh air into the exhaust ports.

Q

Quartz halogen bulb Tungsten filament surrounded by a halogen gas. Typically used for the headlight **(see illustration)**.

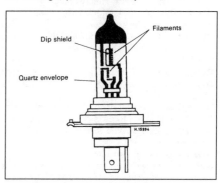

Quartz halogen headlight bulb construction

R

Rack-and-pinion A pinion gear on the end of a shaft that mates with a rack (think of a geared wheel opened up and laid flat). Sometimes used in clutch operating systems.
Radial play Up and down movement about a shaft.
Radial ply tyres Tyre plies run across the tyre (from bead to bead) and around the circumference of the tyre. Less resistant to tread distortion than other tyre types.
Radiator A liquid-to-air heat transfer device designed to reduce the temperature of the coolant in a liquid cooled engine.
Rake A feature of steering geometry - the angle of the steering head in relation to the vertical **(see illustration)**.

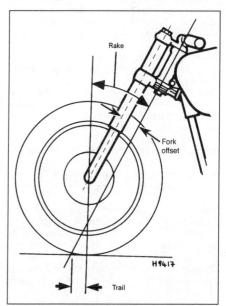

Steering geometry

Rebore Providing a new working surface to the cylinder bore by boring out the old surface. Necessitates the use of oversize piston and rings.

Rebound damping A means of controlling the oscillation of a suspension unit spring after it has been compressed. Resists the spring's natural tendency to bounce back after being compressed.

Rectifier Device for converting the ac output of an alternator into dc for battery charging.

Reed valve An induction system commonly used on two-stroke engines.

Regulator Device for maintaining the charging voltage from the generator or alternator within a specified range.

Relay A electrical device used to switch heavy current on and off by using a low current auxiliary circuit.

Resistance Measured in ohms. An electrical component's ability to pass electrical current.

RON (Research Octane Number) A measure of a fuel's resistance to knock.

rpm revolutions per minute.

Runout The amount of wobble (in-and-out movement) of a wheel or shaft as it's rotated. The amount a shaft rotates 'out-of-true'. The out-of-round condition of a rotating part.

S

SAE (Society of Automotive Engineers) A standard for the viscosity of a fluid.

Sealant A liquid or paste used to prevent leakage at a joint. Sometimes used in conjunction with a gasket.

Service limit Term for the point where a component is no longer useable and must be renewed.

Shaft drive A method of transmitting drive from the transmission to the rear wheel.

Shell bearings Plain bearings consisting of two shell halves. Most often used as big-end and main bearings in a four-stroke engine. Often called bearing inserts.

Shim Thin spacer, commonly used to adjust the clearance or relative positions between two parts. For example, shims inserted into or under tappets or followers to control valve clearances. Clearance is adjusted by changing the thickness of the shim.

Short-circuit An electrical condition where current shorts to earth (ground) bypassing the circuit components.

Skimming Process to correct warpage or repair a damaged surface, eg on brake discs or drums.

Slide-hammer A special puller that screws into or hooks onto a component such as a shaft or bearing; a heavy sliding handle on the shaft bottoms against the end of the shaft to knock the component free.

Small-end bearing The bearing in the upper end of the connecting rod at its joint with the gudgeon pin.

Spalling Damage to camshaft lobes or bearing journals shown as pitting of the working surface.

Specific gravity (SG) The state of charge of the electrolyte in a lead-acid battery. A measure of the electrolyte's density compared with water.

Straight-cut gears Common type gear used on gearbox shafts and for oil pump and water pump drives.

Stanchion The inner sliding part of the front forks, held by the yokes. Often called a fork tube.

Stoichiometric ratio The optimum chemical air/fuel ratio for a petrol engine, said to be 14.7 parts of air to 1 part of fuel.

Sulphuric acid The liquid (electrolyte) used in a lead-acid battery. Poisonous and extremely corrosive.

Surface grinding (lapping) Process to correct a warped gasket face, commonly used on cylinder heads.

T

Tapered-roller bearing Tapered inner race of caged needle rollers and separate tapered outer race. Examples of taper roller bearings can be found on steering heads.

Tappet A cylindrical component which transmits motion from the cam to the valve stem, either directly or via a pushrod and rocker arm. Also called a cam follower.

TCS Traction Control System. An electronically-controlled system which senses wheel spin and reduces engine speed accordingly.

TDC Top Dead Centre denotes that the piston is at its highest point in the cylinder.

Thread-locking compound Solution applied to fastener threads to prevent slackening. Select type to suit application.

Thrust washer A washer positioned between two moving components on a shaft. For example, between gear pinions on gearshaft.

Timing chain See **Cam Chain.**

Timing light Stroboscopic lamp for carrying out ignition timing checks with the engine running.

Top-end A description of an engine's cylinder block, head and valve gear components.

Torque Turning or twisting force about a shaft.

Torque setting A prescribed tightness specified by the motorcycle manufacturer to ensure that the bolt or nut is secured correctly. Undertightening can result in the bolt or nut coming loose or a surface not being sealed. Overtightening can result in stripped threads, distortion or damage to the component being retained.

Torx key A six-point wrench.

Tracer A stripe of a second colour applied to a wire insulator to distinguish that wire from another one with the same colour insulator. For example, Br/W is often used to denote a brown insulator with a white tracer.

Trail A feature of steering geometry. Distance from the steering head axis to the tyre's central contact point.

Triple clamps The cast components which extend from the steering head and support the fork stanchions or tubes. Often called fork yokes.

Turbocharger A centrifugal device, driven by exhaust gases, that pressurises the intake air. Normally used to increase the power output from a given engine displacement.

TWI Abbreviation for Tyre Wear Indicator. Indicates the location of the tread depth indicator bars on tyres.

U

Universal joint or U-joint (UJ) A double-pivoted connection for transmitting power from a driving to a driven shaft through an angle. Typically found in shaft drive assemblies.

Unsprung weight Anything not supported by the bike's suspension (ie the wheel, tyres, brakes, final drive and bottom (moving) part of the suspension).

V

Vacuum gauges Clock-type gauges for measuring intake tract vacuum. Used for carburettor synchronisation on multi-cylinder engines.

Valve A device through which the flow of liquid, gas or vacuum may be stopped, started or regulated by a moveable part that opens, shuts or partially obstructs one or more ports or passageways. The intake and exhaust valves in the cylinder head are of the poppet type.

Valve clearance The clearance between the valve tip (the end of the valve stem) and the rocker arm or tappet/follower. The valve clearance is measured when the valve is closed. The correct clearance is important - if too small the valve won't close fully and will burn out, whereas if too large noisy operation will result.

Valve lift The amount a valve is lifted off its seat by the camshaft lobe.

Valve timing The exact setting for the opening and closing of the valves in relation to piston position.

Vernier caliper A precision measuring instrument that measures inside and outside dimensions. Not quite as accurate as a micrometer, but more convenient.

VIN Vehicle Identification Number. Term for the bike's engine and frame numbers.

Viscosity The thickness of a liquid or its resistance to flow.

Volt A unit for expressing electrical "pressure" in a circuit. Volts = current x ohms.

W

Water pump A mechanically-driven device for moving coolant around the engine.

Watt A unit for expressing electrical power. Watts = volts x current.

Wear limit see **Service limit**

Wet liner A liquid-cooled engine design where the pistons run in liners which are directly surrounded by coolant **(see illustration).**

Wet liner arrangement

Wheelbase Distance from the centre of the front wheel to the centre of the rear wheel.

Wiring harness or loom Describes the electrical wires running the length of the motorcycle and enclosed in tape or plastic sheathing. Wiring coming off the main harness is usually referred to as a sub harness.

Woodruff key A key of semi-circular or square section used to locate a gear to a shaft. Often used to locate the alternator rotor on the crankshaft.

Wrist pin Another name for gudgeon or piston pin.

Note: *References throughout this index are in the form* "**Chapter number**" • "**Page number**". *So, for example, 2•15 refers to page 15 of Chapter 2.*

*Note: References throughout this index are in the form "**Chapter number**" • "**Page number**". So, for example, 2•15 refers to page 15 of Chapter 2.*

Note: *References throughout this index are in the form "**Chapter number**" • "**Page number**". So, for example, 2•15 refers to page 15 of Chapter 2.*

Note: *References throughout this index are in the form* **"Chapter number"** • **"Page number"**. *So, for example, 2•15 refers to page 15 of Chapter 2.*

Haynes Motorcycle Manuals – The Complete List

Title		Book No
APRILIA RSV1000 Mille (98 - 03)		4255
BMW 2-valve Twins (70 - 96)	♦	0249
BMW K100 & 75 2-valve Models (83 - 96)	♦	1373
BMW R850, 1100 & 1150 4-valve Twins (93 - 04)	♦	3466
BSA Bantam (48 - 71)		0117
BSA Unit Singles (58 - 72)		0127
BSA Pre-unit Singles (54 - 61)		0326
BSA A7 & A10 Twins (47 - 62)		0121
BSA A50 & A65 Twins (62 - 73)		0155
DUCATI 600, 750 & 900 2-valve V-Twins (91 - 96)	♦	3290
Ducati MK III & Desmo Singles (69 - 76)	◇	0445
Ducati 748, 916 & 996 4-valve V-Twins (94 - 01)	♦	3756
GILERA Runner, DNA, Stalker & Ice (97 - 04)		4163
HARLEY-DAVIDSON Sportsters (70 - 03)	♦	2534
Harley-Davidson Shovelhead and Evolution Big Twins (70 - 99)		2536
Harley-Davidson Twin Cam 88 (99 - 03)	♦	2478
HONDA NB, ND, NP & NS50 Melody (81 - 85)	◇	0622
Honda NE/NB50 Vision & SA50 Vision Met-in (85 - 95)	◇	1278
Honda MB, MBX, MT & MTX50 (80 - 93)		0731
Honda C50, C70 & C90 (67 - 99)		0324
Honda XR80R & XR100R (85 - 04)		2218
Honda XL/XR 80, 100, 125, 185 & 200 2-valve Models (78 - 87)		0566
Honda H100 & H100S Singles (80 - 92)	◇	0734
Honda CB/CD125T & CM125C Twins (77 - 88)	◇	0571
Honda CG125 (76 - 00)	◇	0433
Honda NS125 (86 - 93)	◇	3056
Honda MBX/MTX125 & MTX200 (83 - 93)	◇	1132
Honda CD/CM185 200T & CM250C 2-valve Twins (77 - 85)		0572
Honda XL/XR 250 & 500 (78 - 84)		0567
Honda XR250L, XR250R & XR400R (86 - 03)		2219
Honda CB250 & CB400N Super Dreams (78 - 84)	◇	0540
Honda CR Motocross Bikes (86 - 01)		2222
Honda CBR400RR Fours (88 - 99)	◇ ♦	3552
Honda VFR400 (NC30) & RVF400 (NC35) V-Fours (89 - 98)	◇ ♦	3496
Honda CB500 (93 - 01)	◇ ♦	3753
Honda CB400 & CB550 Fours (73 - 77)		0262
Honda CX/GL500 & 650 V-Twins (78 - 86)		0442
Honda CBX550 Four (82 - 86)	◇	0940
Honda XL600R & XR600R (83 - 00)		2183
Honda XL600/650V Transalp & XRV750 Africa Twin (87 - 02)	◇ ♦	3919
Honda CBR600F1 & 1000F Fours (87 - 96)	♦	1730
Honda CBR600F2 & F3 Fours (91 - 98)	♦	2070
Honda CBR600F4 (99 - 02)	♦	3911
Honda CB600F Hornet (98 - 02)	◇ ♦	3915
Honda CB650 sohc Fours (78 - 84)		0665
Honda NTV600 Revere, NTV650 & NT650V Deauville (88 - 01)	◇ ♦	3243
Honda Shadow VT600 & 750 (USA) (88 - 03)		2312
Honda CB750 sohc Four (69 - 79)		0131
Honda V45/65 Sabre & Magna (82 - 88)		0820
Honda VFR750 & 700 V-Fours (86 - 97)	♦	2101
Honda VFR800 V-Fours (97 - 01)	♦	3703
Honda VFR800 V-Tec V-Fours (02 - 05)	♦	4196
Honda CB750 & CB900 dohc Fours (78 - 84)		0535
Honda VTR1000 (FireStorm, Super Hawk) & XL1000V (Varadero) (97 - 00)	♦	3744
Honda CBR900RR FireBlade (92 - 99)	♦	2161
Honda CBR900RR FireBlade (00 - 03)	♦	4060
Honda CBR1100XX Super Blackbird (97 - 02)	♦	3901
Honda ST1100 Pan European V-Fours (90 - 01)	♦	3384
Honda Shadow VT1100 (USA) (85 - 98)		2313

Title		Book No
Honda GL1000 Gold Wing (75 - 79)		0309
Honda GL1100 Gold Wing (79 - 81)		0669
Honda Gold Wing 1200 (USA) (84 - 87)		2199
Honda Gold Wing 1500 (USA) (88 - 00)		2225
KAWASAKI AE/AR 50 & 80 (81 - 95)		1007
Kawasaki KC, KE & KH100 (75 - 99)		1371
Kawasaki KMX125 & 200 (86 - 02)	◇	3046
Kawasaki 250, 350 & 400 Triples (72 - 79)		0134
Kawasaki 400 & 440 Twins (74 - 81)		0281
Kawasaki 400, 500 & 550 Fours (79 - 91)		0910
Kawasaki EN450 & 500 Twins (Ltd/Vulcan) (85 - 04)		2053
Kawasaki EX & ER500 (GPZ500S & ER-5) Twins (87 - 99)	♦	2052
Kawasaki ZX600 (Ninja ZX-6, ZZ-R600) Fours (90 - 00)	♦	2146
Kawasaki ZX-6R Ninja Fours (95 - 02)	♦	3541
Kawasaki ZX600 (GPZ600R, GPX600R, Ninja 600R & RX) & ZX750 (GPX750R, Ninja 750R) Fours (85 - 97)	♦	1780
Kawasaki 650 Four (76 - 78)		0373
Kawasaki Vulcan 700/750 & 800 (85 - 04)	♦	2457
Kawasaki 750 Air-cooled Fours (80 - 91)		0574
Kawasaki ZR550 & 750 Zephyr Fours (90 - 97)	♦	3382
Kawasaki ZX750 (Ninja ZX-7 & ZXR750) Fours (89 - 96)	♦	2054
Kawasaki Ninja ZX-7R & ZX-9R (94 - 04)	♦	3721
Kawasaki 900 & 1000 Fours (73 - 77)		0222
Kawasaki ZX900, 1000 & 1100 Liquid-cooled Fours (83 - 97)	♦	1681
MOTO GUZZI 750, 850 & 1000 V-Twins (74 - 78)		0339
MZ ETZ Models (81 - 95)	◇	1680
NORTON 500, 600, 650 & 750 Twins (57 - 70)		0187
Norton Commando (68 - 77)		0125
PEUGEOT Speedfight, Trekker & Vivacity (96 - 02)	◇	3920
PIAGGIO (Vespa) Scooters (91 - 03)	◇	3492
SUZUKI GT, ZR & TS50 (77 - 90)	◇	0799
Suzuki TS50X (84 - 00)	◇	1599
Suzuki 100, 125, 185 & 250 Air-cooled Trail bikes (79 - 89)		0797
Suzuki GP100 & 125 Singles (78 - 93)	◇	0576
Suzuki GS, GN, GZ & DR125 Singles (82 - 99)	◇	0888
Suzuki 250 & 350 Twins (68 - 78)		0120
Suzuki GT250X7, GT200X5 & SB200 Twins (78 - 83)	◇	0469
Suzuki GS/GSX250, 400 & 450 Twins (79 - 85)		0736
Suzuki GS500 Twin (89 - 02)	♦	3238
Suzuki GS550 (77 - 82) & GS750 Fours (76 - 79)		0363
Suzuki GS/GSX550 4-valve Fours (83 - 88)		1133
Suzuki SV650 (99 - 02)	♦	3912
Suzuki GSX-R600 & 750 (96 - 00)	♦	3553
Suzuki GSX-R600 (01 - 02), GSX-R750 (00 - 02) & GSX-R1000 (01 - 02)	♦	3986
Suzuki GSF600 & 1200 Bandit Fours (95 - 04)	♦	3367
Suzuki GS850 Fours (78 - 88)		0536
Suzuki GS1000 Four (77 - 79)		0484
Suzuki GSX-R750, GSX-R1100 (85 - 92), GSX600F, GSX750F, GSX1100F (Katana) Fours (88 - 96)	♦	2055
Suzuki GSX600/750F & GSX750 (98 - 02)	♦	3987
Suzuki GS/GSX1000, 1100 & 1150 4-valve Fours (79 - 88)		0737
Suzuki TL1000S/R & DL1000 V-Strom (97 - 04)	♦	4083
Suzuki GSX1300R Hayabusa (99 - 04)	♦	4184
TRIUMPH Tiger Cub & Terrier (52 - 68)		0414
Triumph 350 & 500 Unit Twins (58 - 73)		0137
Triumph Pre-Unit Twins (47 - 62)		0251
Triumph 650 & 750 2-valve Unit Twins (63 - 83)		0122
Triumph Trident & BSA Rocket 3 (69 - 75)		0136
Triumph Fuel Injected Triples (97 - 00)	♦	3755
Triumph Triples & Fours (carburettor engines) (91 - 99)	♦	2162
VESPA P/PX125, 150 & 200 Scooters (78 - 03)		0707
Vespa Scooters (59 - 78)		0126
YAMAHA DT50 & 80 Trail Bikes (78 - 95)	◇	0800

Title		Book No
Yamaha T50 & 80 Townmate (83 - 95)	◇	1247
Yamaha YB100 Singles (73 - 91)	◇	0474
Yamaha RS/RXS100 & 125 Singles (74 - 95)		0331
Yamaha RD & DT125LC (82 - 87)	◇	0887
Yamaha TZR125 (87 - 93) & DT125R (88 - 02)	◇	1655
Yamaha TY50, 80, 125 & 175 (74 - 84)	◇	0464
Yamaha XT & SR125 (82 - 02)	◇	1021
Yamaha Trail Bikes (81 - 00)		2350
Yamaha 250 & 350 Twins (70 - 79)		0040
Yamaha XS250, 360 & 400 sohc Twins (75 - 84)		0378
Yamaha RD250 & 350LC Twins (80 - 82)		0803
Yamaha RD350 YPVS Twins (83 - 95)		1158
Yamaha RD400 Twin (75 - 79)		0333
Yamaha XT, TT & SR500 Singles (75 - 83)		0342
Yamaha XZ550 Vision V-Twins (82 - 85)		0821
Yamaha FJ, FZ, XJ & YX600 Radian (84 - 92)		2100
Yamaha XJ600S (Diversion, Seca II) & XJ600N Fours (92 - 03)	♦	2145
Yamaha YZF600R Thundercat & FZS600 Fazer (96 - 03)	♦	3702
Yamaha YZF-R6 (98 - 02)	♦	3900
Yamaha 650 Twins (70 - 83)		0341
Yamaha XJ650 & 750 Fours (80 - 84)		0738
Yamaha XS750 & 850 Triples (76 - 85)		0340
Yamaha TDM850, TRX850 & XTZ750 (89 - 99)	◇ ♦	3540
Yamaha YZF750R & YZF1000R Thunderace (93 - 00)	♦	3720
Yamaha FZR600, 750 & 1000 Fours (87 - 96)	♦	2056
Yamaha XV (Virago) V-Twins (81 - 03)	♦	0802
Yamaha XVS650 & 1100 Dragstar/V-Star (97 - 05)	♦	4195
Yamaha XJ900F Fours (83 - 94)	♦	3239
Yamaha XJ900S Diversion (94 - 01)	♦	3739
Yamaha YZF-R1 (98 - 03)	♦	3754
Yamaha FJ1100 & 1200 Fours (84 - 96)	♦	2057
Yamaha XJR1200 & 1300 (95 - 03)	♦	3981
Yamaha V-Max (85 - 03)	♦	4072
ATVs		
Honda ATC70, 90, 110, 185 & 200 (71 - 85)		0565
Honda TRX300 Shaft Drive ATVs (88 - 00)		2125
Honda TRX300EX & TRX400EX ATVs (93 - 04)		2318
Honda Foreman 400 and 450 ATVs (95 - 02)		2465
Kawasaki Bayou 220/250/300 & Prairie 300 ATVs (86 - 03)		2351
Polaris ATVs (85 - 97)		2302
Polaris ATVs (98 - 03)		2508
Yamaha YFS200 Blaster ATV (88 - 02)		2317
Yamaha YFB250 Timberwolf ATVs (92 - 00)		2217
Yamaha YFM350 & YFM400 (ER and Big Bear) ATVs (87 - 03)		2126
Yamaha Banshee and Warrior ATVs (87 - 03)		2314
ATV Basics		10450
TECHBOOK SERIES		
Motorcycle Basics TechBook (2nd Edition)		3515
Motorcycle Electrical TechBook (3rd Edition)		3471
Motorcycle Fuel Systems TechBook		3514
Motorcycle Maintenance TechBook		4071
Motorcycle Workshop Practice TechBook (2nd Edition)		3470
GENERAL MANUALS		
Twist and Go (automatic transmission) Scooters Service and Repair Manual		4082

◇ = not available in the USA   ♦ = Superbike

The manuals on this page are available through good motorcycle dealers and accessory shops.
In case of difficulty, contact: **Haynes Publishing**
(UK) +44 1963 442030   (USA) +1 805 498 6703
(FR) +33 1 47 17 66 29   (SV) +46 18 124016
(Australia/New Zealand) +61 3 9763 8100

MCL18.04/05

Preserving Our Motoring Heritage

< The Model J Duesenberg
Derham Tourster.
Only eight of these
magnificent cars were
ever built – this is the
only example to be found
outside the United States
of America

Almost every car you've ever loved, loathed or desired is gathered under one roof at the Haynes Motor Museum. Over 300 immaculately presented cars and motorbikes represent every aspect of our motoring heritage, from elegant reminders of bygone days, such as the superb Model J Duesenberg to curiosities like the bug-eyed BMW Isetta. There are also many old friends and flames. Perhaps you remember the 1959 Ford Popular that you did your courting in? The magnificent 'Red Collection' is a spectacle of classic sports cars including AC, Alfa Romeo, Austin Healey, Ferrari, Lamborghini, Maserati, MG, Riley, Porsche and Triumph.

A Perfect Day Out

Each and every vehicle at the Haynes Motor Museum has played its part in the history and culture of Motoring. Today, they make a wonderful spectacle and a great day out for all the family. Bring the kids, bring Mum and Dad, but above all bring your camera to capture those golden memories for ever. You will also find an impressive array of motoring memorabilia, a comfortable 70 seat video cinema and one of the most extensive transport book shops in Britain. The Pit Stop Cafe serves everything from a cup of tea to wholesome, home-made meals or, if you prefer, you can enjoy the large picnic area nestled in the beautiful rural surroundings of Somerset.

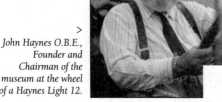

John Haynes O.B.E.,
Founder and
Chairman of the
museum at the wheel
of a Haynes Light 12.

< The 1936 490cc
sohc-engined
International
Norton – well known
for its racing success

The Museum is situated on the A359 Yeovil to Frome road at Sparkford, just off the A303 in Somerset. It is about 40 miles south of Bristol, and 25 minutes drive from the M5 intersection at Taunton.
Open 9.30am - 5.30pm (10.00am - 4.00pm Winter) 7 days a week, *except Christmas Day, Boxing Day and New Years Day*
Special rates available for schools, coach parties and outings Charitable Trust No. 292048